ADVENTURESS

ADVENTURESS

THE LIFE AND LOVES OF
LUCY, LADY HOUSTON

TERESA CROMPTON

The
History
Press

Adventuress: a woman adventurer, specif. one
who seeks to become rich and socially accepted
by exploiting her charms, by scheming, etc.

Collins English Dictionary

First published 2020

The History Press
97 St George's Place, Cheltenham,
Gloucestershire, GL50 3QB
www.thehistorypress.co.uk

© Teresa Crompton, 2020

The right of Teresa Crompton to be identified as the Author
of this work has been asserted in accordance with the
Copyright, Designs and Patents Act 1988.

British Library Cataloguing in Publication Data.
A catalogue record for this book is available from the British Library.

ISBN 978 0 7509 9328 9

Typesetting and origination by The History Press
Printed and bound in Great Britain by TJ International Ltd.

CONTENTS

Acknowledgements

Ancestry (website)

British Newspaper Archive (website)

Cambridge University Library (Stanley Baldwin and Lord Birkenhead correspondence)

Churchill Archives Centre, Churchill College, Cambridge (Churchill correspondence)

City of London School Archives

Cornell University, Division of Rare and Manuscript Collections (Ford Madox Ford Collection, Violet Hunt Papers)

Dr. Peter Crompton

Hansard 1803–2005 – Parliament UK (website)

John Rylands Library, University of Manchester (Ramsay MacDonald Papers)

Dr. Myrddin Lewis, Department of Humanities, Sheffield Hallam University

National Brewery Museum, Burton on Trent

Miranda Seymour

Alan Taylor, Folkestone and District Local History Society

University of Manchester Library (forged Russian letters correspondence)

University of Oxford, Bodleian Libraries, Weston Library, (T.E. Lawrence and Lord Wolmer correspondence)

NOTE ON SOURCES

Lucy Houston began her life in obscurity and ended it as a household name, with episodes of scandal, notoriety and public acclaim along the way; it is inevitable, therefore, that the biographer's source material is varied. The richest mines of personal information are two biographies, written in 1947 and 1958 respectively by employees, newspapermen Warner Allen and James Wentworth Day. These are invaluable as a behind-the-scenes record of Lucy's later lifestyle and her attempts to alter the course of British politics. The present work often draws upon them, and also gleans information from other first-hand accounts written by political associates such as Oswald Mosley and friends such as the writer Eveleigh Nash. Although in her later years Lucy was a prolific correspondent, not hesitating to publish letters of advice or commendation to strangers such as British Prime Ministers, Hitler and Mussolini, relatively few private letters have survived. A number of letters to and from Lucy are held in public archives, however. This biography has drawn upon, for example, her correspondence with Winston Churchill, T.E. Lawrence (Lawrence of Arabia), Stanley Baldwin and the writer Violet Hunt. Much of the information revealed by the archival material – for example, Lucy's attempt to prevent Baldwin making Lord Birkenhead a cabinet minister, her dealings with Scotland Yard about forged letters from Ramsay MacDonald to leading Bolsheviks and her support of the novelist Violet Hunt – has, to my knowledge, never been published before.

There is, however, less hard information about Lucy's earlier life, in the late Victorian, Edwardian and First World War periods. Even when she did confide in others, as readers will soon note, her memory was highly selective, always impressionistic, sometimes deceitful and suspiciously self-serving. This book therefore uses other documentary sources to tell a fuller story of

Lucy's earlier life, and also some episodes of her later life unknown to those earlier biographers, such as her purchase of the forged Ramsay Macdonald letter to the Bolsheviks. The pages of the press, many local newspapers recently having been made available online, have also been helpful, particularly for establishing Lucy's activities and whereabouts. To avoid drowning the text in source notes, rather than identify individual press articles, which were in any case often syndicated and thus appeared in many publications, I have generally referred to 'the press'. Memoirs and biographies used are referred to in the text and details provided in a bibliography. Where archive material is used, referencing is provided in the endnotes.

Despite my best efforts to tell as complete a story as possible, gaps remain. Lucy's childhood and her life as the teenage mistress of Frederick Gretton are largely undocumented and throughout there are periods, such as that of the 'Madame Chabault' episode of 1906–08, where a biographer can only speculate how she was spending her time. Overall, big money leaves a bigger trail, and the task of accounting for Lucy's whereabouts and activity is easier after her marriage to the millionaire Sir Robert Houston. This fact explains the biography's emphasis on the final decade of the subject's lifespan.

1

No Lady

Fanny Lucy Radmall – called Poppy by her family and Lucy by everyone else – never scorned her origins. At the end of her days, as a super-rich woman with a title and a famous yacht, she would boast, 'I'm a pure Cockney, my dear, born within sound of Bow Bells.' The Cockney traits of optimism, determination, quick thinking and humour would characterise all that she did. Her upbringing in Victorian London would exert great influence upon her life. By the time of her birth in the 1850s, London, the capital of the British Empire, was developing rapidly and abounded with optimism and opportunity. For decades people had been flooding into the city from across Britain; the families of Lucy's parents, Thomas and Maria, crafts- and tradespeople seeking to exploit the city's markets, had been among them. Thomas Radmall, born in about 1816, was the son of a stonemason while Maria Clark, born in 1818, was the daughter of a brewer.

With a young population, London had a high birth rate and with it a high level of illegitimacy. By the time of their marriage in June 1840, Thomas and Maria already had two daughters, Margaret and Eliza. Maria was pregnant again when she married and bore another girl, Mary, six months after the wedding. The fact that Maria signed her marriage certificate with a cross indicates that she was illiterate. The lives of the Radmalls, with the frequent changes of occupation and location that indicated economic instability, were typical of the lower classes. They lived at various addresses south of the River Thames until about 1840 but then moved north into the City of London, the capital's historic centre. There Thomas worked firstly as a warehouseman and then as a boxmaker, and later Maria would run a clothes shop from the family home in Shoe Lane in the parish of St Bride.

In April 1843 their first son, Thomas, known as Tom, was born, followed by another girl, Sophia, and then three boys, Alfred, Walter and Arthur. Mary and Alfred had died by the time that Lucy, Thomas and Maria's penultimate child, was born on 8 April 1857 at 13 Lower Kennington Green in Lambeth. In 1861, when Lucy was aged 4, the Radmalls moved once more, for Thomas had risen to become a junior partner in the firm of J.T. Powell and Co., a wholesale woollen-drapers in Newgate Street. Thomas had charge of the warehouse, overseeing the dispatch of orders of cloth to retailers in better parts of London. The Radmalls lived on the premises, sharing the crowded rooms 'above the shop' with two company porters and two female servants. This would be Lucy's home for seven years. In 1862, Maria's last child, Florence, was born. She usurped Lucy's position as baby of the family but was destined to spend her life in the shadow and under the patronage of her big sister.

Outside the family home the streets offered entertainment and drama. Newgate Street itself was a busy trading thoroughfare but had never been a salubrious address; it was described in a guidebook at this time as 'little better than a lane' in a 'greasy' neighbourhood, featuring an 'odorous and insanitary' meat market. Newgate Prison, a gloomy building with high walls, was one of the area's attractions and, until 1868, hangings took place on gallows erected in the street. Either Lucy's parents were happy to allow her the freedom to explore the City of London or they had little control over their strong-willed daughter. Newgate Street was near St Paul's Cathedral and there, she would recount, almost as soon as she could run she played hide-and-seek among the tombstones in the churchyard: 'My playmates were the bones of the City Fathers,' she said. On another occasion she told a friend how she had once led a 'band of little ragamuffins up and down Drury Lane'. In her 70s, out in her Rolls-Royce, she would direct her chauffeur through the maze of little streets that she had known as a child. She knew every inch of the City, she told a companion, for as a child she had 'run wild through its streets like a street arab' until she could not have got lost if she had wanted to. The City, she said, had been her home.

In the wider sphere, lavish expenditure was being made on infrastructure and public buildings. For example, in the year of Lucy's birth the South Kensington Museum (the predecessor of the Victoria and Albert Museum) opened its doors, and the following year the new Royal Opera House was inaugurated at Covent Garden. Communications advanced. In the late 1850s public post boxes appeared, Westminster Bridge was built in 1862, and the following year the world's first underground railway opened, with a line between Paddington and Farringdon Street operated by steam locomotives pulling gas-lit wooden carriages. These developments were a grand display of the power of money.

In later life Lucy would be proud to be labelled 'patriot' but her patriotism would always belong to the England of her youth, when, with London the global centre of finance and commerce, Britain's power and reach was extending ever further. In 1858 the British government took direct control of India to establish the British Raj, or Rule, and India became the 'jewel in the crown' of the Empire and a key source of British strength. Lucy's upbringing in the imperial capital would shape the beliefs and feelings that became a key component of her patriotism in later life. Another strong influence in Lucy's early life was the changing lives of women. Women were at this time gaining an increasing role in public life and Lucy was greatly influenced by stories of Florence Nightingale, then a national icon for her work in the care of soldiers wounded in the Crimean War of 1854–56. Lucy's parents had named their youngest child after the great nurse, and Lucy's admiration of Nightingale would contribute both to the development of her own feminist aspirations and to her later charitable support of hospitals and nurses' welfare.

The regular income and more settled way of living that came with Thomas Radmall's partnership in J.T. Powell and Co. provided a foundation from which the Radmall siblings could advance. As a group they possessed intelligence, ability and a culture of achievement that enabled them to make their own luck; in time each would rise considerably above the social and economic level of their parents. Significant moves into higher levels of society were made by Lucy's brothers Arthur and Tom in the 1860s. In 1862, at the age of 12, Arthur was enrolled in the City of London School, an independent day school for boys from poorer backgrounds. Arthur did well to get in, for it had an excellent reputation and there was a long waiting list for scholarships. He was in the same class as Herbert Asquith, later British Prime Minister, and at the school's annual prize-giving ceremony of 1864 he received a prize for arithmetic – no small achievement in a school known for the quality of its mathematics scholars. Arthur left school that December to become an apprentice accountant. Lucy, meanwhile, may have attended James Allen's Girls' School in Dulwich village, which educated girls from less well-off backgrounds.

But it was Tom, the oldest boy, who was destined to rise the highest and fall the furthest. After leaving school he became one of the many young men who worked as clerks in the City of London, but as he laboured with ledgers and invoices Tom set his mind on greater things. Quick-witted, clever, capable and sociable, he was a person, a friend wrote of him later, who 'could do and did everything well and without trouble'. Short and wiry, at the age of 18 Tom took up rowing, becoming a founder member of the Thames Rowing Club, which had been formed that year at Putney. Racing events were reported in the London newspapers and successful rowers became celebrities of the river; it was something to be associated with the rowing club. Tom's move would allow the young Radmalls to mix with or succeed among social superiors. In time Tom's brothers Arthur and Walter would join, and two of their sisters would marry club members. Tom became a leading member of the club and he and his rowing partner James Catty were so successful that, it was reported some years later, they became 'all but worshipped names between Putney and Mortlake'. Both would serve as club captain.

In 1868, when Lucy was aged 11, Thomas Radmall's partnership with J.T. Powell and Co. was dissolved and he set up in business as a picture-frame maker. At about this time the family seems to have broken up, for Lucy went to live with her sister Sophia in Earls Court; she was baptised at the church of St Matthias there in September 1869. In doctrine the church was 'high', veering towards Anglo-Catholicism, a religious line to which Lucy would adhere throughout her life. The baptismal record shows that she had already swapped her first names, and by this effected an early, if minor, change of identity. A photograph from about this time shows Lucy with small determined eyes protruding slightly from beneath bony, prominent, brows; the strong chin is inclined to be fleshy. There is no indication of her later famed beauty.

In the 1860s Tom Radmall had left clerical work to begin his own business as a wine merchant and restaurant owner, but in 1870 he went bankrupt. Nevertheless he got married that same year. Insecurity about their ages or social status would over the years lead various Radmall siblings to lie on official documents. On Tom's marriage certificate, for example, he gave both his and his father's profession as 'Gentleman'. The term had traditionally been the preserve of the gentry and a right of birth, and the rising middle classes were anxious to have it applied to themselves, but even by the standards of the day Tom was stretching things too far. When, five weeks after Tom's wedding, his sister Sophia married James Catty, her marriage certificate was strikingly different, for Thomas Radmall's profession was more correctly given as 'warehouseman'. A precocious 'Lucy Fanny Radmall' signed with a flourish of confidence beyond her 13 years; Lucy felt grown-up, for education was not compulsory and she had already left school.

After signing Sophia's wedding certificate Lucy all but disappears from the contemporary record for a decade. Many years later she would say that as a 'poor girl' she had worked for her living and gone on the stage as a 'ballet dancer', although others interpreted this as meaning 'chorus girl'. But long after Lucy's death a newspaper would report that she had been a showgirl who appeared at 'bachelor dinner parties', and on one occasion had emerged 'high-kicking, from a huge pie'. Certainly, Lucy's petite form and extrovert personality would have lent themselves to such employment, and the story would also explain how she first attracted the eye of the man who would change her life.

Frederick Gretton, a partner in the prosperous brewing firm of Bass, Ratcliff and Gretton, was fifteen years Lucy's senior. Bombastic and alcoholic, he was also *nouveau riche* and indeed very wealthy. He was brought up in the brewing town of Burton-on-Trent, which owed its fame to the qualities of its spring water. In Tudor times water obtained from a 'Holy Well' dedicated to Modwen, a local female saint, had been found to be particularly suited to brewing; beer made with Burton water became clear without the need for further processing. Small breweries had sprung up and with industrialisation in manufacturing and transportation the beer trade expanded rapidly. As demand grew there were fortunes to be made and Frederick Gretton's father John was one who took advantage of the boom.

John Gretton's background had been lowly. Born in 1792 into a poor Staffordshire family, he had begun his working life as a carter. But when in his early 30s he started work as a brewer for the Bass company, his outstanding capabilities and business acumen ensured that he was soon appointed manager of the malting and brewing departments, and within a few years taken on as a partner. John Gretton inspired affection, respect and admiration, not only for his ability but also for his service to the town. For the following thirty years he would be one of the triumvirate who ran Bass, Ratcliff and Gretton. The company's aggressive exporting across the British Empire meant that by the mid-1850s Bass 'bitter' was the world's best-known beer and a symbol of Englishness, as a contemporary rhyme showed:

John Bull, indeed, would be defunct, or else look very queer,
If Bass and Co. should cease to brew their glorious bitter beer.

Frederick, born in 1839, was one of five children. During his childhood the family still lived in an unpretentious home in Bass's premises on Burton-on-Trent's High Street. He grew up amid great piles of stacked casks, breathing brewing-scented air, and to the sound of locomotives rumbling through the streets pulling trucks loaded with beer barrels. During Frederick's teenage years the value of his father's capital as partner rose dramatically. Money projected the young Grettons into a higher social class but, like Thomas and Maria Radmall, John Gretton and his wife were personally ill-equipped to prepare their children for sophisticated social environments. Frederick attended a small local school but left as a teenager to work in the brewery; he had no opportunity to acquire the polish that a public school and university education had given his financial peers. Contemporary news articles indicated unease and disorientation among the families in Burton-on-Trent as a new generation, the recipients of unearned wealth, arose out of the success of the town's brewing industry. The young people, it was feared, would be unable to cope with the opportunities, perils and pressures that money would bring. As Frederick Gretton would show for one, as they entered higher levels of society and interacted with those who had been born into money, they would bear the stigma of being first-generation rich.

Frederick and his older brother John were expected to dedicate their lives to the service of the company in whose rapid expansion their revered father had played such a prominent role. Indeed, initially both seemed set to follow this path and John junior, being quiet, competent, hard-working and ambitious, seemed a worthy successor. Frederick, on the other hand, was boisterous and sociable, and in his youth participated keenly in the sporting life of the area, rowing and playing cricket for local teams, and leasing a large shooting estate. He and John also joined the local branch of the Volunteer Rifle movement and participated in drill and shooting practice, and it would be shooting that would eventually lead Frederick to Lucy.

In his mid-20s Frederick Gretton became manager of Bass's thirty-two malt houses, supervising 200 employees. It was a responsible position, for upon his department the reputation of the company depended. The work of maintaining the supply of Bass beer in sufficient quantity and quality was no easy task. Pacing the hollow wooden floors of the tall brewery buildings Gretton oversaw the hops and malt, water and yeast as they progressed through the various processes of brewing. Sieving, crushing, mashing, blending, separating, boiling, straining, cooling and fermenting brought forth the end product, which was barrelled up and transported out of Burton by rail. The Bass company continued to grow so that within a few years its annual output reached 720,000 barrels, each containing 36 gallons of beer. This, a newspaper reported, was enough to provide more than half of the human race with a glass each.

Frederick Gretton seemed set for a lifetime in brewing but as a minor celebrity in the town he was closely observed, and the pressure to live up to his father's reputation was a burden. At the age of 27, and rich but restless, he began to cast off the constraints of Burton life and would increasingly become an embarrassment to Bass & Co. and to his family. He began to shift his focus to London, his initial visits to the capital probably made in connection with the Bass premises then under construction at St Pancras Station, but before long he joined the fringes of Victorian London's 'social season', as enjoyed by the upper classes. Wanting to test his skills against a different class of shot he joined the newly formed Shepherd's Bush Gun Club, essentially a betting venue based on pigeon-shooting events using live birds. The all-male membership was cosmopolitan and sophisticated, comprised mainly of aristocrats, military officers and members of prestigious London clubs. Gretton could join on the basis of his money but, despite that fact that he had more disposable income than many of his social superiors, with his wealth coming from manufacturing and trade he had no class. However, he was generous and sociable and those gun club members who would tolerate his company could introduce him to all that London had to offer. Many members were prominent in horse-racing circles and it was probably this connection that introduced Gretton to the lifestyle that would soon consume his interest.

After the death of his father in 1867, Gretton was made a partner in Bass & Co. and he and his brother each held a 12.5 per cent share of the company's capital. With an increased income and freedom from his father's expectations Gretton could live as he pleased, and he increasingly grew away from his brother's steadying influence. While he occupied his father's home, Bladon House, with his unmarried sisters, Frances and Clara, he sought excitement elsewhere and in 1868 took up horse racing and betting. In this way he used money that had originated with the Bass company for purposes that many in Burton thought selfish, reckless and immoral. In particular Michael Thomas Bass, the strait-laced but influential senior partner, disapproved strongly. Frederick Gretton, people told each other, was on the slippery slope to hell but, having found his life's passion, he was not going to give it up for a few critics.

The 'Turf', as the world of horse racing was called, was then in its heyday and England's most popular sport. The headquarters of the exclusive Jockey Club, the Turf's governing body, in Newmarket, was its centre. Beginning to build a stable of racehorses, Gretton adopted 'racing colours' for the jockeys who would ride his horses, choosing the garish scheme of orange jacket with purple belt and cap, and gave himself over to horse racing almost entirely. Most owners were aristocrats, landowners or those such as Gretton who made their money from trade and industry. That the Prince of Wales and many in his circle were Turf enthusiasts greatly raised the prestige of the sport, and involvement offered enhanced social status. Gretton's ownership of horses therefore allowed him to mix with members of the highest society at the many meetings that made up the annual racing calendar. He quickly made a name for himself when in October 1871 his bay colt, Sterling, had a sensational win at Newmarket. The horse became an instant equine celebrity, reported in the press as being 'undeniably the best animal of his age in the world'. Gretton was delighted and when a few months later Sterling won again at Newmarket, he was so proud that he commissioned an equine portraitist to depict the horse in oils.

When in London, Gretton made his headquarters at the Bath Hotel, located in fashionable Piccadilly. As there is no photograph of Frederick Gretton he may have disliked his appearance and avoided the camera – perhaps because he took after his father. A photograph of John Gretton senior shows a dour visage that, by the standards of the day, belonged to a farmer rather than a gentleman. A magazine suggested that, for all his money, Frederick Gretton's figure 'never seemed in harmony with the landscape of Piccadilly'. Gretton, well aware that his lack of manners and polish created a barrier between him and those in higher social circles, surrounded himself instead with people with whom he felt comfortable. He held a kind of court at the Bath Hotel in which he was the centre of a group of cronies and hangers-on, some of them old friends from Burton. With money but no intellectual interests or acquirements, Gretton relied entirely on others for diversion and entertainment. But his desire for constant company, and in particular his generosity as a host, made him vulnerable to sycophants and parasites. Not only did his associates eat and drink at his expense – and at any event hosted by Gretton the drink was sure to flow freely – they also sought betting tips, with which he could be generous when he chose.

While Gretton's wealth may have brought attention from middle- and upper-class women, he seemed comfortable only with working-class girls such as barmaids and chambermaids. Stories went around about Bath Hotel barmaids. One, for example, was that in 1872, when his horse Playfair was due to run in an important race, Gretton offered to put a sovereign on the horse for two of the girls. One asked for the coin instead, while the other took up Gretton's offer and enjoyed a handsome win. Gretton's first meeting with Lucy occurred probably in the early 1870s for, according to James Wentworth Day, who would work for Lucy in the 1930s, she became Gretton's mistress at the age of 16. In later life, to protect her reputation and the secret of her age, Lucy was always vague about the chronology of her early years and the date of the start of their liaison is not known. Lucy once admitted that she had been on the stage for only six weeks before meeting the brewer, but given that she had left school at the age of 12 and gone on the stage soon after, this would have made her only 12 or 13 when she became Gretton's mistress. In this case there would have been no illegality for the age of consent in England was then 12, but such a relationship would hardly have been socially acceptable. If, on the other hand, she did not go on the stage until the age of 16, there is a mystery about her whereabouts in the three or four intervening years. But, whatever the chronology, it seems clear that sometime between the ages of 12 and 16, Lucy met Gretton and was initiated into a new life.

Wentworth Day's account of Lucy's relationship with Gretton was, in part, mere speculation. Having not heard the story of Lucy emerging from a pie he imagined Poppy Radmall in the back row of the chorus kicking her legs and showing her figure, and thereby catching the eye of Gretton watching from his theatre box. He envisaged Gretton as a 'masher' – one of the 'gilded youth' of the day who dressed as a dandy in silk hat and white tie, and inspected chorus girls as though they were 'yearlings at the Newmarket sales'.

In those 'golden, gas-lit nights' of the 1870s, when hansom cabs 'jingled their tiny bells down Piccadilly', the 'mashers' invited the girls to supper at fashionable restaurants such as the Café Royal and Jimmy's, where, in curtained alcoves and private rooms, they plied them with champagne.

Whatever the actual circumstance, Lucy effectively became another hanger-on, preying upon Gretton's amenability and money, and her brother Tom, who at some point in the 1870s became a professional racecourse bookmaker, also joined the group surrounding the brewer. In later life Lucy would acknowledge and regret that in her youth she had been unscrupulous and heartless in her pursuit of money, but the brewer was easy prey for one as young, pretty, vivacious and scheming as Lucy. Yet they were not ill-matched. A friend would write of her in those early days that, 'spontaneous and natural, Lucy possessed the rare gift of wit, which rendered her conversation a delight. Men adored her.' Lucy, then, could provide the amusement that Gretton craved, and with her excellent dress sense she could look the part in any social environment. She was no social threat, for with her low-class origins she would hardly turn up her nose at the source of Gretton's money. But even as Lucy dropped her Cockney accent and moderated her manners, she was still only a counterfeit lady to his counterfeit gentleman.

Did she love him? Wentworth Day would write that Lucy 'fell in love, truly, deeply and sincerely, with her dashing masher'. While this may have been Wentworth Day's invention, Lucy perhaps had some feelings for Gretton for, as an old woman, on the anniversary of his death she would tell her secretary that it was a 'very sad day'. Someone she had 'loved dearly', she said, had died on that day fifty years ago: 'He worshipped me and said that I was the apple of his eye. Now wasn't that a sweet thing to say?' Wentworth Day states that Lucy and Gretton went to France and lived there 'as man and wife for ten or a dozen years', and indeed Lucy did go to Paris. The city was hugely attractive for it was then experiencing the start of the belle époque, the 'Beautiful Era', in which science, technology, fashion and the arts – especially literature, painting, music and theatre – flourished. For Lucy, Paris was the height of sophistication, offering excitement, novelty and French fashions. In addition, for someone in her position, the anonymity and looser moral climate offered a more accepting environment than London, although she did adopt the name of 'Mrs Gretton'. Although Gretton may well have travelled to Paris with Lucy he did not remain there for any length of time, for in 1872 and early 1873 the newspapers report him as being in England as usual, attending races, purchasing horses, sailing in his yacht, or in residence at Bladon House. However, there was no mention in the papers of him being in England from April to October 1873, and it may have been during this period that he and Lucy first went abroad. After that, Lucy may have divided her time between London and Paris, Gretton could not have spent more than a few months at a time out of England at any time prior to his death in 1883.

Why did Gretton and Lucy not marry? The objection may have been on Lucy's side for, as events would prove, she was so clever and tenacious that she would probably not have found it impossible to push him to the altar. She might simply not have liked Gretton enough, or not wanted to chain herself to an alcoholic and throw away the chance to make a better catch – perhaps one with a title. For unknown reasons Lucy was unable to bear children and so she had the freedom to play the field. However, her use of the name 'Mrs Gretton' suggested that she appreciated married status, and indeed in later life she would go to great lengths to attain it. It seems likely, therefore, that it was Gretton who resisted marriage, seeing no reason for it when his mistress provided everything that he wanted from a woman. He was a notoriously suspicious man and perhaps, not without reason, he felt unable to trust Lucy's feelings for him.

Despite his success on the Turf, Gretton was already attracting criticism for his habit of 'scratching', or withdrawing, his horses before the start of races. The press generally attributed this to his desire to maximise his betting wins, and he was condemned as running his horses for profit and not for pure love of the sport as a true sportsman should. But Gretton, brought up in a commercial environment, looked on racing as a business and hoped to make money from it. If he was disliked for bringing the vulgar principles of trade to the Turf, his reputation suffered further when he was compared to his brother, who in 1873 also began a racing stable. But, perhaps with one eye upon appeasing his Turf-averse colleague Michael Thomas Bass, John never placed a bet.

Perhaps envy of Gretton's wealth contributed to the attacks on his racing habits but, lacking family connections and influence, he was unable to command the respect or obtain the silence about his shortcomings that was enjoyed by aristocratic 'Turfites'. Gretton was fair game for the sporting press and from 1873 his name began to appear in the scurrilous gossip columns of the popular weekly, *The Sporting Times*, printed on salmon pink paper and hence known as the *Pink 'Un*. When the *Pink 'Un* exposed not only

Gretton's questionable racing policies but also the company that he kept and his heavy drinking, the negative attention that its 'black sheep' attracted was embarrassing to a family attempting to rise in the social hierarchy. As Gretton's reputation deteriorated, perhaps in part because he kept a mistress, in the spring of 1873 a rift occurred between him and his brother and thereafter they largely went their separate ways. Unfortunately, however, the separation threw Gretton further into the arms of less scrupulous associates.

Lucy's liaison with Gretton gave her entry into the world of the Turf with all its glamour, excitement and gossip. Race meetings provided a good day out in a fairground atmosphere; racegoers could try their hand at the coconut shy, for example, or enjoy the entertainment of banjo minstrels, acrobats and conjurors. A race meeting was an intensely social affair, providing an opportunity to see and be seen. At prestigious events such as Goodwood and Ascot, the Prince of Wales and other members of the royal family were greeted by cheering crowds as they drove to their reserved enclosure in horse-drawn carriages. The more fashionable race meetings served as an arena for women to display the latest styles of the season. Lucy, with no reputation to maintain, could dress to impress. Sixty years later she would recall a gown that she had worn at the Epsom Derby during her Gretton years; entirely covered in sequins and featuring a fish tail, it had been designed to give a 'mermaid' effect. It was, Lucy would recall gleefully, the 'sort of dress no lady could have worn'. Every eye, she remembered, had been upon herself, and the horse racing nearly forgotten. But as the heads turned towards the glistening figure, those not in the know would have asked one another, 'Who is she?' and the whispered reply of 'Frederick Gretton …' would have been enough to enlighten them. As Gretton's mistress Lucy had no real identity of her own but was effectively a manifestation of her lover's wealth, and was hence his property.

In 1874 Gretton placed his stable of thirty horses at the establishment of trainer John Porter of Kingsclere in Hampshire, almost monopolising Porter's business. Early success with Sterling had given Gretton confidence as a judge of horseflesh and as the 1870s progressed he began to spend excessively, and often indiscriminately, on horses. Imagining that an expensive animal was a good one he paid sums of up to £2,500, but throwing money at horses did not guarantee winners. By 1876, after two or three years of lacklustre racing, the press suggested that Gretton had bought a lot of expensive horses for nothing, and commented upon his 'unlucky' racing colours.

But Gretton's luck was about to turn. In 1877 he purchased Isonomy, a bay colt, for the relatively modest sum of 320 guineas. The small but powerful-looking horse had been sired by Sterling, now retired and out at stud. Isonomy showed promise, and Gretton and Porter came up with a plan. The result would become a Turf legend. For a year they kept the colt out of the public eye while Porter prepared him for one race – the Cambridgeshire Handicap at Newmarket in October 1878. Gretton's intention was to pull off a huge gambling coup. Having complete confidence in Isonomy, Gretton backed the horse with large sums, and when Isonomy, a complete unknown with odds of 40–1, crossed the finishing line first by a large lead over a field of thirty-four runners there was an uproar. Gretton received £2,187 in prize money but his betting winnings were thought to amount to £40,000. Gretton and Isonomy were instant celebrities and John Porter's reputation as a trainer was made. At the Bath Hotel, Gretton and his friends celebrated late into the night for weeks on end, and a horse portrait painter was commissioned to depict Isonomy. Over the next two years Isonomy won the majority of the races in which he was entered and no more was heard of Gretton's bad luck.

It was probably during this period that Lucy, calculating that she could benefit financially from Gretton's success, returned from Paris to live in London full-time. Having acquired some of the polish and dress sense of French women, she appeared in London society transformed. In Paris she had made a friend, Eva Thaddeus, who wrote later that Lucy's emergence in London created a 'sensation' because of her 'extreme youth and beauty'. Lucy was 'small, exquisitely made, with tiny waist and beautiful shoulders, her carriage was superb, her head proudly carried; her taste in dress was infallible, coming up to the highest standards of Parisian elegance.' Lucy, wrote Eva Thaddeus, became a 'famous toast and beauty of the late Seventies and early Eighties, in the spacious days when the fair one's health was drunk in champagne from her satin slipper'. Eva Thaddeus had even heard of a 'certain London clubman whose proudest boast it was that on one romantic evening he had kissed "Poppy" Radmall in the height of her beauty'. Having learned fast in Paris, Lucy was able to move in the exclusive circles of the very rich, and years later would relate how she had often seen the Prime Minister Benjamin Disraeli in company, although she had never spoken to him. Lucy may have lived at Claridge's Hotel in Brook Street, Mayfair, an establishment that was the height of fashion, exclusivity and comfort, for she would recall how when she drove up the hotel's carriage sweep people had climbed on the iron railings to look at her. It was a triumph for the girl who only a few years previously had run through the city's streets as a ragamuffin.

When Tom Radmall turned to bookmaking as a quick escape from his financial problems he had a special advantage – his connection with Gretton through Lucy. His business as a professional racecourse bookmaker did well and, while the extent of the relationship between the two men is unclear, Radmall may have owed his success to Gretton's influence and racing tips. By 1878 Tom had done so well that he was able to buy an elegant four-storeyed house, 12 Pelham Place, in the heart of South Kensington. While Lucy was the toast of London society, Radmall became a racehorse owner, purchasing fourteen horses within a few months. He still maintained his bookmaking business and, probably with Lucy's help, expanded it to France. In the winter of 1879–80 Lucy travelled with her brother and his wife to the French Riviera, while in the months of her absence Gretton returned to his sisters at Bladon House.

English visitors delighted in stepping off the train into the warmth and beauty of the Riviera, with its grand snow-covered mountains and coastal panoramas. The Radmalls first attended the annual two-day racing event at Nice which marked the start of the Riviera's winter 'season', occupying the first three months of the year. After the races ended the Nice Carnival began, bringing thousands of visitors the city to enjoy a great procession of floats which paraded the streets, balls and fireworks. As they strolled in the sunshine along Nice's famous Promenade des Anglais among the monied of many nations, did Tom and Lucy Radmall reminisce about the old days? They had come a long way from Newgate Street.

After the Nice carnival the Radmalls, along with many others, moved along the coast to the gambling resort of Monte Carlo in Monaco, where Lucy stayed at the fashionable and expensive Grand Hotel. Monte Carlo, gloriously situated on a rocky slope at the foot of the Alpes Maritime, offered a lovely environment, with one visitor describing the 'azure tints of the Mediterranean, the ethereal blue sky, the tropical plants, the orange and lemon plantations, the luxuriance of the olive and the fig trees'. But a greater attraction that winter was the newly opened Grand Casino with its magnificent decorations, parquet floors, chandeliers and lounges furnished in crimson velvet. The Radmalls were among the first visitors.

Lucy was a keen gambler and in later life it would be said of her that she usually gained more money than she lost. The casino had eight tables – six for roulette and two for *rouge-et-noir* – and the gambling rooms, an observer noted, had a 'hubbub of voices' and a 'general sense of scuffle and turmoil' in an atmosphere that resembled that of a 'thriving city bank'. As Lucy jostled with those pressed three or four deep around the tables, she was among British, French, Italian and Russian gamblers. Monte Carlo drew some whose curiosity overcame their strong disapproval of gambling, and one woman correspondent of the *Dundee Evening Telegraph* was disgusted by the 'foetid atmosphere' of the casino where people stayed for hours, 'every feeling and thought absorbed in the passion which is born of the greed for gold'. Monte Carlo, she wrote, represented all that was 'mischievous, false, and unholy in the world'. There were women 'dressed in the height of Parisian fashion, wearing garments and jewels the price of which may have been the ruin of some youth born for better things'. If Gretton had been born for better things, then Lucy could be classed among them. But the Monte Carlo authorities ensured that there was plenty to please the non-gambler. High-class cultural attractions were provided free of charge and Lucy was probably present at the inauguration of the Opéra de Monte Carlo in the casino's theatre, the Salle Garnier, with a performance by the French actress Sarah Bernhardt, then at the height of her fame. Outside, the casino's terraced gardens were expensively laid out with exotic plants, flowers and trees to provide an exotic environment for visitors from northern climes. One reporter found them too lovely to describe: 'The high rock rising from the sea is draped in fine terraces and white marble balustrades, and all about overhung with palms, acanthi, cacti, myrtles, and all the tropical vegetation of North Africa.' On the lowest terrace was a grassy shooting ground where the best shots from among the world's wealthy took aim at live pigeons fluttering skywards from little boxes. The shooting tournaments were major betting events, and the high-stakes bidding would make Tom Radmall a considerable sum of money in the coming years.

While Lucy was away, back in Burton-on-Trent Gretton felt it politic to show his face and involve himself in the company of which he was a partner, for in January 1880 Bass, Ratcliff and Gretton was converted into a limited liability company. All 32,000 shares, with a value of £100 each, were divided equally between the eight partners. Gretton was now aged 41 but showed no sign of curtailing his prodigal lifestyle. John may have taken the opportunity of this rare trip home to have a brotherly talk, perhaps discussing questions of responsibility and marriage, and if so he may have been indirectly responsible for the step that Gretton now took. In April, with Lucy back in London, Gretton returned to the Bath Hotel and contacted his lawyers, and on 10 April they drew up the terms of a bond that would pay Lucy £1,000 a year for life. As Lucy had turned 23 two days previously, the legacy may have been a birthday present. Given that a well-paid servant might earn £75 a year the provision was generous, and equivalent in today's values to about £100,000 a year. It demonstrated that Lucy was firmly established as Gretton's long-term mistress and favourite.

In the spring of 1880 Isonomy was entered in the Manchester Cup and gave a performance that would go down in Turf folklore. When after a thrilling race the horse passed the post first out of a field of twenty-one a great cheer went up from both those who had won money on him and those who had lost. The press paid glowing tributes, with one magazine reporting that Isonomy's achievement was the 'most wonderful feat of modern, or indeed any time'. As Isonomy went on to score victory after victory, admirers crowded to the Bath Hotel and the drink flowed freely in long nights of celebration for weeks on end. Gretton's life had entered its apogee and he floated on success, full of bravado and his own cleverness. But Gretton was becoming notorious for the conduct and management of his stable, and was further criticised for scratching some horses and not running others. In 1880 the negative press reached a crescendo. Because Gretton apparently failed to heed public opinion the press concluded that he cared nothing for it, but, a friend wrote, beneath his 'ruggedness' there lay a 'sensitive nature' and he could be very hurt by unfair criticism. In August 1880, perhaps to remove himself from the hostile atmosphere, Gretton went to Scotland for the grouse-shooting season, having leased the remote 30,000-acre Ben Alder estate in Inverness-shire. Lucy was probably with him on this first visit and, many years later, she would return to Ben Alder under quite different circumstances.

Gretton's intense involvement in the affairs of the Turf gave him frequent reason to drink – for celebration or consolation – and by 1880 alcohol had him in its grip. He was planning another Cambridgeshire betting coup in November with a colt, Fernandez, brother to Isonomy. However, when his scheme went wrong the extent of his alcohol problem was revealed. In June Fernandez had performed so well in a race that he had shown his form and thereby thwarted Gretton's plans. Blaming the jockey, Tom Cannon, for letting Fernandez run so well, Gretton complained to a friend, Sir John Astley, who wrote a comic account. Gretton met Astley with 'mingled tears of brandy, whisky, champagne, port wine, brown sherry, and other fluids coursing down his face', exclaiming, 'Oh, Sir John! What in the world was Tom Cannon about, to ride such a race as that!' When they met again five months later, on the day before the Cambridgeshire race, Gretton had 'done himself a little extra well (as was not his unfrequent habit)', Astley wrote, and was still 'bemoaning his jockey's uprightness over a glass of scotch'. But worse was in store. During the race Fernandez was in the lead when a mare, Lucetta, swerved across the course towards him, forcing Gretton's jockey to hold Fernandez back. Fernandez did not win and after the race the race stewards investigated the matter. When they decided in favour of Lucetta, Astley wrote, Gretton was furiously angry and 'consumed enough Scotch to wash a bus'.

By the end of 1880 Gretton's health had deteriorated to the extent that he gave the management of his racing engagements over to an old Burton friend, Freddy Swindell. When in November Swindell manipulated Gretton's horses before the Liverpool Cup race the betting public was confused and angry, and the sporting press in an uproar. Gretton, one newspaper commented, had achieved in the public mind 'unpopularity rarely attained in so comparatively brief a career on the Turf as his has been'. It was the last straw for his trainer John Porter, and when he asked Gretton to remove his horses from Kingsclere it was the beginning of the end for the brewer.

Such was Gretton's state of health that his doctors prescribed a sea cruise. He already had a yacht, the *Modwena*, but in 1880 gave it to his brother and bought a larger one, the *Margaret*, ordering it to be fitted out for a Mediterranean cruise for the spring of 1881. Lucy was already in France and perhaps the plan was that she would meet Gretton on the Riviera. But as the *Margaret*, flying a flag in the racing colours of orange and purple from its mizzen mast, waited for Gretton to join it, he had an accident. One night at the Bath Hotel he fell downstairs in the dark and was so badly injured that travel was out of the question, and the Mediterranean cruise was abandoned.

Meanwhile, in the spring of 1881, Gretton's horses won few races and the press commented on his long run of bad luck. By now Isonomy had retired and been put out to stud, and Gretton's other horses were no longer in the first rank; the root cause was generally thought to be their removal from

John Porter's care. In June, with Lucy back from France, Gretton joined the *Margaret* for several weeks but, perhaps frightened of being far from his doctors, only shuttled only between the Isle of Wight and Gosport. Then in August he again visited Ben Alder with a party of friends, one of whom was probably Lucy. But Gretton did not stay long in Scotland, for the Turf acted like a drug. That autumn he was seen at many race meetings but it was the last period in which he attended on a regular basis. In December it was revealed that Gretton's prize money had been only £1,726 that year, whereas it was rumoured that he had spent £40,000 on his horses.

But if Gretton's situation was deteriorating, Tom Radmall's was on the up; on the strength of his foreign winnings in 1881 he had added eleven more horses to his stable. Radmall was becoming a force to be reckoned with on the Turf. Early in 1882 he was once more on the Riviera, and *The Sportsman* noted that the 'genial and popular sportsman' was as well known in sporting circles in France as in England. Radmall had a particularly successful season and upon his return to London in mid-April it was reported that he was 'swimming on a tide of fortune', and in betting at Monte Carlo casino 'Tom Radmall couldn't do wrong'. While he continued to work as a bookmaker, his wealth and aura of luck and success were helping him up the social ladder; in April he was reported as being among the 'many "swells" and leading patrons of racing' at Newmarket. Money, success and status were his, for now.

Early in 1882 Gretton again ordered the *Margaret* to be fitted out for a Mediterranean cruise but by this time alcoholism was reducing him to a state of invalidity, and for a second time his plan came to nothing. Gretton did not attend races during the early part of the season and in April his condition was so precarious that his family chartered a special train from Burton-on-Trent to London. Gretton, it was rumoured, was to be carried home to die. However, he rallied once more. Lucy was almost certainly with him from this time until his death; she could hardly have abandoned him now and besides, she was working to get more money out of him.

Gretton attended Ascot in early June 1882 but by this time, as a friend reported, he was a 'great invalid'. He did not get out of his carriage, and although he drew it up near the finishing line, not one of his horses won a race. Gretton spent most of June and July again shuttling in the *Margaret* between Southampton and the Isle of Wight with friends, but cruising for the sake of his health was futile when he did not remove himself from the temptations of alcohol, and he had 2,000 bottles of wine and spirits stowed aboard the yacht. Despite his poor health Gretton still hoped to attend Goodwood, and the *Margaret* anchored nearby in the Solent off Ryde Pier. On a fine day, it was said, Goodwood racegoers with binoculars could see the white sails of yachts, but if from the yacht's deck Gretton caught a glimpse of Goodwood it would be his last view of a racecourse.

Gretton's illness forced him to give up his peripatetic Turf lifestyle and he leased or purchased 22 Thurloe Square, a five-storey Italianate townhouse in South Kensington. The house was well located in a fashionable area near the Victoria and Albert Museum, fronting the large Thurloe Square garden with its paths and shrubs for the enjoyment of the square's residents. Lucy had probably influenced Gretton's choice, for Thurloe Square was only a short walk from Radmall's more modest home in Pelham Place. Early in August the *Margaret* returned to Southampton and Gretton, too ill to shoot at Ben Alder, let the estate and went to Brighton for his health. His horses were still being entered in races and by now Tom Radmall was playing a major role in the management of Gretton's stable.

In August Gretton had a stroke and on 26 August he hastily drew up a will. The only specific bequests were for the two people who were with him at Thurloe Square at the time – Lucy, and William Pawsey, his 'man servant'. Under the terms of the will Lucy was left £6,000 (£600,000 in 2019 values) per year for life, which probably represented the amount that she calculated would keep her in the style to which she had become accustomed. The residue of Gretton's estate was left to his unmarried sisters Frances and Clara. That his brother John and married sister Mary were not mentioned suggested that Gretton and Lucy regarded them as their particular enemies. The decade that Lucy had invested in Gretton had paid off handsomely; her future was financially secure.

Two distinguished doctors, probably the most expensive in England, were treating Gretton for enlargement of the liver and dropsy, or oedema, caused by alcohol abuse. Sir William Jenner had a great reputation, being Physician in Ordinary to the Queen and the Prince of Wales. Sir Alfred Cooper was a fashionable English surgeon whose patients also included the Prince of Wales. Cooper and Jenner apparently did not believe Gretton's life to be in immediate danger and, perhaps unaware of the *Margaret*'s alcoholic cargo, recommended another cruise. For the third time, therefore, the yacht was put under orders for the Mediterranean, with the voyage to begin shortly after Christmas. Gretton now made the drastic decision to greatly reduce his stable and gave instructions to Tattersalls, the auctioneers, to sell ten horses, including the famous Isonomy. But his change of lifestyle had come too late.

Gretton was well enough to entertain company at Thurloe Square during the second week of November, and spoke of his forthcoming cruise. Then a few days later, on the evening of Wednesday, 15 November, he again sat down to dinner in his dining room at about eight o'clock. Lucy was in the house, and probably with him, when shortly after eating Gretton was seized with a violent fit of coughing which ruptured a blood vessel in his lungs and caused a haemorrhage. Doctors Jenner and Cooper were called with haste but could do nothing, and Gretton died at about twenty minutes to nine. It must have been a harrowing experience for Lucy to wait help-lessly for the doctors while Gretton drowned in his own blood. Lucy acted quickly. Calculating that once the news reached Gretton's family they would descend upon the house, she hurriedly gathered jewellery and valuables and departed for Victoria or Charing Cross railway station, from where she could travel to a south coast port to catch a cross-Channel steamer ferry to France. Gretton's death exposed Lucy in the press, and a newspaper reported with heavy sarcasm that she was 'so overcome by the shock of his sudden death that she felt herself obliged to leave town for Paris the same evening. The painful surroundings were too much for her.'

Gretton's brother and sisters duly arrived to reclaim their 'black sheep' and carry his body home; they placed a terse announcement in the 'Deaths' column of a local newspaper: 'On the 15th inst., Frederick Gretton Esq., of Bladon House, Burton-on-Trent. No cards.' This notice made it seem that Bladon House had been Gretton's habitual home; his life with Lucy at Thurloe Square was obliterated. There was a general consensus in the press obituaries that Gretton had not approached sport as a true gentleman should: 'His career was harmful, for he lowered racing to the lowest business level,' was how one journal put it. References to the cause of his ill health were guarded, however, with one newspaper regretting the 'wreckage of a once stalwart frame'. Another reported delicately that Gretton had 'suc-cumbed to a long illness which might perhaps have been averted had the deceased observed a little more care in his mode of life'. All in all, as another writer mused, it was 'sad to think of a life closed at the early age of 43, with little else in its leisure hours to cheer it but the din of the racecourse and the approving smiles of doubtful friends'.

When the contents of Gretton's will emerged, the public exposure must have distressed and humiliated his family. For one thing, it made his relationship with Lucy the subject of common gossip, and the *Derby Daily Telegraph* referred to the 'fortunate lady who for some time has borne his name'. The press was also quick to imply that Gretton should have left the *Margaret* to John, who was a keen yachtsman but still using Gretton's cast-off *Modwena*. Yet amid all this one can only imagine that the Gretton family must have felt a certain relief that their wayward relative could cause neither himself nor them further embarrassment.

Before long, Lucy returned from Paris to attend to financial matters. Gretton's siblings were unhappy with the terms of the will and threatened to contest it on the basis that Gretton had not been in his right mind when he signed it, or had been unduly influenced. But nothing could be proved and the Grettons were forced to accept the will's validity. Once the financial matters were settled it was agreed that Lucy would receive an annuity of £5,000 clear of tax and duties, while still receiving the £1,000 from the previous bond. She would be paid the annuity quarterly, which equated to four payments per year each of £1,250. Whether as owner or tenant is unclear, but Lucy kept 22 Thurloe Square until 1884.

Lucy now had to deal with the social impact of Gretton's death. While he was alive he had provided protection of sorts but now she was exposed as his mistress, and therefore a person of low morals and hence social status. Isolated, she became the butt of jokes. One, oft-repeated, was an epitaph about a well-known sporting brewer who had left a fortune to his mistress: 'Living he made Beer; dying he made a Poll an heiress.' The joke was a play on words that referred to Apollinaris Water, a popular sparkling German mineral water, while a 'poll' was a mistress. Nevertheless, at the age of 25, Lucy had the advantages of good looks, high spirits, money and freedom, and within a year of Gretton's death she would pull off an astonishing coup. Having obtained for herself a remarkable degree of financial security and independence, Lucy's next moves would reveal a different goal. Gretton had not been comfortable or accepted in the upper ranks of English society, and Lucy wanted a man who was.

2

MISS GRAFTON AND MRS BRINCKMAN

'Lucky' Tom Radmall, as the press called him, had continued to push his way upwards in the Turf elite and by the spring of 1883 such was his social stature that *Sporting Life* listed him among the notable titled owners – the Hungarian Prince Gusztav Batthyany, the Russian Prince Soltykoff and the Duke of St Albans – who watched their horses exercising at Newmarket. But Lucky Radmall was about to be expelled from the gilded world that he had worked so hard to enter. His downfall came suddenly, at the two-day Second Spring Meeting at Sandown Park in Surrey. Radmall had entered his horse Brilliancy in two races. In the first she achieved only fifth place but in the second, having initially lagged behind and entered the final straight last, the horse suddenly surged to win by a length. It was rumoured that a number of influential figures, including the Prince of Wales, had placed bets based on Brilliancy's form as demonstrated in the first race and were angry. Radmall was suspected of asking his jockey to run the mare differently in each race to engineer the outcomes for personal gain through betting. This was a practice known as ramping; Radmall had used it before but now he had been caught out. There was an outbreak of public indignation and the matter came in for close scrutiny in the press, with the *Pink 'Un* commenting that Radmall 'might have had the decency to wait a fortnight' between races. Had he done so there may have been suspicions, but nothing could have been proven. Another newspaper thought that Radmall was either 'very stupid or else very confident to carry out so indecent a "ramp"', and although many others were doing the same thing every week, they were not so 'barefaced and clumsy'.

An investigation was launched by the Sandown stewards – a particularly aristocratic team that included Sir Frederick Johnstone and Lieutenant-General Owen Williams, both friends of the Prince of Wales. But who was Radmall? A diminutive Cockney bookmaker from Newgate Street, the son of a tradesman, who had aspired to cross the social divide to join the ranks of gentlemen while burdened with a disgraceful sister. Radmall was in trouble. After consideration the stewards referred the case to the Jockey Club, the 'high court' of the Turf, and a few days later it was announced at Newmarket that Radmall and his jockey had been found guilty of dishonourable conduct, and that both were 'warned off' the Turf for an indefinite period. Banned from every racecourse in the country, Radmall was not even allowed to run his horses. All the sporting correspondents were agreed that Radmall had got what he deserved, although there was surprise at the heaviness of his sentence and speculation that he had been barred out of spite because he had won £20,000 from a prominent Jockey Club member at Monte Carlo earlier that year. Whatever the case, it was felt that Radmall's aspirations as a financial and social climber had been a contributory factor. He had no choice but to sell off his stable of nineteen horses. He then went to France and bided his time working as a bookmaker.

At about this time Lucy had received the first instalment of her Gretton inheritance and the brother and sister were two of the most talked-about figures related to the Turf. At the height of the Brilliancy scandal the 79-year-old Prince Batthyany, a great friend of the Prince of Wales, had dropped dead at Sandown racecourse. When it was revealed that he had left his six-figure fortune to his mistress, a newspaper commented that were she to inherit, the wrong done would be 'greater than even that of Mr Gretton'. Lucy had already suffered social stigma because of her relationship with Gretton, and now being the sister of Tom Radmall had also become a liability.

With neither Gretton nor her brother to support her, Lucy decided to branch out on her own. For a decade living an assumed life had been second nature and now she planned a new identity for herself as an actress. Obtaining a part in a play was no easy matter for an unknown but, targeting the fashionable Drury Lane Theatre in Covent Garden, Lucy marched in one day early in 1883 and demanded to see Augustus Harris, the young manager. She was undaunted when told that an introduction was impossible:

'I was very good-looking in those days,' she would say when telling the story in old age, and she refused to leave the premises until Harris saw her. Once in his presence she would not leave until he promised her a part in a play; she got a job through being 'such a bloody nuisance', she would recall. Harris, like many a man who would attempt to defy Lucy's will in later years, had realised when he was beaten. It so happened that he was planning the production of a modern drama, *Lady Clare*, for a tour of the provinces. He gave Lucy a role, and even half a century later she would remember her victory with glee, for suddenly everything had become '*couleur de rose*', as she put it.

The plot of *Lady Clare* was concerned with love and money, themes with which Lucy was familiar, and she was given the part of Melissa Smale, the designing and shallow daughter of a vulgar American millionaire. The first scene opens with the pretty but poor Lady Clare in love with her cousin, the worthless Lord Ambermere. But Melissa Smale, Lady Clare's old school-friend, secretly hating Lady Clare and envying her social status, lures the impoverished Ambermere away. Theirs will be a marriage of convenience, for Ambermere wants money and Melissa Smale a title. Lucy was acting the part of an heiress who was outside the sphere of English high society but was able to marry into the aristocracy on the basis of her money; she could not have known then that she would act out the role for real eighteen years later.

A new name offered Lucy a means of escape from the associations of the old one, and she adopted the stage name of 'Miss Lucy Grafton'. Prior to the departure of *Lady Clare* on a provincial tour an inaugural public performance was scheduled for 24 August 1883, for which a newspaper advertisement read:

Lady Clare, the new Drama of Modern Society. This day (Friday) at 3.0, at Crystal Palace, under direction of Mr Augustus Harris. Characters by Misses Lizzie Claremont, Kate Pattison, Daisy England, C.E. Barker, L. Grafton, J. Thompson, Messrs. Augustus Cooke, W.R. Sutherland, H. Parker, E.D. Lyons, Bruton Robins, F. Pemberton, H. Barri Stevens.

Lucy must have been delighted to see her name in print but the secret of her identity had leaked out, and even as she and the other cast members rehearsed their lines and put the finishing touches to their costumes, two *Pink 'Un* journalists were on their way to the Crystal Palace for the performance. Warner Allen, who knew Lucy in later life, would write that during this period the 'fame of no reigning toast was then complete, until it had been consecrated by some witty impropriety in the blushing pages' of that newspaper. The journalists planned to write an extraordinary exposé of Lucy that would be a coup for the *Pink 'Un* and a prime example of the work that made its reputation. They wrote under pseudonyms, 'Stalled Ox' being James Davis, known for his caustic racing and drama commentaries, while 'Pot' was Henry Pottinger Stephens, a journalist and writer of burlesques and comic operas.

The 'witty improprieties' of the *Pink 'Un,* Allen wrote, could only be fully understood by the 'man about town in the know', and certainly readers would need to be 'in the know' about the article that Davis and Stephens would produce, for they never mentioned Lucy's name. To identify Lucy Grafton as Lucy Radmall, mistress and heiress of Gretton, readers would require a good knowledge of current Turf gossip. For this reason much in the article is obscured from the modern reader, although the intention can usually be inferred. With a style that was apparently disingenuous but employed biting humour, sarcasm and devious and oblique references to aspects of Lucy's life, the writers intended to amuse and titillate those who knew her backstory.

The news of the actress's new career had 'crept out somehow', the journalists wrote. 'At first it was only a rumour. It was muttered in Mayfair. Discussed openly in Piccadilly. All the Clubs rang with it. Then it rolled along the Strand, and finally reached Fleet Street.' The rumour, the article reported with irony, was that a 'real live lady, possessing a gigantic fortune of six thousand a year, was going to step down in humility from her lofty pinnacle in society to tread the boards of a provincial theatre'. This lady was an 'enthusiastic aspirant for dramatic fame. Salary was not so much an object as a well-dressed part.' Taking to the stage for 'pure love for theatricals', she was 'endeavouring to elevate the tone of the drama'. If by this point readers had not already guessed her identity, a further clue was given by the suggestion that she had 'amassed a fortune on the Turf. It was whispered that she had inherited her money from a wealthy brewer, to whom she was engaged, but who died before his time.' The keen *Pink 'Un* reader would know for sure who and what was meant.

The writers understood, they stated with sarcasm, that Augustus Harris had secured the 'priceless services of the new amateur' on the strength of his success with Mrs Maddick. In fact, Harris had been criticised for hiring the pretty but talentless Mrs Maddick. As for Lucy, 'although her bashfulness prevented her making a first appearance at the National Theatre, yet Augustus persuaded her to accept an important character in *Lady Clare*'. As Davis and Stephens commented, 'You don't find people every day who, with six thousand a year, are mugs enough to go play-acting at nothing and a half a week, and find their own dresses.'

Expecting, therefore, to see an attractive but stupid and stage-struck young woman, Stalled Ox and Pot had set off to the Crystal Palace. They joked that they travelled in a hansom cab that was 'bright orange with black wheels', a reference to both Gretton's racing colours and those of his brother John. On the way they went along Dulwich Road, passing an 'institution to which the stage is indebted for so much beauty and talent. It is called "The National Training School for Mistresses".' This was probably a reference to the James Allen's Girls' School, which Lucy may have attended. Arriving at the Crystal Palace the men made their way to the theatre but were not impressed with the venue; if they had money they would 'get a better theatre to play in than this inconvenient dirty one'. The few people in the audience included the 'Great Augustus 1, of Drury Lane', and other theatrical figures.

Studying the theatre programme they found the part of Melissa Smale would be played by 'Miss L. Grafton', and, in what may have been a tongue-in-cheek reference to Lucy's previous stage appearances, observed that 'the fact of this being her first appearance on any stage is ignored'. Miss Grafton's entrée in the theatre was quiet, but 'how differently Mrs Langtry made her *début*'. As Mrs Langtry was a former favourite of the Prince of Wales who had become an actress, the comparison could be taken to imply a suggestion that Lucy had also been the prince's mistress, or simply that she had been someone's mistress.

The play began and Stalled Ox and Pot were initially unimpressed. The lead actress made a 'weak and timid' Lady Clare, while Lord Ambermere rudely kept his hat on while talking to the ladies. But at last came the moment the *Pink 'Un* correspondents had been waiting for – the entrance of Lucy as Melissa Smale. Then, a 'nicely figured, pretty little lady appears fussing with a fan'. She was wearing a bodice of shining metal: 'Probably she has changed one of her million pound notes into new three-penny pieces, and had them sewn together.' Lucy had dressed the part of an American heiress. The critics praised her for making an 'intelligent rendering of a somewhat eccentric part'. She acted 'delicately and with spirit', and delivered her lines 'quietly and unassumingly', with an American accent. But after the praise came the attack: if Lucy were not so rich she could have become 'as great a comedy actress as Miss Phillis Broughton or Birdie Brightling'. This was damning indeed, for the actress Phyllis Broughton received poor reviews while Birdie Brightling was an 8-year-old child prodigy who toured the provinces as an 'American Banjo Soloist, Characteristic Vocalist and Dancer'.

As Lucy was not on stage during the last act she came out to sit in the audience. When the play ended the correspondents headed for the stage door to meet her for, Pot joked, he hoped to sell her one of his plays. However, he held out little hope, for the quality of her performance suggested that she was 'not quite so foolish' as he had hoped. But Lucy had already left for her 'castle in Belgrave'. The article ended with a final swipe at Lucy's origins, for the men wrote that on the way home they passed through Kennington Green, her birthplace. Lucy must have realised that her cover had been blown, and the secret circumstances of her private life, just then at a delicate stage, were thrown into a hiatus. She had a week of crisis management ahead.

Meanwhile, after the opening at the Crystal Palace, the company, scenery, and props moved on to Portsmouth for the first engagement of the provincial tour. The opening performance took place on Monday, 27 August at the town's Theatre Royal, and the cast waited anxiously for the reviews. The local press was appreciative; the play was 'mounted, dressed, and acted' with 'perfection', and Miss Lucy Grafton got a special mention as a 'most bewitching Melissa Smale, with the prettiest of nasal twangs beloved of the Yankee'. Another local paper found that Miss Grafton and the actor playing her father made 'quaint amusing Yankees'. The week at Portsmouth ended with the final performance on Saturday, 1 September, the day upon which the damning article appeared in the *Pink 'Un*. While the company decamped to the Theatre Royal at Reading where the next performance was scheduled for Monday evening, Lucy hurried back to Thurloe Square to make preparations for her wedding.

The fact that the wedding was planned at the last minute and it was Lucy, rather than her fiancé, who hurried matters along, suggested that she wished to secure her man before he became aware of the *Pink 'Un* article. If so, she had a race against time. Early on the morning of Monday, 3 September she applied for a marriage licence, which allowed a quick wedding without announcements being made in advance. Lucy swore an oath that she knew of no legal impediment and that for the past fifteen days her 'usual place of abode' had been within the parish of Holy Trinity Brompton in South Kensington. Thurloe Square fulfilled that criterion.

The ceremony took place that same day at Holy Trinity Church. The marriage certificate recorded that Fanny Lucy Radmall, aged 24, of 22 Thurloe Square and of no stated profession, had married Theodore Francis Brinckman, aged 21, gentleman, of 40 Berkeley Square. Lucy had knocked two years off her age to disguise the fact that she was five years older than her groom, and had also given the occupation of her deceased father as 'Gentleman'. Two people signed as witnesses but they seem to have been unconnected with the couple, suggesting that no friends or family members were present. And so Miss Lucy Radmall, also known as Miss Lucy Grafton, had become Mrs Theodore Brinckman, the wife of the son and heir of Sir Theodore Henry Brinckman, baronet.

Years later Lucy would tell Allen that at that moment, when everything was '*couleur de rose*', she had been a 'fool and spoilt it all' by losing her heart and running off with Brinckman. But Theodore Brinckman was quite a catch for any woman, let alone one with the past and family connections of Lucy. Tall, dark, strongly built and impossibly handsome, he came from a wealthy family. The Brinckmans possessed an estate, St Leonards near Windsor in Berkshire, in addition to the Berkeley Square house in Mayfair and property in Yorkshire and elsewhere. Brinckman provided Lucy with not only the security and respectability of marriage, but also a large step up the social ladder.

While Lucy's liaison with Gretton had been hardly surprising, her ensnaring of the son of a baronet was a great feat, the first of the stunning successes that she would make with each of her three marriages. Lucy would confide to Wentworth Day that she had told Brinckman that she was 19, and it was probably the case that he was unaware of her true identity; as far as he knew she was a rich young woman with a large house in Thurloe Square, probably inherited from her 'gentleman' father. Brinckman may not even have known her real name, and by the time he read it on the marriage certificate it was too late. But why had he rushed into marriage? Far in the future, in 1912, the *Chicago Tribune* would look back to this time and report that as a 'mere lad' he had been 'jockeyed into marrying a girl, on the understanding that she was about to become a mother'. Too late he had found out that he had been lied to by a woman who was only after marriage and money. If this was true then the relationship had been going on for some months. But with rumours such as this swirling round London, Lucy had made Brinckman a laughing stock and compounded her own reputation. After marrying in haste the couple would have to live with the consequences.

The young man's family already had its own scandals and secrets, for Brinckman's great-grandmother had been Elizabeth Conyngham, the last in the string of mistresses of King George IV. Elizabeth, shrewd but vulgar, was said to have taken advantage of the besotted King's attachment to promote the interests of her family and secure a baronetcy for her husband. Brinckman's own mother had died when he was aged 15 and Claude, his only sibling, aged 6, but he had had the conventional upbringing of an aristocrat, attending Eton school, joining the East Kent Militia (the 'Buffs'), and at the age of 18 being presented to the Prince of Wales at St James's Palace. The following year, however, Brinckman's life had begun to demonstrate the turmoil and incident that would characterise it for years to come. A major aspect was his problematic relationships with women, for he became involved in three romantic entanglements within two years. His first engagement dragged on for months before an announcement that no marriage would take place, and five months later he was engaged to someone else. However, in March 1883 it was announced that this engagement was also off, and perhaps by this time Brinckman had met Lucy. He celebrated his twenty-first birthday in May that year and with financial freedom, and perhaps under the influence of Lucy, he began to invest in racehorses. In mid-August Brinckman adopted the racing colours of 'Eton blue, brown belt', showing allegiance to his old school.

After the wedding ceremony there was little time before the new Mrs Brinckman, doubtless rejoicing at her victory and new status, hastened to Paddington Station to catch the train to Reading in time for her evening performance as the grasping Melissa Smale. The honeymoon would have to wait. Lucy appeared at Reading all week and also at Southampton the following week. *Lady Clare* continued to receive good reviews, the *Era* reporting that the play had been 'most beautifully staged, and the clever artists have interpreted their parts in a manner deserving of the highest encomiums, receiving unbounded applause nightly'. But after the final performance at Southampton on 15 September Lucy quit, and for the rest of the tour the part of Melissa Smale would be played by another actress.

But although Lucy was now free, she and Brinckman may not have lived together, for in mid-October it was reported that he was suffering from typhoid fever from drinking infected water and was at his father's house in Berkeley Square. Was Lucy tending her sick husband, or staying alone at Thurloe Square? Brinckman's father may still have been unaware of the marriage, or have banned Lucy from his house. She may have feigned a miscarriage, or even have had one that would leave her infertile. By 6 November 1883 Brinckman was well enough to attend a family wedding and a few days later was reported to have gone to Scotland, where the family leased Nairnside, a shooting estate a few miles east of Inverness. But still there was no sign of Lucy.

It took the press almost three months to get wind of the marriage, and then on 24 November the *Pink 'Un* published a small item: 'Miss Lucy Radmall, who benefited so much under the will of Mr Gretton, is about to marry the son of a baronet, and to take the Olympic Theatre. We wish her joy in both enterprises.' If the truth about the new Mrs Brinckman had not been generally known, the *Pink 'Un* had ensured that it was now. The story was such a sensation that it crossed the Atlantic, with the *New York Daily Tribune* reporting on the supposedly upcoming marriage in its 'London Gossip' column. Lucy's alliance with Brinckman had already caused 'much perturbation', it reported, and the marriage rumour had thrown the 'entirety of "masherdom," the sporting world, the front row of the ballet, the ranks of aspiring choristers, the keeper of the stage door at the Gaiety Theatre, and the noble array of county baronets', into a state of excitement. Perhaps Lucy had worked at the Gaiety Theatre as a teenager? There had been great curiosity, the *Tribune* continued, as to what Lucy would do with her Gretton legacy and there had been suggestions that she would either 'own race-horses, start a newspaper, take a theatre, or get married'.

The *Tribune* believed that she was soon to become the lessee of the Olympic Theatre, in London's Strand. Although there was no truth in the Olympic Theatre story, once the rumour began it could not be stopped. The Olympic had been struggling for years, but in 1883 it had been bought by a wealthy woman, Mrs Anna Conover. Although she had no connection with Lucy, the press assumed that they were one and the same. For years to come Mrs Conover would be described as 'Mrs Gretton'; her doings would be muddled with those of Lucy to the detriment of both, and damaging the Olympic Theatre's business prospects.

The hasty Brinckman marriage, with Mrs Conover and Tom Radmall thrown in, was the talk of London. The young man's youthful folly was laughed at and condemned in high-society circles. London had become an uncomfortable environment for the new couple. Four months after her wedding, leaving Florence in charge of 22 Thurloe Square, Lucy embarked with Brinckman on the RMS *Ballaarat,* bound for Melbourne, Australia.

The weather was cold and windy as Lucy, Brinckman and their two servants – a lady's maid and a manservant – departed from London on the *Ballaarat,* a P&O line steamship. Passing through a gale and high seas in the English Channel and Bay of Biscay, the ship continued into the Mediterranean and from there headed east to Malta and then on to Port Said in Egypt. Leaving the Suez Canal, the ship sailed on to Colombo in Ceylon (modern-day Sri Lanka), and then into hot and humid weather, passing through volcanic ash clouds, probably from the eruption of the Krakatoa volcano in Indonesia the previous August. By the time the *Ballaarat* arrived in Melbourne, Lucy and Brinckman had already been away for two months. London, with all its problems, was pleasantly distant.

Which of them had instigated their escape on a belated honeymoon? A sea voyage in which they were cooped up together for weeks on end seemed calculated to lay bare Lucy's deficiencies before Brinckman. Perhaps Lucy felt that his interest was already waning and wanted optimum access in order to shore up their relationship. Alternatively, Brinckman's father may have paid for the Australia trip in the hope that his son's eyes would be opened to his folly. And indeed this may have been what happened. Brinckman was educated and polished but Lucy's Paris gloss was only skin deep, and years later the *Chicago Tribune* would state that the marriage had been unhappy from the outset owing to differences in 'rank and education'.

In the great Victoria Gold Rush of the mid-nineteenth century Melbourne had grown from a village to a rich metropolis in only fifty years. Already by the time of Lucy's visit the city had many fine public buildings that included the Treasury and Post Office, while others were under construction. There was only one really good hotel, Menzies, and so it was probably there that the Brinckmans stayed. The couple would spend two months in Australia, moving on from Melbourne to Sydney where on 22 May they and their servants embarked on the RMS *Zealandia,* bound for Auckland, New Zealand. It was planned that they would sail together from New Zealand across the Pacific to San Francisco but it seems that while Lucy went on with the servants, Brinckman stayed behind. Perhaps they had tired of each other and Brinckman opted to take the quickest route home. The Pacific voyage, of more than 7,000 miles, was expected to take forty-three days, with stops at Fiji and Honolulu, and Lucy arrived in San Francisco on 16 June. From there she made her way across America, travelling to New York by rail, from where she crossed the Atlantic to Liverpool in a luxury liner.

Once Lucy had sailed on the *Baallarat*, her sister Florence, alone at 22 Thurloe Square and bereft of her sister's advice, immediately got into difficulties. Only three weeks after Lucy's departure, and doubtless influenced by the daring and romance of Lucy's secret marriage, she contracted one of her own. The man she married, 21-year-old Harold Wood, was the son of a prosperous Southend corn merchant and must have seemed a good choice to a girl adrift. In February, while Lucy was en route to the Mediterranean, the wedding ceremony took place at Kensington Register Office. The couple would keep their union secret; perhaps the notoriety of her brother and sister meant that Wood dared not present his bride to his family. Afterwards they lived apart – a strange start to a marriage.

Tom Radmall, meanwhile, had spent the early part of 1884 on the Riviera but upon his return in April he was readmitted to the Turf. There were, however, dark mutterings in the press, with an Australian newspaper reporting that had not Radmall been reinstated, 'unpleasant disclosures would have been forthcoming' for he was well connected in the betting ring, and 'viscounts, earls and right honorables don't always find it convenient to settle on a Monday following a bad week'. Adopting new racing colours of 'pink jacket, green sleeves and cap', Radmall set out to claw his way back to his former position both socially and financially, and by the end of the year his new stable was six strong.

3

BECOMING
MRS BROADHEAD

Despite an absence of many months, London was still too uncomfortable for Mr and Mrs Brinckman. And so, upon their return in 1884, they went to live at Newton, a small village 6 miles south of Cambridge, where they occupied the grey-brick Newton Hall, the largest building in the area. The lease on the house had been taken by Brinckman's father and, as residence at Newton seemed almost calculated to drive a further wedge between the couple, that was perhaps his intention. To Lucy, used to London and Paris, Newton must have been anathema. Of the village's 230 inhabitants half were agricultural labourers. The only middle-class inhabitants were William Hurrell JP, who occupied the manor house, three farmers, a shopkeeper, a carpenter, a baker and a publican. Such society was no substitute for the circles in which Lucy had formerly moved, nor the village shop, inn and bakery compensation for the Champs-Elysées. The cerebral atmosphere of nearby Cambridge would also have irked her, for she never had much time for education. However, if the rural environment was uncongenial to Lucy it had many attractions for her husband. Brinckman would make Newton his base until early in 1887 and, an archetype of the 'hunting, shooting, fishing' English gentleman, he immersed himself in country pursuits. He also built up his stable of racehorses at Newmarket, conveniently located less than 20 miles away, and resumed his life on the Turf. The marriage certainly deteriorated at Newton. Ten years later, at the time of their divorce, a newspaper would report that the Brinckmans had separated 'within a year or two'.

The split, however, would not be total for some time and they continued to live together on and off in various locations until 1889.

Lucy had by now given up the Thurloe Square house and it was probably in the early weeks of 1885 that, after months of tedious rustication, she left Newton for Paris. In common with other women of wealth, Lucy visited the French capital each spring to renew her wardrobe; at this time of her life, to be dressed in the latest Paris fashions was of paramount importance. While Lucy was away Brinckman stayed on at Newton but in early March, perhaps seeking the solace of male company, he joined the East Kent Militia and from then until August spent most of his time with the regiment at Chatham in Kent. However, by start of the grouse-shooting season in August he was back at the family estate of Nairnside in Scotland.

The life of Lucy's sister Florence took another peculiar turn in the summer of 1885. After her marriage to Harold Wood, she had lived on at Thurloe Square until Lucy disposed of it, and subsequently gone to live with her mother at Twickenham. Then Wood's father had died, and it was perhaps the removal of paternal disapproval that allowed the couple to reveal their relationship. But, seemingly unable to admit to their existing marriage, Florence and Harold went through another marriage ceremony. This time the wedding took place in a church, announced in the press, and attended by members of both families; it seems likely that their relatives did not know of the earlier ceremony. The couple went to Brussels but, as her divorce testimony would later reveal, even in their honeymoon suite Wood began the physical abuse that Florence would endure for years to come. The hasty marriages of the two youngest Radmall girls were not proving a success.

During 1886 and 1887, although Lucy and Brinckman spent a considerable time apart, by now Brinckman's father was reconciled to Lucy as indicated by her invitation to join him at Nairnside in the autumn of 1886. Then that winter, Brinckman, alone at Newton, threw himself into local social events. A popular figure, just before Christmas he treated eighty cricketers to a 'first class supper of good roast beef, turkey and fowls' at a local inn and was afterwards presented with a silver hunting horn, and hunting flask and cup for his contributions to the cricket club. Having brought bagpipes, kilt and swords from Scotland, he caused great amusement with his performances of sword dances and bagpipe-playing at local social events. Brinckman, still aged only 24, was an all-round good sport.

Meanwhile, the notoriety of Lucy's liaison with Gretton was unfairly impacting an innocent party. The Olympic Theatre was floundering financially as Mrs Conover staged one bad play after another. Aggrieved that she was still being identified as 'Mrs Gretton', she blamed the erroneous connection for many of her problems. In December 1885, unable to bear it any longer, she wrote to the *Era* to give her 'most positive, emphatic, and unqualified denial. I am *not* Mrs Gretton, *I never have been known as Mrs Gretton.*' Indeed, until the painful Gretton rumour had reached her ears she had not been aware that anyone by the name of Gretton, 'either Mr Gretton or Mrs Gretton, or any other Gretton' had ever existed. As the rumours had militated against her success and damaged her interests she offered a reward of £100 for information that would enable her to bring the originator of the slander to justice. The Olympic would stagger on until 1887, when Mrs Conover became embroiled in a legal case over her dismissal of a pregnant though married actress. When the case brought renewed press mentions of 'Mrs Gretton' Mrs Conover instructed her lawyers to place a notice in the *Morning Post*, the *London Daily News*, and the *Evening Standard*. The lawyers stated that the rumours that Mrs Conover had benefited from Gretton's will were calculated to do her 'great injury', and they issued a 'most ABSOLUTE and UNQUALIFIED DENIAL'. Responding to gossip about Tom Radmall and Gretton, they also refuted the statement that a brother of Mrs Conover had charge of Gretton's racehorses. Mrs Conover, the lawyers insisted, had never seen Mr Gretton or received a penny from him. Shortly after this Mrs Conover admitted defeat and sold the Olympic.

Tom Radmall's struggle to rebuild his life on the Turf was also faltering. In January 1886 he made his annual visit to the Riviera but his famous 'luck' had deserted him. Whether Radmall could have succeeded in rebuilding his Turf career will never be known. At about six o'clock on the morning of 23 February, while he was at Monte Carlo, a huge earthquake hit the area. Hotel guests sprang from their beds, pulled on whatever clothes came to hand and hurried outside to gather in the streets. With the initial panic over but with aftershocks feared, many people hastily retrieved their possessions from their hotel rooms and headed for the railway station. But others were unable to obtain train tickets and the casino gardens were crowded with people sitting on chairs, upturned wheelbarrows or on the grass, wondering what to do. Monte Carlo was thought to be safer than elsewhere because the town was higher and built on solid bedrock, and refugees flooded in from other resorts, exacerbating the accommodation problem. As the day wore on preparations were made to spend the night outdoors, and those who could afford it hired horse-drawn vehicles to sleep in. Radmall secured a place in an omnibus which joined other vehicles – carriages large and small, and even a furniture removal van – lined up along a street near the casino.

By the time Radmall was able to leave Monte Carlo he had spent four nights camped out in the omnibus. Suffering from a cold and bronchitis, he arrived back in England on 28 February. On the evening of 10 March he was well enough to give a dinner party at his home for a few friends but it would be his last social appearance. After the party he became seriously ill with typhoid fever and died at home on 20 March. He was 43, the age at which Gretton had died. The golden boy of the Thames and the Turf had come to grief. In later life, perhaps to avoid the stigma of his disgrace on the Turf, or simply because the memories were too painful, Lucy never mentioned her brother.

By this time the Brinckmans were largely living apart. In later life Lucy would attribute the break to her husband's adultery, telling Wentworth Day that even though they were 'devoted' to each other Brinckman ran after another woman and stayed away at weekends: 'He nearly broke my heart. Night after night I cried myself to sleep,' she said, and those sleepless nights had stayed with her all her life. After Brinckman's betrayal, she would say, 'life was never the same again'. But upon reflection she wished that she had not taken 'Theodore's weekends' so seriously: 'I was a little fool then,' she said, and should have 'played him at his own game' and let him think she had a lover, for there would have been 'plenty of volunteers!' But she was 'far too good – and too silly'.

In 1887 Brinckman left Newton and took a house in Alpha Road in St John's Wood in London. Large, detached and with a good-sized garden surrounded by a high wall, the house was convenient for Regent's Park. Brinckman and Lucy lived there on and off. That Alpha Road was only 200 yards from Lord's cricket ground was a great attraction for Brinckman, for he occasionally batted for Marylebone Cricket Club. Another advantage was the proximity to London nightlife, and a story that Lucy told later indicated Brinckman's way of life at that time. One day in the 1930s when Wentworth Day arrived at her home with a black eye Lucy exclaimed, 'What a beauty! My dear husband, Theodore, used to come home with an eye like that early in the morning.' She advised Wentworth Day to go to 'that man in Jermyn Street', and upon seeing his puzzlement exclaimed, 'Don't be a fool.

He paints them out … Theodore *always* had his painted out.' It dawned upon Wentworth Day that Lucy was referring to Sutherland MacDonald, a tattoo artist who many years previously had had premises in Mayfair, only a short distance from Alpha Road.

Alpha Road also suited Lucy, for St John's Wood had long been the residence of those who, for one reason or another, sought privacy, and by the 1880s it was established as the most 'bohemian' area of London, possessing a reputation for tolerance of the unconventional politics and sexual mores of its residents. Lucy could be classed among the *haute bohème*, the wealthy or aristocratic class who had unconventional lifestyles. In St John's Wood Lucy could keep a low profile while at the same time living among people who would not shun her for her past. She had kept up her French connections and often met Parisian friends, including the famous actress Gabrielle Réjane, known simply as Réjane, at Dieudonné's, a well-known hotel in Ryder Street that was frequented by visiting French actors, singers and artists.

In the spring of 1889, at the age of 32 and after five years in a failing marriage, Lucy finally separated from Brinckman. Stress had always affected her badly and it was on the advice of her doctor that she went to live in Paris, and would stay away for three years. Paris had changed since Lucy's Gretton days. Its massive scheme of urban renewal had created wide new boulevards, public buildings, parks and infrastructure. Prosperous and dynamic, it was Europe's most cosmopolitan capital. The sciences were flourishing and there were new movements in the arts: Post-Impressionism, Symbolism and moves towards Modernism. Part of the reason for Lucy's residence in Paris at that time was probably that in 1889 the city was hosting the huge six-month *Exposition Universelle,* the greatest fair of the nineteenth century, that attracted 23 million visitors from around the world. The exhibition marked the centenary of the French Revolution of 1789 and served as a celebration of the advances of mankind as well as of the culture, values and achievements of France. The exhibition's gateway, the Eiffel Tower, constructed for the occasion, was a major attraction.

After her departure for Paris, Lucy disappeared from view for three years. Later she would discuss her experiences there with Warner Allen, who wrote a short chapter dedicated to Lucy's reminiscences of Paris, ostensibly over a period of forty years from the 1870s. However, from a few episodes that can be dated it seems that most of these memories came from the 1890s, and therefore from this *fin de siècle* period. Lucy, Allen wrote, spoke French well and liked to use French phrases. She could tell 'racy stories of the seamy side of life' in Paris, the 'City of Pleasure', with its 'cynical gaiety' and pretence that only pleasure mattered. She was familiar with Paris nightlife – the 'haunts of pleasure and dissipation', as Allen described them, but thought that the undressed women she had seen looked more respectable than the 'half-dressed lookers-on in their low-cut evening dresses'. Allen, who had lived in Paris for a decade from 1908, envied Lucy her knowledge of the Paris of the 'Maison Dorée and Tortoni's, cafés which in my day were spoken of with bated breath as the last temples of Boulevard brilliance in the height of its glory'. Lucy remembered seeing the Prussian statesman Otto von Bismarck dining at Tortoni's.

According to her own account, in Paris Lucy had also often been in the proximity of Edward, Prince of Wales (later Edward VII), but the depth of their relationship can only be speculation. She had first met him, she said, in the studio of the famous French painter Edouard Détaille. On that or another occasion, according to Allen, the 'graciousness' with which the prince paid her compliments had 'won her heart'. She had often dined at the Café Anglais, the prince's favourite Paris restaurant, although she told Allen that she was downstairs while he, as Allen put it, was 'making merry in gay company in the salons above'. On one occasion at least she had socialised with the Prince, for she recalled an anecdote he told about a stag-hunting accident in France that had never been reported in the press. Lucy had also met friends of the prince – the Prince de Sagan and General de Galliffet. She had known 'Polaire', a famous French singer and actress, well enough to ride with her in her carriage, and had been a 'bowing acquaintance' of the society figure and art collector Madame de Polès.

Apart from this account by Allen, nothing concrete is known of Lucy's life until her reappearance in January 1892 at a society wedding in Ireland. The bride was a Conyngham relative of her husband but Brinckman did not attend; the invitation to Lucy suggests that his family both liked her and considered her the injured party in the marriage breakdown. In fact, while Lucy had been out of England she and Brinckman had decided to seek a divorce. She would tell Allen later that she had had no choice – 'there was nothing else for it' – and besides, she knew that she could not provide Brinckman with an heir. Recent legal changes had made divorce easier and the number of cases was rising nationally, but even so it was still so uncommon that in 1893 there were only 387 divorces in England and Wales.

From Ireland Lucy returned to England, and from May to mid-July 1893 she and Brinckman lived together for the last time, at Sandgate in Kent, close to Shorncliffe Barracks, where Brinckman was serving with the Buffs. It was during this period that they worked out the details of their divorce. Obtaining a divorce in 1893 was more complicated than today; under the Matrimonial Causes Act of 1857, while husbands could petition for divorce on the sole grounds of their wife's adultery, wives could only petition on the grounds of adultery combined with another offence, such as incest, cruelty, bigamy or desertion. After the couple left Sandgate they set in motion the events that were the classic method by which divorce could be obtained. Later, Lucy would later tell the divorce court that after the stay in Sandgate she had planned to go abroad, and while at first Brinckman had agreed to go with her he had changed his mind at the last minute and instead gone shooting in Scotland with friends. While in Scotland he and Lucy exchanged letters. On 13 July Lucy asked Brinckman for a restoration of conjugal rights and requested that they live together again, and Brinckman replied, in effect refusing her request. Then Lucy began the next stage by going to the offices of a solicitor and commencing legal proceedings for the restitution of conjugal rights.

For four or five months Brinckman stayed in Scotland shooting stags. His record, bringing down thirty-two animals which weighed an average of 17st ½lb, was one of the best in the Highlands that season. Then, on 21 December 1893, Brinckman was ordered to restore Lucy's conjugal rights within fourteen days; he failed to comply, thereby rendering himself guilty of desertion. After this Lucy was able to petition for divorce on the basis that her husband had deserted her and committed adultery, and in court it would be shown that on three nights in February 1894 Brinckman had stayed at the Queen's Hotel on Brighton seafront with a woman who was not his wife. Armed with evidence of desertion and adultery, Lucy instituted a divorce suit in 21 February 1894. That Brinckman offered no defence was accepted as a tacit admission of guilt and a decree nisi was awarded in July. Later an American newspaper would report that the 'peculiar circumstances' of the divorce attracted considerable attention in London at the time, although public sympathy apparently lay with Brinckman because Lucy had coerced him into marriage.

Once again Florence's life mirrored Lucy's. Harold Wood had continued to use violence against her and Florence had applied for divorce at the same time as Lucy on the grounds of her husband's adultery and cruelty. The case would have attracted little press attention but for the fact that it brought to light the strange affair of the two marriage ceremonies. The press picked up on the story: 'Clandestine Marriage Dissolved', ran the headlines, but no explanation was offered for the reasons for the two weddings. The final divorce decrees would be granted on the same day, 14 January 1895; it was an unusual sister act. Although ostensibly the wronged party, contemporary attitudes to divorced women meant that Lucy and Florence were subject to stigma and projected into social limbo, as an article in the *Lady* explained in 1893: 'Women are terribly mistaken if they think they can go through the Divorce Court untainted if their husbands have had cause to seek separation; or if they imagine that society will receive them afterwards.' In English society, the article continued, 'everyone who is anyone at all knows exactly who is who', and past marriages and relationships were not forgotten. Therefore, unless a divorced woman elected to live 'very quietly', and to visit nobody outside her own family until the matter died down, she would be given the 'cold shoulder'.

Brinckman, as a man, felt able to seek full reinstatement in society. On 6 February, only three weeks after his divorce was finalised, an announcement appeared in the *Morning Post*. A marriage would take place in April between Brinckman and 25-year-old Miss Mary Linton, known as 'Mamie', the stepdaughter of the Earl of Aylesford. The friends and relations of the two families were determined to make the wedding a grand event that would effectively blot out Brinckman's troubled past. The subtext was that his marriage to Lucy had been nothing but a meaningless youthful error, and that by marrying the fair and virginal Mamie, so different from the used Lucy, Brinckman would both seek and declare social cleansing. In an ostentatious display of the value that he placed upon his bride he showered Mamie with twenty jewelled wedding gifts – necklaces, bracelets and rings adorned with diamonds, rubies, sapphires and emeralds. As things turned out, however, the memories of Lucy would not be so easily erased.

A fashionable Mayfair church – St Mark's in North Audley Street – had been chosen for the wedding ceremony, which was scheduled to take place on Saturday, 27 April. But now a scandal engulfed Brinckman. In some sectors of the Anglican Church there was strong feeling against divorce and the remarriage of divorced persons, and the announcement of Brinckman's marriage had disturbed the English Church Union (ECU). The ECU objected to the fact that a man who had been guilty of adultery should remarry in a consecrated church. Father William Black, described in the press as a tall, handsome, charming and resolute man, was a prime mover in the ECU who had on two previous occasions tried to stop the weddings of divorced people. Now he and fellow ECU members made plans to boycott Brinckman's ceremony. The actions of the ECU caused a sensation that reverberated not only in Britain but around the world. The moral and religious questions raised created a crisis in the Church of England and would be hotly debated for months to come. And for Lucy, the effect was once more to bring her unwelcome attention.

On the day of the wedding a contingent of ECU members arrived at the Mayfair church. Father Black, the group's spokesman, was supported by the Duke of Newcastle, a staunch Anglo-Catholic who spoke on ecclesiastical issues in the House of Lords, and Rev. Henry Washington, an Anglo-Catholic vicar. The three took seats in the wooden galleries that lined the chancel. A large number of guests had gathered and members of Brinkman's regiment, the Buffs, lined up to form a guard of honour inside the church. The ceremony began and with Brinckman waiting at the altar, Mamie came down the aisle dressed in white with orange blossom in her hair beneath her lace veil. She was followed by two pageboys, and six bridesmaids wearing dresses of white satin with pale green chiffon bodices all decorated with pink satin ribbons and crowned by large black picture hats trimmed with ostrich feathers and pink roses.

When everyone was in place the vicar began the service but at that point Father Black stood up in the gallery and began a loud protest. Members of the congregation called out 'Shame' and 'Disgraceful', and at length Black sat down and the vicar resumed the ceremony. However, when the vicar reached the part where he recited, 'if any man can show just cause why they may not lawfully be joined together, let him now speak or else hereafter forever hold his peace,' the militant Father Black protested again. Now, *The Times* reported, the commotion became 'intense', and there were many 'expressions of sympathy with the unfortunate bride'. The service halted and from the altar Brinckman and Mamie turned to look up at Father Black. The vicar addressed him angrily, saying, 'Sir, I am here by the Bishop's mandate, and I refuse to hear another word from you.' Embarrassingly, this had no effect and Black then read out a statement in which he declared that there was an impediment to the wedding:

I allege, and am prepared to prove, that one of the parties has his canonical wife living, and that therefore his marriage with any other person is contrary to the law of God and to the doctrine and discipline of the Church of England.

The congregation tried to drown out Black's words but he finished what he had to say, and then he and his companions descended from the gallery and left the church. Outside, according to one report, a friend of Brinckman called Black a 'scoundrel' and threatened to thrash the Duke of Newcastle, but inside, the ECU party having departed, the ceremony was concluded.

The press had much to say about the rights and wrongs of the Father Black incident, which had made the Church of England look foolish and revealed deep divisions within it. It was inevitable that Lucy's name and past history with Gretton and Brinckman should be dragged up and examined afresh. To make matters worse, the vicar told a newspaper that Brinckman had been divorced from his first wife 'under circumstances reflecting no discredit upon himself'. By implication, the discredit lay with Lucy. This put Brinckman in an awkward position and from the fashionable Hotel d'Albe in the Champs-Elysées in Paris where he and Mamie were on their honeymoon, he wrote to *The Times* on 12 May. He deeply regretted, he said, that statements had been made that were 'calculated to injure and annoy my former wife, who was unrepresented and had nothing to do with the proceedings'. He wished to state that he had given 'no instruction, indirectly or directly, to make any imputations against that lady', but nevertheless felt that an apology was due from him as a 'gentleman and an Englishman' for statements made without his authority. Brinckman then continued: 'We were both very young when we married, but as regards it turning out unfortunately I was entirely and solely to blame.' Through it all, he said, Lucy had treated him with the 'utmost consideration' and he was 'truly sorry that anything has taken place calculated to give pain to an innocent lady, whom I shall always honour and respect'.

But the damage had been done and Brinckman would long be remembered as the 'guilty divorcee' and Lucy as the woman who had lured him into an unsuitable marriage. As for Mamie, having been exposed to extreme embarrassment and humiliation during the wedding ceremony, she had also to endure her new husband praising his first wife and admitting his prior adultery from their honeymoon suite. The Brinckman marriage scandal stung the Church of England to the extent that it changed its laws so that no vicar would be obliged to allow his church to be used for the remarriage of a person whose prior marriage had been dissolved on the grounds of adultery or crime. A guilty divorcee, declared the Archbishop of Canterbury, could instead have a civil marriage so as to not 'murder other people's religious sentiments'.[1]

Now that there was a new 'Mrs Brinckman', Lucy took an old and pleasantly anonymous Brinckman family name to become 'Mrs Broadhead'; her former identity was thus wiped out. As divorced women, Lucy and Florence clung together for mutual support. While they could still claim the respectability of the title of 'Mrs', their divorced status carried stigma, but they had the compensation of their divorce settlements. The Brinckman family had arranged a trust for Lucy and she bought 52 Portland Place, a smart ten-bedroomed townhouse in a prestigious address in central London. It was advertised in the *Morning Post* in November 1894 as an 'excellent moderate-sized Town Mansion, with stabling, in capital order, and fitted with modern improvements and sanitation, comprising electric bells, speaking tubes, dinner lift, tiled hearths and stoves, and hot and cold supplies to top of house'. It featured a handsome drawing room with decorated ceiling, a large dining room, a library, and stables at the rear with accommodation for four horses and a coach-house for two carriages. The location was excellent; the street was wide and elegant, and the residents were superior. The writer Frances Hodgson Burnett, already well known for her novel *Little Lord Fauntleroy*, lived at number 63 Portland Place, and the Conservative politician the Earl of Lathom, at number 41, was one of several titled neighbours.

The house at Portland Place would be Lucy's main residence for five years and she lived, according to Eva Thaddeus, 'quite quietly' with the 'very pretty' Florence and a 'small circle of intimate friends'. In 1897 Lucy bought two horses – Duke, a black gelding, and Duchess, a black mare – and a Victoria carriage to go with them. The elegant Victoria was the favourite vehicle for ladies; it featured a seat for two passengers, and a coachman's seat in front. At the north end of Portland Place there was a broad gateway into Regent's Park and doubtless Lucy and Florence were a regular feature of the park's Carriage Drive. Lucy may also have appeared on a bicycle; with cycling fashionable in the 1890s she joined the Kensington Ladies' Cycling Club, the most exclusive women's cycling club in London.

The small circle of friends who shared the Portland Place house with Lucy and Florence during 1896 and 1897 included Eva Thaddeus and her husband, the Irish society portrait painter Henry Jones Thaddeus, known as Harry Thaddeus. In 1893, already pregnant with his child, Eva had divorced her first husband to marry him. The handsome Thaddeus was a charismatic figure possessed of considerable charm, and his reputation was well established through his portraits of such figures as the Prime Minister William Gladstone and Pope Leo XIII. The Thaddeus family survived on money from portrait commissions but were often in financial difficulties, and would have welcomed Lucy's invitation to occupy some of her eight spare bedrooms. During this period, too, Lucy was sometimes invited to dine by Lieutenant-Colonel Nathaniel Newnham-Davis. Well known in London for his articles on food, high society, the theatre world and the Turf, he combined business with pleasure by hosting friends to dine at restaurants and hotels such as the Savoy, Romano's and Pagani's, as well as more modest establishments. Lucy's wide circle of acquaintance and knowledge of life in London and on the Continent would have made her a valuable asset to Newnham-Davis in his news- and gossip-gathering activities.

In the summer of 1897 Queen Victoria's diamond jubilee was celebrated. Marking sixty years of Victoria's reign, it was also intended as a celebration of the British Empire, then at the height of its power. At the age of 78 the Queen was the most powerful figure on earth, ruling 450 million people – more than a quarter of the world's population. The jubilee festivities lasted a fortnight but the highlight came on 22 June when a great procession of seventeen carriages carried members of the royal family and the leaders of British dominions and imperial states on a 6-mile route through the heart of London. The marching men of the British and colonial armed forces in their dress uniforms made a splendid display, with the *Daily Mail* reporting: 'Up they came, more and more, new types, new realms at every couple of yards, an anthropological museum – a living gazetteer of the British Empire.' Cheering spectators lined the route beneath fluttering Union Jack flags and bunting. Lucy enjoyed it all enormously. Afterwards, for the first time, she used the press to promote an idea, writing to the *Morning Post*:

Sir, I think that while everyone has been rejoicing during this wonderful Jubilee time, a little fun and amusement ought to be given to those who by their untiring energy and good temper have helped so considerably to make everything go off so successfully – I mean the Police – and it is with great pleasure that I send you £100 towards affording them a little recreation. I have no doubt that many others must share my appreciation of this most deserving and hard-working class of the community, and I hope that you will receive several more contributions towards giving the Bobbies a little enjoyment after their hard work. — Yours, &c, LUCY BROADHEAD. 52, Portland-place.

But Lucy's cheque created difficulties, and two weeks later the *Morning Post* reported that instead of funding recreation Lucy had now kindly consented for the money to be donated to the police orphanage at Twickenham. But perhaps her letter had had an effect for the police authorities granted the officers involved in the jubilee celebrations an extra four days' pay.

A bright point in the Portland Place period was Florence's second marriage. Her new husband was Arthur Wrey, a stockbroker's clerk, the son of a baronet, Sir Henry Bourchier Toke Wrey of Tawstock Court in Barnstable, Devon. Wrey was ten years younger than Florence and far from being the heir to the baronetcy; of fourteen siblings he was the sixth of eight boys. The wedding took place on 11 December but on the marriage certificate Florence told a spectacular lie, by giving her age as 29 when she was 35. Although members of Florence's family added their signatures there were no Wrey witnesses; the family was an old and respectable one and its members were perhaps not overly delighted to find themselves attached to a divorced Radmall. But the marriage, although childless, would be marked by the apparent devotion of the couple to each other and to Lucy. Florence's marriage deprived Lucy of her sister's constant companionship and broke up the Portland Place circle. After the wedding Lucy would shuttle to and fro between London and Paris but in May 1899 her horses, Duke and Duchess, were advertised for sale 'in consequence of ill-health' of the owner.

Although on her own account Lucy had many lovers, during the six years that followed her divorce from Brinckman the name of only one romantic interest has emerged. Through Harry Thaddeus Lucy had got to know the author and explorer Henry Savage Landor, grandson of the poet Walter Savage Landor. Henry travelled widely and wrote books about his experiences in remote regions. One, published in 1893 and entitled *Alone with the Hairy Ainu: or, 3800 Miles on a Pack Saddle in Yezo and a Cruise to the Kurile Islands* had been such a success that its author was received by Queen Victoria. Because of Landor's youthful and delicate appearance, his accounts of dangers and privations during his travels were often disbelieved and yet, Thaddeus wrote, his friend was 'quite a lion', possessing 'courage, will, and powers of endurance'. For all that he could not, apparently, persuade Lucy to marry him. One day Landor went to Eva Thaddeus in 'despair' because Lucy had rejected his proposal of marriage, and so intense was his passion that Eva found it hard to dissuade him from killing himself. Landor never would marry and years later, shortly before his death in 1924, he showed Eva Thaddeus an old photograph of Lucy and declared that 'she was the love of my life'. But Lucy had her eyes set on higher things than Landor, however romantic his lifestyle and profound his devotion. She was determined to climb the social ladder by making an advantageous marriage but, hampered by her background, would not see an acceptable opportunity until 1900.

4

LADY BYRON

The man who would become Lucy's second husband could hardly have been more different from Gretton or Brinckman. He bore a title that was a household name; his forebear, George Gordon, the 6th Lord Byron, was the celebrated poet of the Romantic movement. Renowned for his personal beauty and style of dress, the poet had become the talk of London, both celebrated and criticised for his flamboyant lifestyle, debts and love affairs. Immortalised by early death in Greece in 1824, Byron's legend lived on in the public mind. Many versions of the idealised 'Byronic' hero, characterised by passion, arrogance, self-destructive tendencies and dislike of social constraint, had subsequently appeared in literature and the arts. At the end of the nineteenth century Byron remained an intensely interesting figure to those impatient with the social and moral restrictions of high Victorian life. Books were written, lectures delivered and statues erected in his honour. The public devoured accounts of Byron's homes, hairstyle, corpse, clothing, servants, swimming prowess, diet and dog's grave; and the sale of a Byron relic – perhaps a letter or a lock of hair – was commonly reported in the press,

In 1870 the illustrious title had passed to the 9th Baron, George Frederick William Byron, a 14-year-old grandson of the poet's cousin; it was he whom Lucy would marry. Born in December 1855, George Byron had in his youth followed a traditional path for an aristocrat, attending Harrow School, joining the West Suffolk Militia, being presented to the Prince of Wales at St James's Palace, and studying at Christ Church College at Oxford University. Once Byron turned 21 he came into his inheritance but the amount was relatively modest, and paucity of finances would be a key theme of his life. Despite his limited income, however, Byron's famous name greatly increased his social value, and in 1878 he became a protégé of Benjamin Disraeli, 1st Earl of Beaconsfield, then in his second term as Prime Minister. As a young man Disraeli had idolised and modelled himself upon the poet Byron, emulating his lifestyle to the extent that he ran up large debts and then contracted a marriage to a wealthy woman in order to pay them off. Disraeli subsequently invited the young Byron to parties and it was perhaps through his influence as a favourite of Queen Victoria, that in July 1878 Byron attended a state ball at Buckingham Palace. But although the invitation was a great honour, Byron would never be comfortable in grand company.

Byron's life was dogged by comparison with the poet; for good or ill he lived in the shadow of his predecessor. Although Byron practised writing his signature so that it resembled that of the 9th Lord Byron, in every other respect he was comically un-Byronic, bearing little resemblance in either appearance or character. Short and slight of build, he had a cast in one eye and a small, sparse moustache. Gentle, kind, reserved and whimsical, he was also nervy, eccentric and quixotic, and suffered from chronic indigestion. But while there were great differences between the two Lord Byrons there would also be parallels. Both had inherited the title at an early age, become writers, and amassed huge debts. The 6th made a marriage of convenience as a solution to his financial problems, and like his mentor Disraeli the 9th Baron would follow suit.

Such was the aura associated with the name 'Lord Byron' that the 9th Baron was often blamed or ridiculed for not living up to the image of the 6th. On one occasion, for example, he and his friend James Gilbart-Smith had gone to a department store on Oxford Street to run an errand for Byron's mother. When Byron gave his name, Gilbart-Smith was horrified at the way in which people 'stared and mobbed … I could never have thought such a thing possible'. For this reason Byron often kept his identity a secret. He was a keen writer of articles on current affairs for newspapers and journals, but in his modesty and dislike of trading on his name, most of his output appeared under pseudonyms such as Bryon.

Byron divided his time mostly between London and Wickham Bishops, Essex, where he had a house, High Hall. In Essex he involved himself in local Conservative politics and gentle sports such as cricket and cycling, and, as was expected of an aristocrat, served as a patron and committee member of clubs and societies. When in London Byron was something of a man-about-town, joining several gentlemen's clubs, attending the House of Lords, and taking part in charitable efforts. The saving of money was a common theme of his activities and in 1882 he was appointed chairman of the National Thrift Society, the aim of which, he explained at a meeting at the society's headquarters at Finsbury Circus, was to 'decrease the improvidence of the working classes of this country and lead them into habits of thrift and forethought'. These were words that would come back to haunt Byron. His public works drew attention and in May 1885, at a dinner in aid of the University College Hospital, he was seated on the top table with the Prince of Wales. Having gained entry into the highest circles it would seem that Byron had put himself among people and into situations that he found uncomfortable. In 1885 he brought it all to an abrupt end by taking himself off on a holiday to Australia. On an eight-month trip he would follow the route that Lucy had taken two years earlier, going on from Australia to New Zealand and then San Francisco, before sailing home across the Atlantic. Like the Brinckmans, he seems to have made a deliberate retreat from the pressures of society. Upon his return Byron's life began a new phase. He did not re-enter high social circles but confined himself to people and environments with which he felt comfortable. He spent less time in London, while in Essex he took up the game of quoits and went more deeply into local politics, serving as president of Wickham Bishops Conservative Association, the meetings of which were held in the village schoolroom.

But the years were passing and, despite numerous opportunities to marry, Byron remained single. In 1890, at the age of 35, he had a skirmish with matrimony when he became engaged to 23-year-old Winifred Massey, the daughter of an agent for a firm of Manchester yarn agents. As her father was from the lower middle class and associated with trade, Winifred was far below Byron in the social scale. But 1890 ended and 1891 passed, and there was no announcement of a wedding date. Was Lord Byron going to get married or not? By the standards of the day he had treated Winifred badly for, as he had neither married her nor publicly cancelled the engagement, she had been left in limbo and exposed to ridicule. But at last, in May 1892, an update appeared in the press that the engagement was definitely still standing, but after this there was no further announcement. What was Byron thinking? Perhaps the matter was too difficult and embarrassing to cope with and he hoped that if he did nothing the problem would go away. At the end of 1893 Winifred married a young chartered accountant from Sale; it was a much more suitable match.

The chain of events that led to Byron's marriage to Lucy began innocuously enough during the last weeks of 1894. Staying at a hotel near Malvern, he received a letter from a Mrs Georgiana Kingscote asking for his help. Georgiana had class and credibility, being the daughter of the Right Honourable Sir Henry Drummond Wolff, a highly regarded diplomat and former friend of Byron's mentor Disraeli. She was married to a respectable army man. Kingscote insisted upon coming to Malvern, where she explained her financial predicament and persuaded Byron to help her. She gave him a strong incentive by a promise to introduce him to an American heiress who was planning to visit England in search of a titled husband. If Byron married the heiress, Kingscote said, he could buy back Newstead Abbey, the ancestral home that the great poet had sold off back in 1817. This idea appealed but the American heiress proved to be a myth. Eventually Kingscote moved in for the kill, borrowing money from Byron and persuading him to act as a bank guarantor, which sucked him down into a morass of debt. In fairness to Byron, he was one of many of Kingscote's victims; she had also duped others who included two Oxfordshire vicars, her brother-in-law and a host of London moneylenders. In 1899, £50,373 in debt, Byron filed for bankruptcy. Bankruptcy was deeply shameful, bringing humiliation and disgrace not only upon the person involved but also upon their family. The disgust of Byron's mother was indicated when in March 1899, shortly before the opening of her son's court proceedings, she made a will that left everything to her other children. The will would never be revoked; her rejection of her eldest son was final.

A high-society bankruptcy, especially one involving a woman, was a good story and his was reported around the world. During the hearings at Chelmsford curious revelations made Byron a national laughing stock. The evidence of Kingscote's contempt were particularly humiliating and her letters to Byron, read out to the amusement of the court, made eye-catching headlines. Written to a man who was bankrupting himself for her benefit, they were extraordinarily rude and demonstrated Kingscote's controlling techniques. The biggest laugh in court was raised by a note which read, 'I have decided to do nothing more, and you can go bankrupt or not as you like, for there is no bigger cad in England than you are, or bigger idiot.'

It was no wonder that the *Essex Newsman* commented, 'We never knew, till we read this case, one half of the meaning of the phrase about "adding insult to injury".' The *Essex Herald* expressed surprise that Byron had parted with his money so easily when he was an 'authority' upon thrift and a prominent member of the Thrift Society. This irony had probably also not escaped Byron. Not unnaturally, the press struggled to understand how Byron could have been such a fool but between the lines was the question of whether there had been a sexual motivation. Kingscote was neither young nor good looking but, reported the *Chicago Tribune*, she was a 'smart, stylish, and dashing woman'. However, when it became apparent that there had been no sexual element, Kingscote's success was put down to extreme powers of persuasion.

By the autumn of 1899 Byron's bankruptcy procedures were drawing to a close. Byron lay low, for his situation was bad indeed; he had debts that he could not pay, was estranged from his family and embarrassed to show his face in public. He had only one remaining asset – his title.

The story of a manipulative woman extracting money from a man would have been deeply interesting to Lucy and she must have followed the case of Lord Byron and Mrs Kingscote closely. She realised that it presented possibilities for the bankrupt Byron, the holder of an ancient and aristocratic – if tarnished – title, was unmarried. If Lucy were able to exchange her money for the title of 'Lady Byron' she could cast off the ambiguous state of 'Mrs Broadhead', become a peeress, and enjoy all the benefits and privileges that that entailed. Becoming Lady Byron would not stop gossip but it was better to be talked about behind her back as Lady Byron than as Mrs Broadhead. And besides, in the five years since her divorce no better prospect had appeared.

When Lucy wanted something she took great pains to get it. She must have made careful enquiries about Byron but found nothing to deter her, and it was probably in the second half of 1900 that she enlisted a trusted friend, perhaps Arthur Wrey, to act as intermediary and convey her proposal to Byron. The message was that Lucy would pay off his debts and in addition give him an allowance of £300 a year if he agreed to marry her. Lucy was offering Byron what he needed most: an opportunity to extract himself from his financial obligations with honour and to achieve financial security. Given his circumstances, the shame of an alliance with a woman of Lucy's background was immaterial; one woman of dubious standing had ruined him and now another would be his salvation. When he accepted Lucy's proposal, she had pulled off another amazing coup.

In preparation for the wedding, Lucy gave up 52 Portland Place.[2] Always impatient, she made the wedding arrangements quickly and in secret. The ceremony was scheduled to take place on 1 March 1901, and in order to comply with a legal residency requirement, in the preceding weeks Byron lived at the grand Langham Hotel in Portland Place. The wedding would take place in the fashionable All Souls Church situated only a few steps from the hotel. On the marriage certificate Byron was identified only as 'George Byron' and his rank as 'Gentleman'. Lucy, as 'Fanny Lucy Broadhead', gave her address as 9 Wedderburn Road in Hampstead, the home of Florence and Arthur Wrey. For the second time on a marriage certificate Lucy entered untruths, giving her age as 36 when she was 43, and the rank of her father again as 'Gentleman'. The faithful Wreys signed the certificate as witnesses; they were probably the only guests in attendance.

After their wedding the newlyweds went abroad immediately. In Paris Lucy maintained an apartment at the Hotel Fortuny in the Avenue Malakoff, a prestigious address between the Bois de Boulogne and the Arc de Triomphe and near the Auteuil racecourse, where Tom Radmall had raced his horses. The Hotel Fortuny was discreet, secure and high class, and it was probably there that Lucy and Byron spent the early days of their honeymoon. It may also have been during this visit that Lucy drove with her friend, the actress Réjane, through the Bois de Boulogne in Réjane's famous two-seater brougham carriage. It was drawn by two glossy black mules that had been a gift from the King of Portugal. Pedro and Pepita, with their harnesses hung with jingling bells and bunches of violets, were a well-known sight on Réjane's shopping trips in the Champs-Elysées.

Although Lucy may have stayed on in Paris, Byron was back in London after three weeks and, doubtless galvanised by Lucy's encouragement to rise above the shame of his bankruptcy, reappeared in the House of Lords in March. However, no news of the marriage came out until 6 April, when the *Essex Newsman* reported that 'a marriage is arranged and will shortly take place between Lord Byron and Mrs Broadhead'. By that time the Byrons had been married for five weeks, but announcing their engagement after the wedding was probably intended to deflect attention for longer. Then on 22 April *St James' Gazette* reported in its 'Rank and Fashion' column that 'the marriage of Lord Byron to Mrs Broadhead took place very quietly last week, owing to the bride being in delicate health. Lord and Lady Byron are travelling on the Continent.' Lucy probably gave this notice to the press after her return to England.

If Byron had not had a title Lucy would never have married him, for he was not the sort of man that she found attractive. Although they lived together, there was little romance and probably no intimacy between them; Lucy would later confide in Wentworth Day that her second husband had been a 'nice man ... quite harmless', but 'terrified' of her. On his side, Byron once commented to his friend Gilbart-Smith that people cared about only two things: money and health. Everything else was an emotion, and love, the strongest, was 'only an excrescence, like the measles – mainly acquired in order to be subsequently proof against it'. Perhaps he was thinking of Winifred Massey. It was not, then, love that Byron felt for Lucy but, Wentworth Day wrote, a 'dog-like devotion' – an indication of the gratitude that he felt. But the Byrons were not wholly mismatched. They were of a similar age and both short in stature, and Lucy, well dressed and familiar with the ways of high society, would not disgrace Byron. Having herself been the butt of gossip and unwelcome press attention Lucy also understood Byron's desire for privacy. While she encouraged him in his charitable and political activities, he informed her political and patriotic views and encouraged her to write for the press.

Marriage brought Lucy a change in lifestyle; paying off Byron's debts required economy and for several years the couple lived relatively modestly in Fitzjohn's Avenue in Hampstead. But the marriage also brought Lucy a huge perk. Queen Victoria had died in January 1901 and the coronation of the Prince of Wales as King Edward VII was scheduled to take place in Westminster Abbey on 9 August 1902. As a peeress, Lucy had the right to attend. Having first met Edward in Paris, she was now to see him crowned as King. The coronation would be the grandest of events and national excitement was extreme. Taking place in the capital of the British Empire, it was planned as a huge piece of imperial theatre designed to send the world the message that Britain possessed an innate right to rule the lands that comprised the British Empire.

The great day dawned. The old abbey, which had hosted the coronation of every English monarch since 1066, was prepared and even by eight o'clock in the morning the attendees, of whom there were about 8,000, had begun to arrive. The Byrons reached the abbey before nine o'clock, wearing the full regalia required by protocol. As a male peer, Byron's rank as baron was indicated by two rows of ermine spots on the white cape of his crimson robe. He also had a silver coronet lined with crimson velvet and styled with six silver balls on its rim. As a baroness Lucy was allowed a 1-yard train with a 2in edging on her dress (a duchess, for example, was allowed a train 2 yards long with a 5in edging). The Byrons walked down the nave, their scarlet and ermine robes contrasting effectively with the deep royal blue of the carpet. When they reached the empty thrones that awaited the King and Queen they separated. Byron turned to the right, to join the peers who sat in order of rank on raised tiers, while Lucy turned to the left to join the peeresses. The women, *The Times* reported, were adorned with every type of female finery: lace, satin, jewels, velvet, flounces, cloth of gold, tassles, brocades, embroidery, stomachers, bows, tiaras, corsages and aigrettes. Lucy had determined to look the part, for *The Times* would report that 'Lady Byron's kirtle front was draped with old duchesse lace, and her pearls were superb. She wore her famous black pearls, and the front of her bodice was festooned with rubies and diamonds.'

While everyone awaited the arrival of the royal couple, Lucy had ample opportunity to observe the splendid scene. The spectators were seated in tiers, with members of the House of Commons in galleries above the transepts. Among them, but not yet known to Lucy, was Robert Houston (pronounced House-ton), MP for West Toxteth in Liverpool, who many years hence would become her third husband. Lucy may, however, have spotted John Gretton, Frederick Gretton's nephew. Sitting in the midst of it all, how did she feel? It was a proud moment; she had won this great privilege by her own efforts and, although many present would have known her life story, Lucy was well able to brazen it out.

When Edward and Alexandra at last entered the abbey and made their way down the nave all eyes turned to them. Alexandra came first preceded by the Queen's regalia – sceptre, crown and ring – carried by the lords of her household. Her rich purple velvet dress was lined with white satin and adorned with diamonds and pearls, while her cloth-of-gold train was so long that eight pageboys were required to manage it. Next came the King's regalia, and then Edward himself. It was a marvel, wrote an observer, to see the 'supreme ease' with which Edward wore his heavy crimson robes, and with what 'resolute, regal bearing' he trod.

Once the royal couple were seated on their thrones the ceremony proceeded. Alexandra was crowned first, and at the moment the crown was placed upon her head by the Archbishop of York the peeresses took out their own coronets to put them on. A newspaper reported that it was a 'charming as well as a curious sight to see all those white arms clasping all those fair heads, and to watch busy fingers deftly fastening the coronets in their places'. The peeresses struggled for so long that it became 'slightly amusing'. Edward was crowned next, then stayed motionless upon the throne with the sceptre in one hand and the orb, 'that emblem of world-wide sway', in the other. At this moment Edward's throne was the centre and focus of the world's mightiest empire. Then a great cry of 'God save the King' went up, trumpets and drums sounded, and to add to the effect the abbey's electric lights were switched on. It was, reported a newspaper, a sight 'never to be forgotten by any present, and many were deeply moved'. Outside, the abbey bells rang, cannons were fired and crowds cheered.

A new friend of Lucy, the celebrated novelist Marie Corelli, had also been in Westminster Abbey at the special invitation of the King, who was a fan of her work. Corelli was then at the height of her fame and for Lucy such a friendship was a prestigious connection indeed. Corelli had published her first novel, *A Romance of Two Worlds*, in 1886. It had become highly popular and she had gone on to become the author of other bestsellers such as *Barabbas: A Dream of the World's Tragedy*, and her best-known *The Sorrows of Satan*. Although Corelli's popularity has not survived, in her day her books sold far more than those of contemporaries such as Arthur Conan Doyle, Rudyard Kipling and H.G. Wells. Yet Marie Corelli was disliked by many, and, in particular, literary critics, women writers and the press. For this she had only herself to blame for she used her novels – a curious mix of romanticism, biting social commentary and satire – as a platform for criticism. Corelli believed that she had a personal calling to reform British morals but she was a vain woman with a high opinion of herself and her own abilities, and did not hide the fact. Although, as Lucy would discover, Corelli could be spiteful and vindictive, she was devoted to Bertha Vyver, with whom she shared her life and her home, Mason Croft in Stratford-upon-Avon.

On the face of it, Corelli and Lucy did not seem natural friends for there were a number of topics upon which they could not have seen eye to eye. For example, in a lecture given in February 1902 Corelli had condemned high-society women gamblers as a 'shame and sorrow' to their sex. She also criticised such women for pretending to patronise British trade while ordering their clothes and house furnishings from Paris. Lucy was guilty on both counts. Another potential point of contention was men; when asked why she had not married, Corelli had replied that she had no need: 'I have three pets at home which answer the same purpose as a husband. I have a dog which growls every morning, a parrot which swears all afternoon, and a cat that comes home late at night.' But association with Lady Byron had a fascination for Corelli, who was a staunch defender of the great poet's memory. She believed him to have been a genius, and through Lucy Corelli could gain access to the elusive 9th Baron, who carried a little of her idol's blood in his veins. But there were other points in common. Lucy and Corelli were of a similar age and both had overcome humble origins to become self-made women – strong-minded, determined and outspoken. Both had lived in Paris in their youth, although Lucy's experience had been quite different from that of Corelli in a convent school. They shared a cult of youth, beauty and an interest in clothes, although as Corelli was squat, plump and not 5ft tall, and dressed as a much younger woman, Lucy was more successful with clothes.

A few days after the coronation Marie Corelli and Bertha Vyver departed for Scotland, going first to Aberdeen where they intended to purchase a pair of Shetland ponies. The animals were black, reminiscent of Réjane's mules and also of Duke and Duchess from Lucy's Portland Place days. Lucy, with her superior knowledge of horseflesh, may have acted as Corelli's advisor. Corelli had also commissioned a phaeton carriage and when later the ponies arrived at Stratford-upon-Avon, the daily carriage ride of Corelli and Vyver would became a feature of life in the town. Tourists would gather outside Mason Croft to watch the women depart with the coachman perched high behind them, but Corelli holding the whip and reins.

By September Corelli and Vyver were at the Invercauld Arms Hotel at Braemar in Deeside where Lucy, Countess Somers and Lady Kennard joined them. Corelli had invited the women as her guests for the great sporting Highland Gathering scheduled for 11 September, which would be attended by the new King and Queen. In his youth the poet Byron had lived near Braemar for a time, and doubtless Corelli delighted in pointing out to Lucy the sites connected with the man whose name she bore. The day of the Highland Gathering arrived. The weather was perfect, and Corelli's party joined thousands of spectators in a large field near the River Dee. The day began with the gathering of the clansmen – the Balmoral Highlanders, the Farquharson Highlanders and the Duff Highlanders – before the commencement of the games. From a large grandstand the crowds watched the competitions of

Highland dancing, jumping, vaulting, foot racing, hammer throwing and caber tossing. In the afternoon, led by the massed bagpipe bands of the clansmen playing the cheerful 'Invercauld March', King Edward and Queen Alexandra, seated in an open carriage drawn by four grey horses, were greeted by cheers and the waving of handkerchiefs. As a friend of the King, Corelli, together with her party, would have been presented to the royal visitors.

The excitement of the coronation and the Braemar games over, Lucy settled into her role as Lady Byron. She cultivated the manner of the *grande dame* and, joining circles of wealthy and aristocratic women, embraced the organised philanthropy and charity work that enabled them to display both femininity and status. Lucy sat on committees, participated in social functions to raise money for good causes, and lent her patronage to charity events such as balls and bazaars. Bearing such a name, Lucy also acted as a patroness of the arts and involved herself in artistic circles. In her guise as patroness of the arts, Lucy became a theatre devotee, and at the end of 1902 a newspaper reported that Lady Byron and Marie Corelli were the two most 'inveterate matinee goers' in London. While previously having had little interest in poetry she now promoted Byron's memory; the role sat oddly, for Lucy's literary tastes had always been 'lowbrow'. As her own output would later demonstrate, her idea of poetry was derived mainly from nursery rhymes, hymns and comic songs.

In December 1902 Corelli invited Lucy and Byron to stay at Mason Croft. Even those who disliked the author commented upon the attractiveness and charm of her house, with its Elizabethan drawing room, palm-filled lounge and old walled garden accessed by a charming ivy-covered arch. Following this visit the Byrons went on to Essex for a grand ball given by the Earl and Countess of Warwick at Easton Lodge. About 500 guests attended – the cream of society from Essex and beyond – and Lucy and Byron had invited their own group that consisted of General Hemming (a cavalry commander at Aldershot) and his wife; Florence and Arthur Wrey; and William Wynyard, an old friend of Byron from his Essex militia days.

Byron's life had stabilised. He was free of debt, had £25 a month spending money, and Lucy on hand to strengthen his backbone when she felt the need. With all these advantages he blossomed and embraced the intellectually vibrant community life of Hampstead with its many artists, scientists and writers. He made new friends in the world of publishing and literature, including Max Pemberton, who lived in the same street. Pemberton was editor of *Cassell's Magazine*, which published the work of well-known writers such as Robert Louis Stevenson, P.G. Wodehouse and Rudyard Kipling. It was perhaps through this connection that Lucy first came into contact with Kipling, who would later influence her life. Byron also renewed his interest in local politics, becoming a vice-president of both the Hampstead Conservative Association and the Constitutional Club. Taking up philanthropy once more, he associated himself with the City and East London Battalion of the Boys' Brigade, and later would participate in a campaign to endow a cot in Great Ormond Street Hospital for Sick Children. Lucy, influenced by Byron, took up writing and the *Boudoir*, an illustrated magazine, published an article by her entitled 'Neatness in Costume'. In July 1904 the Byrons holidayed at the Imperial Hotel at Hythe after which Lucy toured Normandy and Brittany by car with her friend Constance, Countess de la Warr. Lucy was back in England in October 1904 when she heard the news that the car that she kept at the Hotel Fortuny in Paris had been involved in an accident. A French newspaper, *Le Petit Parisien*, reported that three employees of Lady Byron, out for the evening in her car, had hit a merchant's cart, mounted the kerb, and collided with a tree.

According to Wentworth Day, Lucy always regretted her divorce from Brinckman and to the end of her life he would remain 'first in her heart'; from 1904 she began to reopen lines of communication. Following his controversial wedding in 1895, he and Mamie had had three children – two boys and a girl – but after a decade the marriage was deteriorating. Although Lucy was approaching the age of 50 she may have felt that a reunion would be no bad thing, for Brinckman had attractions that Byron lacked. To obtain a divorce from Byron would be difficult but not impossible; he might agree to be paid off. And so when in February 1904 Brinckman's great-aunt Elizabeth, Countess of Winchelsea, died, Lucy sent a floral tribute with a card that read 'In fond remembrance from Lucy (Lady Byron).' Then, in mid-November 1904, she made another move in Brinckman's direction when she accompanied the Duchess of Bedford to St Saviour's Hospital for Ladies of Limited Means in Osnaburgh Street, near Regent's Park. The hospital was run by the Reverend Arthur Brinckman, Brinckman's uncle.

In 1905 Lucy's friendship with Marie Corelli reached its height and in March the two women holidayed together at the fashionable Devon resort of Sidmouth. In May the headline 'Venice on the Avon' appeared in the press. Miss Corelli, it was reported, was now the 'proud possessor of a real

Venetian gondola propelled by a genuine Venetian gondolier'. Decorated with bronze emblems of Venice and the Adriatic, at 24ft long the gondola was two-thirds normal size but was still the most exotic craft on the Avon, outshining the humble Stratford punts. It was perhaps with the intention of showing off her gondola that Corelli issued a second invitation to Lucy that summer. Lucy took the train to Stratford with Eveleigh Nash, a publisher, whom Corelli had also invited. In his autobiography Nash recalled that upon their arrival Corelli met them at the railway station, but while Lucy was taken to Mason Croft, Nash was consigned to a hotel. This mystified Nash but he suspected that Corelli thought it would not be 'safe' for him to sleep in the house of an unmarried woman, and in particular as he had travelled to Stratford with an 'attractive married lady guest', i.e. Lucy. Perhaps Nash and Lucy were not above Corelli's suspicion. Nash would also recall that one evening after dinner Corelli entertained her guests at the piano, but when she sang 'Within a Mile o' Edinburgh Toon' Nash could hardly keep a straight face. Her performance, he said, resembled a 'funny turn' from the old days of the music halls. Certainly the song, popularised by the well-known high-soprano opera singer Adelina Patti, had some difficult high notes.

The Stratford weekend was only the prelude to a much greater act of patronage on the part of Corelli, for she had invited Lucy to accompany her on a visit to the luxury yacht *Erin*, which belonged to Corelli's friend Sir Thomas Lipton. The wealthy Lipton, who had started from nothing and built up a nationwide grocery chain, was a favourite in royal and aristocratic circles. A friend of King Edward, his social year was filled by visits to Buckingham Palace, Sandringham, Balmoral and the royal yacht *Victoria and Albert*. Charming, witty and amusing, Lipton was popular with women but was something of a cipher, for he had never married nor had any apparent romances. Lipton used hospitality as a means of showing his social status; in addition to the British King and Queen and other members of the royal family he had, as he boasted in his autobiography, hosted 'practically every Royal personage in Europe and of illustrious men and women in every walk of life on both sides of the Atlantic'. An invitation to the *Erin* was therefore highly prestigious.

Now, with Lipton fresh from a voyage to visit his tea estates in Ceylon and a cruise in the Mediterranean, the *Erin* had arrived at Cowes by 1 August 1905 to join hundreds of other yachts for an event of great national significance – the visit of the French naval fleet. Five days of celebrations and festivities were planned on a massive scale as part of the Anglo–French *entente cordiale*, a series of agreements signed by Britain and the French Third Republic in 1904. The Cowes event was intended to convince the French of England's good intentions and to impress upon the world that the *entente cordiale* was binding. As Lipton's guest accommodation aboard the *Erin* was occupied, Corelli and Lucy stayed at the stylish South Western Hotel in Southampton. However, from the yacht the women had a privileged view of the proceedings.

The festivities were to take place in the Solent off Southampton and Portsmouth, and at Cowes on the Isle of Wight. On Monday, 7 August at Spithead, the British massed their Channel fleet with its cruiser squadron and torpedo-boat destroyer flotilla to receive the visitors. When the French fleet arrived, the massed military craft stretched for 3 miles and with their decorations, colourful awnings and flowers and plants on the decks, the ships made a splendid sight. The royal yacht *Victoria and Albert*, with King Edward on board, formed the focal point of hundreds of civil craft owned by British and foreign yacht owners that had gathered for the celebrations. What followed was an extraordinary piece of imperial theatre and an exercise in rapprochement that would be a masterstroke of diplomacy and triumph for Edward, and yet it was all done on the cheap: the visit of the French had been timed to coincide with the annual Cowes Regatta and therefore the yacht owners, both British and foreign, would have been there anyway.

With the basic ingredients to hand it needed only the presence of royalty plus a dark night, fireworks and innumerable fairy lights to work imperial and geopolitical magic. Celebrations continued for three days in a carnival atmosphere with fireworks, banquets and balls on board the ships and ashore. The highlight of the festivities was the illumination of the massed craft and the shorelines at nightfall. At nine o'clock the firing of a signal gun from the royal yacht heralded the start. First the display of the *Victoria and Albert* was switched on, lighting the yacht in red, white and blue, happily the patriotic colours of both Britain and France. Then it was the turn of the other vessels and suddenly, reported a newspaper, 'out of the black shapeless void of the sea sprang into being a fairy fleet, the lines of the English and French men of war being illuminated like magic'. Each yacht owner had their own scheme of illumination and several newspapers singled out Lipton's *Erin* for special mention. Lucy and the other guests on board would have gazed upwards as the yacht's name was spelled out in green electric lights suspended from the masts, while the main mast showed the French *tricolor*. Lucy remembered the scene and years later would use her own yacht to give out a quite different message.

The *Erin*'s cabins were occupied by Lipton's friends, who included Wilson Marshall, an American yacht owner; Edward Morris, a millionaire Chicago beef-packer, and his wife Helen; and Robert Houston, the unmarried ship owner and MP. However, the *entente* was hardly *cordiale* between Lucy and Marie Corelli aboard the yacht. Corelli was outshone, for Lucy's undoubtedly superior attractions meant that she received more attention from the men. Corelli watched with growing irritation and jealousy as Lucy flirted with the eligible Houston and Lipton, and perhaps with the American men too. As a result a great rift developed and after they left the *Erin* the two women, formerly such fast friends, never saw each other again. After this both felt in need of a restorative holiday and Corelli went abroad to a spa resort, while Lucy went to Harrogate with Byron. Perhaps in his quiet ways and gentle humour Lucy found solace and sympathy after the unpleasantness with Corelli. However, the novelist's friendship had served Lucy well while it lasted.

5

IDENTITIES

The death of his father had brought the lately promoted Colonel Sir Theodore Brinckman, now 3rd Baronet, a greatly increased income and with the freedom to do as he pleased, he took a mistress. By early 1906 Brinckman had hired a new valet, Frank Easton, and it was from Easton's evidence, given at Brinckman's later divorce proceedings, that the main facts about the mistress are known. A Frenchwoman, she went by the name of Madame Marguerite Chabault. The affair had already begun by the spring of 1906 and the pair would travel and live together on and off for the following two years. Who was 'Madame Chabault'? Nobody of that name was known in English society. She appeared from nowhere and would in time disappear without trace; the name was false. She might have been a woman whom Brinckman met in Paris or Monte Carlo. She could have been Elisabeth Bergerand, the French woman whom Brinckman would later marry. However, it is also possible that Madame Chabault was Lucy.

By 1906 Lucy was 48 years old and had been acting out the role of *grande dame* for four years. She may have felt stifled by its constraints and tired of the vigilance required to maintain the persona expected of a baroness. Byron was boring, but being Madame Chabault offered challenge, excitement and fun. By renewing her relationship with Brinckman in a romantic escapade that involved costume, a foreign accent and deceit, Lucy would be able to revive the glamour of her Lucy Grafton days. As Madame Chabault she would roll back the years and once more enjoy horse racing and gambling with a man whose appearance was something to be proud of. If Lucy had wished to conduct an affair as Lady Byron she might not have been able to keep it secret, and she had no wish to humiliate Byron. But in the disguise of a Frenchwoman she could carry out an illicit intrigue in anonymity.

It is not difficult to imagine Lucy taking on the role of Madame Chabault; it was the sort of thing that she would do. But it would be an extraordinarily risky undertaking, for, apart from the effort of staying in character in public, Brinckman and Chabault visited places such as Monte Carlo where Lucy might be recognised. However, she had the motivation as well as the necessary money, skills and, crucially, daring. While there is no hard evidence that Madame Chabault was Lucy there is also no evidence that she was not, for during the period of Brinckman's affair there is little independent sign of Lucy; as Lady Byron she carried out few reported engagements and activities. In addition, at the times when Brinckman was known to be with his mistress Lady Byron's movements are not at any time accounted for, and there were even occasions upon which they were in the same vicinity. However, once Brinckman's affair was over, Lady Byron re-emerged in society.

The affair may have begun in August 1905. Early that month Brinckman and Mamie were staying at the fashionable Hotel Metropole in Folkestone, and during the third week of August the Byrons also checked in; the visits of the two couples may have overlapped. In April 1906 Brinckman and Mamie went to the Ritz Hotel in Paris but once in the French capital Brinckman decamped to an apartment at 19 Boulevard Flandrin, conveniently located near the Bois de Bolougne and the Auteuil racecourse, where he lived with Madame Chabault for some weeks. Whether or not Lucy was at the apartment, she would have already been in Paris for her annual wardrobe visit. From Paris Brinckman returned to England with Chabault and for periods during May and June they lived at the Hotel Metropole in Folkestone. During this time Lord and Lady Byron appeared at a polo tournament at Fulham, and Brinckman was also in London for he was presented at St James's Palace to mark his succession to the baronetcy. He then returned to the south coast and for a week or two commanded the Buffs during their annual training at Shorncliffe Camp, while 'Lady Byron and suite' were at the Grand Hotel in Dover, only 10 miles along the coast from Shorncliffe.

After the Buffs' training period, Brinckman and Madame Chabault together went to Aix-les-Bains in France, a resort popular for its thermal baths, where they stayed for a few weeks. Returning to England in July, they were at Newmarket racecourse and then at Ascot. But then the death of Brinckman's sister-in-law caused him to focus on his family, and in August he and Mamie went to Scotland, where Brinckman had rented 15,000 acres of the Auchnafree moors in Perthshire for grouse shooting. Brinckman felt the need to keep up appearances but in reality his marriage was almost over. From September to November 1906 Brinckman and Chabault stayed at the Boulevard Flandrin flat on and off, and Lucy was certainly in Paris during this period for in October she gave evidence in a court case involving a valuable string of pearls, giving her address as a hotel in Avenue Kleber, that was only half a mile from the Boulevard Flandrin. By 22 November Brinckman and his mistress were back in London where they stayed at the Great Central Hotel in Marylebone until 3 December, and during this period a legal Deed of Separation was drawn up between Brinckman and Mamie. This done, Brinckman and Madame Chabault departed on a foreign tour, travelling from Paris to Algiers, and by the end of February they were at Monte Carlo, where Brinckman took part in the pigeon-shooting competitions.

With the Chabault affair intensifying in the summer of 1907, Brinckman made changes in his life, reducing his stable and resigning his commission with the Buffs to become the battalion's honorary colonel. In July he was once more in Aix-les-Bains with Madame Chabault but by the 'Glorious Twelfth' of August they were in Scotland for the grouse-shooting season. This year Brinckman was a guest at Cabrach Lodge in Banffshire, while Chabault stayed a few miles away over the hills. The *Banffshire Journal's* report of 6 August that 'Madame Chabault, of Paris, arrived at Cornihaugh last week for the season', forms the only evidence in the press that Brinckman's French mistress existed. The Cornihaugh estate was known for its fine fishing and the cost for the season would have been considerable. Quite how Chabault occupied her time at the remote lodge, or how often Brinckman left his friends to go over the wild moors from Cabrach to see her, is a mystery.

By the end of October the couple were again in Paris, where Brinckman attended the Auteuil autumn race meeting. Then in January, after a few weeks back in England, they went on to Monte Carlo, where they had taken a villa. The weather was glorious and the season busy, and Brinckman, in his element, again took part in the pigeon-shooting contests. But the Madame Chabault affair was coming to an end. Lady Byron was in London at the end of January, attending the London and Paris Dress Exhibition at Earl's Court. She was among thirty-four duchesses, viscountesses, countesses and ladies who were patrons of the two-week event. The exhibition, said the advertisements, featured 'Lovely Gowns and Hats and everything connected with a Lady's Wardrobe', and the best Paris and London fashion houses were in attendance, displaying and selling clothes. After this excitement Lucy needed a holiday, and when the exhibition ended she went to Hastings. Meanwhile, Brinckman would remain in Monte Carlo until the end of the shooting events in mid-April. In early June, on his way home, he attended the Auteuil Grand Steeplechase in Paris, but if he saw Madame Chabault there it was for the last time. The affair had run its course, having cost them both much time and money, and ultimately resulting in nothing.

With the disappearance of his mistress Brinckman attempted a reconciliation with Mamie. At Auteuil he had met up with his old Boer War colleague Lord Dudley, who was shortly to travel to Australia to take up his appointment as governor-general. Dudley invited the Brinckmans to visit him in Sydney. On 7 August, when he would normally have been heading for the Scottish grouse moors, Brinckman, together with Mamie and her maid, departed from London on the RMS *Orontes*, bound for Australia. For a couple whose relationship was rocky at best the undertaking to live at close quarters on board ship for months on end was risky. By replicating his Australian honeymoon voyage with Lucy of twenty-five years previously was Brinckman trying to mend or end his marriage? Or was he simply escaping the clutches of the persistent Madame Chabault? The trip did not go well and the Brinckmans made the return journey separately. After this, with his second marriage finally at an end, Brinckman went to live abroad.

Calls for female suffrage, 'Suffragism', were growing in England and the old hierarchy of aristocratic male rule in parliament and church was being increasingly challenged. In 1903 Emmeline Pankhurst and her daughters Christabel and Sylvia had founded the Women's Social and Political Union (WSPU), the main aim of which was to obtain votes for women in elections. The WSPU's protests, which resulted in arrests and imprisonments, had by 1906 aroused strong feelings both for and against the cause. Marie Corelli was one prominent woman who opposed the enfranchisement of women, arguing that women already had sufficient power over men. Real women, Corelli said, possessed the 'natural heritage' of their sex, which was the 'mystic power to persuade, enthrall, and subjugate' men. The vote would signal the loss of 'all true womanly power, reserve, and dignity'. Besides, she said, through their influence women were already the 'very head and front' of the government and had no need to join the male sphere of politics personally. Suffragettes had sacrificed their 'birthright – the right to claim men's devout reverence, faith, and loyalty', and there was no romance in brandishing umbrellas and screaming for the vote.

Corelli was by no means alone in her views, and Lucy was one of those who agreed with her. Allen would later describe Lucy as a 'past mistress' in the 'arts of getting what she wanted out of men and reducing them to subjection to her slightest whim'. The Women's Anti-Suffrage Movement, formed in 1907, argued that the majority of British women did not want the vote. Antagonism between the sexes was wrong, the organisation believed, because the roles of men and women were not antagonistic or identical, but complementary. Like Corelli, members believed that the ability to vote would destroy women's 'real influence'. To prove the point the movement organised a national petition and collected 37,000 signatures in a fortnight. It was reported in early March that the campaign had been highly successful and that Lady Byron had 'written expressing her entire sympathy with the cause'. At this point in her life, it seems, Lucy was still confident in her ability to bend men to her will.

In 1908, perhaps as a result of the ending of the Chabault affair, Lucy began a new phase of her life. She bought a house from her sister Sophia Catty that would be her home until her death thirty years later. Myrtlewood, situated in a secluded location in North End on the very edge of Hampstead Heath, was a white-painted detached Georgian building set in a large garden, with stables and staff accommodation. Although only a short walk from the Bull and Bush public house, traditionally a popular destination for East Enders on a day out, it offered Lucy the quiet retreat that she would increasingly need. She renamed the house 'Byron Cottage', but it seemed strange to give such a name to a house of that size, and stranger still not to care that 'Lord and Lady Byron of Byron Cottage' sounded absurd. The move to Byron Cottage brought new associations. Next door lived Juliana Hoare, aunt of the future cabinet minister Samuel Hoare; Juliana would come to have a great influence upon Lucy.

In the six years leading up to the outbreak of the First World War in 1914, Lucy stayed mainly in England, focusing on local and national causes. She was over the age of 50 and whereas she had previously preferred 'influence' over men to the vote, she now changed her mind. In the free-thinking atmosphere of Hampstead, Suffragism interested those in the literary and artistic circles in which Lucy moved. Social rigidities were softening and class solidarities beginning to be put aside. *Grande dames* were shifting away from the old practices of patronage and moving towards independence of mind and lifestyle. The WSPU offered a course of action that would address problems head-on rather than following the old pattern of paternalism that might only change them gradually. Whatever the reason for her change of heart, in 1908 Lucy joined the WSPU. That year the movement adopted the colours of purple, white and green, and held a huge rally in Hyde Park reportedly attended by 300,000 women; Lucy may have been among them.

Lucy still guarded her looks carefully and in 1909 posed for a series of portrait photographs with Bassano, the leading society photographer of the day. One was published in *England's Beautiful Women*, a limited-edition volume that featured royal and titled women. In the head-and-shoulders portrait Lucy wore a large fur hat, a dark dress with lace edging under a fur coat and a long string of pearls. Her interests were given as music, gardening and 'occult science'. The caption writer had done his or her best, describing Lucy as a 'charming woman with lovely red-brown hair, brown eyes with very long eyelashes, and a fair complexion'. But 'charming' was not 'beautiful'. Although Lucy was in a three-quarter pose and looking away from the camera, the slight malformation of her right eye that would later become increasingly visible can be noticed.

With the rise of interest in women's issues it was coming to be recognised that the work and activities of women of all classes had value, and in the summer of 1909 a 'Women of All Nations Exhibition' was staged at Olympia. It was still mainly aristocratic women who possessed the necessary money, skills and influence to organise such an event, and Lucy was one of the titled patrons. The exhibition would promote the pursuits of women both inside and outside the home. Among the features were Girl Scouts and 'lady billiard players', while a woman gave an 'exciting' demonstration of putting out a fire with a fire extinguisher. Nevertheless, reported the *South London Press*, 'as baby is undoubtedly King of the home, baby is to have a whole section of the exhibition to himself'. This was a crèche – a 'little paradise of babies of all nations. There are Chinese babies, Japanese babies, Italian babies, negro babies, and wee mites from the social wilds of North-East London.' There was also a nursery school where visitors could watch children being taught 'simple prayers, the arranging of flowers, care of plants and living creatures, drawing, kindergarten games, and hygienic exercises'. As a patron Lucy would have attended the exhibition's first day but on the second, 1 September, the death of Byron's 83-year-old mother put a stop to social engagements for a time, although Lucy did not attend the funeral. When the will was published it was revealed that his mother had left Byron's former residence, High Hall, to his sister Margaret, while her Langford estate in Essex went to his brother Charlie. As for the rest, Margaret got the diamonds and Charlie the silverware, and the money – £17,295 – was divided between the two. Byron's mother had left her oldest son not even a keepsake.

Lucy had an extensive social life, her friend Eva Thaddeus wrote, entertaining well-known writers, artists and musicians at Byron Cottage. She was still a leader of fashion, and in 1910, when the latest French fashion in 'Chantecleer' hats arrived in London, Lucy bought the first, featuring a feathery arrangement resembling a bird, with natural-coloured plumage, beak, comb and eyes. In June 1912, when the famous Russian ballerina Anna Pavlova bought a house in Hampstead, Lucy gained another friend. By this time she had also become close to the writer Violet Hunt, the daughter of Pre-Raphaelite artist Alfred William Hunt. Violet had been brought up among artistic and literary figures including John Ruskin and William Morris, while the writer Oscar Wilde had reportedly wished to marry her. In the 1890s she had published novels, *The Maiden's Progress* and *A Hard Woman*, and was now a keen Suffragette. Known for her rakish personal life and many lovers, Hunt was then gaining notoriety for her liaison with novelist and literary editor Ford Madox Hueffer (later known as Ford Madox Ford). Despite the fact that he was her junior by eleven years and married, Hueffer lived with Hunt from about 1910 to 1918 and during this period Hunt's home in Campden Hill would become the gathering place of writers such as Joseph Conrad, D.H. Lawrence and Henry James. In about 1911 Lucy purchased a holiday home, 4 Radnor Cliff in Sandgate near Folkestone, and at the end of the year lent it to Hunt and Hueffer, who stayed there for some months.

In May 1910 King Edward died suddenly. The shock to the nation was immense. Theatres were closed, cricket matches cancelled, and newspapers gave many black-edged column inches to the late monarch's life and death. The Edwardian era had come to an abrupt end. At this time Lucy was involved with the development of the Hampstead Garden Suburb, an experiment in urban planning. The scheme aimed to create a pleasant living environment for people of all income groups, providing good social and educational facilities, low-density housing and wide and tree-lined roads. To cut down noise from bells only one church was planned – a large red-brick Anglican church dedicated to St Jude-on-the-Hill – which would crown the garden suburb's highest point. Situated about a mile from Byron Cottage it was built to the design of the well-known architect Edwin Lutyens, a Hampstead resident. Despite Lucy's interest in 'occult science' she was a practising member of the Church of England, and when in April 1910 the foundation stone of the Lady Chapel of St Jude's church was laid it was Lucy, as a member of the church building committee, who presented the Earl of Crewe with a silver trowel for the purpose. The coronation of King George V and Queen Mary was scheduled for 22 June 1911 and as part of the celebrations a great four-day Empire Fair was held in Hampstead. The fair had a Tudor theme and the stalls were run by women dressed in appropriate costume; Lucy assisted at a stall that sold fancy needlework, pottery and baskets.

Lucy was becoming increasingly involved in women's issues. The unity of purpose of women who wanted voting rights engendered a sense of sisterhood that diminished social barriers, and in June 1912 Lucy took part in a charity fundraising event that demonstrated their new freedom and confidence. 'Alexandra Day', a celebration of the fiftieth anniversary of the dowager Queen's arrival in England, showed the power of the new ideas. On behalf of hospital charities, 10,000 women of all classes went out on the streets of London to sell artificial flowers, targeting major thoroughfares, government buildings and railway stations. The event could have been seen as a protest against militant Suffragism, for the flower sellers were carrying out a non-political and charitable activity that was essentially feminine and paternalistic in the traditional manner. However, they were also wearing the white dresses that were the hallmark of Suffragettes. Even though it was but a gentle demonstration of their freedoms, the flower sellers were doing a daring thing by standing unprotected on the streets of London and interacting with unknown men. Lady Byron was reported as selling flowers in the Haymarket with Lady Maud Wilbraham, and then in Trafalgar Square with Mrs Alfred Yorke. Alexandra Day gave a mixed message, both affirming the cause of women's rights and the caring role of woman as charity workers. In effect, high society had showed its approval of the concept of rights for women, as long as they confined themselves to a traditionally female activity such as flower selling – even if they did walk the streets to do it.

In September 1912 Lucy made a political intervention in the press on behalf of the cause of women. The occasion was a speech given by the Chancellor of the Exchequer, Lloyd George, in his home village of Llanystumdwy in Wales.

When a number of women interrupted by shouting 'Votes for Women' the crowd turned upon them, stripping one to the waist and attempting to throw another into the river. The disturbances were widely reported, and Lucy wrote to the press to say that while she had never sympathised with militant methods, the only crime that the Suffragettes had been guilty of was calling out 'Votes for Women!' It was 'shameful' that women could be treated so outrageously in a Christian country, she said, and could only incense 'even the most rabid anti-suffragist' and hence further the cause of woman's suffrage.

In 1912, with the government showing no sign of relenting on the issue of votes for women, the militant wing of the WSPU began a new campaign of violence. In March the police raided the WSPU offices and Emmeline Pankhurst was arrested and sentenced to nine months in Holloway Prison. Lucy's admiration for Mrs Pankhurst and her belief in the Suffragist cause was such that she continued to support the WSPU and stood bail for women who were arrested. However, in October 1912 Lucy demonstrated her opposition to the turn to militancy by making an appeal to its most prominent advocate, Christabel Pankhurst. Lucy's lively and down-to-earth open letter was entitled 'A Scolding for Christabel':

Dear Miss Christabel Pankhurst,

The name 'Christabel' is a charming one. It conjures up a vision of youth and beauty, and it suits you, for you are young, beautiful and brilliantly clever, and because you are exceptionally gifted I feel I must scold you! Nobody likes being scolded, so I will try and do it as nicely as I can. When I first became interested in woman's suffrage I found that although many old-fashioned people thought it 'very shocking,' the majority were ready to admit its justice. In parliament you had more friends than foes. The government was constantly worried and hampered by your unexpected and unwelcome attentions, and when Winston Churchill was completely silenced by a pretty girl ringing a big dinner bell the world laughed. He was almost as ridiculous as when he called out the army to deal with the Sidney Street burglars.

As long as you adopted amusing methods you advertised the cause and steadily gained sympathy from all classes; but alas! you were not content when all was going so well. Some evil spirit whispered in your ear. 'Militancy!' and what has been the result? Since the fatal day when every one was horrified to hear of refined women descending to the level of hooligans by smashing the windows of innocent shop-keepers (many of whom previously were sympathisers), the word 'Suffragette' became a synonym for a vulgar, violent, virago. The cause you love is turned into a ribald jest for the mob to mock at and the refined to shrink from! Why will you advocate this suicidal policy? You say in the *Suffragette* that you have no great reverence for numbers. How do you propose to gain women's suffrage unless you can command the sympathy and support of women, the majority of whom are dead against your methods? Your vehement vindication of violence has made the cause so unpopular that now you are completely misunderstood. You have done much, but you do not seem to see that a little worldly wisdom is necessary. Leave violence to the vulgar and try tactful tactics once more. Forgive me for this lecture. My sympathy is with you, but as you love the cause leave militancy – the argument of prehistoric man – to those who know no better.

LUCY BYRON.

PS You say 'Violence is necessary. Violence keeps us before the public.' But is there no other way? I will make you a sporting offer. If you will induce 670 of your friends each to buy a parrot and teach it to say 'Votes For Women,' by the 16th of next December, I will promise to supply the violet and white cages for them and send them to each member of Parliament wishing him Happy New Year, if women get the vote! Don't you think that might prove as persuasive as setting fire to their houses?

Lucy's letter caught the public imagination and, as many agreed with her, it received a considerable and generally positive press response. However, the alliterative term 'vulgar, violent, virago' would be used against Lucy in later years.

When Christabel did not take up the parrot offer Lucy pursued the idea herself, or so she would tell Wentworth Day. She bought 615 parrots and cages, and painted the cages red, white and blue. Her plan was to teach the parrots the phrase 'Votes for Women' and then deliver one to each MP in the House of Commons at the same time on the same day so that all the birds could screech the phrase together. Yet, she told Wentworth Day, the parrots defeated her – the only thing that ever had: the 'damn birds wouldn't keep in time. They were as bad as a lot of women.' In another personal effort, inspired by the power of WSPU speakers such as Mrs Pankhurst and Flora Drummond, Lucy launched her own speaking campaign. On Sundays and public holidays, she told Wentworth Day, she would drive out from Byron Cottage on to Hampstead Heath with her carriage and pair of horses, and draw an audience with her appeals for support for the cause.

By May 1913 the country was in an uproar because of the extreme actions of militant women Suffragists. Newspapers routinely printed lists of the latest attacks under headings such as 'The Week-end Outrages by the Crazy Suffragettes'. It was reported, for example, that women had booby-trapped roads with pieces of leather filled with nails and stamped with 'Votes for women', and a death threat and bomb had been delivered to a magistrate who had convicted Suffragettes at Bow Street Court. Lucy had joined the New Constitutional Society for Women's Suffrage, one of the many more moderate organisations that were starting up across the country, and on 25 June she lent the gardens of Byron Cottage for a well-attended fundraising event in aid of the society. 'Old Music and Dancing in the Open Air' and 'Miss Margaret Morris and her Dancing Children' were the main attractions. The sideshows included a 'lightning sketch artist', a silhouette artist and a palmist. Women viola players, perhaps appreciating the irony, entertained the audience with music from *The Taming of the Shrew*. It was all a far cry from militancy.

Lucy did not attend the garden party for that day was also Alexandra Day, and she was again selling roses in central London. A *Tatler* photographer snapped her in St James's Street wearing a white dress and face veil, and holding a collection tin and a large tray of blooms. Twenty years later Lucy would tell Wentworth Day that at this time she was still beautiful and, although in her mid-50s, looked only 30. She remained, she said, 'one of the best-looking, best-dressed women in London'. However, the *Tatler* photograph shows that her figure was beginning to spread. The day was a great personal triumph for Lucy, for her achievement in obtaining a donation of £100 for a single rose was widely reported.

With Alexandra Day over, Lucy departed for Sandgate where she would stay for several months. The break from London may have been owed to the desire to disassociate herself from the violence that had given Suffragism a bad name. Lucy found Sandgate residents more congenial and developed a close friendship with Lady Marie Bancroft, a former actress and theatre manager in her mid-70s. Lady Bancroft and her husband Sir Squire Bancroft, who lived a few doors from Lucy, were legendary for their development of Victorian theatre, firstly as managers of the Prince of Wales Theatre and later the Haymarket Theatre. As with others of Lucy's women friends, Marie Bancroft's early life had been unconventional. The daughter of a travelling actor, she had two illegitimate children before her marriage and had subsequently worked her way to a successful career and a title.

At Sandgate there was plenty of entertainment of the light-hearted variety that Lucy loved. In June she, together with the Bancrofts and other titled residents, were patrons of a Grand Garden Fete. Opened by local MP Sir Philip Sassoon, it featured a fairground, donkey races and tableaux scenes of classical dances from the court of Versailles and *Alice in Wonderland*. The Folkestone Operatic Society gave a concert, local children did morris dancing, and there were prizes for the 'Ugliest, Prettiest, Fattest, Smallest, and the best Dressed Dog'. In July, Lucy and the Bancrofts attended a garden party given by the mayor of Folkestone, and then in November Marie performed in a comic sketch to a large and enthusiastic audience, including Lucy, at a charity performance at the Pleasure Gardens Theatre in Folkestone.

Disillusioned with the WSPU, Lucy took up a new cause. Apart from a common enthusiasm in the theatre and its personalities going back to the 1880s, she and Marie Bancroft shared an interest in alternative health regimes. Lucy was reported to be a devotee of sleeping outdoors in a summer house: 'Really fashionable people,' an article stated that year, 'do not dream of sleeping under a roof at this time of the year' but instead took their beds into the garden. This practice was not only good for the complexion but also cured insomnia and had a 'remarkably steadying effect on the nerves'. Lucy's passion for fresh air would continue until the end of her life. That autumn she issued advice on health and domestic issues in the press. Women, she said, needed so little to keep them fit and well but, she was sorry to say, it was mostly the better off who were willing to give up luxuries. Lucy herself had renounced 'tea, coffee, butter, bacon, meat, drinking at meal-times, white bread and pastry, all alcoholic drinks and salt'. As a result, she reported, she was free from indigestion and in much better health. It was possible for the 'frugal minded' to save more than half their food budget but still be well nourished if they were prepared to change their eating habits. However, it was perhaps galling for housewives struggling on a small budget to be given domestic advice by a wealthy peeress however well meaning.

As a result of her willingness to engage with the press, Lucy became a 'go-to' person for opinions on domestic and social matters. One topic on which the press solicited her views was the craze for the tango that swept Britain in 1913. The 'Dance of Moral Death', as it was often described, involved close physical contact and the entwining of limbs, and many considered it shocking. But influential society hostesses embraced it, the Waldorf Hotel in London held tango teas, and Selfridges department store held a tango ball. In December 1913, when the *Gentlewoman* magazine surveyed peeresses for their views, most were opposed. The Duchess of Norfolk, for example, thought the dance 'foreign to our English nature and ideals', while Lady Layland Barratt found it an 'immodest and suggestive dance, altogether impossible for any girl of refinement or modesty'. Lucy, however, was not wholly in agreement. Although, she said, the tango was 'acrobatic' and often 'ungraceful', it was good exercise. It was a 'romp – the physical expression of the age, the result of undisciplined, unrestrained, youthful exuberance', but as for its being 'suggestive', she wrote 'to the pure all things are pure'. This can scarcely have ingratiated her with Lady Layland Barratt.

As the year 1914 began few can have suspected that in eight months' time Britain would be at war. Back in London Lucy continued her busy life-style, in January celebrating the Russian Christmas Day at a party given by Princess Bariatinsky at the Ambassadors Theatre, and a couple of weeks later attending a musical matinee at Claridge's Hotel. While Suffragettes continued to carry out high-profile violent attacks, Lucy, seeing herself as a voice of moderation and reason, again sought influence by advocating political means. Her article, entitled 'A Cabinet Minister for Women', appeared in the March 1914 issue of *The Nineteenth Century*, and in it Lucy appealed for the creation of a 'woman's council' to be formed by peeresses and represented in parliament by a cabinet minister. Presumably Lucy imagined herself in that role, for in May a newspaper reported that she was 'closely in touch with prominent politicians'. However, male politicians seemed uninterested in women's suffrage, Lucy wrote, and this being the case she thought it foolish for Suffragists to blind themselves to the fact that the vote was still a long way off.

But Lucy had not disassociated herself from the WSPU entirely, for in June she contributed £10 to its 'Self-Denial Fund', by which for a week members did without items such as cocoa, tea and coffee, and donated the money saved to the cause. But that month it was reported that the police were considering taking action against those who supported the WSPU on the grounds that they were financiers of militancy. To this the organisation retorted that if the authorities did so they would be 'putting their heads into a hornet's nest', for wealthier donors had influential relatives who would not stand back and see them prosecuted. Lucy quickly put out a press release making it clear that although she gave money to the WSPU she had repeatedly denounced militancy, feeling strongly that it was damaging the cause. Her gentler methods were demonstrated when a week later she hosted another fundraising garden party for the New Constitutional Society for Women's Suffrage, billed as a 'women's pastoral entertainment'. Lucy was also connected with the National Union of Women Suffrage Societies, an organisation of 100,000 members that advocated legal and peaceful methods.

But such things were about to be put aside. The assassination of Archduke Franz Ferdinand of Austria on 28 June 1914 by a Serbian nationalist had triggered a crisis which had escalated, until on 4 August Great Britain declared war on Germany; the Great War had begun. The outbreak of war put Suffragettes in something of a quandary, for their cause had been subsumed by a greater one. Essentially, Suffragette leaders accepted that the campaign for voting rights would have to go on hold for the duration of the war.

6

WAR WORKER

With the declaration that Britain was at war a wave of patriotism swept the land and hundreds of thousands of men hurried to enlist in the army and navy. The war effort was wide open for personal and individual participation, and many were eager to give of their time, money and good cheer. Hampstead residents sprang into action. The Grand Duke Michael Romanov, for example, offered Kenwood House, his great mansion on Hampstead Heath, as a military hospital, while his daughters set up a knitting scheme. Sir William Lever, the soap manufacturer, fitted up his home to receive wounded officers while local residents provided furniture and funded the purchase of medical equipment. The famous composer Sir Edward Elgar signed up as a local special constable but also began the composition of 'Carillon' – music to be performed for the benefit of Belgium, which had been overrun by German troops.

Lucy, now aged 57, was among the prominent women who responded immediately to appeals to help the country. Initially she joined with others, continuing her pre-war interests of women and healthcare by supporting Princess Mary's appeal for providing soldiers and sailors with a Christmas gift. But not for long was Lucy content to take a back seat, and after a few weeks she sought personal involvement in national affairs. Her contribution to the war effort was to take an independent and ambitious course. Her first scheme was for the welfare of nurses and, while others made offers of accommodation for nurses on leave, Lucy went one step further. Taking a large house in Tanza Road, Parliament Hill, she set about creating a home-from-home for nurses. Calling it the 'Bluebird's Nest', she intended it to provide every comfort and convenience. The home was furnished with consideration towards fraught nerves, with the bedrooms decorated in a restful blue. The sitting room featured a large model of a bluebird donated by Lady Bancroft. A cook-housekeeper and housemaid were hired to do all the work so that visiting nurses had only to rest and recuperate. The garden opened directly on to Hampstead Heath, affording quiet walks and fresh air.

The Bluebird's Nest was up and running by the spring of 1915 and Lucy promoted the home in the press, and in particular in the *Daily Mirror* and *The Times*, which belonged to the newspaper empire of Lord Northcliffe. In a period in which the newspaper was still the main means by which the public obtained news, individual proprietors had enormous power to influence popular opinion. Whereas before the war Lucy can have felt little sympathy with Northcliffe because of his strong opposition to Suffragism, she now found herself in accord with his right-wing and virulently anti-German views. Lucy's relationship with Northcliffe's newspapers was symbiotic. For example, in 1914 Lucy supported the *Mirror*'s appeal on behalf of soldiers based in the Tower of London with the gift of 100 blankets, while the *Mirror* printed her appeal for donations of reading matter for the Bluebird's Nest.

While Lucy had intended the Nest to be a haven of peace, at the planning stage she could not have foreseen the extent to which the war would come to Hampstead. Early in 1915 maimed men began to be seen in the streets, and in January that year Germany brought the war to England with a bombing campaign by Zeppelin airships. The British people had no previous experience of aerial attack; the great majority had never seen an aircraft, whether airship or aeroplane, and some even did not believe that such things existed. The first attack on London came in May, when an airship meandered over the city dropping bombs here and there, killing only seven people but inspiring fear and awe. In November anti-aircraft guns were set up in the stableyard at Kenwood House and other weapons erected on Hampstead Heath. It was all too close to Byron Cottage for comfort.

Lucy worked out her own original schemes for targeting specific problems faced by soldiers serving overseas. At Christmas, upon hearing that soldiers at the front in France had cigarettes but no matches, Lucy dispatched a consignment of 100,000 boxes. With each one labelled 'A match for our matchless troops, from Lady Byron', 100,000 men could appreciate her munificence, as could readers of the newspapers that reported it. Lucy also sent 1,100 brown woollen pullovers to the 9th Battalion of the Buffs, each garment accompanied by a card that read 'A warm greeting from Lady Byron'. She publicised letters of appreciation, as for example from a soldier who returned the top of a matchbox with a note saying that it had been through 'Ypres, Hazebrouck, Silvester, Cappel, and Morbecque, and the matches have done as good service as the troops'. It was all most gratifying. The press wrote of Lucy appreciatively and in March 1915 reported that she was one of the people who was working hardest on behalf of British soldiers. The war brought Lucy many new contacts and one of her 'great supporters', according to Eva Thaddeus, was Rudyard Kipling, the journalist and writer. Lucy met Kipling many times, visiting him at Brown's Hotel in Mayfair, where she learned from the great imperialist about Britain's relationship with its war allies. In those days Kipling's famous poem, 'If', was constantly upon her lips, but especially the lines:

And lose, and start again at your beginnings;
And never breathe a word about your loss.

Of Byron there was no sign but it is unlikely that so staunch a patriot did not try to do his bit. He may have been working for the War Propaganda Bureau, otherwise known as Wellington House or MI7(b), which operated in the strictest secrecy from Buckingham Gate in central London. It employed writers to produce positive propaganda that was planted in the press to keep up public morale. MI7(b) was directed by Charles Masterman, a former cabinet minister who knew many people in the literary world. Workers came and went but of those known to have worked at Wellington House during the war, several were friends or acquaintances of Lucy and Byron. These included, in addition to Kipling, Ford Maddox Hueffer (Violet Hunt's partner), J.M. Barrie, Sir Arthur Conan Doyle, H.G. Wells and G.K. Chesterton. It is quite possible that Byron, as a prolific writer of newspaper articles, was called in to work with them.

A few months into the war, rich and titled people were looking further afield for recipients of their patronage. Thomas Lipton, now in his late 60s, had already volunteered the *Erin* to transport equipment and medical staff to a hospital in France. Now, in 1915, he gave the yacht for the service of the ravaged country of Serbia. It was loaded with equipment, supplies and chests of Lipton's tea for Serbian hospitals, and lorries and ambulances were lifted on to the same decks from which Lucy and Marie Corelli had watched the

1905 *entente cordiale* celebrations. Afterwards Lipton donated the *Erin* to the Admiralty but in April 1916 it would hit a mine and the famed yacht, aboard which Lipton had entertained so many illustrious figures, sank to the bottom of the Mediterranean.

Lucy, too, interested herself in other countries affected by the war and in 1915 joined the committees of organisations set up to help Poland, Montenegro and Italy. She was chair of the high-profile Great Britain to Poland Fund, serving alongside the Lord Mayor of London and the fund's star, the actress Madame Lydia Yavorska, the wife of a cousin of Tsar Nicholas II. By the summer Lucy had also joined the committee of the Montenegrin Red Cross and Relief Fund, along with the Queen of Montenegro, Thomas Lipton, and the Russian ambassador to Britain. Serving on the British Committee in Aid of the Italian Wounded, in company with the Archbishops of Canterbury and York and Sir Arthur Conan Doyle, Lucy raised money to buy twenty-five ambulances. Her involvement, a newspaper commented, was 'peculiarly fitting' because the name of Byron was still revered in Italy. Then, in June 1915, Réjane visited London for a performance in aid of both convalescent camps in Normandy and a fund for Gondolier-Soldiers' Wives in Venice. This 'All-Women Matinee' was attended by a large audience headed by Queen Alexandra, and Lucy was prominent among the titled women. The most memorable act, it was reported, was a 'magnificent' recital by Réjane of 'Chantons, Belges, Chantons', a poem set to Elgar's 'Carillon' music. Réjane's performance of what the *Stage* described as the 'classic War piece – a very epitome of the grief and glory of Belgium', was 'beyond all praise'.

British feeling against Germany and Germans grew as the war progressed and in March 1915 the Anti-German League was formed to combat German trade and influence. Intending to weaken the German Empire, the league urged the public not to purchase German-made articles, employ a German, or use shops, banks or hotels in which German labour was employed. Sentiments were compounded when in April 1915, during the Second Battle of Ypres, Germany used poison gas on a large scale for the first time. Then, on 7 May 1915, the British ocean liner RMS *Lusitania* was sunk by a German U-boat off the south-west coast of Ireland, resulting in the deaths of 1,198 civilians. Feelings boiled over and Rudyard Kipling declared that there were only two divisions in the world, 'human beings and Germans'. Germans living in Britain became a target for hatred; there were protests and rioting around the country, and demands that the government take immediate steps to intern or deport all alien enemies, naturalised or not. Lucy stoked the fires of wrath by writing two letters to *The Times,* attacking the writer H.G. Wells for his condemnation of anti-German protestors. There were 40,000 Germans living in England, 'free to plot and spy', Lucy pointed out. But demands for their internment had been disregarded until ordinary Britons, 'goaded beyond all endurance' by the sinking of the *Lusitania,* took matters into their own hands. Lucy's letters contained a clear, if indirect, criticism of the government: 'How much longer are our rulers going to delay justice? An eye for an eye, a tooth for a tooth, is the old law of Moses.' In the days of Queen Elizabeth I, she wrote, Germans were so detested that the Queen turned them all out of the country, and 'all the bells in all the towns and ports of Merrie England rang out joyous peals to see them off!'

In part, resentment against Germans was caused by frustration at British weakness, for while Germany had been preparing for war for years, Britain lagged far behind. Military planners had been caught short and a particular problem was the shortage of artillery shells on the front lines of battle. A government department was created to deal with what became known as the 'Shell Crisis', and in May 1915 David Lloyd George was appointed Minister of Munitions. Lloyd George took rapid action to increase production, setting up new factories across the country. More factory workers were needed but as casualties mounted more men were required in the armed forces; there was only one solution to the munition worker shortage. When Mrs Pankhurst, knowing his past opposition to her cause, received an invitation to meet Lloyd George she was astounded. But, as an indication of the gravity of the national situation, Lloyd George was remarkably frank. Treating Mrs Pankhurst as a person of influence and credibility, he explained the seriousness of the munitions shortage and explained that women were needed to work in factories. He offered the Suffragette leader £3,000 for the cost of organising what would be a great piece of political theatre. A procession, he suggested, in which women demonstrated their willingness to work, and in particular in munitions production, would increase the acceptance of working women by men.

It took Mrs Pankhurst a remarkably short time to activate Suffragettes to organise the 'Give us Work' procession, which was scheduled for Saturday, 17 July. The culmination was to be a carefully staged meeting at the Ministry of Munitions between Lloyd George and a deputation of high-profile women. The members included Emmeline Pankhurst, WSPU organiser Annie Kenney, the celebrated concert singer Madame Clara Butt, Lucy and seven others. The event received wide attention and, because it had the backing of both the King and government, was universally approved in the press.

On Saturday afternoon 40,000 women gathered on the Thames Embankment to begin the march in wet and windy weather. According to police estimates, 100,000 spectators lined the streets between Blackfriars and Westminster; many were men, who, according to one report, were 'slightly inclined to chaff'. The route took the marchers along Piccadilly, up Park Lane to Oxford Street, on to Oxford Circus, Regent Street, Haymarket and Northumberland Avenue before returning to the Embankment. Heading the procession was a girl dressed in white who carried the flags of the Allies bunched in her hands. After her another girl carried the flag of Belgium. These two were followed by women representing Belgium, France, Serbia, Montenegro, Russia, Japan and Italy. The women of the deputation, includ-ing Lucy, came next with Mrs Pankhurst, who, it was reported, looked frail and was enveloped in a big mackintosh topped by a dowdy mauve hat. But she received a great ovation and even the police smiled and saluted her with respect. How times had changed! Behind these leading Suffragettes came many women including hospital nurses, all-women brass bands and 1,000 marchers carrying banners bearing slogans such as 'Men must fight and women must work', 'We mean to save our country' and 'To keep the Kaiser out let us make shells'. To make the point that women had stamina they had been instructed to walk fast, and the procession went by almost at the double.

The march completed, the women rallied at Whitehall Gardens and the deputation was received by Lloyd George in his office at the Ministry of Munitions. He used the press coverage to set out his plans – already fully developed – for the employment of women: 'Without them victory tar-ries, and victory which tarries is victory whose footprints are the footprints of blood,' he declared. Men had to drop their prejudices about working women, and he assured men that they would get their old jobs back once the war was over. Lloyd George then went outside to be greeted by a great ovation. One woman called out, 'We want the vote,' to which Lloyd George replied, 'Yes, but we want you in the shell factory first.' Clearly a deal had been done: if Suffragettes gave their support for the war effort they would get the vote when the war ended.

The government's request for women to join the workforce confirmed that the war still had many months to run. Men who had marched off to fight were creeping back maimed and disabled, to be termed 'broken heroes'. In September 1915 the Battle of Loos brought a fresh wave of casualties and the press debated what could be done with and for men who had been invalided out. In October a group of church people in Bristol proposed the formation of a 'League for the Marrying of Wounded Heroes', the object of which would be to save 'broken fighting men from lives of loneliness'. One of the group wrote to the press saying that it was intolerable that a man who had offered himself in the service of his country should have no alternative but to spend his 'broken life in grim untended loneliness or the grey depression of an institution'. It was better to have died on the battlefield than be forever denied the 'joys of family life'. Surely, the correspondent believed, many 'noble-minded, patriotic women' would be glad to marry such men and, as the broken heroes had 'risen to heights of moral heroism', their offspring were likely to be 'of the very best, such as the nation needs'.

The question was widely debated, but views were mixed. A Manchester newspaper thought that such soldiers should be encouraged to reproduce, for the replenishment of the nation's racial stock should not be left to those who were so physically imperfect that they had not been allowed to join the military services in the first place. But others made fun of the idea, with one journalist joking that the suggestion had excited widows and spinsters, and some women who were 'fair, fat, and forty' felt that they were back in the running and were making 'covert inspections at their mirrors'. When the press sought the opinion of prominent women, Lucy declared herself in favour. It was a woman's character, she said, to care for the helpless, and thousands of women would welcome the opportunity. It would also be an excellent thing for quiet girls who would not otherwise meet men, not that Lucy had ever had that problem. But other voices were less enthusiastic. The Marchioness of Townshend thought the idea 'ridiculous', and said that she would have a low opinion of a girl who made herself available in this way. Sylvia Pankhurst, who was opposed to marriage in principle, said bluntly, 'No love, no marriage.' As for the broken heroes themselves, nobody asked them, but an Australian newspaper humorously commented that 'if he is going to be married to someone he has never seen, or even perhaps someone he has seen, he will want to go back to the front'.

Lucy commented, too, on the death of British nurse Edith Cavell, who had been court-martialled by the Germans in Belgium, found guilty of treason and, despite international appeals for mercy, executed by firing squad in October 1915. In this way Cavell became the best-known female casualty of the war and a powerful propaganda tool for the Allies. Making a donation of 100 guineas to the Cavell memorial fund, Lucy was quoted in the *Daily Mirror* as making an appeal that the nurse should not have given her life in vain:

> If love of country had been instilled into the minds of our 'slackers' when they were little children, there would be no slackers to day. But Britain, alas! has utterly neglected to teach her children patriotism, or to honour our dead heroes.

By early 1916 the sense of urgency of the early months of the war had faded and Lucy turned her attention to new matters. Those in high society still held social functions, although all were now in aid of the war effort, and Lucy supported the Countess de Morella in arranging a festival in aid of Allied hospitals in France, and hosted a large lunch party at Claridge's Hotel for the Montenegrin Relief Fund. Her guests included her friends the Bancrofts and Sir Roper Parkington, consul-general for Montenegro. But Lucy did not forget serving soldiers. The war was dragging on and in an attempt to combat the demoralisation that was setting in among troops Lucy sent a consignment of footballs to the Western Front, each inscribed with the words 'Simple mirth keepeth high courage alive'. Some of the footballs, a *Sunday Mirror* correspondent reported a few weeks later, were already war relics, for he had seen one that has been deflated by a stray bullet as the owner carried it not far from the firing line.

Lucy was by now a prominent public figure, and was invited to sit on the platform at a high-profile meeting at the Mansion House in March 1916. With more men joining the armed forces the role of women was expanding further and this meeting, organised by the Criminal Law Amendment Committee and the Women's Police Service, considered the question of women serving in the police force. Then, as economic constraints began to bite, it became a patriotic duty to restrict food consumption. Lucy responded to a report that the guardians of Thetford workhouse in Norfolk had decided that margarine was not good enough to give the inmates. She wondered why this was, for she herself had been eating margarine for some months and knew many women who had done so since the beginning of the war. The Sainsbury's chain of food shops jumped at the advertising opportunity:

> Sound and sensible Economy. The Lady Byron has been speaking well of margarine, so well, indeed, milady surely referred to 'Crelos'! So excellent is Sainsbury's 'Crelos' that it has won more 'really nice people' to the use of margarine than has any other brand. Ninepence per pound. Still only at the branches of Sainsbury's.

The Battle of the Somme began on 1 July 1916, with 19,240 British soldiers dying on the first day alone. Lucy continued her war efforts, on 18 July hosting a garden party at Byron Cottage in aid of the Sailors and Soldiers Tobacco Fund, to which wounded soldiers were invited. Lucy entertained the men in her terraced gardens, and a *Sunday Mirror* correspondent reported that the first terrace had only pink flowers – roses, snapdragons and Betsie's pretties – while the next was a blue 'heaven-garden', with larkspurs, delphiniums and love-in-the-mist. The third was a 'sun garden' of yellow flowers, and after the war it would be reported that Lucy had started a 'yellow flower cult', with marigolds prominent in the windows of fashionable florists. The *Mirror* reported rapturously on the 'too beautiful afternoon', nothing was too good for the wounded men, and Lucy waited on them personally: 'My dears, she serves her guests with strawberries and cream from no mean plates or dishes, just great ewers and basins of beaten silver.' Lucy had arranged entertainments for the men and enlisted the services of a clairvoyant, a palm reader and a horoscope expert, as well as Miss Constance Holmes who told 'Character by Physiognomy'. The following month Lucy again opened her home and garden to host a tea and garden party for mothers of soldiers. The *Illustrated War News* published photographs which show Lucy manning a tea urn while sober-faced women, some dressed in the black of mourning, ate their sandwiches and cake. The party, as the newspaper commented, was an 'admirable and kindly idea', although this perhaps suggested that it had not been a success.

Although women now had careers in many fields, one exception was the clergy. While women preachers would not have been tolerated before the war, social attitudes were changing and the question of women entering the pulpit was taken up by the press. The *People* reported that the matter had caused a 'tremendous hullabaloo' in the Church of England, and when the *Weekly Dispatch* sought opinions on the matter it found that men were more opposed to the idea than women. Lucy, perhaps remembering her own past, suggested, not with perfect logic, that if Jesus Christ had considered Mary Magdalene, a sinner, to be worthy to wash His feet with her tears, then it could not be argued that a woman was unworthy to be a preacher. Christ, she declared, did not set limitations upon women or countenance different moral laws for them, and spirituality was 'sexless'. The debate rumbled on until the following year, when Lucy would make a further contribution in the *Daily Mirror*. Doubtless meaning herself, she said that it was an acknowledged fact that women were more spiritual than men. All those 'inspired by the spirit of truth to deliver a message' were the 'chosen vessels of the Almighty'. If, she argued, it was wrong for women to preach, God would not have given women the necessary gifts of understanding, intuition and eloquence.

German airship raids on London had continued and in the summer of 1916 Lucy escaped to her house in Sandgate, where she would stay for some months. She lived next door to Bithia Croker, the author of forty-four novels of Victorian romance, and when Lucy was without a cook Mrs Croker kindly sent round a hot meal every day.[3] Lucy and Lady Bancroft were often seen together, and in September the *Daily Mirror* reported that the two were warmly welcomed whenever they visited the military hospital. The women, noted the newspaper, were 'not of the dull kind'. While Lucy was out of London a method was found of bringing down German Zeppelin airships with incendiary ammunition and with the threat abated, Lucy returned to London. There she launched her 'Give Him Socks' campaign, a particularly helpful and practical scheme because soldiers were issued with only one spare pair. Announcing it in the *Daily Express*, Lucy wrote:

> I have been asking friends returning from the front the greatest need of our soldiers. They tell me flat the most insistent, ever-recurring, and never satisfied want is – socks! To have to wear dirty socks, stiff with mud and slime, is a discomfort often felt to be the last straw of their misery. Millions of pairs of socks are wanted, so in popular language I beg one and all to 'Give him socks.' Please send as many pairs of socks as you can to Lady Byron, Byron Cottage, Hampstead Heath, who will gratefully acknowledge them and forward them to the troops.

Lucy added that a 'little word of affectionate sympathy and the name of the donor sent with each parcel will greatly enhance the gift'. In October the *Daily Mirror* published a photograph of Lucy and women helpers knitting at Byron Cottage amid piles of donated socks. There was no limit to the demand: 'Send me more and more and more,' Lucy appealed. Her sock campaign was a great success.

In the autumn of 1916, now almost 60, Lucy progressed to making direct interventions in political issues, presenting herself as an outspoken voice of common sense and unafraid to enter spheres that had traditionally been the preserve of men. Her willingness to court controversy and make personal attacks on public figures prefigured her political campaigns of the 1930s. Lucy's first target was Lord Bryce, with whom she had served on the committee of the Great Britain to Poland Fund the previous year. James, 1st Viscount Bryce, now aged 78, had gained considerable status through a long and highly respectable record of public service, and was friend and counsellor of King George V. But when, in October 1916, Bryce made remarks that were interpreted as demonstrating sympathy with Germany his views were strongly repudiated in the press. Lucy, in her capacity as a vice-president of the British Empire Union (the new name of the Anti-German League), joined the fray. With what the *Newcastle Journal* described as 'something of the snap of language' associated with the name of Byron, she wrote to the press criticising Bryce. If he met a mad dog, Lucy asked, 'would he consider killing it "indulging in revenge?" One need not hate Germans, but the natural instinct of self-preservation prompts one to protect oneself against them.'

In December 1916 when Wilhelm II, the German kaiser, made moves to end the fighting, the *Daily Mirror* denounced Germany's dove of peace as a 'Blood-Stained Eagle'. Lucy jumped in to denounce the kaiser who, she told the *Mirror*, reminded her of a 'third-rate quick-change artist, but in his disguise of the Prince of Peace he has forgotten to hide the cloven hoof'. The only answer to the kaiser's 'impertinent' proposals, she said, should be an 'intimation that Peace can only be arranged when we arrive in Berlin, or when the German army arrives in London'. Lucy's last outburst of 1916 was an attack on an economy drive started in December by the National War Savings Committee. While, the press reported, the campaign was aimed at women of all classes, those in the middle and upper classes were expected to take the lead. Lucy, however, did not approve. The economy campaign, she told the *Daily Mirror*, was 'senseless and extravagant', and exhortations to economise had already cost the nation thousands of pounds. Why should the onus be on women, she asked? Would it not be better to remove the temptation to purchase by stopping shopkeepers from displaying goods that were intended to 'tempt frivolous femininity into extravagance'? The only sensible solution was to prohibit tradesmen from selling anything that was not a necessity.

However, Lucy's participation in national debates was about to be curtailed. Byron's brother Charlie had inherited Thrumpton Hall in Nottinghamshire from his aunt, the Dowager Lady Byron, and in the second half of February 1917 he invited Byron and Lucy to stay. Towards the end of the month, perhaps fired up by religious conversations with Charlie, who was an Anglican minister, Lucy wrote to *The Times* from Thrumpton to contribute to a debate on the nature of spiritual truth. Such truth, she said, could only be revealed to those capable of receiving it but, 'alas! the gift of understanding and the gift of the Spirit seem to have been denied to our spiritual pastors and masters of today'. As for dead soldiers, nobody could doubt that they were 'happy and glorious in the Great Beyond', for they had sacrificed their lives for their country and by this means had reached a 'much higher plane on the straight and narrow path leading to salvation'. But by this time Byron had contracted influenza, and by early March he was seriously ill. There was much against his recovery. Not only was it an unusually cold March that year but Thrumpton Hall was heated only by coal fires. It was not a good environment for an invalid with a chest condition whose lungs had been weakened by decades of heavy smoking. However, Byron seemed to pick up and was able to resume his writing for *The Times*, and Lucy turned her mind once more to national affairs.

Isolated in the wilds of Nottinghamshire, she read news reports on moves by the Ministry of Food towards food rationing. Lord Devonport, who headed the ministry, preferred a system of 'Voluntaryism' rather than the introduction of formal rationing. Devonport recommended the weekly consumption per person of the 'three most important staples', which equated to 4lb of bread (or its equivalent in flour), 2½lb of meat, and ¾lb of sugar. He placed the nation 'upon its honour' to observe these conditions for if each consumer reduced their consumption then rationing could be avoided. Lucy was one of many people who thought that voluntary rationing would not work and would only delay the introduction of compulsory rationing, and she wrote to the *Pall Mall Gazette* to make a fierce attack. Voluntaryism in food consumption, she wrote, would allow 'undesirable aliens', Germans and 'food hogs' to buy what they wanted while 'honest, self-sacrificing, and patriotic English-women' would suffer. With characteristic dogmatism she denounced Voluntaryism as 'vile and evil' and Germany's 'best friend'. Lucy blamed the influence of the Labour Party for the policy, and this – her first public criticism of socialism – foreshadowed the attacks that would feature so strongly in her campaigns of the 1930s.

Suddenly, on 30 March, Byron's chest condition deteriorated and he died. Lucy was thrown into mourning and ordered two black dresses from London; she would later boast that in her observance of wartime economy they were the first dresses that she had purchased since the outbreak of war. Byron's funeral took place at Thrumpton early in April in bitterly cold weather, and he was buried in Thrumpton churchyard. Byron's final exit went almost unnoticed in the press, although Charlie's assumption to the title of the Reverend and Right Honourable the Lord Byron raised a little interest, with the *Tatler* remarking that it was difficult to imagine a vicar holding the title that had once belonged to the 'naughtiest man of his day'. After the funeral Lucy stayed on at Thrumpton for some weeks. She enjoyed Charlie's company and he, Wentworth Day wrote, had the 'greatest liking for his volcanic sister-in-law'. Lucy may have given a fleeting thought to marriage but ultimately the prospect of life as the wife of an eccentric vicar in an isolated village, with all the onerous constraints and duties involved, was not attractive.

With summer approaching, Lucy returned to London. In Byron's lifetime she had honoured his status as a peer and now as his widow she conformed to the standards and traditions of mourning by withdrawing from society. Byron's death drew a line in Lucy's life for it marked the end of her heavy involvement in war-related activities. Perhaps shaken by the ease with which death had overtaken Byron, Lucy became a founder member of the People's League of Health, the object of which was to raise health standards in Britain and the Empire. She was also greatly pleased when she was made a Dame Commander of the British Empire (DBE) for service to her country during the war, one of only five women to receive that honour. To mark the event Lucy sat for another studio portrait photograph. Still wearing mourning clothes, she has a peculiar appearance. The effect of her headdress is part wimple and part nurse's scarf; perhaps Lucy wished to give the impression of dedication, spirituality and self-sacrifice. Her expression seemed calculated to convey both suffering and compassion, the head tilted to show a sympathetic nature. The two sides of the face were different. The right showed the squint that was becoming increasingly apparent, but there was a slight smile on the lips and a general impression of softness and warmth. The left side, however, was much more alive and, while it revealed Lucy's famed beauty, the eye is shrewd and questioning and the lips determined, even stubborn.

When Lucy re-emerged into public life in early 1918 she turned her mind to new topics – and to husband-hunting. Brinckman had married again in the spring of 1913, to Elisabeth Bergerand, known as 'Brownie'. If Lucy had posed as Madame Chabault it would have been particularly galling to be usurped by a genuine Frenchwoman, but even had she still wanted Brinckman she must have recognised that it would be difficult to compete with a woman seventeen years her junior. Ever afterwards, Wentworth Day noted, Lucy nursed an 'unquenchable hatred' for Elisabeth. With Brinckman out of the running, Lucy looked around for other candidates.

7

A Real Man

As 1918, the final year of the Great War, opened, British morale was low. In Russia the overthrow of the Tsar in early 1917 had brought in a provisional government but this had been overthrown by the Bolshevik party under the leadership of Vladimir Lenin. Subsequently the Bolsheviks had withdrawn Russia from the war, leaving Germany in a strong position. But while the mood in Britain was subdued, when Lucy re-entered the public sphere after her period of mourning she was not. Misjudging the atmosphere, Lucy directed her energies scattershot at random causes and her fighting talk appeared anachronistic and her interventions directionless. Rather than an influential figure, she now appeared something of an eccentric. But while she had lost the benefit of Byron's quiet advice, she had gained another and far more belligerent influence – the Liverpool shipowner Robert Houston. The fact that, at the age of 65, and four years Lucy's senior, Houston was regarded as a 'confirmed bachelor' did not deter her when there was a fortune to be won, and even by 1918 Lucy had wormed his way into his confidence.

The Victorian period had seen the rise of new classes of wealthy people, prominent among them brewers such as Gretton, merchant bankers and shipowners. Robert Houston was one of several shipowners who accumulated great fortunes in their own lifetime. A tough, hard man of great ability, he had built up his business from nothing through sheer determination and hard work. 'Impossible' was a word that Houston did not recognise, and he would not tolerate weakness in himself or others. He had been only in his twenties when he started his own company, R.P. Houston and Co., operating cargo services between Liverpool and the River Plate (Río de la Plata) in South America. His business went from strength the strength and in 1898 the Houston line became a subsidiary of the British and South American Steam Navigation Company. New services were added and offices established in London, New York, Cape Town and Buenos Aires. Houston's success, his obituary in *The Times* would state, had been 'one of the most striking individual developments in the modern history of shipping'.

Up to 1899 Houston operated only a few ships, but the outbreak of the Boer War in South Africa changed everything. By offering the right services in the right place at the right time, and with amazing efficiency, Houston obtained War Office contracts and emerged from the Boer War as a millionaire and one of the country's largest shipowners. With a seemingly miraculous knowledge of every detail of his business, he supervised and directed everything from his Liverpool headquarters. But in his drive to infiltrate the South African cargo trade Houston had made bitter enemies among a group of Liverpool shipping lines, which included the Union Castle Line, the White Star Line and the Clan Line, which dominated the trade. Once the Boer War ended Houston fought them for a greater share and, claiming that there was a conspiracy against him, litigated in numerous trade altercations. He discovered a bright young lawyer by the name of F.E. Smith, later Lord Birkenhead, who was then building a practice in Liverpool. Smith helped Houston force his way into the South African trade and the two men became close friends.

Houston also sought political influence and in 1892 was elected MP for Liverpool West Toxteth, a seat that he would hold uninterrupted for thirty-two years. Tall and solidly built, with black hair and beard, piercing eyes and a rough voice, he became as legendary a figure in the House of Commons as he was in the shipping world. His outspokenness and refusal to mince words ensured that his contributions were noticed but also meant that he was not universally liked. His friend T.P. O'Connor would write of him that with his 'strong lips, his beetling brow, his defiant eyes, his defiant expression; and when it came to fighting – and he was never out of a fight – he had all the ferocity and still more of the tenacity of the bulldog'. Houston's political speeches were characterised by patriotism and dislike of socialism, and he pressed his appeals for governmental action regardless of party political considerations. But, *The Times* reported, while Houston could be 'extremely unpleasant' he could also be 'very good-natured', and was known by his friends as a 'good-humoured and generous host'.

As the First World War began, Houston, at the age of 60, was already dogged by the ill health from which he would never be free. The nature of his illness was not stated but heavy smoking and alcohol consumption may have contributed. Immersed in shipping arrangements imposed by war conditions, he became a strong and persistent critic of the government's handling of various aspects of the war. In the business sphere, Houston's decisions were put into effect with lightning rapidity, and he soon became bitter and frustrated at the seeming inefficiency and negligence of the government. Unfortunately for officials, with his encyclopedic knowledge of merchant shipping and world trade, Houston usually had a better grasp of the facts than they did. As his obituary in *The Times* would state, in his 'splendid self-confidence he regarded every Admiralty official as an ignorant, incompetent ass'. His attacks did not increase his popularity and Houston again believed, as with his Liverpool shipping rivals, that there was a conspiracy against him, and even that he was being poisoned to keep him away from the House of Commons. Whatever the case, the poison theory was a good excuse for the physical weakness that Houston so hated in himself.

Houston particularly deplored the loss of British ships to German submarines, and when the British passenger liner *Lusitania* was sunk in 1915, Houston, it was reported, was rendered 'almost speechless with indignation' against the Germans, so that he could only repeat, 'The damned scoundrels! The damned scoundrels!' Suggesting in a letter to *The Times* that Britain's 'nerveless and lethargic' wartime government was slow to deal with German submarines, he worked out a plan for personal intervention, offering up to fifty awards of £2,000 each to British-born masters of British-owned merchant ships for every German submarine that their ship sank.

Houston's forthright ways and outspokenness appealed to Lucy and he stood for much that she admired; he was, she said, a 'real man' who 'never wasted time or money'. However, it would take her six years to get him to the altar, and later she would admit that Houston had been a 'hard nut' to crack. He was, she would reflect, a difficult customer, but she boasted that she had 'never been afraid of a mere man'. Houston was not used to anyone standing up to him but Lucy was 'not one of his shareholders to be silenced and browbeaten', she told Wentworth Day, and was 'more than a match for him'. But the truth was that for several years she was by no means sure of eventual success; she kept her eyes open for other candidates, as an incident that occurred at about this time showed. Thomas Lipton and his friend the distilling magnate Thomas

Dewar, being unmarried and among the country's richest men, were obvious targets for Lucy's matrimonial ambitions, and Wentworth Day gave his own account of a conversation between the two that suggested they felt pressured by Lucy. 'We must marry her off, Tommy!' Dewar said to Lipton. 'It's not safe to have her about loose.' Both agreed that there was only one person who could master Lucy – Robert Houston. 'Ask him to stay,' Dewar urged, 'and ask Poppy at the same time. I'll guarantee she sinks him on sight.' This was written long after all concerned were dead but, given the dogged and ruthless nature of Lucy's pursuit of Houston, it seems likely that Lipton and Dewar had indeed conspired to deflect her predatory attentions.

Adopting some of Houston's aggression, in January 1918 Lucy made a controversial and poorly received statement on the subject of votes for women. It was by now generally accepted that women would be given the vote in recognition of their wartime contribution, and indeed parliament was working on reform of the electoral system. Lucy, however, fearing that certain anti-Suffrage peers might sabotage the legislation, declared in the press that a man who voted against the emancipation of women had 'no right to call himself a Christian'. The *Sketch* was indignant: 'That, and nothing less, is Lady Byron's opinion.' It retorted scornfully that it could not understand what Lucy or anybody else meant by emancipation. 'What do they want? What more can we give them?' the paper asked. Men had suffered out of all proportion to women in the war, and women appeared far from 'miserable, down-trodden, unappreciated, and "unemancipated"'. When the Representation of the People Act was passed in February 1918 it extended the right to vote to nearly all men over the age of 21, but only to women who were over the age of 30 and who met certain property qualifications. But even though women were still not politically equal to men, they now made up 43 per cent of the electorate.

In an attempt to flatter Houston and create common ground between them Lucy shadowed the shipowner's interests, for example, in food supply. By January 1918 Britain had only enough wheat stocks to last six weeks and, with food shortages causing long queues outside shops, the *Daily Mirror* printed Lucy's solution. She advised that once a queue had formed shopkeepers should 'call out from an upper window to the police below just how many persons could be served with each commodity'. A policeman would then count off the appropriate number of people and disperse the rest. To those so dispersed Lucy's advice would be, 'Keep smiling. If the dear fellows fighting can do that, so ought we when we have to do without things.' This homespun suggestion attracted little attention.

Food shortages worsened and by July 1918 householders were required to use ration books for the purchase of meat, butter, margarine, lard and sugar. With people having to do more with less, Lucy championed the humble potato. If the vegetable was respected, appreciated and understood, she wrote in the press, much could be obtained from it. A crucial fact to grasp was that the most valuable and nutritious part was just below the skin, and yet that was what most people either threw away or gave to their pigs. Recommending that potatoes be cooked in their skins, she gave a recipe for a 'delicious' soup made with four large potatoes, two chopped onions, a pint of milk, grated nutmeg and pepper. Lucy may have been right about the potato's nutritional value but there was something ridiculous about a peeress giving out recipes for potato soup. At the same time Lucy was in the news for her donation of valuable jewellery to the Red Cross, to be auctioned at Christie's salerooms in aid of the charity's funds. Lucy had previously donated a tapestry panel from the time of Charles I which had fetched £220, but now she gave what the *Graphic* described as the 'most remarkable' suite of jewels. It comprised a pendant/brooch that featured a 'wonderful cat's eye' 1in in diameter, surrounded by twelve large diamonds and accompanied by matching earrings. Lucy told the *Mirror* that the set had been purchased for £1,500 thirty years previously (her 'Mrs Brinckman' days), but she hoped it would fetch more now. However, these hopes were dashed when it made only £1,500. Perhaps the set was out of fashion.

In August 1918 the Allies broke the German advance and pushed through German lines. Faced with the prospect of defeat, in early October the German government wrote to Woodrow Wilson, President of the United States, effectively requesting an armistice. Lucy, feeling that Woodrow Wilson might need help in coming to a decision, sent him a pithy telegram:

> Dear President Wilson, – I am only a woman, but if I were you I should return the German peace Note with one vulgar, but forceful, little word written across it – 'Piffle'.

This attracted much attention and the *Birmingham Gazette* made the tacit suggestion that Lucy's term 'vulgar violent virago' could be applied to Lucy herself. Indeed, Lucy was out of alignment with the direction of international affairs for an armistice was agreed, to take effect on 11 November. The war had lasted for four years and four months. In the United Kingdom 6 million men had been mobilised, of whom more than 700,000 had been killed. Lucy would never forget that fact.

The war had also taken a toll on Houston's business. He had lost five ships to German submarines and mines, and the rest of his fleet was old and worn. He was 65 and in poor health; it was time to retire. Lucy would tell Wentworth Day that Houston acted upon her recommendation to sell his business at the 'top of the boom' at the end of the war: 'If he'd listened to the advice of certain other people, he would never have been worth the fortune that he left,' she recalled. He always took her advice, she boasted: 'That's the real mark of a big man – I mean, that he'll take the advice of the woman who loves him, provided she has common sense.' Therefore R.P. Houston & Company and the British and South American Steam Navigation Company Ltd were sold to the Clan Line, the transaction going through on 1 November 1918. However, the change in ownership was kept secret and the ships retained their names and livery. Houston was loath to admit that he had given up his life's work. Also, as he was an important employer in his West Toxteth constituency he must have calculated that if the sale were known he would lose votes.

With the war over, Houston, freed from his business commitments, had newfound leisure and vast wealth, but he was not a happy man. He had worked hard all his life but, T.P. O'Connor wrote, ultimately it had destroyed his health and left him only 'sad and depressed', for his money could not reach the 'core of disappointment and something like despair which was within his breast'. However, the liquidation of Houston's wealth made him more attractive to Lucy and, weakened by age, illness and depression, he was rendered vulnerable to her predations. Lucy was also at a loose end. Perhaps her misjudgment in the 'Piffle' episode had had a salutary effect, for now she limited her press comments to less controversial matters. At that time there was much agonising about the role of women, for the war had changed attitudes, not least among women themselves. During the war years they had enjoyed higher status, more work opportunities and wider contact with men from outside their social sphere. As their economic value had increased, their view of themselves had altered and their horizons widened. Having won the vote and been freed from a variety of confinements, many women did not want to turn the clock back. Writing in the press about the '*dernier cri*' girl – the very latest type of post-war young woman – Lucy conceded that the 'modest, demure maid is a drug on the present girl market', i.e. was no longer in demand, and she blamed men for encouraging girls in their behaviour. However, she pointed out that although society allowed men to misbehave, it had different standards for women:

> We shall soon hear fond parents, in glossing over their daughters' faux pas, saying, 'Of course dear Daphne is a bit wild, but girls will be girls, and when she settles down and marries some nice, domesticated, good man, she may be all the better for having sowed her wild oats'.

It was said, Lucy argued, that the 'reformed rake' made the best of husbands, so why should not his female equivalent make the best of wives? This was an unconventional view for a woman in her 60s to hold in 1919.

In February, Lucy also participated in a debate in the *Morning Post* on the question of domestic workers. The post-war girl, with her newfound freedoms, was unenthusiastic about entering domestic service and Lucy suggested ways in which the social status of household duties could be raised. She advised that the 'detested old feudal word' servant be scrapped, along with the terms 'cook', 'parlourmaid', 'housemaid' and 'kitchenmaid'. Instead there should be a new universal name – 'home-bird' – and domestic workers should be addressed as 'Miss' and spoken of as 'young ladies'. Such changes, Lucy argued, would remove the 'servant' stigma and ensure that housework appealed to all classes of women. Her suggestions drew a lively but not altogether approving response.

Lucy also spoke out on the vexed question of fashions. The war had reduced restrictions on women's bodies as well as on their behaviour. In 1914 tight corsets and hobble skirts had been in vogue, but during the war the requirements of working life, as well as cloth shortages and economy measures, had made it a patriotic act to wear clothes that used fewer resources. Having come to appreciate the new simplicity and freedom of movement women were loath to revert to restrictive styles, and fashions were growing even skimpier and looser. The 'bare-back' fashion, which began in 1919, evinced particular attention. Asked her opinion, Lucy advocated modesty. Evidently, she said, women hoped that the bare-back dress would make them more attractive to men, but they were mistaken. Perhaps remembering episodes from her own life, Lucy said: 'My experience is that even the gayest Lothario prefers a woman who makes at least some pretense at modesty.' Again she pointed the finger at men: 'I hate saying it, but the men are really and truly to blame. The lure of the eye is more potent than the lure of the heart, and consequently the womanly woman is a back number.'

Lucy spent much of that autumn and the winter of 1919–20 quietly at Byron Cottage, spending part of the time researching and writing an article that would appear in the spring in the *British Dominions Year Book*, a publication that discussed political and social issues of the day. Lucy's article,[4] entitled 'Woman and the Problems of the Future', written in her capacity as vice-president of the British Empire Union, was mainly concerned with the position of women in society and in particular their employment. She began by stating that having gained the vote, women were a new factor in politics and would, she hoped, introduce a 'softening influence' and 'practical common sense'. The political outlook for women was 'most brilliant' and, if well-organised, they would become the 'greatest power the world has ever known'. Already the 'inefficient male' had been silenced, for now she seldom heard the trite retort, 'How like a woman!'

Turning to the question of work, Lucy attacked women leaders of the 'so-called' Labour Party for teaching the doctrine of Bolshevism and deceiving uneducated women with 'impossible ideals', for in reality Labour did not want women taking the jobs of men. Then she made a somewhat muddled argument. The home was the 'vital centre of world happiness', she said, and women had been entrusted with its preservation. But while she was in favour of women having careers, the integrity of home life was under threat from women seeking not work but entertainment outside the home. As a result children were not being taught 'morals or manners', and the 'old-fashioned virtues of honesty, truthfulness, and courtesy' were disappearing. Girls' schools, Lucy continued, should teach cooking, cleaning and the 'proper and intelligent care of infants'. Young people should also receive the knowledge of 'discipline and military training' that would enable them to fight efficiently in the defence of their country. Morris dancing, too, should be taught from an early age and included in every festive occasion to help to make England 'Merrie England' once more. But most of all, Lucy concluded, boys and girls should be trained in patriotism, for England and its Empire were in trust to them.

In the spring of 1920 Lucy was again involved in fundraising activities. In March she sat on a committee formed to raise £10,000 to provide a 'country house' and pension for Mrs Pankhurst and her daughter Christabel in recognition of their role in Suffragism. Then in April she was invited to join a committee formed to raise the £10,000 required to buy and open to the public the former home of the poet Keats in Hampstead. The connection to Lucy – that Keats had been a friend of the poet Byron – was somewhat tenuous but the committee was prestigious, its members including Lucy's old enemy Lord Bryce, Edward Elgar and the well-known writers J.M. Barrie, Robert Bridges (the Poet Laureate), Thomas Hardy and H.G. Wells. At the same time Lucy continued her interest in international affairs, being involved with the British Empire Union in its efforts to build a 'new world' by promoting British influence and goods over those of Germany. She also worked with the social reform group the National Political League, among the aims of which was to educate the nation about the dangers of Bolshevism. That spring, too, Lucy served on the Council of Welcome for Rev. Frank North, former chaplain of St Andrew's Anglican church in Moscow. Having been forced to flee Russia by Bolshevik forces, North had become something of a national hero in Britain, and his experiences and testimony fed into Lucy's increasingly virulent anti-Soviet feelings.

In the summer of 1920 Lucy again disappeared from the public eye, and it is possible that she went to the United States to meet Sir Thomas Lipton, who was competing in the America's Cup race to be held at New York in mid-July. It would be the veteran yachtsman's fourth challenge for the trophy and he expressed himself confident of victory with his yacht *Shamrock IV*, in particular because it had a 170ft mast – higher than Nelson's Column in London – and hence a large area of sail. In New York Lipton chartered a steam yacht, the *Victoria*, and gathered friends, including Thomas Dewar, on board to watch the racing. A series of photographs was taken on the *Victoria* on 15 July and a number show an unidentified woman who may have been Lucy. Short and dark haired, she had Lucy's stance of jutting out her chin, either to show confidence or to hide a double chin, and her smile turns up at the corners in the way that Lucy's did. While other women aboard the *Victoria* were wearing straw hats decorated with flowers, bows or feathers, the woman has a hat of the dark and furry tricorn style that Lucy had worn both for the Bassano portrait in 1909 and for another photograph published in the *Sunday Mirror* in 1916. She is accompanied by a man with high cheekbones and small eyes that suggested a family likeness; if the woman is Lucy the man was probably her brother, Arthur Radmall.

Several of the photographs show Lipton and his guests on deck, posing for the camera. Lipton is in the front row with the unidentified woman to his left, a position of honour that would befit an old friend such as Lucy. Yet neither seems comfortable. In every photograph the woman smiles too broadly, as if determined to show that she is enjoying herself. But Lipton, usually the ever-charming 'ladies man', is not playing to the camera. His posture, which suggests anger and resentment, is neither polite nor considerate to either the woman on his left or on his right. In a seeming display of disrespect and domination his legs are spread so wide that his body space invades that of his neighbours. His arms, tightly folded across his chest in a defensive pose, create a physical and psychological barrier. It is clear that Sir Thomas has no intention of making the smiling woman Lady Lipton. In the event, the *Shamrock* did not win the America's Cup. Deeply disappointed, Lipton would wait another decade before making his fifth and final challenge.

When the coal industry had been nationalised during the First World War, wages and working conditions had improved, and when the war ended miners wanted things to continue in the same way. However, Lloyd George, now Prime Minister, intended to denationalise the mines, which would mean wage cuts and longer working hours. Strike action was threatened. Houston turned his mind to the subject and linked the problems in the coal industry with food shortages. When in May the government announced that it was raising the price of coal, Houston argued in the House of Commons that if output was increased British coal could be traded for Argentinian wheat, thus relieving food shortages in Britain. As unrest continued and strike action loomed there were accusations that Bolshevik agents and Russian money were fuelling the agitation. In early September Lucy, then at Sandgate, became so engaged in the question that, under the auspices of the National Political League, with which she was still involved, she went out into Folkestone and Hythe to ascertain the views of local women. Not surprisingly, Lucy told the press that the women she interviewed were against strike action and had frequently described miners as 'selfish brutes'. The time had come, Lucy felt, for women of all classes to unite and demand that the government made strikes illegal. It was intolerable, she said, that the few could exercise 'tyranny' over the many.

Lucy then sent out an extraordinary rallying call to the women of England, effectively setting herself up as their self-proclaimed spokeswoman. 'We women,' she announced, 'have been waiting for the men to come forward, but they do not seem to have the pluck to make any move against the miners.' She proposed a 'war of women' against striking miners, with shopkeepers refusing to sell them food or drink and miners' wives refusing to 'cook, clean, or cater' for their husbands. But Lucy had failed to understand the closeness of mining communities, or appreciate that most women would stand by their men. She pressed on, calling for wives from every coalfield in the country to attend a rally in London in September. Not surprisingly the turnout was disappointing and a resolution to condemn the miners met with a mixed reception. The campaign had failed, and on 16 October newspaper headlines declared, 'Miners' Strike Begun!' However, as consolation, by this time Lucy's efforts to secure Houston seemed at last to be paying off, for, as the strike began, she left the country for a cruise in his new yacht, the *Liberty*.

8

LADY HOUSTON

The Edwardian heyday of the luxury yacht was over, but the craft still retained their allure. An invitation to join the *Liberty* would give Lucy all the advantages of yachting as well as continual access to Houston. Houston had purchased the yacht for the sake of his health and as a reward for his lifetime of hard work. She was a 12-year-old twin-screw steamer and, at 268ft long and requiring a crew of at least sixty-three, one of the largest and grandest private yachts afloat. The epitome of comfort and elegance, she was painted white with gold decoration on its bows and possessed what one newspaper described as an 'arrogant loveliness'. The master bedroom, very large and decorated in grey and blue, occupied the full width of the yacht, and the five en suite passenger cabins were decorated in white with green carpets. The large dining room gave views of the sea on all sides. There was also a library, drawing room and smoking room, and below decks staff quarters in addition to a well-equipped gymnasium and a three-bed hospital ward. The yacht also boasted a 25ft tender complete with passenger cabin.

The *Liberty* had a romantic history. She had been built in 1908 for the American newspaper proprietor Joseph Pulitzer. Suffering from depression, blindness and acute noise sensitivity, Pulitzer had had the *Liberty* customised to cater for his needs. Double-thickness doors were installed, the deck ran from stem to stern without any inconvenient projections, and the yacht's speed was limited to 12 knots. During the First World War the next owner, Lord Tredegar, had given the *Liberty* as a Red Cross hospital ship, and afterwards taken her twice round the world before the huge cost of upkeep forced him to put her on the market. The *Liberty* was already an anachronism, for in the post-war economy there were few rich enough to maintain her; Houston probably drove a hard bargain before closing the deal in September 1920.

Houston dressed the part: on the quarter deck, it was reported, with his yachting cap pulled down well over one eye he looked the 'jolliest of buccaneers'. It was probably on this voyage that Houston, well aware of Lucy's intentions, said to his captain William Goodwin, 'Mark my words, Goodie, she's after my bloody money!' But it was no romantic cruise for two, for Houston had also invited two close friends, Sir Warden Chilcott and F.E. Smith, who by that time had the title Baron Birkenhead and the position of Lord Chancellor. With his brilliant mind, Birkenhead seemed to have a great future ahead of him; he had recently turned down the offer of the prestigious post of Viceroy of India. Houston retained a great affection for his old friend, whom he habitually called 'Boy', and at about this time told him that he intended to leave him £1 million, and showed him the will to prove it.

Lucy, as the only woman on board, was probably rather isolated among three men who had much in common, all being Liverpool MPs as well as keen yachtsmen. Lucy, considered opinionated and outspoken, would have expected to take a full part in political discussions. While Birkenhead, as his son later wrote, was delighted by the 'frivolity' of good-looking women who were prepared to flatter him, he strongly disliked 'earnest' women and those with a 'serious intellectual appetite', resenting their intrusion into tradition- ally male spheres like politics. Lucy was therefore anathema to Birkenhead, and mutual dislike arose between them.

At this time, according to Birkenhead's son, Lucy was already on 'terms of intimacy' with Houston; her intentions were obvious to Birkenhead. The two feared the other's influence over Houston, and further antipathy arose when one day on the yacht Birkenhead made a remark that he would live to regret. Apparently Lucy had said to him archly, 'Lord Birkenhead, I've got a silly sort of fancy to tell you the story of my life,' but he replied, 'My dear lady, if you do not mind I would rather postpone that pleasure.' On Lucy's part it was probably a friendly approach, for the offer of her life story – so sought after by others – was a form of flattery of Houston's close friend, but Birkenhead probably felt that he has heard more than enough from her already. The damage was done; Birkenhead had offended Lucy and, realising that he opposed her relationship with Houston, she determined to destroy the friendship between the two men.

By early November 1920 the *Liberty* had reached Naples, where Birkenhead and Chilcott disembarked, doubtless much to Lucy's relief. The yacht then headed south to Palermo on the island of Sicily, called in at the port of Tunis, and from there sailed north to the French Riviera. In December the yacht was at Cannes, where Lucy enjoyed a busy social life at the height of the season. There is no sign that Houston accompanied her ashore; he was probably too ill to venture from the yacht. During the cruise no letter or article from either appeared in the press, a silence that may have been in part owed to the fact that Houston was hoping for a knighthood. His past attacks on the government had counted against him and it was in the interests of both to maintain a discreet silence.

The Riviera retained its old magic. It was the third season after the war and tourists had returned in force, with many prominent people to be seen strolling in the sunshine. Among them were Sir Jesse Boot, owner of the famous retail chemists chain, and his wife Lady Boot; Florence Boot, later Baroness Trent, would become a close friend of Lucy, as would Molly Fink, otherwise known as the Ranee of Pudukota. The ranee, an Australian, was the wife of the Rajah of Pudukota, a small principality in southern India. As the British government of India had refused to recognise his mixed-race marriage, the rajah had accepted a substantial allowance to remain in exile, and he and the ranee lived a life of pleasure. 'Madcap Molly', as she was known, danced until dawn, piloted her own motorboat in the Mediterranean, and had the reputation of being the best-dressed woman on the Riviera.

By the end of January 1921 the *Liberty* had arrived at Monte Carlo and moored below the casino. There was something of a frantic atmosphere that season, as if, amid the post-war uncertainty and economic problems, people were determined to evoke a remembered golden age. There were many new faces and a reporter, observing diners at a restaurant, concluded from their expensive meals and loud laugher that they were 'war-profiteers'. The casino, judging the new mood, provided gilt top hats, squeakers and soft toys; one titled woman took a toy lamb to the gambling tables and smacked or petted it according to her luck. The thoughtless gaiety of the 1920s had arrived. Amid this rather desperate merrymaking, and with the Monte Carlo season in full swing, two new English visitors arrived – the 10th Lord Byron and his new wife, on their honeymoon.

Once Charlie had inherited the title he had become the object of increased female attention and, approaching 60, had found himself courting Lady Anna

Fitzroy. Anna was a soft target for Charlie's shy approaches. In her mid-30s, she was plain, awkward and retiring; Charlie, for all his oddities, was a good catch. Having married in January, the new Lord and Lady Byron arrived in Monte Carlo in February, checking into the fashionable Balmoral Palace Hotel. It seemed an uncharacteristically daring and extravagant move for Charlie but perhaps Lucy and Houston had paid for the trip as a wedding present. By April Charlie and Anna were reported to be 'yachting guests', and were probably staying aboard the *Liberty*. With Lucy to act as hostess, the *Liberty* now became a meeting place for the rich and influential. The yacht was a great draw in itself and the desire for an invitation did much to overcome reservations about the characters of Houston and Lucy; that spring the Countess Torby, wife of the Grand Duke Michael Romanov, and King Gustav V of Sweden were among their guests.

With the Riviera season drawing to a close, Lucy arrived back in England in April or May 1921; in her absence two of her Sandgate friends, Lady Bancroft and Bithia Croker, had died. After his return, Houston reconnected with Birkenhead, who had been elevated to viscount but now got into hot water. A general election was approaching and in June the *Manchester Guardian* reported that Birkenhead, Winston Churchill (now Secretary of State for the Colonies), and others had discussed forming a new party and forcing the ageing Lloyd George to retire as Prime Minister. The report was embarrassing for those involved and when challenged by the press Birkenhead said that the *Guardian* article was 'from beginning to end a far-rago of wild invention', but this did not quite amount to a denial.

That summer Lloyd George was staying at a remote holiday home, Flowerdale, overlooking Gairloch Bay in Wester Ross in the north-west of Scotland. It was 600 miles from London and communications were difficult, but when political problems in Ireland necessitated a cabinet meeting, Birkenhead and other ministers had to make the journey. Birkenhead needed to smooth things over with Lloyd George by having a private talk before the other ministers arrived, and with the land journey being uninviting Houston offered to deliver him to Gairloch Bay in style by sea. Apart from having to explain the cabinet plot incident, Birkenhead may also have wished to advocate for an honour on behalf of Houston. On 14 September the *Liberty* arrived at Gairloch early in the morning with Houston, Birkenhead and Lucy on board, and anchored in the bay. The yacht's tender deposited Birkenhead at Gairloch's little jetty, from where he walked to Flowerdale and knocked on the door. Lloyd George was having breakfast and was not expecting him: 'Good gracious,' he was reported to have exclaimed, 'Where did you come from and how did you get here so early?' In response Birkenhead pointed across the bay to where the *Liberty* lay a few hundred yards offshore. Lloyd George was shocked at the easy breach of his security measures and by sunset a British destroyer had joined the *Liberty* in Gairloch Bay.

A few days later the other cabinet ministers had gathered. Winston Churchill arrived on 20 September and was accommodated on the *Liberty*, and on 21 September Lloyd George and a house guest, his friend Sir George Riddell, visited the yacht for lunch. The Prime Minister's acceptance of Houston's invitation probably signalled his agreement to award him an honour. The *Liberty*, Riddell wrote in his diary, was a 'magnificent affair, a small floating palace. Houston and Lady H. kind and hospitable.' This suggests that Lucy was giving the impression that she was Houston's wife. Having played a role at the heart of political affairs, the *Liberty* left Gairloch Bay after a stay of ten days and on its return journey called in at Douglas Bay on the Isle of Man where, it was reported, Houston, Birkenhead and Lucy spent the day touring the island. Houston would be named in the 1922 New Year's Honours list, and the Houston baronetcy of West Toxteth in the city of Liverpool was created on 17 January. With Houston now 'Sir Robert' his wife would become 'Lady Houston' – a further incentive for Lucy to marry him.

A story told by William Ogden, a well-known Mayfair jeweller, gives an indication of Houston's relationship with Lucy by this time. One day, Ogden wrote, a large and 'sinister-looking stranger' entered his shop wearing a huge astrakhan coat. The stranger picked out a necklace worth £20,000 and asked Ogden to accompany him to Hampstead to show it to someone; of course he meant Lucy. Ogden, not knowing that the man was Houston, was suspicious and made excuses, saying that he preferred that the person should come to him. At this Houston laughed, either because Lucy would not like that, or because he could tell he was not trusted. Years later, still delighted by the thought of Houston's infatuation and her own cleverness, Lucy would tell Allen the story of her 1922 birthday gift. Houston had arranged for a jeweller's shop in Regent Street to send an assortment of items on approval from which she could make her choice. However, she was most particular about jewellery and liked it to be distinctive. When the items arrived at Byron Cottage she found nothing to tempt her for, although expensive, the selection was 'ordinary and dull'. Houston rang later and asked what she had chosen but Lucy retorted that she had sent 'all that rubbish' back to the shop. Houston was hurt: 'Why, Poppy, there was a pearl necklace there worth twelve hundred pounds. Any woman would be proud to wear it.' To this Lucy replied, 'You had better find her then and give it to her. I'm not any woman and I won't have it.'

Just then a Bond Street jeweller rang and asked if she would be interested to call and see a unique necklace of matched black pearls, for which the lowest price would be £100,000. Lucy loved black pearls and went to view them. Later Houston rang again, still crestfallen, and Lucy told him about the pearls but said that they cost too much for him. This was a calculated move because Houston did not like to be told there was anything he could not afford. He gasped when he heard the price but, she told Allen, she had the pearls the next day. 'Poor Robert had not a chance against me. He was a child in my hands, for by that time there was very little about men and how to manage them that I did not know.'

A general election was scheduled for November 1922 and Houston, now the oldest Conservative MP in Lancashire, fought and won another campaign. The Conservatives were victorious nationally and Lloyd George was replaced as Prime Minister by Andrew Bonar Law. Houston was again sworn in to the House of Commons and seemed to be back on form, giving long speeches on strikes and German trade competition, but his contribution in December to the debate on exports to South America was to be his last.

Birkenhead had watched Lucy's growing influence over Houston with alarm but, well aware of his opposition to her, Lucy was determined to eject him from Houston's life. As a result of her actions, at a time when his days in the thick of British politics were coming to an end due to his infirmity, Houston also lost one of his dearest friends. By the time that Birkenhead was elevated to the rank of earl in November 1922, his relationship with Houston had already deteriorated. The ostensible reason was a quip made by Birkenhead to the effect that Houston dyed his beard. When it was widely repeated Houston was deeply offended and became a laughing stock in the House of Commons, and Wentworth Day later implied that it was Lucy who had told Houston the story. Birkenhead would take no more cruises on the *Liberty*. But in any case Houston was too ill to travel and in February 1923 Lucy went to Cannes alone. Houston's health was now so poor that he was considering stepping down as MP, but by September he had recovered sufficiently to embark on the *Liberty* once more. Lucy was with him but the yacht would not venture out of British waters. At one point she moored off Sandgate, where Lucy purchased another house, 8 Radnor Cliff, just a few doors uphill from the old one. The new house was larger, having seven bedrooms, and its terraced gardens reached down to the seashore. Lucy perhaps hoped that she could entertain Houston there.

In May 1923 Bonar Law resigned as Prime Minister to be replaced by Stanley Baldwin, who called a general election for December. In West Toxteth, Houston struggled to fight his ninth and last campaign. His sole opponent was a Labour candidate, Joseph Gibbins, and although in the previous election Houston had won with a large majority, now he scraped in with a majority of only 139 votes. Nationally, the election resulted in a hung parliament and the Labour Party came to power, with its leader Ramsay MacDonald as Prime Minister. Houston, calculating that he faced defeat at the next election, announced his resignation in April. He then departed on a cruise in the *Liberty*, and Lucy was probably aboard as the yacht headed for Jersey. The island had no income tax or death duties and Houston, well known for his abhorrence of taxes, wished to establish domicile there. He bought a house, Beaufield, a relatively modest residence for a millionaire, standing alone in an elevated position in the St Saviour district, overlooking the town of St Helier and beyond that the sea. Houston would spend parts of 1924, 1925 and 1926 on Jersey but while residence seemed a good idea at the time, the island eventually became the setting of a nightmare that would be played out in public.

Houston's business, parliamentary seat, health and friendship with Birkenhead were gone. Although he was tough Lucy was tougher and, with little left apart from her, he finally gave in. It was probably at Beaufield that summer that the couple, lounging on the verandah or in the rose garden, planned their wedding. Lucy, of course, knew how to arrange matters as it would be her third secret ceremony. They returned to England in September and the *Liberty* sailed for the Mediterranean with only the crew on board. Meanwhile, Lucy departed for Paris where she checked in to the Trianon Palace, a luxury hotel set in quiet grounds within sight of the former royal palace of Versailles. There she would stay for more than two months while she waited for Houston, who was in England having an operation. Unwell herself she went out little, but occupied her time writing articles for the *Daily Mirror* and dealing with her correspondence.

One person to whom Lucy wrote was Stanley Baldwin, leader of the Conservative Party, who seemed set to become Prime Minister at the next general election, scheduled for October 1924. One issue being debated on electioneering platforms was the question of agriculture and food production, and it was on this subject that on 16 October, a fortnight before election day, Lucy sent Baldwin her unasked-for advice:

> Dear Mr. Baldwin, I see that you have again referred to the suggestion I sent you at the last election namely that you intended to enquire into the high price of food, but as you considered that suggestion of mine worthy of notice perhaps you may not object to what I [next?] propose – I am quite sure that you would gain every woman's vote if you now declared that you had gone into the matter (it can be gone into in a few hours by anyone taking the trouble to find out the price of meat sold at Smithfield Market – the price milk is sold by the farmers) & you can now promise a sensational drop in the prices of these two articles of food, & also a considerable drop in other foodstuffs. This can easily be done in one day by any intelligent person – if you wish to verify my statements and you could then promise the women that if they voted Conservative their food would cost them half what it now costs for no retail dealer can complain if you limit their profit to 50 percent, and that would mean all & more than I say – Hoping dear Mr. Baldwin that these suggestions will be of some use to you, & also wishing you a bumping majority (I believe you will get it) Yours sincerely, Lucy Byron. Please excuse pencil scrawl but I am an invalid writing in bed.[5]

This letter was received by Baldwin's private secretary, Geoffrey Fry, who attached a lapidary and sarcastic note: 'An invalid lady wishes Mr. Baldwin to promise to reduce the price of food in one hour which he could easily do.'[6] Fry also added a small, precise cross above the word 'lady', perhaps a private code to indicate that the writer was no lady. Fry replied, however, stating that the letter would have Baldwin's attention and addressing his letter to 'Miss Lucy Byron'.[7] It seems that Fry did not recognise Lucy as Lady Byron.

The general election took place, the Conservatives won by a large majority and, as expected, Stanley Baldwin became Prime Minister. But with Houston still delayed in England, Lucy wrote to Baldwin again. In this letter (which is unavailable), she attempted to persuade Baldwin to deny Birkenhead a cabinet position but this failed, for on 6 November Birkenhead was named as the new Secretary of State for India. However, a few days later Lucy made another attempt to damage Birkenhead. Writing to Baldwin again, she headed her letter 'Strictly Private & Confidential':

> Dear Mr. Baldwin, You know what I told you a few days ago about a certain bounder whose name begins with 'B' the enclosed letter which I send you to read and which please return to me – reasserts & confirms all that I then told you. You will see his opinion of you – where I have marked it. What a false brute he is! Yrs sincerely, L. Byron.[8]

Lucy enclosed a private letter written by Birkenhead to Houston on 31 October that year, presumably having been taken from Houston's possession without his knowledge when he arrived at the hotel. There must have been consternation in Baldwin's office when the identity of the 'bounder' was realised.

In his letter Birkenhead, addressing Houston as 'My Dear Friend', expresses great respect and affection. His family, he says, has been distressed to hear that Houston was still in so much pain and that his left arm seemed likely to be permanently affected. He hopes that a long spell of Mediterranean sunshine will put him right, and invites him to bring the *Liberty* to Madeira, where Birkenhead will be holidaying that winter. This, he said, will 'certainly bring great happiness' to his family. In political matters, Birkenhead is pleased by the 'stupendous' triumph of the general election, although at the time of writing his own cabinet position has not yet been settled. However, he has given 'most anxious consideration' to Houston's opinion and decided to accept the position either of First Lord of the Admiralty, Secretary of State for the Colonies or Secretary of State for India (the post he would receive), or even serve again as Lord Chancellor. He expresses his hope that Winston Churchill should be appointed to the cabinet. Then comes the damning criticism of Baldwin that had so excited Lucy: 'It is of course a tragedy that so great an army should have so uninspiring a Commander-in-Chief. But this cannot be helped; and I think he will be well under control.'[9]

Lucy's glee over Birkenhead's negative comment about Baldwin was palpable but her action was, to put it mildly, unprincipled. She had betrayed Houston's trust and sought to damage the career of one of his closest friends. In doing so she was taking a risk that Houston would learn of her betrayal; and although word did indeed leak out, there is no evidence that it reached

Houston. Birkenhead was at that time grieving the loss of his brothers, both of whom had died that year, and in such circumstances Lucy's behaviour was particularly heartless. After her death it would be written that Lucy was 'implacable in her hatreds, insatiable in her kindnesses', and certainly she was implacable in her campaign against Birkenhead. Her attempt to undermine him foreshadowed her attacks on politicians Ramsay MacDonald, Anthony Eden and Baldwin himself a decade later.

Meanwhile, Fry had asked the Metropolitan Police to ascertain the identity and investigate the background of Baldwin's correspondent, and Special Branch duly launched covert enquiries at Lucy's hotel. Lucy's identity as Lady Byron was then confirmed, although Special Branch may not have known that when she gave her age as 57 on the hotel register she had knocked off ten years. Special Branch also set a watch on Lucy, perhaps by means of a chambermaid and the hotel's mail staff, and it was reported that she spent most of her time writing and was regarded as 'eccentric'.[10]

Presumably oblivious to being spied on, Lucy finalised her wedding plans and at last, on 12 December 1924, the marriage of Lucy Byron and Robert Houston took place at the British consulate in Paris in the presence of two friends. Lucy's years of effort had paid off. When the news came out a few days later the British press expressed surprise, for Houston's visit to Paris had been believed to be merely part of his convalescence. His age also attracted comment: 'Bachelor Septuagenarian Baronet Married', ran a headline. The newlyweds, too unwell to travel immediately, stayed on in Paris for some days after the wedding and on 17 December Lucy saw Dr Farquhar Buzzard, a highly regarded doctor who attended members of the royal family. But by the end of December they had reached Marseille and joined the *Liberty*, which had been anchored there for weeks. They then departed on their honeymoon, sailing along the Riviera to St Maxime across the bay from St Tropez. There the *Liberty* stayed for some weeks, and Lucy described their surroundings in a letter to Violet Hunt. They were moored, she wrote, in a 'lovely little spot, quite tucked away in a little backwater of the sea, and the scenery is charming, with mountains each side of us, and woods of fir trees and mimosa – the fragrance of the scent of them is most delightful'.[11]

The marriage, a friend of Lucy would write later, had been a 'genuine match of affection'. On Houston's side, despite being a 'victim of a particularly painful form of disease which slowly sapped his strength', he became, a friend would relate, a 'much happier man' after his marriage. Although

Lucy had achieved her desire, still she could not rest in her campaign against Birkenhead. Fretting at Baldwin's lack of response, she wrote to him again in January 1925 from St Maxime. Now using the name 'Poppy Houston', Lucy reminded Baldwin that although 'all the time a wretched invalid' she had taken the trouble to warn him that Birkenhead was 'no friend' of his. Referring to Birkenhead's letter that she had previously enclosed, she feared that it had not reached Baldwin, for:

> Of course you would have answered it by now, especially as the enclosure was a letter not addressed to me & I wanted it returned. Will you kindly let me know if you ever received it? I was Lady Byron when I wrote but have since married Sir Robert Houston. I am heart and soul for you & helped you very considerably during the Election through my colleagues of the National Political League – we get at the women – Of course you may not have got my letter or on the other hand you might have thought I was mistaken in what I told you – but unfortunately my information is only too true about B.

Even though Baldwin had not returned the first purloined letter, Lucy, unabashed, now enclosed a second. Given that she had now achieved her ambition of marrying Houston, this second letter was gratuitously vindictive. The new enclosure had been written to Houston by Joan Smith, the widow of Birkenhead's brother, on 1 November 1924. With regard to the result of the general election, Mrs Smith wrote, 'I am sure Fred [i.e. Birkenhead] has done a lot to save the country from the Ramsay MacDonald crowd. He seems to have made such wonderful speeches.' But then came the sentence that had caught Lucy's eye: 'Now that dreadful Baldwin must be got rid of.' Joan Smith, Lucy told Baldwin, was 'evidently quoting' Birkenhead. But the underlining and inverted commas that emphasised the sentence appear to have been added by Lucy. The effect of doctoring the letter was to make it seem that Joan Smith was quoting Birkenhead, whereas in truth the negative opinion of Baldwin was Joan Smith's own.[12] Nevertheless, Lucy wrote to Baldwin:

> I don't see how you can explain away that & I think you will now feel that I am a true friend – in letting you know how grateful your friend B is!! – Of course I need not say to a gentleman that this is absolutely

entre-nous but alas! there are some people the more <u>you</u> do for them the more they hate you – and B's ambition is to oust you & become P.M. himself (of course the country would never have him!).[13]

Lucy asked that Baldwin acknowledge receipt of her letters, and reiterated: 'I do not wish you to allude to the information herein given <u>please</u> as this is quite private but you may rely on me in the future to keep you posted of any news that may be useful to you.'[14] Baldwin would not have wanted that. and perhaps to forestall further communication Fry replied tersely on 15 January 1925: 'Madam, The Prime Minister has asked me to send you this line to let you know that he received the private letter which you wrote to him recently, and also one of a previous date.'[15] With this Lucy had to be content, and she would have the aggravation of seeing Lord Birkenhead continue as Secretary of State for India until 1928.

At the same time that Lucy was writing to Baldwin, she was also corresponding with Violet Hunt. Lucy had lent her Sandgate house to her friend in December 1924 and Hunt would stay there on and off until 1926. It was an arrangement that suited them both, for while Hunt acted as a house-sitter she could live cheaply and have a quiet place to write. Three letters, affectionate in tone, that Lucy wrote to Hunt between late December 1924 and 12 February 1925 from the *Liberty*, poste restante St Maxime, survive. Lucy's letters suggest that the Houstons were living the secluded life of invalids, for Lucy says that she is 'much worried' about Houston who is 'not so well poor dear', and she has sent for a specialist from Paris. Lucy herself, she tells Hunt, has been 'most horribly ill, no sleep and nearly crazy with insomnia'. However, she was well enough to ask Hunt to arrange for Mrs Constantine to scrub all the stone floors in the Sandgate house once a week, and polish the wood in the Oak Room with homemade beeswax and turpentine.[16]

Hunt was at that time embroiled in a messy legal dispute. Some years previously she had separated from her lover Ford Madox Hueffer (by now known as Ford Madox Ford) but, still obsessed, she had continued to use the name 'Mrs Hueffer'. However, in doing so she stepped on the toes of Ford's legal wife, Elsie, who was claiming damages for libel. When the case of Hueffer v. Hunt was heard in the High Court of Justice and the judge found against Hunt, Lucy sent a note:

Dearest Violet, I am <u>so sorry</u> <u>how I wish</u> you had taken my advice long ago and dropped the beastly German name! Well now you've got to and pay into the bargain … I only just wanted you to know that I was sympathising with you dear. Stay on at No. 8 as long as you like.[17]

Lucy's sympathy was not without reproach, and perhaps to make a point she addressed her letter to 'Mrs Violet Hunt' despite the fact that Hunt was not married. But naming conventions were on Lucy's mind, for in answer to Hunt's question as to whether she would now be known as Lucy Byron or Lucy Houston, Lucy replied, 'neither, dear Violet, the name that I have always been known by in my family has been Poppy since I was a baby, so I am going to be Poppy Houston'.[18]

From St Maxime the *Liberty* moved along the coast to Cannes, where disaster befell Lucy in February: it was reported that, going ashore, she had lost a handbag containing '£25,000 in cheques, cash and jewellery, the greater value being in the jewels'. In March or April the Houstons returned to England but, with four houses and a yacht between them, they seemed unable to settle and moved rapidly from place to place. At Sandgate Lucy had the idea of buying Saltwood Castle, a damp and crumbling pile owned by Herbert Deedes. His son, William Deedes, later well known as a journalist and newspaper editor, wrote that one day Lucy walked into the drawing room where his parents were having tea and announced, 'I have come to buy the castle!' Deedes had never understood why his father refused her offer. Then in August the Houstons moved on to Scotland, where Houston had taken the shooting lease of the Ben Alder estate. Forty-five years after first going there with Gretton, Lucy returned to Ben Alder Lodge. The splendid countryside, with the loch on one side and the great sweep of the Grampian hills on the other, gave Houston a new lease of life and, with Ben Alder Forest possessing perhaps the finest deer country in Scotland, he was reported to be having 'first-rate sport' shooting stags.

From Ben Alder, in September and October, Lucy wrote two further letters to Violet Hunt at Sandgate. Hunt had complained of irritations and Lucy, again irked by her friend's lack of backbone, advised, 'I am sorry you are bothered by tiresome people whom you do not care for. Why not shut yourself up and not see anybody? That is what I always do when people bother me.' Meanwhile Lucy was enjoying the peace and solitude of Ben

Alder; it was 'lovely', she said, up in the mountains with no other habitation for miles. Lucy was still struggling with 'many tiresome ailments' but was sleeping better, and rejected Hunt's suggestion of hypnotism, for she had tried it often without success. But towards the end of October Lucy's health suffered a reversal when the nurse who had been giving her injections of 'warm oil' made the oil too hot. Lucy was ill for a week and the carelessness of the nurse made her very angry, for she had been doing so well before.[19]

The Houstons left Ben Alder in October and travelled south to Harrogate where, despite Houston's apparent stamina at Ben Alder, his health took a serious turn for the worse. Although warned by his doctors that a move might prove fatal, on 15 November he made a sudden dash for Jersey. Chartering a special train that consisted of only a saloon car and a luggage car, he, Lucy and their servants travelled from Harrogate to Southampton dock. There Houston had chartered the fastest boat that served the Channel Islands, the large new luxury passenger steamship the *St Helier*. Houston, a newspaper reported, had to be carried from the train across the network of railway tracks to the steamship in an 'invalid chair'. But he appeared in good spirits, smoking a cigar and insisting upon supervising the loading of the luggage. Houston's hurry, it seems, was that he had realised that if he did not arrive in Jersey within twenty-four hours his domicile would lapse. Racing against time to save £2.8 million in death duties, he reached the island with only an hour to spare. But although Houston had saved his widow a fortune, the crossing had been his last journey.

Details of the five months that followed the arrival of the Houstons in Jersey are scanty. The *Liberty* was brought to St Aubyn's Bay and the couple spent most of their time living aboard, intending to sail as soon as Houston recovered. But both were in poor physical condition and Lucy's worries over her husband exacerbated her own ill health. In December 1925 and January 1926 Houston made two wills. In the first, which dealt with his Jersey property, he left everything to Lucy, while the second will disposed of the rest of his estate. One day, Lucy later told Wentworth Day, Houston entered her stateroom on the yacht, handed her a draft of his will, and said, 'You'd better have a look at it. I've left you quite a lot of money.' Houston departed, leaving the will for Lucy to read, but when she found that she was to receive only £1 million she tore up the document and threw it on the floor. It was 'quite comic', Lucy recalled, when Houston returned, looked at the paper 'aghast', and then at Lucy. 'If I'm only worth a million, then I'm worth nothing at all,' Lucy declared. Houston remade his will leaving her £6 million. 'After all – why not?' she asked Wentworth Day, 'I'd doubled his fortune for him!' The will contained no mention of Birkenhead, whose son wrote later that Lucy had 'forced' Houston to strike his name out; by that time, it seems, he was in no fit state to withstand the pressure she applied.

At some point in their relationship, and it may have been at Jersey, Lucy twice nursed Houston back to life when the doctors had given him up for dead. Lucy thought much of her own healing ability which, she said, was possessed by only one or two people in each generation: 'It's something in my fingers and in my make-up. Nervous disorders respond to it.' Later she would attribute her own and Houston's illness to a 'plot' for, she told Wentworth Day, there were 'bitter enemies behind the scene' as Houston's will 'didn't please everybody'. Could Lucy have thought that Lord Birkenhead was implicated? She suspected poison and one day Houston was 'white and gasping', and his tongue black. Lucy gave him an emetic and he vomited immediately: 'Castor oil, my dear! The finest cure for everything,' she told Wentworth Day, but after this episode she tasted Houston's food at every meal. But despite Lucy's healing touch, castor oil and the attentions of several well-known doctors, by March both were in a serious condition, with Lucy suffering from severe jaundice. When Violet Hunt received no reply to two of her letters to Lucy she wrote with concern to Houston's solicitors and on 8 April received a reply: 'Lady Houston is, we understand, very ill at present, and doubtless that is why you have had no reply.'[20] But if Lucy was very ill, Houston was worse, and he died aboard the *Liberty* on the morning of 14 April. Lucy's hard-won marriage had ended after only sixteen months, and the most difficult period of her life had begun.

9

SIX-MILLION WIDOW

After Houston's death Lucy remained aboard the *Liberty* seriously ill. Help arrived when Arthur Radmall, Arthur and Florence Wrey, and George Appleton – Houston's friend and business partner – hurried to Jersey and arranged the funeral. Had she been in a healthier state herself Lucy might have demanded a post-mortem, but as it was Houston was buried on 16 April 1926, only two days after his death, in the cemetery of St Saviour's parish church. Lucy broke down completely and, as grief, depression, delirium and paranoia overwhelmed her, she felt that she was imprisoned and that her nurses were guards. She dared not sleep for fear that they would smother her with pillows; if they murdered her, she told them, they would be hanged. But somewhere in the midst of her misery, she recalled years later, she prayed with 'all her heart and all her soul', crying out, 'Oh God, help, help, help.' After this, a 'light broke into her darkness, a voice restored her courage', and Lucy knew it was the 'gift of God'. Her mental agony was replaced by faith and a voice told her to 'be brave and fear not'. This spiritual experience, Lucy said, brought a profound change over her and marked the last 'turning point' in her life. Previously rooted in the material world, she became convinced of God's presence and His concern for her welfare and salvation.

Confined to her sickbed, Lucy was spared from seeing the press coverage in the aftermath of Houston's death. The saga of the 'Houston millions' had begun and his fortune, estimated to be £6–7 million (£342 million to £399 million in 2019 values), was the subject of intense speculation. The press confidently printed stories that a cabinet minister would inherit a large sum, and nobody was in any doubt that this meant Birkenhead. The reports must have been difficult for Birkenhead's family to bear, for his wife Margaret wrote to Lord Beaverbrook, 'What do you think of the papers giving us old H's fortune? We knew only too well that the old B. had done us out of every penny when she married him.' By 'old B.' Margaret meant Lucy, and her use of the term possibly suggests that she had come to know of Lucy's 'name begins with B' comment to Baldwin, although Margaret presumably had a different word in mind. Houston's solicitors contradicted the story that he had left a large legacy to a cabinet minister, but Lucy was too ill to gloat over her enemy's public humiliation. On 27 April the solicitors informed Violet Hunt that Lucy was in a 'very bad state' and was likely to be found insane as a result of the forthcoming court enquiry. Alarmingly, their letter ended, 'The medical men also seem to think she will not last very long.'[21]

When seeking domicile in Jersey for tax purposes Houston had not taken into account the extent to which it would render him and Lucy subject to the island's laws. On 24 April, ten days after his death, the Jersey Royal Court ordered that six 'principal residents' of the parish of St Saviour were to board the *Liberty*, interview Lucy, and then give evidence as to whether or not she was capable of managing her own affairs. All of those chosen were men, and three were doctors. Lucy had been unaware of the ruling and was shocked and indignant when the party entered her cabin. The interview went so badly that the reports of the witnesses were universally damning, with one stating that it was impossible to hold a rational conversation with her, and that she had 'definite delusions'. The message was clear: Lucy was insane. Trapped within a web of legal procedures, she was declared to be incapable of looking after herself or her property, and the Attorney General appointed Sidney Crill, Houston's Jersey solicitor, to curate her affairs for a year. This ruling effectively made Lucy a prisoner on the island and was so restrictive that she was forbidden to even send or receive letters. The fragility of Lucy's condition had put her at the mercy of others in a way that she had never before experienced; she found it intolerable.

Houston's wills were processed and the first, concerning his Jersey property, presented no problems: Lucy inherited Beaufield. It was the second will, pertaining to the bulk of Houston's estate, that interested the world. He had appointed Lucy and George Appleton as his executors, and Lucy was to receive the *Liberty* and four-fifths of his estate, of which £100,000 was to be given immediately. The will described Lucy as Houston's 'beloved wife, whose self-sacrifice, devotion, care, and wonderful intuition, on two separate occasions saved my life, when the doctors despaired'; it rather seems that Lucy had contributed some text herself. Among other bequests Houston left £50,000 plus one-fifth of his estate to Appleton, and £50,000 to be distributed among those employees of Houston's companies who were in service on or before 31 October 1918. When the will was proved on 20 April, Appleton acted alone for Lucy, who, reported the *Daily Express*, was still 'dangerously ill'.

Meanwhile, with speculation that Houston's estate was not liable for death duties, journalists who had probably never seen payment of their personal tax demands as a patriotic duty condemned Houston for his duplicity. *The Times* declared that Houston was the 'artful tax-dodger' who had designed to evade paying tax to the England 'under whose laws and institutions he had amassed his fortune'. He had had no 'sense of decency and patriotism' and his actions carried the 'stigma of bad citizenship'. The slurs on Houston's patriotism would have incensed him had he known. *The Times* was pleased that 'the Houstons of this world are fortunately few', and hoped that the Treasury would find a loophole. A remedy was indeed being sought by Winston Churchill, then Chancellor of the Exchequer, who declared in April in the House of Commons that he would take all necessary steps to secure payment of death duties 'legally due' on Houston's estate. Even so, however, Churchill probably knew that procuring such duties in fact would not be possible.

It was not until mid-May that Lucy was out of danger but the Houston inheritance was a major news story, bringing light relief to the national gloom over the nine-day General Strike. There was a surprise development when a new claimant for Houston's money emerged in the form of Cecil Skinner, a 34-year-old printer who lived in a Liverpool council house. Skinner, who had engaged a solicitor and adopted 'Houston' as his middle name, claimed that, as the shipowner's grand-nephew, he was the principal heir. In questioning that Houston's will was a true expression of his wishes, and doubting that the shipowner could have prepared a will, Skinner seemed to imply that Lucy had either influenced Houston's will or had written it herself. Later, in June 1926, things were further complicated when it was revealed that four aunts of Skinner were also making claims.

By then Lucy was strong enough to begin trying to take power over her situation, and persuaded one of her nurses to smuggle ashore and send off telegrams to several well-known doctors requesting that they visit her.

Having done this, Lucy moved from the *Liberty* to Beaufield. The medical experts came, made their assessment, and departed, and on 21 June Lucy issued a statement to the effect that they had found her normal mentally and physically; it had been jaundice that had caused her confusion and convalescence in England was advised. This announcement caused a sensation on Jersey but the verdict of the doctors had to be accepted by the Royal Court. A hearing was scheduled for 26 June and, anticipating with glee her imminent release from the clutches of the Jersey authorities, Lucy herself attended. But escape would not be so easy. The court considered the doctors' report but after deliberation decided that local witnesses would also have to be heard. Lucy collapsed in court, declared that it was unfair, alleged that there was a conspiracy against her and had to be helped to her car.

As Lucy remained restlessly at Beaufield the *Liberty* sat temptingly in the harbour below. Knowing that if she could sail beyond Jersey waters she would be physically outside the jurisdiction of the court, Lucy made plans to escape but, it was reported, the authorities got wind of her scheme and took legal possession of the yacht as it was ready to depart. However, there is an alternative version of events: two later accounts suggested that Lucy did indeed escape on the *Liberty*. One, which appeared in a Scottish newspaper in 1962, stated that immediately after the doctors had gone Lucy persuaded one of her nurses, Kitty Pentreath, to help her. Kitty rowed out to the *Liberty* at night while Lucy, wearing a fur coat over her nightdress, sat in the stern of the small boat urging, 'Row, Kitty, row harder. I'll settle £50,000 on you if we dodge these devils.' These details sound plausible. Further in support of this account, Comyns Beaumont, an employee of Lucy in the 1930s, would relate that when he asked Lucy if she had escaped to England in a small boat at night she replied, 'Certainly. I landed at the bottom of the garden of my house at Sandgate.' Then she laughed: 'That spiked their guns. No one has ever held me against my will and never shall.' But there was no mention of this at the time, and if Lucy had escaped she must have returned to Jersey shortly afterwards of her own free will, having made her point to the island's authorities.

Lucy was certainly at Beaufield towards the end of June, for she invited a number of reporters to tea, intending to sway public opinion in her favour. Houston's money, she told them, was 'nothing but a curse', but still she had received none of it – not even the £100,000 that was supposed to be released to her immediately – and had not a penny in her purse. She was also not allowed access to her own private income of £6,000 or £7,000 per year, and her jewellery had been taken away. Yet despite her sorrow and illness after Houston's death, Lucy said, her mind had been 'razor-like in its sharpness', and now she had the 'pluck of a hundred red women'. This comparison of herself with Bolshevik women can have done little to convince readers of her sanity. She continued, with spirit, that she did not care how much money she spent on obtaining her freedom. She refused to be beaten, she said, and had arranged for her doctors to attend the next court hearing to attest to her sanity in person. The newspaper reports that resulted from the interviews made Jersey look bad, and the *Daily Express* reported that the Channel Islands were earning a 'thoroughly unenviable reputation' from the 'medieval absurdity' of their constitution. The system by which a 'perfectly sane' woman was 'branded as a maniac on the casual opinions of a few neighbours' deserved only 'compurgation and the ordeal by fire', and the islanders were unfit for self-government. The tide was turning in Lucy's favour. Her doctors were present when the Jersey Royal Court met again on 3 July. Lucy attended with her sister Florence. Despite wearing mourning clothes she appeared, it was reported, cheerful and confident. The court heard Lucy's specialists, curator Sidney Crill, and relations, friends and neighbours testify to her state of health. As all agreed that Lucy was sane and capable, the Attorney General had little choice but to declare that she no longer needed a curator.

Lucy had fought the Jersey authorities and won, and as she left the court she told the many women who congratulated her, 'Oh! I am so very, very happy now. Thank God! Thank God!' However, she was still so weak that she could hardly stand and clung to her brother and a friend for support. That afternoon, just before stepping into the *Liberty*'s launch, Lucy told a reporter, 'I am going back to my own country a free woman. Freedom is more to me than millions of money.' But after eight months of suffering Lucy was badly shaken, and would take a long time to recover.

With serious financial and legal problems to face, for the following five months Lucy hid herself away on the yacht and worked through them. The *Liberty*'s first stop was Dinard in Britanny, where Lucy would stay for some days, but by the end of July the yacht was in Southampton Water. There Lucy gave a press interview, addressing the reporter from her bed. On no account, she said, would she return to Jersey for the strain there had been 'terrible' and she was suffering from a 'nervous breakdown'. Lucy's doctor Sir Thomas

Horder had ordered complete rest, and every day her bed was carried out on deck from where she watched the passing ships.

Upon hearing of Lucy's release Violet Hunt wrote her a letter, to which Lucy replied, 'Oh! What <u>hell</u> it has been! – all as you say of course a <u>plot</u>. There is one thing certain that the lunacy laws are a <u>disgrace</u> which all women must work to have altered.' Lucy was exhausted and her financial affairs, she told Hunt, were 'chaotic', for the Jersey authorities were still retaining her own private money as well as Houston's.[22] As a sign of defiance Lucy ordered a Southampton ships' chandler to make a new burgee, or two-pointed pennant, for the *Liberty*. It featured the motto *Nemo me impune lacessit*, which Lucy freely translated as meaning 'Whoever hits me, I hit back – harder.' Robert Houston would have approved. That summer, indicating Lucy's state of mind, the *Liberty* charted an erratic course. On 25 August she yacht arrived in Torbay where Lucy watched yacht races from the deck, and from there moved to Brixham for a few days, then on to Weymouth Bay, and at last, on 20 September, arrived at Sandgate. The *Liberty* anchored near Lucy's house, from which furniture was removed and taken on board the yacht. When the yacht sailed on it was reported that Lucy planned a long Mediterranean cruise, but this was Lucy's ploy to evade attention. Instead the *Liberty* went back to Weymouth and anchored well out to sea; Lucy stayed on board for weeks, never once going ashore, while she waited for the Jersey court to process legal matters.

The Jersey authorities had ordered that items of jewellery given to Lucy by Houston should be kept on the island and a jeweller in St Helier had been holding necklaces, brooches, rings and earrings to the value of £146,000. Lucy wanted them back. In November she wrote to the jeweller asking him to bring the jewels to her. The man conceived a plan to evade the Jersey customs authorities. Wrapping the items in cotton wool, he put them in a wicker market basket and covered them with potatoes from his garden. At the ferry terminal he passed through customs unopposed and embarked for Southampton. On board the ferry he asked the purser to put the basket in the safe, telling him that the value of Jersey potatoes in November was like gold. At Southampton Lucy had fixed matters with British Customs and when the jeweller arrived he was escorted by two detectives across Southampton Water to the *Liberty*. On board he carried the precious basket straight to Lucy's stateroom, where he was well rewarded for his efforts. In December, despite having said that she would not return to Jersey, Lucy boarded the mail steamer ferry from Weymouth to spend Christmas and New Year at Beaufield. Although it was reported that she was selling her island property this would prove not to be the case; Lucy would not let Jersey off that easily.

In January 1927, once she had gained power of attorney over Houston's estate Lucy left for Paris, returning to the Trianon Palace Hotel where she began to reorganise her personal affairs. One day she wrote a will in which she listed her sister Florence, her niece and many foundations and charities as the recipients of her fortune. At about this time she gave ownership of Byron Cottage to her nephew Hugh Catty, and from then on occupied the house as a tenant. In March Lucy returned to Jersey and *The Times* reported that she would make Beaufield her home, but the truth was that she intended to be a thorn in the flesh of the local authorities. After her death an Australian relative would tell the press that Lucy had 'owned the whole of the island of Jersey' and if this were true, buying up the island was Lucy's revenge. In July, Houston's gravestone was installed. Remembering his Scottish ancestry, Lucy had chosen a large Celtic cross and on its base inscribed the words:

This cross is raised by his sorrowing wife to the memory of Robert Paterson Houston Baronet, who died most mysteriously, on the 14th April 1926. My Robert, my dear dear Robert.

The inscription created indignation: 'Medically there was no mystery about the cause of death, and the use of the word by Lady Houston is much commented on,' remarked the *Northern Whig*. But when questioned by the press Lucy replied that she could not reveal anything yet but had discovered 'certain telegrams which point clearly to strange events just before my husband's death'. Although the ecclesiastical authorities had at first objected to the inscription she had convinced them that it was justified, she said.

Lucy was now one of the richest, if not *the* richest, woman in England and the press dubbed her the 'six-million widow'. She had fought all her life to obtain money but now, Allen would observe, she valued it 'more for the pleasure of giving it away than for what it would buy'. Cecil Skinner's claim of being Houston's principal heir had failed but Lucy voluntarily offered him and his aunts £50,000 each, and also increased the amount of some other legacies. In the summer of 1927, feeling sufficiently recovered to travel to Scotland, she took the lease of the Ben Alder shooting estate where only two years previously she and Houston had spent their last autumn together. Meanwhile the Treasury had been trying to claim death duties on Houston's estate, but the matter had dragged on for so long that Lucy was weary of it. One day she was seized by an impulse to take matters into her own hands. Gathering pen and paper she wrote a long telegram to Winston Churchill, which began:

> Lady Houston presents her compliments to the Chancellor of the Exchequer, and begs to inform him that as an act of grace on her part she desires to present to the British Government her share of the English death duties on her late husband's estate which would have been due had he been domiciled in England.

Lucy's term 'act of grace' reinforced the point that the estate was not legally liable. Ben Alder Lodge had no telephone but within three minutes of dashing off the telegram Lucy had dispatched a messenger to the post office 7 miles away. She followed up with other telegrams but they caused consternation at the Treasury, where there was uncertainty as to their authenticity. The Treasury hardly dared believe its luck.

When the news got out the press anticipated that Lucy would hand over £3 million but she had specified that she would pay 'her share', i.e. half of that amount, and indicated that if the Treasury pursued its claim for the larger sum it would get nothing. Her offer, Wentworth Day believed, was prompted by her admiration of Churchill, and had a socialist government been in power she would not have parted with a penny. In what followed Lucy insisted on dealing only with Churchill personally. As chancellor, Churchill had been under continual criticism for his financial policies and Lucy's gift was a great personal triumph. As she would tell Allen, 'Winston was delighted. He knew he could never have got it out of me by law; it was a free gift on my part to my country.' In a few days, via telegram, Lucy and Churchill reached an understanding.

Meanwhile, Lucy wished to issue a press statement, and invited a reporter to Ben Alder. He found her alone, reclining on a couch on the lodge's verandah where, it was whispered locally, Lucy sunbathed in the nude. Although the Ben Alder estate was one of the most expensive in Scotland, Lucy so craved peace and quiet that she had not allowed shooting that year, and the grouse and deer roamed free. Except for her secretaries and servants, Lucy told the reporter, there was no one with her. Wanting to be a 'hermit of the hills' she had shut herself away to be alone with her memories, and she recited lines from the local 'Song of the Badenoch':

Of wonderful love tales, of old tragedies,
Filling the heart with pity and the eyes
With tears of rare remembrance; and old songs
Of love's endurance, love's despair, love's wrongs,
And triumphs o'er all obstacles at last,
And all the grief and sorrow of the past.

Every line in the song, she said, applied to herself and recalled so many memories.

In her early years Lucy had preyed on others in her quest for money but now, as the mistress of millions, she herself had become the prey. One of her reasons for coming to remote Ben Alder, she told the reporter, was to evade people who had 'designs' upon her and her money, but even here she was pursued by sackfuls of begging letters. At first Lucy had tried to investigate all the claims but many times when she had given substantial help she later found that she had been tricked. The 'most beautiful and most pathetic letters', she discovered, were written by the worst offenders, scoundrels who possessed 'all the arts of obtaining money and sympathy'. But perhaps the main purpose of Lucy inviting the press to Ben Alder was to provide herself with a kind of life insurance. She kept a photograph of Houston's tombstone close by and glanced at it occasionally during the interview. Then, raising herself up on her couch, she said, very slowly and deliberately, 'People are still conspiring against me – people whose action brought me nigh to death's door after my husband's death – and I am not going to allow myself to be robbed of a single shilling by one of them.' In making her suspicions public Lucy presumably intended that her persecutors would be aware that others knew of their intentions. With her time at Ben Alder drawing to a close, Lucy hosted the traditional end-of-season ball at Newtownmore Public Hall for her house staff and the Ben Alder gamekeepers and ghillies, although the services of the latter had not been needed that year.

Once back at Byron Cottage, Lucy resumed negotiations with Churchill, and so therapeutic had been her holiday that some of her natural buoyancy, humour and charm returned. Dispensing with legal and financial advisors, she requested that she carry out negotiations with Churchill in person. And so, at half past five on the evening of Saturday, 29 October, Lucy arrived at the Treasury building on Horse Guards Road for the first of two visits. The windows in the imposing façade of the deserted building were unlit but the building had been kept open specially. Although the meeting was supposed to be secret the story had leaked out and at least one reporter was waiting outside as Lucy stepped from her Buick car bundled up in a fur coat. Lord Hailsham, the Attorney General, arrived a little later, followed by Churchill who went straight upstairs to his grand office where Lucy, Hailsham and two private secretaries waited. It would be, the press reported later, 'one of the most extraordinary secret meetings ever held in Whitehall'. The talks would continue for over an hour. Over cups of tea Churchill tried to persuade Lucy to hand over £2.5 million but, as she later related, she 'argued and bargained' and 'wheedled and bullied' Churchill into accepting her lower offer of £1.5 million – the equivalent of £85 million today – still an enormous sum. A second meeting was scheduled at which Lucy would put the cheque into Churchill's hand. When she emerged from the building a reporter asked for a statement but Lucy, taken aback, replied, 'However did you know I was here? No, I must not say why I came here, or what I have been doing.'

Twelve days later Lucy returned to the Treasury with her cheque book in her handbag, and Churchill himself later told Wentworth Day what happened. He was in his office with Lord Hailsham when suddenly the doors were thrown open and 'in swept the British Boadicea – ridin' in an invisible chariot, with unseen scythe-blades mowin' down hordes of unguessed enemies!' Lucy gave Churchill the 'sweetest smile' then looked at Hailsham even more sweetly and said, 'I see you have your lawyer with you, Mr. Churchill. Why? I left mine outside in the car!' Hailsham took the hint and departed, leaving Churchill with Lucy, in his words, 'alone, unarmed and defenceless'. With Hailsham gone Lucy flirted outrageously. Sitting opposite Churchill at his desk she took out her cheque book and asked to borrow his pen. Writing out the cheque she looked up at him: 'Tell me, how many noughts are there in a million? I've never written a cheque as big as this before,' then added archly, 'don't you think you'd better come and guide my hand?' Churchill replied that she was quite capable of doing it without his help, but Lucy told a reporter afterwards that she had got 'so muddled up with the bewildering array of figures that the Chancellor had to extricate me from my difficulty on two occasions'.

Having signed the cheque, Lucy handed it across the desk and said, 'Now, haven't I been a good girl? Don't you think I deserve a kiss?' To this Churchill replied, 'You do. But you won't get it! You'll get a cup o' tea instead!' Over tea, Churchill would recall, Lucy 'prattled away, full of schemes and plans for bettering the country'. She was, he mused, a 'grand old lady – the greatest gentleman-adventurer alive'. However, some months later Churchill revealed an ulterior motive for Lucy's apparent generosity. Certainly, he wrote to a Buckingham Palace official, she wanted to 'win some mark of the royal favour', and several times during the death duties negotiations she had reminded him that she was 'conferring an immense gift upon the State' and so 'ought to be treated as was the late Baroness Burdett-Coutts by being made a Peeress in her own right'.[23]

When the news emerged the press questioned Lucy eagerly and she took the opportunity to boast that she had done what no woman had ever done alone before. Without a single expert advisor, she said, she had approached the chancellor and by a few telegrams and two interviews achieved what would have taken lawyers and financial authorities a year or more. She had written the cheque with a 'joyful heart' and without admitting any legal liability. The next day, 11 November 1927, Churchill announced triumphantly in a cabinet meeting at 10 Downing Street that he had received Lucy's cheque. Lord Birkenhead was in the room; one can only guess at his feelings. To ensure that there was money in the bank to honour the cheque, Lucy personally directed the sale of Houston's securities. She was, she declared, the 'only woman in the world' who had ever carried out such financial dealings entirely alone. With the financial matters settled, Lucy contemplated her future and in November a newspaper reported that she was soon to enter politics. But Lucy, now aged 70, was in no physical condition for that and the idea would not materialise. However, the report indicated the way in which her ideas and interests were developing. But for now, having overexerted herself, in mid-November she took to her bed at Byron Cottage and gave instructions that she was not to be disturbed.

INTO THE JOLLY OLD LIMELIGHT

he upkeep of the *Liberty* was hugely expensive and caused Lucy end-less vexation. However, she loved the sea, and the yacht provided her with a quiet retreat and also a form of continuity with her life with Houston. Lucy made a number of changes on board. Rather than using Houston's grey and blue master suite, she converted the dining room on the main deck into her bed-sitting room. With windows on all sides it was light and airy, and in it she spent much of her time when aboard. By December 1927 the *Liberty* had been lying idle for a year but suddenly, shortly before Christmas, Lucy gave orders to prepare for a cruise to France. On Christmas Day she left London with a handful of staff to join the yacht at Southampton, but the country was in the grip of the 'Christmas Blizzard' – one of the worst storms of the century in the south of England. Snow lay 10ft deep in central London and elsewhere villages were cut off by drifts of up to 20ft. Lucy arrived on the south coast to find that in the Arctic condi-tions all Channel crossings had been suspended; nevertheless, she gave orders for the *Liberty* to sail. When the captain advised her that the risk was too great she retorted, 'We keep straight on!' The sea, she declared, was 'England's heritage – not England's mistress'.

Predictably, the Channel crossing was terrible. Furniture, equipment, crockery and crew were thrown about while Lucy not only had to be tied to her bed but the bed itself had to be lashed down. The *Liberty*, a newspaper reported, 'came nearer to being lost than in her whole varied sea life', and had she not been the 'largest and most seaworthy' private vessel in European waters she might not have survived. But when Cherbourg was reached at last Lucy remarked blandly to the captain, 'I told you that the sea was our servant.' From Cherbourg the *Liberty* went along the coast of Normandy and on 29 December turned into the River Seine, steaming about 70 miles inland to moor on a quiet reach of the river a few miles from Rouen. There was nothing in sight but bare trees, desolate hills and the occasional passing boat; the trips made by the yacht's motor launch to Rouen for supplies were the only connection with the outside world.

Lucy's New Year of 1928 was cold and cheerless. She had deliberately sought solitude but without company to amuse her she stayed alone in her cabin watching the passing steamer traffic through the windows, which were always kept wide open. With time on her hands and still paranoid Lucy brooded and after a few days, unable any longer to contain her feelings or the urge to communicate, she again contacted the press. When a reporter arrived Lucy made various announcements. She was on the yacht, she said, to recuperate from the huge task of selling Houston's securities but she had also left London to escape the 'enormous' number of begging letters which, since her complaint at Ben Alder the previous year, had only increased. She also repeated with emphasis her belief that there had been 'something sinister' about Houston's death. After this Lucy went to Paris and the Trianon Palace Hotel, while the *Liberty* returned to Southampton to take on stores before departing for the Mediterranean.

From Paris Lucy went by train to Marseille where she, together with two or three women friends, joined the *Liberty*. Revisiting the site of her honeymoon three years previously, Lucy ordered the yacht to moor in the bay of St Tropez. The Riviera environment and the company of friends revived her spirits, and on 4 March she wrote Winston Churchill the first of several private letters that she would send over the coming years. After the death duties meetings she felt in a position to give the chancellor her advice, telling him that she wished to whisper in his ear what her 'intuition' told her should be done with the budget – although in her letter she did not elaborate on what that was. She then criticised his cabinet colleagues. Austen Chamberlain, Secretary of State for Foreign Affairs, had made a 'gaffe', but then he always did look an 'awful ass', she said. As for Stanley Baldwin, he had openly scolded one of his own followers for 'telling the truth about the P.O.' Meanwhile Birkenhead, whom Lucy must have known was Churchill's close friend, never opened his mouth without 'putting his foot into it!' Churchill was the 'only gentleman' among them, and she hoped that he would not be influenced by such 'duffers and bounders'. Ironically, she concluded by saying that she would not thrust her advice upon him, but wished him luck: 'You know I told you I had been a mascotte to you & I have, haven't I?'[24] Churchill's short reply was a masterpiece of tact: 'I am very much obliged to you for your letter; and though I cannot agree with your harsh comments on my colleagues, I will bear in mind the advice which you give.'[25]

At the end of March the *Liberty* moved on to Cannes but all was not well in the yacht's galley, for there had been six chefs in as many weeks. The press put this down to Lucy's demands that everyone conform to her 'strong will', but while she did indeed make life difficult for her kitchen staff, the real reason for the rapid turnover was that she feared she was being poisoned. Dismissing the last of the series of chefs, she moored the yacht for several weeks close to La Favourite, the beautiful Cannes villa belonging to the Rajah and Ranee of Pudukota. During this period La Favourite's chef prepared Lucy's meals at the villa and a sailor was sent from the *Liberty* to collect them. After about four months on the *Liberty*, by the end of May Lucy was back at the Trianon Palace Hotel in Paris.

Then disaster struck the rajah and ranee. Having collected their 12-year-old son from boarding school in London they had set off to return to Cannes. But in Paris the rajah became ill, and following two operations on an obstruction of the intestines he died, at the age of 53. The ranee was devastated. Once back in London, Lucy visited her and said, 'Now, my dear, you will no longer be needing any of your pretty coloured dresses, so you can give some to me. As you are fatter than I, but wear your skirts shorter, they will be just right.' It was perhaps in compensation for the dresses that when the ranee visited Byron Cottage Lucy handed her a cheque for £1,000, saying, 'You look so sad, my dear Molly. Now go and buy yourself something pretty to cheer yourself up!'

That summer of 1928 Lucy felt able to re-enter London society. On 4 July she attended a high-profile reception at the Mayfair Hotel in honour of 'Women Pioneers of Empire', at which the bulk of the awards were made to women aviators. They included the Honourable Lady Mary Bailey, who, having gained a pilot's licence only two years previously, had become the first woman to fly across the Irish Sea and had also set a world height record of 17,283ft in the light aircraft category. In her speech the chairwoman remarked that while athletic records proved that women had only about three-quarters of the physical ability of men, a 'non-athletic woman' could fly a light aeroplane. Lucy also spoke, and a snippet was published in a Suffragette newspaper under the heading 'Wit and Wisdom'. Women, Lucy quipped, had been pioneers since the beginning of time, for 'did not Eve take the first bite of the apple?'

Enthused about the potential of flight, later in July Lucy made the first of the donations that would earn her the name 'England's Lady Bountiful'. Her gift to Emilie Hinchcliffe, widow of a pilot who had disappeared while attempting to cross the Atlantic in a single-engined plane, was heralded by a telegram which read, 'So sorry to hear that you are penniless. Am sending you a cheque for £100 – Lady Houston.' That summer Lucy gained further attention by renewed reports of her spending the night in a summerhouse among the trees in her garden. Built on brick stilts, the wooden structure had a roof but no walls yet it was said that despite sleeping here in all weathers Lucy had never caught a cold. After these airy nights, she told the press, at six o'clock in the morning she would sometimes put on an old coat and walk out on to Hampstead Heath to talk to tramps: 'They think I am one of them, and we have some very interesting talks.' This remark was widely reported and caused considerable amusement.

After a holiday on Jersey, Lucy departed for Scotland in August, again leasing Ben Alder. Her visit this year would be very different for she entertained a large house party that included Captain Theodore Brinckman (hereafter 'Theodore'), the elder of her former husband's sons. Lucy had lifted the ban on shooting in Ben Alder forest and late in August Theodore brought down two large stags. However, even in Scotland Lucy was so persecuted by begging letters and requests for money that she again sought the help of the press. The number of letters was overwhelming, she complained, up to 600 per day even though some were addressed only 'Lady Houston, Scotland', or even just 'Lady Houston'. The letters, Lucy said, came from all over the world and were often written in languages that she could not understand. Some contained pamphlets, books, poetry and music for which she was requested to pay, while others were pleas for her to take out patents or finance businesses. But most were purely begging letters, such as, 'Dear Lady Houston – send me £250. This is very urgent. Do not delay.' Others were more sophisticated and included large packets with twenty-page letters, family histories, birth and marriage certificates, and photographs of the writer's family. 'And the funny thing is,' Lucy said, 'that they always ask me to return these photographs, and get really abusive if I do not.' Scores contained offers of marriage from men young and old who, Lucy said, thinking her foolish, hoped to make money out of her. The letters had broken down Lucy's health in London and disturbed her holiday. 'Tell people to leave me alone,' she asked a reporter, adding in a resigned tone, 'yet I suppose they never will leave me alone, now.'

The problem was not that Lucy did not want to give, but that she wanted the recipients to be deserving. She believed that her money was a sacred trust from God and that she had been given the responsibility of spending it. Unable to deal with the letters herself, and often doubting her ability to donate wisely, over time she would work out ways of ensuring satisfactory distribution. One method was to forward requests to the Charity Organisation Society and give only to cases that it determined to be genuine. She would also come to rely upon the judgement of her Hampstead neighbour, Juliana Hoare, giving to any cause that she recommended. However, Lucy also made personal donations to individuals, and often to poor people who had been reported in the press as having performed some small heroic deed. She wrote to them enclosing one or more £5 notes and a handwritten message: 'With Lady Houston's compliments and love. She would like you to know that she admires your pluck.'

If Lucy was careful with giving she was also careful in personal expenditure, and indeed could be stingy over small items. In later life she would say that once she became super-rich she spent far less on herself than when, as Lady Byron, she had been merely well off. Even so, she was still capable of squandering large sums. For example, Wentworth Day recounted how she had once refused to sign some share transfer documents despite being warned that if she failed to do so she would lose money. Six weeks later she remarked casually to her secretary, 'You know those papers I wouldn't sign for Mr Girling? Well, I lost £20,000 over that. I suppose some people worry over a thing like that.' Lucy could afford such a cavalier attitude, for she knew that her investments would soon regenerate the loss.

That summer Lucy made another large expenditure when her enthusiasm for Highland life and her thriving relationship with the Brinckmans led her to purchase her own Scottish property. The 10,384-acre Kinrara estate in Inverness-shire had a number of advantages over Ben Alder, being only 3 miles from Aviemore railway station and much closer to the Brinckmans at Nairnside. The white twenty-bedroomed house looked out over the unruffled waters of Loch Ericht and the Spey valley to the mountains beyond. The moors and loch offered much sport – pheasants, grouse, salmon, trout and the famed Kinrara red deer. Returning to London after the shooting season, Lucy continued her philanthropy with sums large and small. In October, for example, she donated £10,000 to provide a window for Liverpool Cathedral in memory of Houston. In November she sent a cheque for £100 to Lady Zia Wernher, daughter of Grand Duke Michael of Russia, who was organising a cabaret ball in aid of disabled Russian and British children. That month Lucy also bought the archives of Ronald Ross, who had been awarded the Nobel Prize for achievements in the field of malaria research. In 1916 Lucy and Ross had been members of the Poetry Society but the scientist had since fallen on hard times, and having paid him £2,000 Lucy presented his papers to the British Museum.

Now, two years after Houston's death, Lucy had regained her equilibrium and ebullience and at the age of 71 a new phase of life was opening. Lucy made a tentative foray into the political sphere in December but unfortunately, by her attempt to muscle in on a joke between two prominent male Tory figures, she embarrassed herself in public. The right-wing newspaper proprietor Lord Rothermere had challenged Sir William Joynson-Hicks, Home Secretary, to a bet of £100 to £10 that the Conservatives would lose the forthcoming general election in May 1929. Joynson-Hicks had replied that instead he would bet Rothermere 'two hats to one' that the Conservatives would win with a large majority. A newspaper quipped that if Joynson-Hicks won he would get the better deal because he wore a silk hat, whereas Rothermere sported a bowler. Rothermere responded by saying that Joynson-Hicks was 'talking through his hat', for he knew well that the Conservatives had no chance of victory. Lucy weighed in. Was Lord Rothermere willing, she asked in the press, to make the money bet with Lady Houston but in thousands instead of hundreds of pounds? Rothermere's reply to the press was crushing: 'Lord Rothermere has not the pleasure of the acquaintance of Lady Houston and never makes bets with strangers. He is not making any more bets on the Election.'

Rothermere may have put Lucy down, but she was thick-skinned and her craving for political engagement was unabated. Taking on Houston's mantle Lucy stepped forth, dedicating his money to an all-consuming battle on behalf of Britain and its empire. Armed with Houston's money Lucy had nothing to prove or fear and no reputation to preserve and, like her late husband, she would give no credit to an enemy. With compromise out of the question she intended to engage in a fight to the death. Lucy was by nature a woman of extremes and her feeling for her country became fanatical, leading her to hate all that she believed was seeking to undermine it; the root of the evil, in her opinion, was Bolshevism. She saw politics in quasi-religious terms as a cosmic struggle in which she and the British nation were on the side of God, engaged in a battle against the forces of Satan, as represented by Bolshevism, coming out of Soviet Russia. Lucy, frustrated at the diminishing of Britain's power and stature in the world, believed that honest and loyal Britons would share her views of what was in the country's best interests. When they failed to do so she concluded that they were traitors operating under Soviet influence. In her view British socialists were simply watered-down Bolshevists and either the dupes or the willing servants of Moscow.

At the end of 1928, therefore, in the self-appointed role of national scourge of socialism, Lucy made a major attempt to undermine its doctrine when she thrust herself into the disputes that continued to surround the coal industry. Industrial unrest, changes in coal production and European markets had put the industry in difficulties. As output fell wages were cut, working hours increased, pits closed and mine workers were laid off. On Christmas Day Edward, Prince of Wales, having been disturbed by a recent visit to depressed mining areas, made a live radio broadcast on behalf of the Miners' Relief Fund, and Lucy listened in from Beaufield. The prince's moving appeal, in which he described the grim conditions of unemployed miners and their families, brought a wide response, but the largest donation was from Lucy, who gave £30,000.

But her generosity had a sting in the tail. In a New Year message of her own to the miners, Lucy said that she had been glad to respond to the appeal made by 'our dear, wonderful Prince of Wales'. However, while her heart was full of 'goodwill and sympathy', she wanted to give them a 'little advice'. Lucy's advice was also reproof. It was crystal clear, she insisted, that the miners had been reduced to their present plight by 'mischievous men' who were 'not fit to black your boots'. She meant socialist trade union leaders. Lucy reminded the miners that she had once urged their wives to try to persuade them not to become involved with union leaders, 'but alas, you would not listen'. Trade unions had brought only suffering and Lucy advised miners to think for themselves for she was sure that most had 'plenty of common sense if you would only use it'. Their New Year's resolution, she declared, should be to 'send all trade unions to the place where all bad people go'. In Russia, she said, hordes of starving, diseased and uneducated children roamed the streets, 'So you can tell your "Red" leaders this who try to persuade you into Bolshevism.' Finally, she advised the miners to vote for the Conservatives who would, she said, bring back prosperity to 'poor old England'.

This patronising letter brought Lucy strong criticism in the press and the miners themselves were particularly bitter, with one writing to the socialist *Daily Herald* that Lucy's donation should be sent to the 'place where she thinks trade unions should be sent'. A miner's wife from Leeds thought Lucy's message an insult to the patriotism of miners: 'More power to the trade unions!' her letter concluded. When Lucy was interviewed at Beaufield in mid-January 1929 she admitted that she had received a number of abusive letters but she remained defiant: 'I care nothing for such attacks ... for I feel that I have merely given the men advice which should have been given them by persons in authority.'

A few days later, on the point of leaving Jersey for the Riviera, Lucy gave the press a Biblical-type parable. It presented an idyllic past in which mining had been a prosperous industry and miners well paid and happy until the devilish 'serpent of discontent called trade unionism' had crept in. The serpent abolished contentment and high wages and ruined the industry while his followers worshipped him, crying, 'Great is trade unionism, whose name is ruin.' Then, said Lucy, the serpent 'preened his tail and winked his eye' while his supporters applauded and cried out, 'We must be much more miserable before we are truly happy,' to which the serpent replied, 'So you shall ... Vote for Socialists at the coming general election.' A columnist of the *Daily Herald*, the country's leading left-wing newspaper, took a sardonic view of Lucy's parable, commenting, 'I think she deserves full marks for that little effort, does Fanny Lucy. People get good money on the music-halls for being half as foolish.'

Meanwhile, Lucy was compiling a large dossier of information about the past history and political activities of prominent socialists. In 1930 the results of Lucy's research would be published as a book entitled *Potted Biographies: 'Lest We Forget', A Dictionary of Anti-National Biography*, which revealed the pacifist activities of many members of the Labour Party during the war, foremost among whom was its leader Ramsay MacDonald, twice British Prime

Minister. Lucy regarded it as monstrous that pacifists such as Macdonald, who had opposed the First World War, should now be entrusted with the country's government. That they should support the Bolsheviks, who had taken Russia out of that war, executed its royal family and declared its intention to export its revolution internationally, further confirmed Lucy's view of Labour politicians as traitors and revolutionaries. From 1929 she waged a campaign against the Labour government and from 1931 was to campaign against the Conservative Party's strategy of forming a coalition with the Labour Party.

In February Lucy and a party of friends and relatives were cruising in the Mediterranean aboard the *Liberty*, calling at ports on the European and north African coasts. At Monte Carlo Lucy socialised with the King of Sweden and the Prince of Monaco, but the problems of England and the horrors of socialism were never far from her mind. Another general election was approaching and in April, from the yacht, Lucy sent the British press a cringeworthy appeal to the 'young and beautiful girls of England'. The country, she wrote, was in deadly danger of being destroyed by socialism but girls had an opportunity to use their votes to help their country. How 'thrilling' and 'romantic' it would be, Lucy declared, when they saw the announcement in large type in the press: 'England Saved from Socialism by Girls.' Not surprisingly the *Daily Herald* again made fun of Lucy. 'Listen to Fanny, Girls!' ran the headline of an article which commented that 'Fanny Lucy has broadcast an appeal to "the young and beautiful," and only a churl would suggest that she is not entitled to do so.' It was an unkind jibe. Despite all Lucy's warnings Labour won by a clear majority and party leader Ramsay MacDonald was again sworn in as Prime Minister. Remaining in office until 1935, he would become Lucy's pet hate. When Lucy left the Mediterranean that summer it would be for the last time. Not only advancing age and deteriorating health but the expansion of her interest in national politics, in particular her concern with the threat of socialists in government, would from now on keep her closer to home.

In June Lucy wrote to King George V to offer him and Queen Mary £300,000, the interest of which they could donate to charities of their choice. The King was tempted to accept but was concerned about negative consequences and so, knowing Churchill's connection with Lucy, he asked Sir Frederick Ponsonby of the Privy Purse Office to consult Churchill on the matter. Ponsonby wrote to Churchill, asking for his advice and setting out his own objections to Lucy's offer.[26] Firstly, he feared that Lucy would publicise her gift, and secondly suspected that her real motive was to procure an honour. Ponsonby was also concerned that if Lucy's offer was accepted the royal couple would become merely the distributors of money from the 'Houston fund', while Lucy got the credit. Churchill replied immediately, confirming that Lucy did indeed desire an honour and would be 'certain' to make her gift public. However, he said that within the past two years Lucy had offered Queen Mary a charitable donation and the Queen, after consulting Churchill, had accepted it. But in this case he recommended a rejection, although he suggested that if Lucy continued to lead a 'godly, righteous and sober life' and to make donations to good causes, she would eventually 'establish a claim' to a royal honour.[27]

When the King rejected Lucy's offer she became so ill that she chartered a steamer to bring a Paris specialist to Beaufield in July. It was the first of several occasions on which the rejection of funding for a patriotic project was followed by a health crisis. By August, however, Lucy was sufficiently well to travel to Kinrara for a two-month holiday. Brinckman was already at Nairnside and Lucy was developing a peculiar relationship with his sons. She was 'devoted' to them, Wentworth Day would write, and from the way in which she spoke he often thought that she regarded them almost as her own. Certainly she would later describe them to reporters as her 'stepsons', and indeed some newspapers would believe that they were her own children. Lucy became particularly close to Theodore and it was probably in 1929 that she bought her way into his life by gifting him the Kinrara estate. Theodore, now aged 30, had adopted a military career and become a captain in the Life Guards. But while Theodore was short, with buck teeth and protruding ears, Brinckman's second son, Roderick Napoleon, known as 'Naps', a soldier in the Grenadier Guards, had inherited a good measure of his father's looks and physique. One day in the 1930s, when Lucy heard that there might be a corpulent visitor to Byron Cottage, she would say to Wentworth Day, 'I don't want any fat men about the place. They should be like my step-son, "Naps" Brinckman. There's a man for you! Straight as a gun-barrel. And oh! So handsome. He looks just what a soldier should.'

The Wall Street Crash of October 1929 and the subsequent collapse of the American financial markets brought economic depression to Britain. Unemployment rose sharply and support for socialism increased. When in November 1929 diplomatic relations were renewed between the Soviet

Union and Britain, a new Soviet ambassador, M.G. Sokolnikoff, arrived in London. Lucy was incensed. She wrote to the *Morning Post*, declaring: 'With all my heart, with all my soul, with all my strength, I denounce the iniquitous recognition of Satan's emissaries by the present Government.' Everyone with the love of God in their hearts should vow that 'vile and blasphemous' Soviet diplomats should not be allowed to 'pollute the air of England breathed by the Faithful in the Lord'.

The following month, still furious at the creeping advance of socialism, Lucy launched into the affair of the Hull tramwaymen. The object of her wrath was Hull city council. In the city's municipal elections in November socialists had gained a majority and subsequently begun a house clearing, causing bitter local feeling when they cast aside many longstanding public servants. As part of the purge they also intended to put out of work 115 tramway workers, specifically men who had volunteered to help keep the city's tramway system running during the General Strike of 1926. Back then the workers had been promised permanent employment, and they were now planning legal action for breach of contract. The city council had not calculated on the level of public attention that the case would receive. The local press denounced the council's desire to fire the tramwaymen as a scandal and merely revenge for the failure of the General Strike. Councillors, reported the *Leeds Mercury*, had made an unparalled 'display of malice, naked and unashamed', and the humiliation and injustice suffered by the men was a 'very dirty business'.

The matter came to national attention on 12 December when Margaret Bondfield, Minister of Labour and Britain's first female cabinet minister, stated that she had no authority to intervene. Lucy picked up on this, telling the Press Association that if Miss Bondfield could not insist upon justice being done then her title should instead be 'Minister of Injustice to Labour'. Bondfield, Lucy declared, pretended to be the friend of the working classes but nobody could feel anything but disgust at her 'unwomanly attitude' towards the 'brave fellows' who had stepped in to help the citizens of Hull when those whose duty it was had 'failed and slunk away'. Lucy's support of the tramwaymen met with general approval but, having criticised the Labour government, Lucy then turned her wrath on the Conservatives. They had done nothing to protect the tramwaymen, she said, and it had been left to a 'poor little woman to fight their battle for them'. Did the Conservatives feel proud of themselves, she asked?

When there was still no action, Lucy threatened Hull city council with legal action, saying that she would cheerfully take upon herself the 'burden of this very unequal fight', which she was sure she would win. The councillors retorted that they would not be dictated to but in reality, as some of Lucy's other opponents would find to their cost, they had bitten off more than they could chew. Lucy's threat had changed the game and the *Daily Express* advised the councillors to give in. Any defeat was humiliating but this one, the *Express* reminded them, would be more so than most because the victory would 'rest with a woman'. Perhaps even the *Daily Herald* approved of her actions, for it commented only that 'our dear old friend Fanny Lucy, Lady Houston, has got herself into the jolly old limelight once more. It seems to be pretty Fanny's way.' When the Hull city council subsequently backed down and an amicable solution was reached, Lucy had won a resounding victory.

While the Hull affair was in progress Lucy made two attacks on the Prime Minister, Ramsay MacDonald. British rule of India was under pressure from Indian nationalists and there had been an assassination attempt on the viceroy, Lord Irwin. Lucy believed that British weakness encouraged Indian unrest and in January 1930 she wrote a personal letter to MacDonald. 'Not because I love you, but because I see grave danger ahead in India, I am sending you as a New Year's gift − an idea,' she began. The attempt on Irwin's life had proved that 'cowardice and truckling to treason' did not work and in Lucy's view Lord Lloyd, who as governor of Bombay from 1918 to 1923 had quelled unrest by imprisoning Gandhi, was the man to sort things out in India. If MacDonald was wise, Lucy said, he would recall Lord Irwin, the Viceroy of India, and go down on his knees to Lord Lloyd and beg him to step in. This offensive letter was only the beginning of MacDonald's woes with Lucy.

Lucy Radmall. (Bassano)   'Mrs Gretton'. (Bassano)

Monte Carlo casino in the 1890s. (Retrieved from the Library of Congress)

"Theodore."

Clockwise from right: Theodore Brinckman.
(The Picture Art Collection/Alamy Stock
Photo); The ninth Lord Byron (Public domain);
Lucy as Mrs Brinckman. (Public domain)

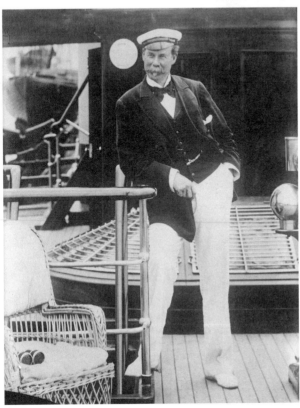

Thomas Lipton aboard the *Erin*, 1902. (Retrieved from the Library of Congress)

Lady Byron, 1909. (National Portrait Gallery)

Lady Byron in mourning, 1917.
(© Imperial War Museum (WWC D12))

The *Liberty*. (Public domain)

Robert Houston. (The Picture Art
Collection/Alamy Stock Photo)

F.E. Smith, Lord Birkenhead.
(Retrieved from the Library
of Congress)

Stanley Baldwin and Winston
Churchill, 1925. (Retrieved
from the Library of Congress)

One of the Schneider Trophy Contest Supermarine S.6B aircraft at Calshot. (Public domain)

Lucy with Schneider Team Members. (Royal Air Force Museum)

Ramsay MacDonald and his daughter Ishbel. (Retrieved from the Library of Congress)

'Mt. Everest Conquered!' (Westland Aircraft Works)

Wentworth Day (far left) with the *Saturday Review* street sellers. (Public domain)

Lucy's idol, Edward, Prince of Wales, *c.* 1920. (Retrieved from the Library of Congress)

Anthony Eden, Lucy's 'Prince of Ineffectuals'. (Retrieved from the Library of Congress)

Oswald Mosley with Benito Mussolini. (Public domain)

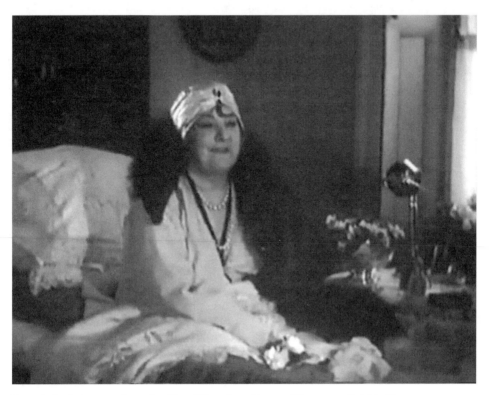

Lucy in bed. A scene from the film *Wings Over Everest*. (Gaumont–British Picture Corporation Ltd)

The Saturday Review 26.12.36

Reduced to

2D.

LADY HOUSTON

Writes to KING GEORGE

THE SATURDAY REVIEW

Edited by Lady Houston, D.B.E.

Volume 162

26th December, 1936

To His Majesty King George VI

Your Majesty,

I was glad, Sir, to read your rebuke to those who have tried to insinuate that you supplanted the late King gladly.

Knowing as I do that the moment when at last you were most unwillingly persuaded to do this was the saddest and blackest moment of your life.

The Archbishop of Canterbury's disgraceful attack on your brother must have hurt you deeply, as it has all those who love and mourn him.

THE ARCHBISHOP AND MR. BALDWIN WILL—AS LONG AS ENGLAND REMAINS—FOR EVER BE HELD RESPONSIBLE FOR THE DASTARDLY MANNER HE WAS DRIVEN BY THEM OUT OF THE COUNTRY.

Mr. Baldwin has said that a "Democratic Government" must always be two years behind a country governed by a Dictator. That is why the "Saturday Review" and its readers have for months past tried to

(Continued on page 805)

Lucy's last issue; the *Saturday Review* of 26 December 1936. (Author's collection)

11

WERE I PRIME MINISTER

L ucy spent the Christmas of 1929 at Beaufield, but her health was so poor
that on 29 December she sent for Lord Dawson Penn, the King's physician. Returning to Byron Cottage she hired a new secretary, Miss Bessie
Ritchie. Aged about 45 at this time Miss Ritchie, wrote Wentworth Day,
was a 'practical, hard-working, God fearing Scotswoman, full of common sense
and womanly charm'. Lucy became fond of Miss Ritchie, who would serve
as her long-suffering but loyal secretary and friend until a short time before
Lucy's death. Then, early in February 1930, with Miss Ritchie and a handful of
other staff, Lucy joined the *Liberty* and went to her favourite hideaway spot on
the River Seine. In the weeks of her stay there she was busy, making charitable
donations including one of £100,000 to St Thomas's Hospital in London to
create a fund to be known as the 'Lady Houston Gift'. On 20 March, feeling
unwell, she scribbled a second will which stated simply, 'I leave all I possess to
Miss Hoare of North End House in N.W. to do with as she in her great good-
ness of heart thinks best. Signed Fanny Lucy Houston.'

When aboard the yacht Lucy had a set personal routine. Every morning
she had a cold bath, or at least a scrub down with cold water, and afterwards,
behind a screen set up on the deck furthest from the shore, she would walk
up and down, naked, for half an hour while the crew and staff remained
below decks. Sun and wind on the skin, she believed, was highly benefi-
cial to the health. Later, Lucy spent a considerable amount of time with
Miss Ritchie, who first read out extracts from the daily press and then
begging letters. Lucy was popular with her crew for she paid well; on her
birthday and at Christmas every man received a £5 note. She could also be

demanding; the system of bells installed by the yacht's first owner was still in operation and enabled Lucy to summon any member of staff or crew at any time. Once, at two o'clock in the morning she got no reply from the quartermaster who was supposed to be on duty she lost patience and rang all the bells; the entire staff hurried to her cabin. As a former crew member wrote, when Lucy had one of her tantrums: 'Look out!'

Encouraged by her success in the affair of the Hull tramwaymen Lucy wanted greater participation in public affairs, and in that peaceful location on the Seine plotted her next moves. The best way to promote herself and her views was through the national press, she believed, but she was frustrated that the newspapers refused to publish her work, or misrepresented her by printing it only in part. The only way to communicate freely, Lucy believed, was to have her own newspaper. She studied the newspaper world, taking all the national daily papers and forming an opinion on each. The *Daily Herald,* for example, had 'excellent' articles, she told Miss Ritchie, and had it not been socialist would be a '*very good* newspaper'. She visited every newspaper office in London and kept contact details of editors, reporters, feature writers and lobby correspondents. In particular she admired R.D. Blumenfeld, former editor of the *Daily Express.* An old friend of Rudyard Kipling and a strong critic of socialism, Blumenfeld was one of the few men of whom Lucy stood in awe, and she described him as the 'Wise Man of Fleet Street'. Another favourite was Oscar Pulvermacher, then night editor of the *Daily Mail*; at about this time Lucy asked his advice on buying a certain Sunday newspaper. She hoped, she said, to get Churchill to write leaders for £100 a week, but what did Pulvermacher think of the newspaper? He advised her that the cost would be too high and, although money was not her first priority, Lucy's respect for Pulvermacher's opinion was such that she took his advice.

Seeking another route to newspaper ownership, Lucy invited Comyns Beaumont, editor of the *Bystander,* to the *Liberty.* Admiring his political stance, she hoped that they might work together. Beaumont, who had never met Lucy, was greatly excited by the invitation. In his later account he described how he met the *Liberty*'s launch at Rouen and was taken along the Seine at high speed until, rounding a bend, he beheld the great white and gold yacht sitting alone on a wide stretch of the river. On board he was received by the captain, and so impressive was the 'almost semi-regal' atmosphere that surrounded Lucy that Beaumont wondered how to behave when he entered 'the Presence'. At length Beaumont was conducted to a large saloon at the far end of which, 'embowered in hothouse blossoms, and shaded by subdued lights', sat Lucy. But as he approached she gave him a friendly smile – her smile was 'most attractive', he thought. She also appeared much younger than her 73 years, although he observed that she could 'never have been beautiful in a classic sense'. Tied around her head was a pink silk bandeau pinned with a glittering jewel and from the sides peeped 'little golden curls', which Beaumont may not have realised were part of the wig that Lucy now always wore. A sable cloak was draped over her shoulders against the chill of the afternoon. When Lucy expressed the hope that the meeting might prove worth both their whiles Beaumont turned on the charm: 'It would be well worth my while, Lady Houston,' he said, 'if only to have the pleasure of meeting one of the most remarkable women of the time.' They talked on general topics until lunchtime and Beaumont found Lucy 'affable, understanding, direct, and despite her plutocratic surroundings, definitely homely'. Her eyes 'twinkled with amusement or flashed indigna-tion' according to the circumstances, and when she laughed the corners of her mouth turned up 'impishly'. He formed the opinion that while the general public believed that Lucy was 'crazy', she was in fact 'extremely level-headed if decidedly unconventional'.

At teatime Beaumont met Lucy again, and as she poured him tea from an enormous silver pot she brought up the matter of the newspaper. Beaumont had prepared a dummy edition and the talk went backwards and forwards, with both having clear ideas about the contents and price, and the type and social class of readership at which it should be aimed. They even decided upon a name, the *Pepper Pot*. Eventually they reached an agreement: 'Together we shall triumph!' Lucy declared, 'I always succeed when I set my mind to a task, and I shall play a big part in it. How soon can you start? There's no time to waste with Ramsay MacDonald and Baldwin on the rampage!' Beaumont warned her that there would be many matters to attend to but Lucy replied, 'Well, get on with it. I am impatient when I make up my mind.' Beaumont departed in a state of exhilaration but even on the return Channel crossing doubts set in. Later, after a further conversation with Lucy, he realised that a subtle approach would not satisfy Lucy and that the new journal would have to be 'brutally frank and outspoken'. He suspected that Lucy would not allow him the final decision on publication policy and as editor he would be held responsible for her statements that Ramsay MacDonald was a traitor. Lucy was annoyed when Beaumont subsequently backed off.

At the end of June 1930, Lucy left France for Jersey, where she attended the inauguration of a new Southampton-to-Channel-Islands air service operated by an amphibious craft that could take off and land on both land and water. Lucy's friend Florence Boot, alias Lady Trent, who had retired to her native Jersey, hosted a tea party to celebrate. She and Lucy were close and sometimes went on picnics together. Lucy favoured cliff tops, where she could take advantage of the health-giving properties of sea air. It was the duty of her chauffeur to lug Lucy's camp bed up the hill from the car, and then Lucy removed her coat to reveal only a brassiere and a pair of short shorts beneath. 'Why shouldn't I sun-bathe?' she was said to have retorted to someone who expressed concerns about Peeping Toms: 'If people look, they'll only see a fat old woman lying here.' Thus established in a lonely but breezy location, the two friends would partake of cold chicken and salad, fruit pie and cream, Guinness, and coffee from a Thermos flask.

There would be no visit to Kinrara in 1930 but in August Lucy joined the *Liberty* for the Cowes Regatta. Perhaps the attraction was Sir Thomas Lipton, and Lucy may have wished to commiserate over their mutual friend Thomas Dewar, who had died earlier that year. In his will Dewar had left Lucy a painting, *Gypsies Gathering Sticks*, by George Morland. From Cowes the *Liberty* went to Start Bay in Devon, where Theodore came aboard. A keen cricketer like his father, he was playing for the Marylebone Cricket Club that summer in matches around the country. If Theodore was not free to go to Kinrara, Lucy would go to him. In September, Lipton, now aged 81, entered *Shamrock V* in the America's Cup race but once again his yacht was defeated and Lipton was bitterly disappointed. Admiring her old friend's spirit, Lucy sent a rhyme to the *Bystander*:

Here's to the sportsman so happy and gay
Whom everyone loves though he's eighty
We drink to his health and we drink to the day
He brings back the Cup – though it's weighty!'

But Lipton would never bring the cup home and died the following year with his ambition unfulfilled.

Unemployment had now reached 2 million and, blaming Ramsay MacDonald and his government, Lucy sent an article to the *Bystander*. The dole was 'degrading', she said, but she had a solution: 'Were I Prime Minister, my first act would be to train the many hundreds of poor fellows (despised by others and despising themselves, now in the hateful position of being paupers on the dole), to be *soldiers*.' Dressed in khaki, Lucy continued, the men would take pride in themselves as soldiers of the King and every girl would think, 'By gosh! These are *men*!' But, Lucy continued, the Labour government was ruled by Soviet Russia, which therefore ruled England, and she hoped that the British people would soon realise this and turn out the 'wolves in sheep's clothing'. Lucy concluded her article with another rhyme:

There are two sorts of people in this world,
Two sorts only that matter:
Those who build up and achieve,
And those who drag down and shatter –
Socialists belong to the latter.

Earlier in life Lucy had gained money, status and social advancement through alliances with men and now, although her cause was different, her methods were similar. From 1930 she kept in close contact with a number of men and one or two women whom she admired and sought to use in pursuit of her agenda. In addition to figures such as Pulvermacher and Blumenfeld, who advised her on current affairs and the newspaper world, peers and politicians were useful tools for her political intrigues and patriotic campaigns. There was a small number of men whom Lucy believed embodied her ideal of the strong and active patriot, and where she could she promoted them.

The man in whom Lucy had most faith was Lord George Lloyd. Then aged 50, he would for a time become her greatest hope for England's future. Short, arrogant, ruthless and full of nervous energy, Lloyd drove himself and others hard. His career entranced Lucy. As governor of Bombay he had imprisoned the Indian nationalist leader Mahatma Gandhi, and during the First World War he had worked with Lawrence of Arabia. Then, as high commissioner of Egypt in the 1920s, he had ruled with an iron hand. Having ambition but relatively little money, Lloyd was susceptible to Lucy in his desire for financial help, and perhaps also on account of her flattery. Her faith in him was boundless; he was the one man, she believed, who could rescue the country and Empire from the lethal grip of socialism. Later a journal would suggest that Lloyd had been born 200 years too late, and would have been more suited to the days when the British Empire was 'on the make, not the brake'. The same could have been said of Lucy, but their similarities would militate against a harmonious relationship.

On 11 November 1930 Lucy wrote to Lloyd insisting that the position of prime minster was in the 'gutter of Socialism' but could be won by any man with 'pluck and determination'. Why, Lucy asked, should not that man be Lloyd himself, for nobody could govern England as well as he. She set out her recipe for success. It could be 'so easy' to gain political power, she wrote, for all Lloyd would have to do was to 'talk, talk, talk in the House of Lords, day after day, week after week, picking up every dirty unworthy trick and action of the Labour Government and exposing it'. He was not well known by the public, she complained, and should put himself constantly in the limelight.[28] But while Lucy wanted Lloyd to become Prime Minister, he himself believed that Churchill was the natural leader of the Conservative Party. Lloyd's main ambition was to become Viceroy of India, a role that would have suited the autocratic side of his nature, but Lucy did not intend to let his wishes stand in the way of her will.

From behind the scenes Lucy made efforts to push Lloyd forward, in a letter urging Pulvermacher to promote Lloyd in the *Daily Mail* as a 'new man' in politics, and adding, 'Sir Robert used to say I had a flair for politics'.[29] In December Lucy wrote to Pulvermacher telling him that unless Lloyd was repeatedly pushed down the throats of the general public 'they would not listen to him if he were the Archangel Gabriel'. Lloyd should be 'advertised and rubbed into their thick intelligences. He cannot do this himself – but you can.' If, she urged, Pulvermacher agreed to act he would be doing the 'greatest and most splendid service' to his country.[30] In January Lucy wrote again to Pulvermacher. Although Stanley Baldwin was being attacked on all sides he refused to resign as Conservative Party leader and now, Lucy wrote, it was up to her and Pulvermacher to get rid of him: 'What fun!! And at the same time, the only way to save the country.' Baldwin was the 'greatest asset' of socialists and the country was helpless as long as he stayed in power: 'What a brute he is!' Lord Lloyd, who knew Baldwin well, had told Lucy that she was 'perfectly right' about him, for the Conservative leader was 'oozing conceit from every pore'. Lucy ended by inviting Pulvermacher to visit her on the *Liberty* later so that they could 'plot together!!' Nobody would know where the yacht was – 'No one ever does, when I go there. They will think I am on the Riviera.' In fact, the *Liberty* would be on the Seine.[31]

On an even higher level than her respect for Lord Lloyd were Lucy's feelings for Edward, Prince of Wales. In her view he was the gallant and romantic 'Prince Charming' who could do no wrong and would inherit the rule of the world's greatest empire. Her devotion was blind and uncritical. She kept his photograph in a silver frame and would have done anything for him. In recognition of her support for his charities, on 28 October 1930 Edward received Lucy at St James's Palace. It would be the first of several meetings, for in the coming years Lucy would meet Edward, as Prince of Wales and later as King, privately at both St James's Palace and at Clarence House; he also visited her at Byron Cottage.

At Beaufield over the Christmas and New Year period Lucy had followed in the press the sorry tale of the Schneider Trophy competition, a biennial international air speed race. In 1929 Britain had won the competition for the second time and was due to host the next contest; if it won again it would keep the coveted trophy for good. In 1929 Ramsay MacDonald, as Prime Minister, had indicated that the government would support the 1931 contest, but early in 1931 the government seemed to back-pedal on the grounds of money, feeling that in the currently depressed financial climate the expenditure could not be justified. Without the government's support it seemed almost certain that there would be no Schneider competition. Surprise, indignation and criticism came forth from aviation enthusiasts, the aviation industry and nationalists. The Air Ministry's claim that financial reasons were behind its withdrawal was condemned as short-sighted and illogical, and it was said that the money spent would advance scientific research, boost exports and improve RAF morale, while a British win would prove the country's prowess as a technologically advanced nation, strengthen the Empire, and advance imperial trade and communication.

Pressure mounted as the political right blamed the socialists in the government for their shortsightedness. An important voice in the opposition to the government's intransigence was an air pioneer, the unusually styled Colonel the Master of Sempill. In September 1930 Sempill had set a new record by piloting his plane non-stop from London to Stockholm in twelve hours, and Lucy considered him the bravest man in the world. When the Schneider row was at its peak Sempill took action. Flying to Jersey, he explained the situation to Lucy at Beaufield, and when he asked if she would put up money to fund the competition she agreed immediately. Lady Houston, commented the *Scotsman* when the news came out, was becoming 'celebrated for her dramatic entries upon the scene'. Lucy's reasons for supporting the competition, she informed the press, were 'purely patriotic' and in particular she wished to boost the Royal Air Force, of which she was 'very proud'. She was tired of the 'lie-down-and-kick-me attitude' of the socialist government, which was 'down with the Navy, down with the Army, down with the Air Force, down with our supremacy in India, and down with that wonderful man, Lord Lloyd, because he knew how to rule wisely in Egypt'.

Lucy's belief that MacDonald was behind the government's failure to support the Schneider contest raised her hatred to new heights, and her offer gave her a platform in the press from which to launch a virulent campaign against him. At the end of January Lucy told the press that the government's 'paltry excuse' that they could not afford to host the race made her blood boil with indignation. British people were not 'worms to be trampled under the heels of Socialism', she wrote, and an Englishman was 'equal to three foreigners'. The socialist government, she said, was doing its utmost to make Britain a 'third-rate Power'. Meanwhile, with only eight months to prepare, at the Supermarine Aviation Works near Southampton designer R.J. Mitchell was working on ways to increase the speed of planes that would compete in the Schneider race, scheduled to take place in the Solent on Saturday, 12 September.

As Lucy was making plans to leave Jersey for the *Liberty* she came under fire in a speech by Frederick Montague, Under-Secretary of State for Air. Montague criticised Lucy for wanting the government to spend money at the expense of the 'desperately poor'. Lucy, Montague said, had the 'bad taste to exhibit the worst sides of her political and class prejudice', and he then gloated that she would have to tolerate a socialist government for some time to come. For people such as her, he said, the Labour government was merely a 'hateful interlude, during which only the barest pretence at social decency' was required, but one day the country's workers, the heart of the nation, would stand up against the 'impudence of the present ruling class'. Lucy's swift riposte, widely published, was withering:

> Poor Mr. Montague. I must indeed be a bitter pill for you to swallow after having done everything you possibly could to dish our airmen and prevent them taking part in the contest for the Schneider Trophy to find that you are now dished yourself by a woman's patriotism.

Sarcastically, she added that she had 'foolishly thought' that he would at least have 'tried to assume a virtue, if you have it not, namely, that of attempting to behave as a gentleman'. The right-wing press, concerned that Lucy might withdraw her offer, sprang to her defence and her old friend Sir Philip Sassoon, now chairman of the Royal Aero Club, turned on Montague in a speech in his own Folkestone constituency. Piling one epithet upon another, Sassoon said that Montague's words had been 'astonishing', 'gross and uncalled for', an 'outburst of vulgarity and spite', a 'contemptible' demonstration of 'prejudice and bad temper' and an 'astounding display of bad manners and bad blood'. The country was fortunate that Lucy was 'larger minded than her detractor'.

In February 1931 Lucy joined the *Liberty*, informing the press that she was heading for the Mediterranean but instead departing for the River Seine. There she would remain until June while preparations went ahead for the Schneider event. Lucy had a large, shabby and old-fashioned handbag that she took everywhere. One day in April 1931 Lucy and Miss Ritchie had visited the bank in Rouen and returned with a wad of £350 in £5 notes; the bag also contained important papers and the great emerald engagement ring that Houston had given Lucy. Lucy had stepped from the launch on to the *Liberty*'s gangway and Miss Ritchie was following with the handbag when the launch lurched and the handbag was thrown into the river. Miss Ritchie watched in horror as it hit the water, came open, and disgorged some papers. While Lucy, oblivious, continued up the gangplank, the launch's crew snatched the sinking bag and rescued as many papers as they could. Miss Ritchie was terrified and feared that the money and the ring had fallen out. Back in Lucy's cabin, she asked Lucy, 'Why don't you wear that lovely ring Sir Robert gave you? It always suits that dress you're wearing so perfectly.' To this Lucy replied, somewhat absently, 'Yes, my dear, but where is it? I can't remember where I put it.' Miss Ritchie took the handbag to the window to search the contents and was greatly relieved to find the bundle of bank notes and the ring still inside.

It may have been this year, too, that Lucy had a visit from William Ogden, the jeweller whom Houston had once intimidated in his shop. So valuable a customer was Lucy that Ogden travelled to the *Liberty* in France in person with samples. Lucy had a necklace of white pearls that she loved to add to and Ogden brought four dozen pearls for approval, each with a value of about £300. Sitting up in bed Lucy sorted them out, chose the ones she wanted, and screwed up half a dozen poorer ones in a piece of cotton wool. A few minutes later, Lucy asked Miss Ritchie to tidy up and throw the cotton wool overboard. Later she missed the discarded pearls, but when Miss Ritchie realised the truth Lucy only remarked casually, 'How very stupid of me. Well, I must pay him for them. That's all there is to that.'

Lucy was still aggrieved by Montague's insults and in March, from the Seine, she wrote to Ramsay MacDonald lambasting Montague for insulting her and suggesting that an apology was due. Montague wanted Lucy off his back and a few days later in the House of Commons stated that he appreciated her 'generous and patriotic' Schneider gift. But if Montague had thought that this would mollify Lucy he was sadly mistaken. What she wanted was not an appeasement, but revenge. She wrote to Montague and released her letter to the press. While her tone was humorous, Lucy belittled Montague with biting sarcasm. She was 'embarrassed and bewildered', she wrote, at his words in the Commons: 'What does it mean? Has the leopard changed his spots? Are you beginning to see the error of your ways? Are you sorry and want to be forgiven?' He must once have been a music-hall quick-change artist, she said: 'When I was a young girl my favourite exercise was turning over head and heels every morning before breakfast, but later on I was warned that only in ones youth should this acrobatic feat be indulged in.' She was willing to let bygones be bygones if he strove to make the Royal Air Force first in the world. Tongue-in-cheek, Lucy said that were she not of a 'meek and lamblike disposition' she would institute a libel case and would enjoy cross-examining him personally, and in that the late Houston had said that she was 'deadly'. Montague may have wished that he had kept his mouth shut; little more would be heard of him in relation to the Schneider Trophy contest.

The summer was approaching and Lucy had taken up a new interest: horse racing. Her involvement with the Brinckmans had turned her mind back to the race meetings of her youth and she purchased a horse which ran in Theodore's name. Reflecting Lucy's current enthusiasm for the Royal Air Force, it was called Air Marshal. Envigorated by her return to the Turf she wrote to Pulvermacher in high spirits: 'Here is an adventure! I am horribly ill, but two days ago I decided to see Ascot once again and have secured a house at the side of the course and a box, No. 110. So if you go, do look me up in my box.' Lucy had been out of high society for eight years, she told Pulvermacher, and hence would be an 'unknown quantity. What fun!'

As the decision to go to Ascot had been made on the spur of the moment, she would attend straight from the *Liberty*.'If you see someone looking very nautically attired, you will know it's me!'[32]

Lucy had rented Huntingdon House on the west side of Ascot racecourse; it was a large property, for she had several guests in her party. Charlie Byron was among them and acted as her escort at the four-day event. The first day was bright and sunny and the women racegoers were turned out in fashionably large hats which flapped in the breeze. Lucy had a ticket for the royal enclosure, where she mixed with members of the house party from Windsor; the King, Queen and Prince of Wales were there. The women's pages of the press reported Lucy's visit: 'It has been most interesting to see Lady Houston at Ascot this year. Social gatherings of this type do not, as a rule, appeal to her.' But she had 'seemed thoroughly to enjoy Ascot, and, surrounded by members of the party she was entertaining there, did the whole programme very thoroughly'. Lord Byron acted as her guide and during her visits to the paddock Lucy was 'rarely alone, generally being engaged in animated conversation with notable folk who had been presented to her'. When word went round that she was present people were 'very anxious to have her pointed out to them', but especially those interested in aviation. Never again would Lucy be so well received by so many.

With the excitement of Ascot over, Lucy returned to the *Liberty* and departed for Jersey on 29 June. Despite an eye complaint, she wrote to Pulvermacher, she planned to attend the Goodwood races at the end of July and had already taken a house for the event: 'Getting very sporting!'[33] There would be no visit to Kinrara that year but in any case, Lucy was too busy to take a holiday. The Schneider Trophy contest was fast approaching and the forty or fifty men of the High Speed Flight, captained by Squadron Leader A.H. Orlebar, had gathered at RAF Calshot, situated at the end of Calshot Spit which projected out into the Solent. With Lucy's money the Supermarine company had built two new seaplanes which had been nicknamed 'Fanny' and 'Lucy' after her. Despite their quaint nicknames the Supermarine aircraft were at the cutting edge of aviation technology. The calibre of the French and Italian teams, against which the British were to compete, was unknown, but there was an atmosphere of 'silent confidence' at Calshot. In late August or early September the *Liberty* arrived in the Solent ready for the race, and Lucy hosted T.E. Lawrence as a guest on board. Lawrence – Lawrence of Arabia – was a legendary figure for his work during the Arab Revolt in the First World War but, seeking anonymity, was serving in the RAF under the name of T.E. Shaw. Lucy had probably met him via Lord Lloyd, for the two had remained friends since their war service together in the Arab Bureau.

The task of organising the Schneider contest was huge but by the end of August the 31-mile course was prepared. It was triangular in shape with the start and finish at Ryde and the turning points, at St Helen's Point off the Isle of Wight and at West Wittering, were marked by bright orange pylons 60–80ft high. The pilots would fly it anticlockwise seven times and spectators could view the race from the coasts of the mainland and the Isle of Wight: Portsmouth and Southsea were planning for 500,000 visitors. The event was expected to receive patronage at the highest level, with the Prince of Wales attending and Ramsay MacDonald and other members of the cabinet viewing from on board the aircraft carrier *Courageous*. RAF and navy craft would serve as patrol boats, starting vessels, rescue vessels and First Aid stations. Pleasure steamers, ocean-going liners and private yachts had reserved positions in the Solent and planned to entertain people on board, while the *Liberty* would occupy a prime viewing position near the westerly turning point at Ryde Middle.

But with British arrangements well in hand and time running short, spirits were dampened at Calshot because France and Italy had not confirmed their participation. When they at last did so at the end of August the announcement was greeted with joy and Calshot became a hive of activity, but then, on the very day that the foreign teams were due to arrive, both pulled out. It was a shattering blow. Lucy's response was typically down-to-earth: 'What a fiasco!' When asked why she thought the foreign teams had dropped out, she quipped, 'I think it must because they haven't got a Lady Houston.' But perhaps pressure had been exerted at high levels in order to deprive Lucy of glory. But then it was realised that if the British team flew around the course alone they could claim the trophy outright. Lucy anticipated a 'very thrilling and heartening event' but the truth was that the British had to make the best of a bad job. Now that the event had been downgraded to a British flyover Ramsay MacDonald was not scheduled to attend, and the Prince of Wales cancelled a promised visit to Calshot and stayed on in Biarritz with friends. On 10 September, two days before the event, Lucy went ashore from the *Liberty* to meet the Schneider team. She commiserated with Orlebar on the 'maddening' withdrawal of the French and Italians, but admired the 'artistry' of Britain's blue and silver Supermarine S6.b aircraft, saying that she took their mechanical perfection 'for granted'.

By now Lucy's friends and relations were gathering on the *Liberty*. They included a number of young people, among whom were her niece, Cicely Radmall and the two sons of Lucy's friend Lady Cynthia Colville, Woman of the Bedchamber to Queen Mary. It was typical of Lucy, Wentworth Day wrote, that when she invited her 'favourite step-son' Roderick Brinckman, she added, 'You can bring two friends with you – but make sure they are good looking!' The Ranee of Pudukota and her son also stayed on board for ten days, and when Comyns Beaumont arrived he found himself among a cheerful and enthusiastic party. Lucy was in high spirits but never a day passed without her hurling invective at Ramsay MacDonald. 'He is not even fit to black the King's boots,' she declared, and one day at teatime when cutting a cake she remarked, 'I wish this were Ramsay MacDonald's head!'

The great day arrived and the Solent and Spithead area were crowded with boats while the *Liberty*, festively arrayed in flags, was in place near the Ryde Middle turn. Unfortunately the weather was misty, wet and windy. Few spectators had turned out and with visibility reduced to only 1 mile it was not a good day for flying. The decision was made to reschedule the flight for the following day. To the relief of everyone, Sunday, 13 September dawned bright and clear. Spectators arrived in great numbers and the coastlines were black with people. The flyover began and the Supermarine seaplane completed the course successfully, with an average speed of 340.08mph, beating the previous best speed of 328.63mph. In the national gloom the event had literally given people something to cheer about, and the Schneider Trophy belonged to Britain for all time. That evening the *Liberty* was brilliantly lit up, with the word VICTORY picked out in lightbulbs and displayed amidships in letters 6ft high. Lucy could not then have guessed, Allen wrote, that the Schneider Trophy flight had been the 'supreme moment' of her life. During the Second World War it would be believed that her funding had been crucial in the development of R.J. Mitchell's Spitfire, which would contribute to British victory. Lucy was dubbed the 'Fairy Godmother of the RAF' until the day of her death, Wentworth Day wrote, and all RAF aircraft that flew over Byron Cottage or the *Liberty* dipped their wings in salute to the woman who had saved British honour and raised the prestige of the air force.

As a gesture of thanks for financing the event the Admiralty had offered Lucy naval moorings between Portsmouth and Cowes. With the *Liberty* lying near a busy sea route plied by ferry boats, Lucy had an idea. She gave orders for the VICTORY sign to be taken down and the words TO HELL WITH RAMSAY MACDONALD displayed instead. That night when the sign shone brightly out over the sea the port authorities were horrified, and the port admiral of Portsmouth called on Lucy to request that she remove the offending message. Lucy was all smiles as she argued that what she did on her yacht was her own business, but the official replied that the Admiralty could not turn a blind eye to her violent attack upon the Prime Minister. When Lucy refused to take down the sign the port admiral said that he would have to remove the *Liberty* by force. 'Thank you, Admiral,' Lucy replied calmly. 'It seems to be the only way, doesn't it?' The yacht was towed to another mooring from where the sign shone out across the Solent uncontested. Within a couple of weeks, exhausted after all the excitement, Lucy retired to the Seine. Basking in the success of her Schneider venture, she wrote to Oscar Pulvermacher:

> Dear Editor, You have been doing me proud in the *Daily Mail*. So dear and nice of you. I am *prostrate* with popularity! I have come here to hide and recover (pray keep it dark). Sack loads of letters, taking hours even to open and everyone enthusiastically delighted. I am told all the young men *adore me* for what I have done. Now, after a little breathing space, my next move must be to get this Government out and it's going to happen.

With the Schneider Trophy contest over, at the age of 74 and with chronic ill health, Lucy threw her energies into preparing for the general election that was due on 27 October 1931. Aboard the *Liberty* she worked out a two-pronged strategy by which she would give financial backing to favoured political candidates while at the same time undermining Ramsay MacDonald. Returning to Byron Cottage, she launched her campaign by announcing that she would support anyone willing to stand as an independent Conservative. Eleonora Tennant, a society figure, responded and her husband Ernest Tennant accompanied her to Byron Cottage. In his later account he wrote that he thought Lucy a caricature of a 'once beautiful barmaid putting on a "grand manner act"'. Although Eleonora committed herself to standing for the Silvertown division of West Ham, a strongly Labour dockland constituency, she and Lucy were equally strong in character and Lucy soon withdrew her support, leaving Eleonora to continue on her own.

Lucy's second strategy, that of attacking Ramsay MacDonald, gained national attention. In the previous general election of 1929, MacDonald had stood as a Labour candidate to win his seat at Seaham with a huge majority. In its efforts to address financial problems caused by the great depression, MacDonald's second Labour government had lost the support of much of his own party. His decision to head a new National Government of all parties in August 1931 had caused a split in the Labour Party, which then mostly deserted him. To consolidate the National Government's position MacDonald had called a general election; he was standing for Seaham again but this time as a National Labour candidate. The constituency, centred on the small coastal town of Seaham in County Durham, contained twelve coal mines, and 80 per cent of the voters were from mining families. The area was depressed and the *Daily Herald* reported that it seemed that the one hope and inspiration of the people was 'Labour idealism'. Seaham had previously been a safe seat for MacDonald, but things had changed. The Prime Minister had not only been ejected from the Labour Party but had earned the wrath of voters by his support of cuts in unemployment benefit – and there were 5,500 unemployed miners in his constituency.

Another factor was Lord Londonderry, who owned three mines in the area. It was reported that MacDonald, who had long preached the nationalisation of mines, was now on the same side as the right-wing Londonderry; certainly he had put him in the cabinet. Complicating the connection was MacDonald's rumoured affair with Londonderry's wife Edith, and some felt that MacDonald was turning into a Tory. It was by no means clear that he would keep his seat.

MacDonald and his daughter Ishbel received a cool welcome when they arrived at Seaham in mid-October for the election campaign. Local feeling was running high and a reporter saw the slogans 'MacDonald, traitor' and 'MacDonald, baby-starver' chalked on a wall. Even the socialist *Daily Herald* gave him a bad press. MacDonald, it reported, 'argues, pleads, is defiant, angry, full of compassion for the distressed', but his audiences of Seaham miners were 'sullenly apathetic', and no wonder, for what he said did not ring true. MacDonald's opponents were William Coxon for Labour, and George Lumley, a communist. Coxon, a respected village schoolmaster, was favoured by the *Herald* and also supported by some local Conservatives, as they did not have their own candidate.

The political parties had recognised the vote-catching value of moving candidates speedily between speaking engagements and it was planned that aircraft would play an important role in election campaigning. Two Puss Moth aeroplanes, it was reported, were to be supplied for MacDonald and Ishbel, and it was perhaps this that gave Lucy the idea for a madcap scheme. The strange story of Lucy's Seaham escapade began early on the morning of 16 October, ten days before election day, when she telephoned her great-niece 'Boo' Catty, who was still in bed. Boo must have been bemused by Great-Aunt Lucy's order to immediately charter an aeroplane and fly to Seaham with Cicely Radmall, Lucy's niece. When they arrived, Lucy instructed them, they should arrange for one of them to be adopted as an independent candidate to fight Ramsay MacDonald.

At eight o'clock that same morning Captain Gordon Olley, a charter pilot employed by Imperial Airways at Croydon Airport, received a telephone call from a young lady who wished to be flown to Seaham. Olley, as Imperial Airways' oldest pilot, had clocked up a million flight miles, and Boo Catty's request was all in a day's work. When Olley met his passengers at Hendon airport with his de Havilland 50 single-engined biplane he was surprised to find that they were 'almost school girls'; in fact, both were under the age of 20. The girls climbed into the enclosed four-seater cabin along with the flight engineer while Olley sat behind in the open cockpit. As Wentworth Day commented, it needed little imagination to picture the 'bewildered plight of these two charming but courageous girls, dispatched by air – in the days of flying orange boxes – to fight the Prime Minister of Britain, at the behest of the most militant aunt in the world'.

The morning was bright and clear as the de Havilland ascended from Hendon to begin the 230-mile flight to Seaham. Two hours later, Olley circled Seaham and brought the plane down in a field about a mile and a half from the town. He, Boo and Cicely got out and walked to the nearest road, where Olley flagged down the first car that came along, the driver of which happened to be the special correspondent of the *Daily Herald*. It seemed too much of a coincidence. The paper opposed MacDonald and had a large readership. If Lucy gave it an anti-MacDonald story it would be an excellent means by which to influence socialists against him. It seems not unlikely, therefore, that she had tipped off the newspaper. Indicating the two young women, Olley told the reporter that he had brought them from London: 'They are anxious to get to Seaham Harbour as soon as possible.

Could you give them a lift?' The reporter agreed, and on the way gathered that the girls had come on behalf of a Conservative or Conservatives to help Mr MacDonald. They did not know what they were going to do but knew the matter was urgent, and asked to be dropped at the Conservative headquarters. When told that there was no such thing, and that MacDonald had 'practically no chance of holding the seat', they seemed surprised. Once at Seaham the puzzled reporter dropped the girls off and went on his way.

Alone in a strange town, Boo and Cicely went first to the post office from where they made a long telephone call to Lucy. Then, acting upon her instructions, they asked for the 'Mayor of Seaham', and when told that there was no mayor asked to be directed to the vicarage. The vicar was out but the girls talked to his wife; but when questioned by the *Herald* reporter later she would not reveal the content of the conversation. Later, when the girls met Captain Olley and told him that they wanted to get back to Brighton or Shoreham, he said that it was too late to make the flight that day. At half past seven, therefore, they caught the train to Newcastle, and when the dogged *Herald* reporter followed their trail he found that they had taken first-class sleeping berths on the night express to London. The following morning Boo and Cicely went directly to Byron Cottage where they recounted their adventures. When they had finished, Boo asked, 'Can I go back to Mummy now?' to which Lucy had nodded and replied, 'You can go.'

Meanwhile, the *Daily Herald* correspondent eagerly filed his report, which was printed under the headline 'GIRLS' SECRET AIR DASH TO SEAHAM. RAF PILOT MYSTERY.' The story caused an immediate sensation and urgent questions were asked of the Air Ministry, the Prime Minister's office, and Lucy — were they supporting Ramsay MacDonald's campaign? Lucy's plot, inadvertently or deliberately, had made it appear that public money was being used to help the Prime Minister, for the reporter had mistaken Olley's Imperial Airways uniform for that of the RAF. The Air Ministry issued a flat denial that the RAF had been involved. For the Prime Minister's office Miss Rosa Rosenberg, MacDonald's private secretary, also gave an emphatic denial, adding that the two women had chartered the aeroplane for 'non-political business'. They had been forced down by fog before reaching their destination, and had happened to land in the Prime Minister's constituency. Miss Rosenberg stressed that they had 'nothing whatever to do with the constituency. It was a pure accident that they landed here.' Rosenberg had not been wholly truthful.

Lucy was less forthcoming. When asked by the *Daily Herald* whether she had arranged to send the women to Seaham, she made a carefully worded statement, released on condition that it was printed in its entirety. Lady Houston, it read, could assure the newspaper that 'had she sent the two young ladies who went to Seaham Harbour, it would most certainly not have been to help Mr MacDonald, whom she utterly distrusts'. She then took the opportunity of attacking MacDonald and calling for new leaders for Britain. What had Lucy's intention been? Boo and Cicely had been quite unprepared, with no workable plan, but perhaps that had not mattered if Lucy had been simply wanted to tarnish MacDonald in the eyes of voters. If she had achieved nothing else, the episode had enabled her to criticise MacDonald in the pages of the *Daily Herald*.

On 18 October MacDonald hit back indirectly at Lucy in the press when he advised voters that it was essential that they understood the tactics of opponents, for any 'red herring' to withdraw the attention of electors from vital issues was 'nothing but humbug'. Lucy, doubtless thinking that it was MacDonald himself who spoke 'humbug' or deceptive talk, added the word to her political armoury. Four days before election day Lucy had sent the *Liberty* to display its sign TO HELL WITH RAMSAY MACDONALD off the coast near Seaham. But when the votes were cast and counted, MacDonald had won 55 per cent of the vote and so was returned as MP, albeit with a greatly reduced majority. Across the country the Labour party suffered a huge defeat but nevertheless MacDonald was reappointed as Prime Minister. The National Government was confirmed and, as a coalition that consisted mainly of members of the Conservative Party, the National Labour Party and the Liberal National Party, it would last until 1939.

During November and December Lucy was ill, it was reported, with 'influenza following a nervous breakdown'. When she had recovered she launched a new round of attacks against socialist influence. In in a scathing article in the *Sunday Express* she explained that MacDonald's policy was clear and simple: 'It is only emptying the pockets and bringing down to beggary one half of the community – in order to pay for the pauperisation of the other half.' With MacDonald, she said, Russia was 'always sacrosanct'. Since the First World War he had followed Russia faithfully until now 'filthy Russian grease, filled with ticks (masquerading as butter)' was being dumped in England. She ended: 'Oh, you 555 Conservative members, are you not ashamed of yourselves? Why, the whole lot of you have not the pluck of one little woman.' Then, on New Year's Eve 1931, Lucy addressed the 'Dear People of England' in a letter to the *Bystander*. England, said Lucy, was in 'crying need' of a leader who acknowledged the difficulties that the country was facing and who would work to solve them. Indeed, she wrote, 'I modestly suggest that you might do worse than your humble servant, Lucy Houston.' She backed this up by announcing that the following year, 1932, she would pay income tax for 'patriotic reasons'. As she was domiciled in Jersey she had no need to pay but, she said, she was considering the nation's need.

R.J. Mitchell, designer of the Schneider Trophy seaplanes, was working for Supermarine on its Civil Flying Boat – a huge six-engined craft that would operate cross-Atlantic passenger services. But in January 1932, even as the aircraft's giant skeleton was still surrounded by scaffolding, the government cancelled the project on the grounds of economy. For a comment on the story Lucy was a natural person to ask and she used the opportunity to abuse politicians. This 'further degradation', she said, made the Conservatives in the government look like a 'lot of performing poodles, who stand up on their hind legs and lick the hand that cracks the whip'. She suggested that they 'adorn their Marcelle-waved hair with a white feather, and stick a red flag in their buttonholes'. The cancellation, she added, was a disgrace and a humiliation, in particular as England's money was going to help its enemies, Russia and Germany. Lucy advised people to withhold their taxes until the government agreed to give no more money either to Germany or to 'that useless, stupid League of Nations', and to make a proper outlay on the armed forces. Nevertheless, she did not offer to pay for the Civil Flying Boat.

Lucy then joined the *Liberty* and sailed for the River Seine, where Philip Inman, house governor of Charing Cross Hospital, visited her hoping for a donation. He was shown in to Lucy's cabin and as she rose to greet him he was struck by the 'unusual forcefulness of her glance. Her eyes were deep-set and piercing. They had that looking-through-you quality which challenges the strong and subdues the weak.' Assuming that a man who worked for a hospital would have medical knowledge, Lucy fixed her visitor with this gaze and said by way of a greeting, 'Tell me, Mr Inman, what do you think of castor oil?' Inman, a resourceful man, replied diplomatically that it was a 'most excellent thing in the right circumstances'. While Lucy gave him a lecture on the pros and cons of taking it orally and by injection Inman listened patiently, wondering how to extract money from his hostess. When at last he was able to explain the purpose of his visit, Lucy was pleased: 'So you came especially to talk to me,' she said. Writing a cheque, she handed it to Inman who, glancing at it, was delighted to see that it was for £1,000. But suddenly he recalled a story he had heard that when Lucy had given her death duties cheque to Churchill she had flung her arms around his neck and kissed him; Inman was pleased when this did not happen to him. It was not until he was on the train to Paris that he noticed that the cheque was unsigned. Returning to Rouen the next day, he found that Lucy had been taken ill and was on the point of leaving for Versailles for medical treatment. It took Inman three days and many telephone calls before he was able to see her at the Trianon Palace Hotel and obtain her signature.

Lucy had left the Seine for the last time and from now on would keep the *Liberty* in British waters. Going on to Beaufield, on 1 March she replied to a letter from T.E. Lawrence. He had written to Lucy that she consistently 'bullied the Government' with the result that politicians were now doing what she wanted. This had amused Lucy, who commented: 'My experience is that the more you bully the Government and get the better of it – as I have done on several occasions – the more polite they become.' The truth was, she said, that the government was 'rather frightened' of her but she wished she could do more for England and would keep on 'fighting the good fight to the bitter end'. Many people whom he might think disliked her for her plain speaking actually respected her for it. But for now, she said, she would be a 'perfect lamb' until she was in better health. She added a PS: 'My chauffeur is becoming impertinent (Rolls-Royce). Can you tell me where to get another man? Forgive my asking, but you know everything, so I hope you won't mind.'[34] But something in Lucy's tone suggests unease; her humour seems a little forced and her apology uncharacteristic. Perhaps Lawrence was failing to respond sufficiently to her charm.

There may have been truth in Lucy's claim that politicians were frightened of her for in February Stanley Baldwin, in an attempt to deflect her unwanted attention, had engaged in social diplomacy. At an 'at home' party at 11 Downing Street the guests had included two ambassadors, Viscountess Astor, Lady Diana Cooper and Mr and Mrs Arthur Wrey – Lucy's sister Florence and her husband. A few weeks later, Florence would again be at Downing Street for a charity garden party. But if the Baldwins hoped to influence Lucy through Florence they would be disappointed.

In 1931 Sir Philip Sassoon had become Under-Secretary for Air and discovered the parlous state to which the government's economies on military aviation had reduced the country's defences. When he informed Lucy, such was her concern that Sassoon advised her to make an offer of £200,000 to buy forty aeroplanes for the air defence of London. In March 1932, from Beaufield, Lucy took action. A gale was sweeping the island when she called Miss Ritchie to her bedside and handed her an envelope containing a cheque for £200,000. She instructed Miss Ritchie to take the cross-Channel ferry, go to the private residence of Chancellor of the Exchequer Neville Chamberlain in Eaton Square, and give him the letter personally. Miss Ritchie, perhaps not overly delighted to have this mission foisted upon her, did as she was told. When Chamberlain opened the letter and saw the cheque he looked astounded but very pleased, and Miss Ritchie had the impression that he would accept Lucy's offer. But Chamberlain did not respond immediately and in the coming days Lucy impatiently sent several requests for an answer. One read: 'A cheque of mine for £200,000 has been kicking around your office for the last month and I have not even had the courtesy of an acknowledgement.' Still hearing nothing, on 9 April she went public with the story in an open letter to the chancellor that included the words:

> On the sad heart of Mary – Queen of England – sorrow wrote the word 'Calais.' On my heart love has indelibly written the word 'England,' and this love of my Country makes me bold and not afraid to speak the truth – for the truth is ghastly – England is in deadly peril – her pride has been dragged down into the dust by Socialism.

After months of meditation, Lucy wrote, she was tired and distressed. She had repeatedly asked God whether she was right to fight for the glory and welfare of England, but always the answer came, 'Yes. You are right. Fight on.' It was 'treachery', she said, to cut England's defence forces further: 'No, no, no, Mr Chamberlain. You must not allow this to be called economy. This is no economy. This is a base betrayal of the people's safety.' Evil spiritual powers, Lucy wrote, were mustering against England and in two years Russia would have an army 30 million strong. Money was being wasted on building labour exchanges when £5 million would secure the defence of the nation, and Lucy had offered £200,000 of it. The publicity spurred Chamberlain into action to reject Lucy's offer. The problem seemed to be that she had set conditions on how the money should be spent, but where 'essential State services' such as defence were concerned the government wished to retain freedom of action and decision. However, Chamberlain suggested that if Lucy removed her stipulations he might yet accept the money.

Lucy was furious. She replied immediately, pulling apart Chamberlain's letter point by point in a biting and sarcastic response. 'Please forgive me,' she wrote, 'I evidently have made a mistake. I thought you were a Conservative, but I cannot imagine a Conservative refusing my offer of £200,000 for the Army, Navy, and Air Force so ungraciously. I wonder whether you have consulted them?' But Lucy did not forget that behind Chamberlain was MacDonald, and privately she fumed to Miss Ritchie that the 'old humbug' hated her so much that he would not take her money. In retaliation against MacDonald, Lucy wrote a leaflet entitled 'What the Prime Minister has Done for England', and had tens of thousands of copies distributed across England. The gist was, of course, that MacDonald had done nothing. Lucy listed his 'evil deeds' in pushing his socialist agenda, for example by trying to foment strikes during the First World War in order to force the government to make peace with Germany. MacDonald had also blocked the Schneider Trophy competition but, 'I, fortunately, was able to step in and prevent this', boasted Lucy. England, she said, had never had an internal enemy 'so implacable, so ruthless, so pitilessly cruel'. She accused Conservative MPs of 'cowardly complacency' in going along with a socialist Prime Minister. Why, she asked, should not Lord Lloyd replace MacDonald, for he 'at least would not empty your pockets to give to Russia'. He was a 'true' Conservative, not a 'humbugging creature' who was bent on ruining the country. 'Three cheers for Lord Lloyd!' she ended. MacDonald, vain and touchy, was angry, and his secretary Miss Rosenberg telephoned Lord Lloyd to ask him to stop Lucy writing such material. Lloyd replied haughtily that he had no influence with Lady Houston but even if he had he would not use it in that fashion. He ended by telling Rosenberg that 'at least Lady Houston is a patriot – which is more than your Prime Minister is'.

The rejection of her defence offer upset Lucy so much that when she arrived back at Byron Cottage from Beaufield in April she was reported to be 'seriously ill'. Her heart had been weakened by the worry, Miss Ritchie told the press, and she was tossing in her bed 'grieving for Britain, and is inconsolable. Her inability to move official circles has proved a great shock to her nervous system. She would give her last farthing to help Britain.' In effect the message was that Lucy's illness was the government's fault. Meanwhile, Miss Ritchie said, thousands of letters by every post congratulating her on her patriotism, many expressing 'extreme disgust' at the chancellor's rejection. One well-wisher was the Prince of Wales, for his comptroller telephoned Byron Cottage to express the prince's regret at Lucy's ill health.

But despite her illness Lucy was building her own racing stable, and chose 'red, with blue sleeves and cap, and white belt' as her racing colours. She named some of her horses herself and in October 1931 sent a telegram to R.B. Bennett, the Canadian Prime Minister, whom she greatly admired, asking his permission to name a horse after him. Bennett agreed to this tribute providing, he said, the horse was a 'good' one. R.B. Bennett was a good one – the best horse Lucy ever owned. He became her great favourite because she thought him as 'courageous and spirited' as his namesake. In July 1932, while the Imperial Conference was taking place in Ottawa, R.B. Bennett won at Gosforth Park and Lucy sent the Canadian premier an embarrassing message:

> Humble greeting from R.B. Bennett, of Newmarket, winner of the North Derby, to his great namesake. May the greatest Derby of the British Empire be now at Ottawa with Free Trade within the Empire, reciprocity, and bumping prosperity. For Britons, both man and horse, are the most glorious race the world has ever produced, and all Britons should feel as proud of their pedigree as I am of mine and of being called R.B. Bennett. God save the King, and three naighs for Ottawa. (Signed) His hoofmark, R.B. Bennett.

At this time Lucy's relationship with R.D. Blumenfeld was still familiar and easy. In June 1932, for example, she sent her regrets at having to cancel a meeting with him. She had been so looking forward to it, she said, but had caught a nasty chill and spent the night 'smothered up with hot water bottles and hot towels trying to get warm – so I dare not leave my bed today – How I hate being always ill!' But by mid-August she had departed to Jersey, where she would stay for several weeks, and from there asked Blumenfeld's help in finding an employee. The man must be a staunch Conservative, she said, but also able to edit the newspaper that she planned to buy and act as her political agent, for she had a plan to intervene in by-elections.

It was a tall order but Blumenfeld knew just the man: James Wentworth Day. And when at the same time Lucy independently asked the Master of

Sempill whether he knew anyone suitable, he too recommended Wentworth Day. Wentworth Day was then 33 years old. Educated at Cambridge University, he had served in France in the First World War and then worked in a variety of roles in a number of national newspapers, but just now was at a loose end. One day Sempill asked for his company on a flight to the Channel Islands, and they took off one bright morning in August 1932 from Hanworth aerodrome to land on the Jersey golf course some hours later. A car, long, sleek and with curtained windows, met the men and drove them up winding lanes to Beaufield. There they were shown into a 'long, pleasant, chintzy drawing-room' to meet a 'bright, charming woman with a disarming smile, brilliant brown eyes' and an 'air of command'. This was Wentworth Day's introduction to Lucy. He recalled later that he had 'never been more impressed by any one person at a first meeting'. With her regal manner and silk turban, Lucy commanded attention. Although 75 she looked a 'hand-some' 45, and was 'sheer dynamite'. She talked like a 'machine-gun, flaying the Government of MacDonald for its weakness'. Lucy was also favourably impressed with Wentworth Day, but six months would pass before she would give him a job.

Towards the end of August, when Lucy left Beaufield, it was for the last time. She perhaps abandoned Jersey because her money had diminished to the point where it was no longer necessary to maintain domicile for tax reasons, or because she had purchased enough of the island to satisfy her desire for revenge. Although she would keep the house on until her death, apart from a housekeeper no staff were kept there; as people continued to write to Lucy at that address, many hundreds of letters would pile up in the rooms, unopened.

BORN TO STRIFE

By mid–September 1932 Lucy was at Kinrara where she entertained a large house party. She also invited Lord Clydesdale who, at the age of 29, was an MP, boxing champion and pilot, to visit her. Clydesdale, who would later become 14th Duke of Hamilton, had an ambition to fly over Mount Everest for the world's highest peak, known as the 'Mistress of the World', was still unconquered by land or air. Advances in aviation technology had made overflight of the mountain seem within reach and it had been the dream of pioneering aviators in Britain, Germany, Italy and America. However, many in Britain felt that for the sake of imperial prestige, if anyone should attempt to fly over the summit of Everest it should be the British. Some months previously Clydesdale and his associate Colonel Latham Stewart Blacker had sketched out plans for a flight backed by a group that included the Master of Sempill, Colonel P.T. Etherton and John Buchan. When the scheme had run aground owing to financial problems, Clydesdale had been given the task of approaching Lucy for, as he was young, good looking and the son of Lucy's old Suffragette friend Lady Hamilton, it was thought that he would have the best chance of success. He had met Lucy earlier that year and she, enthralled by the romance of the scheme, had agreed to assist in principle. Their discussions during the Kinrara visit would mark the beginning of the Houston-Everest Expedition which, in Lucy's lifetime, many would regard as her most significant achievement.

Upon his arrival Clydesdale charmed Lucy by dressing in his kilt; he looked like 'Bonnie Prince Charlie – a true Scottish chief in all his panoply', she told the press. In Lucy's bedroom after dinner they discussed the Everest adventure and Clydesdale set out its benefits, which were as imperialist as even Lucy could have wished. Everest was the last great air challenge, but Clydesdale's desire to conquer the mountain by air was not just because it was there. The overflight, he said, would be the ultimate imperial achievement, in particular promoting British prestige in India. Whereas Indian nationalist leaders were telling the people that the British were becoming degenerate, the flight would prove that they were still virile and energetic. Britain's right to rule would be reasserted and the flight would also harness modern technology as a symbol of national prestige to provide a practical display of British supremacy. These arguments were music to Lucy's ears and she offered Clydesdale £100,000. 'What a lucky boy you were to catch me in the right mood to help you,' she would remark to him later.

The Houston-Mount Everest Expedition project went ahead and the flight itself was pencilled in for April 1933, but the *Tatler* wondered why it was that it had been left to Lady Houston, a private individual, to finance the scheme and hence promote Britain: 'The suspicion that something must be wrong in the country whose major enterprises must be financed by one person cannot be avoided. It seems that Governments of Great Britain can interfere, but can never help.' On Lucy's part, the Everest project spurred her to new attacks on the government in general and Ramsay MacDonald in particular, and her article 'Failure', which appeared in the *National Review* on 1 October, drew a rare response from the Prime Minister in the House of Commons.[35] He had seen, he said, an article by a 'lady who signs herself "Lucy Houston," and she is not only "Lucy," but very lucid as well'. Perhaps thinking it better that people should laugh with him rather than at him, MacDonald quoted Lucy: '"The Spider of Lossiemouth" ["whoever that may be", he added] has so woven his web as to entangle every Imperialist fly.'

From Kinrara in October and November, Lucy sent a barrage of telegrams and letters to Lord Lloyd urging him to push himself forward in politics. Indeed, galvanised by her funding and encouragement, he was at that time becoming increasingly prominent through articles, radio broadcasts and speeches in the House of Lords and around the country. Warning of the dangers presented by the League of Nations, the Soviet Union and Indian independence, Lloyd called for rearmament in Britain; he was described by one newspaper as an 'independent thinker, a forceful speaker, and a hard hitter'. Lucy was delighted with Lloyd's rise and behind the scenes was agitating for him to aim higher, urging him to make moves towards becoming Prime Minister. However, at the same time Lucy believed that Blumenfeld was trying to block Lloyd. On 21 October she sent Lloyd a telegram: 'Blumenfeld is against you I beg of you not to listen to him now is the moment to strike my intuition which always plays me true says this do be guided by me.'[36] She followed this up with a longer note. Blumenfeld, she wrote, was against her but he was '*wrong*. I pray you not to heed him – you know how right I have always been.'[37]

In a further letter she advised Lloyd that if people asked him whether he wanted to be Prime Minister he should say 'yes at least I am not a traitor and at best I believe the country wants a MAN who loves it and I believe I could save England in this its deadly peril. Don't be talked down I implore you.' In another she wrote: 'My advice to you is that now is the moment for action and very strong action.' She recommended that he run a speaking campaign in the north of England with others such as Henry Page-Croft and Colonel John Gretton (Gretton's nephew) who were sympathetic to their cause. 'I have prepared the way for you by recommending you as you know therefore am sure you would receive a great reception,' Lucy said. Lloyd's campaign, she suggested, should be entitled 'What we all Want is Prosperity' and should set out the 'good old fashioned conservative policy' which, Lucy was convinced, was the only thing that could save the country: 'The people are aching for a leader they can trust.'[38] The next day she wrote again to put even greater pressure on Lloyd: 'You are the right man to be PM,' she insisted, and if he was, she reasoned, why should he not say so? He should go round England and get people to follow him, his motto being *L'audace toujours l'audace et encore l'audace* ('Audacity, then again audacity, always audacity').[39]

But perhaps Lloyd found Lucy's intense efforts to manipulate him intolerable, for he was planning to leave the country. Whether by coincidence or design, Lloyd had recently been appointed a director of the British South Africa Company and in early December he and his wife left England for a three-month tour of Rhodesia (modern-day Zimbabwe) to learn about the potentials of copper production. Lloyd was not the first man to seek to evade Lucy's attentions and he must have hoped that by the time he returned to England she would become preoccupied with other matters. Perhaps Lloyd's departure upset Lucy, for after it, back at Byron Cottage, she suffered from vertigo so bad that her Christmas engagements were cancelled. But when a midnight matinee was held in aid of Charing Cross Hospital, Lucy sent a donation of £1,000 and a telegram that included a rhyme entitled 'My Aim':

I strive for all, for I was born to strife,
And, being fearless, strife has saved my life.
But now I strive as I have never striven,
To bring this dear land one step nearer heaven.

It was not until 7 January 1933 that Lucy at last asked Wentworth Day to work for her. Telephoning him before he had even got out of bed, she demanded furiously, 'Have you seen what they're doing to that poor man in East Fife?' This was a reference to Mr J.L. Anderson, a farmer who was standing as an independent candidate in a by-election in the Scottish constituency. Anderson had been bitterly attacked in the press, and Lucy asked Wentworth Day to go and fight for him. But Wentworth Day, a keen sportsman, had arranged to go pheasant shooting with his friend Lord Mandeville at Kimbolton Castle over the weekend. Lucy would have none of it: 'If a thing's worth doing, it's worth doing at once,' she snapped.

And so Wentworth Day hurried round to Byron Cottage, where he found Lucy striding impatiently up and down the drawing room wearing a crimson dressing gown and a silk turban that had a large emerald pinned to it. They set to work. Lucy had written a pamphlet entitled 'Free Trade!' for distribution in East Fife but Wentworth Day had to fight with her over the removal of six 'glaring' libels. With that settled, Lucy rummaged in her handbag and gave Wentworth Day £60 for expenses. It was, she said, the weekend housekeeping money, and her servants would have no wages and she would have nothing to eat. Wentworth Day dashed off to a printer and requested a rush-job for thousands of Lucy's pamphlets plus hundreds of copies of a large poster, to read 'Lady Houston's Advice to East Fife'. He then hastened to King's Cross to catch the night sleeper to St Andrews, the main town in the East Fife constituency. From now on Wentworth Day would get no rest. Once hired, he wrote later, he became Lucy's 'spokesman, "personal representative," political buccaneer, editor and general whipping-boy'.

The next day Wentworth Day stepped down from the train at St Andrews to find the town deep in snow. He sprang into action, hiring a Highland pipe band and taking on twenty unemployed men to put up placards and post Lucy's pamphlets – there were three – through every letterbox. The pamphlets must have amused or bemused the town's citizens. The 'Free Trade!' one included the text:

The spiritual home of politicians must be – Hades! For the Bible tells us that Satan is the Father of all Liars. And – FREE TRADE – is about the biggest LIE that was ever invented.

During the First World War, Lucy continued, Ramsay MacDonald had supported Russia, but it was Russia which had dragged the tsar and his family into a 'filthy dungeon – knee deep with human blood and entrails – and FOULLY MURDERED THEM'. If politicians were so fond of Russia they should be sent there, 'en route for their Spiritual Home', Lucy said.

A second pamphlet, entitled 'Trickery', stated that Lucy considered it a trick by the Conservative central office to put up a National Liberal candidate in East Fife. What the people there really wanted was a Conservative farmer to represent them, because he understood that the hopeless and bankrupt position of local farmers was owed to Ramsay MacDonald's 'criminal want of interest'. The third pamphlet was 'Lady Houston's message to the Women (You may let your husband read this if he is good)'. In it Lucy blamed socialism and the Labour Party for the ruination of farming and the nightmare of unemployment that had brought workers near to starvation. As for Liberals, they were 'bare faced swindlers', while the National Government was a 'sham, a fraud, a humbug, and a make-believe, and is most certainly not national'. Lucy appealed to readers to return to the old true Conservative policy and 'stop playing about with three different parties at once' in the National Government.

As Wentworth Day began his campaign, on 9 January Lucy wrote again to T.E. Lawrence in reply to a letter from him. Lawrence had told Lucy something about Lord Londonderry which had 'utterly disgusted' her but, she said, Londonderry was 'entirely under the thumb' of his wife, who 'as all the world knows, is devoted to the Spider of Lossiemouth'. Lucy suggested that Lawrence join the *Liberty*, for she had discharged Captain Sinclair, who had turned out to be a 'wrong 'un'. Against doctor's orders, she told Lawrence, and 'still beastly ill', she had been writing anti-MacDonald material, and enclosed a copy of what was probably the 'Free Trade!' pamphlet. 'I am doing my worst against Ramsay, as you see,' she wrote. 'I hope it will help to oust him, but he is one of Satan's own disciples.' Lord Lloyd ought to be 'on the spot fighting, but he is away at distant Bulowayo, where I sent him an S.O.S. the other day'. She signed off, 'Yours very tired, but full of mischief,' and added a PS: 'I am now boycotted by the whole press – evidently <u>by order;</u> this is the freedom of the Press.'[40]

Wentworth Day would spend a total of ten days in East Fife, holding six meetings a day and speaking himself hoarse. He also had to spend five nights on the Flying Scotsman sleeper train while commuting between St Andrews and London in order to consult Lucy in person; she did not trust the postal or telephone services. Convinced that her telephone lines were tapped and her telegrams read, she adopted various methods to try to evade the government 'spies' whom she believed were watching her. Therefore, when Wentworth Day sent a telegram to Byron Cottage it had to be addressed to Miss Ritchie and signed 'Vickers' (Lucy thought that that company made good guns) and when he rang her they used the same false names. Wentworth Day's life became further complicated when Lucy set him to fight on a second front at the same time. A by-election campaign was being fought in the Liverpool Exchange constituency with the election day set for 19 January, two weeks before that of East Fife. One dark, wet evening, Wentworth Day attended a Labour meeting held in a 'packed and dingy hall with the trams clanging outside, the cobblestones glistening and class-hatred sizzling'. When he called out and insulted the Labour candidate as a foreigner and a criminal, the response was electric. He was chased from the building and down the street where he slipped on wet cobblestones and narrowly escaped being run over by a tram. His glasses were smashed and he had blacked an eye, but he scrambled to his feet and escaped down a side street.

When he reported to Lucy at Byron Cottage the next day she was curious to know what the socialists and communists of Liverpool thought of her. Recalling the 'blistering obscenities' that had been uttered, Wentworth Day was embarrassed: 'Dreadful names,' he replied, 'I couldn't possible tell you.' When Lucy asked why not, he said, 'Well – er – you're a woman, after all.' 'Heavens!' Lucy replied, 'I've had three husbands and God knows how many lovers – I ought to know *what* men say.' Then, fishing about in her capacious handbag, she took out a crumpled envelope of cheap paper. Inside it was a badly written letter. Patting the blond curl that peeped out below her turban, and with a 'sly, anticipatory' look, Lucy read out the first line: 'You old whore from Camden Town …' She lowered the paper and turned to Wentworth Day with a 'guileless, dimpling smile' and remarked sweetly, 'And, d'you know, my dear boy, I don't think I've ever been to Camden Town in all my life! *Now*, perhaps you'll have the moral courage to tell me what they *call* me.'

Sporting the black eye sustained at Liverpool, Wentworth Day went to Pratt's Club and had just sat down to dinner when Winston Churchill arrived with a friend. Greeting the room with his usual 'Good evening, noblemen and gentlemen,' Churchill cast a penetrating eye on Wentworth Day and introduced as his guest Admiral of the Fleet Sir Roger Keyes. To Keyes he said, 'This is my young friend, Wentworth Day – Lady Houston's kept man! You observe the love token in his eye?' Recalling this years later, Wentworth Day said that he had never lived it down. Next morning he told Lucy the tale. 'Tell Mr. Churchill, my dear,' she chuckled, 'that I am flattered. So should *you* be too! Tell him also, that alas, it's twenty years too late.'

Wentworth Day returned to East Fife but his punishing schedule in the freezing air of Scotland was taking its toll. On his tenth day in the constituency he held sixteen open-air meetings conducted from a 'flying squad of cars with pipers, drummers and flute players to collect the crowds'. It was the last straw; he went down with double pneumonia. The next morning a telegram arrived from Lucy, which read:

> So sorry hear you are ill dear boy all because you overwork told you not to overwork don't be a fool remember castor oil the panacea for all ills take a teaspoonful in half an orange then you won't taste it bottle follows by post get your own orange love Lucy Houston.

The bottle did indeed arrive and Lucy even rang the hotel manager to check that Wentworth Day had taken his dose. With Wentworth Day out of action there was little more that Lucy could do in East Fife, and when the votes were counted on 2 February it was found that despite – or perhaps because of – Lucy's support, Anderson had obtained only 4,400 votes and the Liberal National candidate had won by a large majority.

In another effort to influence public opinion, in February Lucy wrote to Randolph Churchill, the 21-year-old son of Winston Churchill, who was writing a series of articles for the *Sunday Express*:

> I always read what you write every Sunday – because what you write is worth reading but I am sorry to see that you – young as you are – are showing the cloven hoof – or shall I say the fatal flaw of the Churchills' character.

His fault seemed to be that although two weeks earlier he had been 'preaching Conservatism' he was now 'lauding Liberalism'. 'Now my dear boy,' Lucy continued, 'take an old woman's advice and make up your mind which Party you stand for and fight for it – tooth and nail – and never have a word to say in praise of your opponent.'[41] Randolph replied two days later. He had long admired Lucy, he said, for her opposition to MacDonald and her campaign for a 'genuine' Conservative Party, and was therefore distressed that she had detected in him the 'cloven hoof'. He hastened to assure her that she was mistaken, for, rather than lauding Liberalism, he had merely been praising the courage and enthusiasm of some young Liberals with the purpose of motivating the young men of the Conservative Party. With an audacious piece of flattery he added, 'Sometimes I have felt that you and I are the only two real Conservatives left in this defeatist world. We must not start detecting the cloven hoof in each other.'[42]

During the winter much work had been done on the planning of the Houston-Everest Expedition. The organising committee was distinguished and included Earl Peel, a former Secretary of State for India, as chairman, and Colonel Etherton as honorary organising secretary. Other members were Maharaja Jam Saheb of Nawanagar, Chancellor of the Chamber of Indian Princes; John Buchan, the novelist and politician; R.D. Blumenfeld as Lucy's representative; and Lord Clydesdale as chief pilot. There were a number of political snags, one being that the kingdom of Nepal did not want the responsibility of making rescue efforts in the event of a mishap over Nepali territory. However, assistance had been offered by the India Office and the Government of India, while the Air Ministry was also lending its support. Lucy, meanwhile, was closely involved at every stage of the planning; indeed, *The Times* reported that she was the 'moving spirit' of the project. But when the newspaper reported that she had proved a 'most valuable ally and counsellor', it was a polite way of saying that she had poked her nose into everything. Samuel Hoare, at that time Secretary of State for India, would write later that Lucy had had to be 'constantly humoured'. RAF officers had to keep her updated but were embarrassed when she received them at Byron Cottage 'dressed in a pink silk nightdress and lying on a highly decorated bed'.

It was probably during the winter of 1932–33 that two young American brothers, Stewart and Joseph Alsop, visited London. They stayed at the Cavendish Hotel in the City of Westminster, and twenty years later wrote an account of their time there for the *New York Herald Tribune*.[43] The Cavendish was run by Rosa Lewis, whose family origins were similar to those of Lucy although she was ten years younger. Lewis had worked her way up via her culinary skills and bought the Cavendish in 1902. By the early 1930s, the Alsops remembered, the hotel was a fashionable 'half-bar, half-salon', and Lewis, in her mid-60s, still retained a little of her beauty. With its 'decidedly odd clientele', the Cavendish was an interesting place for foreign visitors. The famous society painter Augustus John might walk in, or guests coming from a court ball, the women 'glittering with diamonds' and wanting a drink after closing hours. In the midst, Rosa Lewis presided with an air of 'rakish grandeur'.

During the First World War Lewis had cleverly developed a system whereby rich guests paid for the entertainment of military personnel, and it was because of this tradition that Lucy patronised the Cavendish after the Schneider event. The Alsops saw her there frequently, always escorted by young RAF men. When Lucy came in Lewis would murmur to other guests, ''ere comes the old trout again! Richest woman in England, she is! Now I arsk you, has the good Lord any brains, the way he hands money out?' But Lewis was polite to Lucy's face for she valued her custom. The Alsops, too, gained a bad impression of Lucy for she seemed 'one of the very oddest fish' among the strange array of guests. They described her as a 'plump, rad-dled, foolishly bedizened middle-aged woman, strangely hung about with jewelled chains and little bits of lace and unexpected clumps of silk flowers'. It was not a kind observation, although 'middle-aged' was generous, for Lucy was in her mid-70s. Her escorts 'submitted and even heavily responded' to her 'continuous flow of coquetry' and often, when she had drunk a little too much champagne, her chatter would be 'rather appallingly transformed into girlish flirtatiousness'. Lucy, the Alsops remembered, had been 'more ludicrous than pathetic' and as 'nutty as a fruitcake'.

By the end of January 1933 the Everest plans were well advanced. It was arranged that the expedition would travel to Purnea in the state of Bihar, 160 miles from Mount Everest, where it would establish a base camp from which the attempt over Everest would be made in two adapted Westland biplanes. The pilot was seated in an open cockpit while behind him the observer/cameraman would occupy a separate, closed cockpit. For the purposes of photography and filming the observer's cockpit would have windows on either side and in the floor. The round trip between the Purnea base and Everest was expected to take six hours, in which time the planes would climb to 36,000ft. As the expedition was 'all-British', using only British aeroplanes, engines and material, it represented an acid test of the nation's aeronautic expertise. Breathing apparatus had been developed, and the danger of frostbite would be countered with heated suits. Electrical heating was also needed for goggles, cameras and the aeroplanes' valves. Disaster could not be ruled out and measures for an emergency landing had been taken; 'iron rations' and stoves for heating and cooking were to be carried. But the hard truth was that for much of the time the aircraft would be out of radio contact, and even if the occupants managed to survive a landing in the high mountains, rescue would probably be impossible.

On 9 February the dismantled Westland aeroplanes were packed into crates and loaded into the SS *Dalgoma* at London docks for the long sea voyage to Karachi in British India; the team members would make their way by different routes. Three small Moth aeroplanes, which would be used for reconnaissance and communications in India, were piloted to India by Clydesdale and two others. Flying with the airmen would be *The Times* special correspondent attached to the expedition, and the wife of the expedition leader, Air Commodore P.F.M. Fellowes. When Lucy first heard that Mrs Fellowes was accompanying her husband she was furious. Ringing Blumenfeld, she told him that *she* was financing the expedition and he had no right to allow a woman to go without her permission. Blumenfeld saw red and said to Miss Ritchie, 'Tell Lady Houston that if she wants to criticise me, I don't want to have anything more to do with her.' When Miss Ritchie relayed this message Lucy burst into tears: 'Oh! He's such a dear, good man. I wouldn't upset him for anything. Go straight down to the *Daily Express* in the car at once and see if you can pacify him.' When Miss Ritchie was shown into Blumenfeld's office and explained her mission, Blumenfeld smiled broadly and said, 'I don't envy you your job, having to run round London trying to pacify people like me! Now pop back to Lady Houston and tell her from me that she's a very naughty girl – but I'll forgive her this time and love her still.' When Miss Ritchie delivered this message Lucy clapped her hands with delight.

As the planes and team made their way to India, Lucy returned her attention to by-election politics. Wentworth Day's next destination was Rotherham, where a by-election was to be held on 27 February. Again he heckled at a socialist meeting and was chased outside and rolled in the snow by women who stuffed Lucy's pamphlets down his trousers, nearly pulling them off. The next

by-election would be at Ashford in Kent, where the polling day was scheduled for 17 March. When Wentworth Day went to Byron Cottage to receive
his instructions he found Lucy sitting up in bed stitching scarlet ribbons on
to white cloth to make a banner for the campaign. At Ashford there was an
independent witness to Wentworth Day's campaigning, whose anecdote suggested that matters were not always as lively as Wentworth Day remembered.
W.F. Deedes, a cub reporter only 19 years old, had been sent to cover the
by-election for the *Morning Post*. One afternoon in the High Street he saw
Wentworth Day standing on a soapbox, 'addressing a solitary farming figure
in a tweed hat who held his collie by a piece of binder twine'. As Deedes
arrived, the 'dog lay down, settled its head on its forepaws and closed its eyes'.
The most eventful meeting was the one advertised by Lucy's great banner,
36ft long, which spelled out the message: HEAR THE TRUTH ABOUT
THE PRIME MINISTER. COME TO LADY HOUSTON'S MEETING
AT THE COUNTY THEATRE TONIGHT. Wentworth Day hired twelve
men to parade the banner around the town and that evening 1,200 people
crowded into the theatre, where Wentworth Day was the only attraction.
He set out the Prime Minister's record during the First World War, quoting
MacDonald's views of Russia and his denunciations of Britain. Lady Houston,
Wentworth Day announced, would give a reward of £5,000 to anyone who
could prove that in the war MacDonald had been paid by Russia to foment
strikes and unrest in England: 'I brand the Prime Minister as a traitor to this
realm,' he thundered.

Meanwhile the Everest Expedition team was gathering at the Purnea base
camp and, *The Times* reported, it had aroused 'immense interest' throughout India. When a reconnaissance flight was made towards the Himalayas,
local people were so amazed at their first sight of an aeroplane that they
took cover. There was a superstitious feeling about the expedition, for as
the preliminary flights began the hill people thought that the gods of the
mountains would not allow the aeroplanes to invade their territory. Once
it became apparent that this was not the case they knelt and worshipped
the 'Flying Gods' as they flew overhead. There had been objections to the
overflight of Everest on the grounds that it would amount to 'blasphemy' to
look down upon the summit, and the British team members had a strange
sense that they were alien interlopers forcing their way uninvited into an
ancient land. Later, in their book about the Everest flights, Clydesdale and
his team member Flight Lieutenant David McIntyre would write that those

who had seen the mountains could more easily appreciate Hindu beliefs that they were the 'sacred places of the gods'.

When the team had settled in at the base camp they made trial and reconnaissance flights, and waited for optimum weather conditions in order to make the attempt. On 26 March Fellowes took *The Times* correspondent up in the Puss Moth to reconnoitre the area. 'We had a clear view of the peak of Everest and the surrounding mountains from 100 miles away', wrote the newspaper man, who watched high winds blow great plumes of snow off the crests of the mighty peaks. Finally, on 3 April the wind died down and everything came together. In favourable meteorological conditions the two Westland aeroplanes took off at 8.25 in the morning. One was piloted by Clydesdale and the other by McIntyre, who carried Mr Bonnett, a cinematographer from the Gaumont Film Corporation, which was intending to make a film of the expedition. Everything went smoothly until Bonnett stood on his own oxygen pipe and fractured it, but he managed to tie his handkerchief round the hole and continue. However, whether for this or other reasons the expedition's cameras did not function for part of the flight and not all the hoped-for pictures were captured. Even so, the great objective was achieved: the two planes circled Everest several times, allowing their occupants to see what nobody had ever seen before. Despite the camera problems, magnificent photographs of Everest were obtained including a close-up of the pinnacle showing its southern slopes. Britain's previous land expedition to Mount Everest had ended in disaster in 1924 with the disappearance of climbers George Mallory and Andrew Irvine on the mountain, and the ridge where it was believed their bodies lay was specially photographed in case there was any sign of them.

Great was the relief and rejoicing at Purnea when the two planes returned after three and a quarter hours. The object of so many months' work had been achieved. The Central News agency telephoned Lucy who, perhaps prostrated by the stress of waiting, was seriously ill in bed, to inform her of the victory. Telegrams of congratulations flooded in but it rankled with the Everest team that they had not collected all the photographic material they had hoped for, and the press began to mention the possibility of a second flight. This made Lucy highly agitated, as the aeroplanes had been insured for only one attempt; she feared that another would end in disaster, in which case she would consider herself personally responsible for loss of life and the dependents of the dead. Lucy tried everything in her power to stop a second flight, characteristically bombarding all involved with telegrams from Byron Cottage. One, to Clydesdale, was widely reported in the press:

> The good spirit of the mountain has been kind to you and brought you success. Be content. Do not tempt the evil spirit of the mountain to bring disaster. Intuition tells me to warn you that there is danger, if you linger.

The expedition's London headquarters also sent numerous telegrams discouraging a second attempt, and as the messages grew more urgent gloom descended on the Purnea team, until finally Air Commodore Fellowes reluctantly gave orders to start packing up.

But then, as the story was told later, Fellowes fell ill with fever and those under him began to conspire. Two elements were needed for a clandestine second flight – good weather and the continuing illness of Fellowes. He had given permission for a short filming flight on condition that the Westlands flew at all times within gliding distance of flat land, but his team decided to interpret this liberally. Going to the aerodrome early in the morning, Clydesdale and McIntyre together agreed to disregard orders and took off. Some hours later the Westlands arrived back at Purnea after a second flight and the truth came out: 'EVEREST FLOWN AGAIN. CLIMAX OF THE EXPEDITION. AN UNAUTHORISED ADVENTURE. SUCCESS AT ALL POINTS,' read *The Times* headline. According to the correspondent, the second flight had been a 'piece of magnificent insubordination. Made in uninsured aeroplanes, and without authority from home it was carried through with the greatest success.' Lucy was 'furious', Wentworth Day wrote. Disregarding the extraordinary pluck and daring of the second attempt, which she would normally have considered virtues, she instead felt that she had been 'defied, ignored and flouted'. However, the photographs from the second attempt revealed a hitherto unknown feature – a mysterious flat black heart-shaped area about 200ft across and 6,000ft below the summit of Everest. The conclusion was reached that it was a 'hot lake' created by warm spring water, and Lucy would be particularly pleased when in 1936 the Nepali government named it *Parvati Tāl*, the 'Lady of the Mountain', in her honour.

THE *SATURDAY REVIEW*

Disgusted with the National Government and the complacency of the Conservatives, Lucy came up with a plan. One day early in 1933 Wentworth Day arrived at Byron Cottage to find her with a look of mischief on her face. She handed him a cheque made out to Lord Lloyd for the sum of £10,000, which she intended to be the first instalment of £100,000 that she would dedicate to founding a new political party, or at least turning out the current government and forming a new one with Lloyd and Winston Churchill at its head. These two, Lucy believed, were the only men who could save England. Wentworth Day took the cheque to Lloyd's house in Portman Square and was shown into a large room where signed photographs of George V and Queen Mary, Lawrence of Arabia and Indian princes and rajahs stood about. Lloyd sprang to his feet and strode across the room to greet him. Wentworth Day thought him 'alight and alive', and had never met any man who made such an 'instant impact of purpose, courage, and magnetic personality. The heroes of Ancient Greece were alive again.' Lloyd said, 'You've a letter for me. I wanted to meet you. I know Lady Houston well – a great woman, a great patriot. I admire her intensely.' His voice was 'clipped, staccato, nasal, compelling'. Wentworth Day handed over the cheque and explained what Lucy wanted him to do with the money. Lloyd looked hard at Wentworth Day, who then understood why 'Arabs and Indians looked on him as a king' and 'plotters quailed before those eyes'.

Lloyd said that he could not accept the money if it came with the condition that he form a new party, but he could use it to launch a nationwide campaign against the India Bill. By this he meant the Indian White Paper then under consideration in parliament, which proposed measures that were in effect a further stage in the process of the transfer of power to the people of India. Did Wentworth Day have any influence with Lucy, Lloyd asked? Wentworth Day replied that he could only urge her to accept Lloyd's view: 'She believes in you utterly.' They talked for an hour and from that time forward were close friends. Back at Byron Cottage, Lucy agreed to what Lloyd had suggested and then gave Wentworth Day an arch smile and asked, 'Don't you think he's perfectly adorable? He walks like a tiger. Did you notice when he crossed the floor?' Lucy boasted that when Lloyd visited Byron Cottage and she kept him waiting he paced the drawing room or the hall impatiently, but once in Lucy's room he was in no hurry to leave.

By this time Lucy had found a publication that was willing to allow her a strong voice. The *Saturday Review of Politics, Literature, Science, and Art*, more commonly known as the *Saturday Review*, had been established in London in 1855 as a Conservative weekly journal. Becoming popular and respected, it had featured the work of such distinguished writers as Anthony Trollope, H. G. Wells, George Bernard Shaw and Oscar Wilde. By 1933 the journal had long been in decline but was regularly publishing Lucy's articles. In March, for example, under the heading 'Knaves or Fools?' she attacked the National Government for 'ineptitude' so clumsy that it would be amusing were its effects not so serious. Prime Minister Ramsay MacDonald, Foreign Secretary Sir John Simon and Conservative Party leader Stanley Baldwin were 'England's three greatest knaves (or fools)', and until they were out of office England was in 'deadly peril'. But the fact that the *Saturday Review* printed such material despite the risk it presented suggests that Lucy was already giving the journal financial support.

In April Lucy retired to the *Liberty*, lying at anchor between Sandbanks and Brownsea Island in the mouth of Poole Harbour, at a site which had replaced the Seine as Lucy's favourite location. Thomas Horder, eminent physician of the rich and famous, made regular visits from London and sometimes stayed overnight on the yacht. He had been raised to the peerage as Baron Horder in January that year but Lucy spared nobody. On one occasion, when Lucy sent for him in the middle of the night, he found her sitting up in bed wide awake with Miss Ritchie at her side: 'I can't sleep, Lord Horder,' she said. 'You must give me something to make me sleep. This poor old head of mine keeps going round and round.' Horder had come prepared and, taking a small bottle from his pocket, tipped a capsule into his hand. Lucy was not pleased: 'What do you mean by handling the stuff you're going to give me? Throw it over the side immediately. Really! For a doctor you ought to know better.' Horder slunk to the open window, threw out the pill, then put a second capsule into a spoon. His manner of approach to Lucy obviously betrayed his feelings, for she snapped, 'What do you think you're doing? Feeding the lions at the Zoo?' The presence of Miss Ritchie, who later related the story, was an added humiliation for the doctor.

At Poole Harbour Lucy sent for Wentworth Day; it was his first visit to the *Liberty* and he found the great white yacht in a wide bay surrounded by hills and woodland. Other yachtsman sailing past, he said, 'little realised that aboard that decorously silent ship an old lady was plotting the overthrow of the Government'. He was conducted to Lucy's room where she had just 'polished off a chop and was finishing a Guinness'. She got straight to the point: 'I want you to buy a newspaper for me, my dear.' She would be proprietor, she said, and Wentworth Day editor, and they would get various sympathetic writers who would include Comyns Beaumont and 'all the wise men', by which she meant Winston Churchill, Lord Lloyd, Leopold Amery and Henry Page-Croft, among others. The newspaper, Lucy insisted, must carry her message into every home in Britain.

Later they had tea on the *Liberty*'s after-deck at a table covered by a Union Jack cloth, and discussed newspapers that might be for sale. One was the *Saturday Review*, the owners of which, journalists Guy and John Pollock and Warner Allen, had tried to restore its prestige but succeeded only in losing money. They were ready to sell. Negotiations ensued and a price of about £3,000 was agreed. Debentures and shares then had to be sold and bought, and for Wentworth Day this meant many visits to the *Liberty* and long talks with Lucy. From this time Lucy would keep the yacht close to the shore for better access to a post office for telegrams and mail; later she would have a telephone landline strung across to the yacht. By early May the sale had gone through and Guy Pollock had agreed to stay on as editor, with Warner Allen working under him. Lucy's acquisition of the *Saturday Review* changed her life dramatically. Over the next three years she would expend great sums upon the journal and work for it with gusto. It immediately cast off its former identity and was given a new tagline, 'The Paper that Puts the Empire First', and at the end of May Lucy set out her views in a leading article:

I belong to no political party. If Communism meant prosperity for England, I should be a Communist. I am described in the *Daily Mail Year Book* as Lady Houston, Patriot, and I am more proud of this description than I should be of the greatest honour that could be bestowed on me.

Also in May, with Lucy's money Lord Lloyd launched his campaign to highlight the importance of India to Britain. He arranged a meeting at Manchester Free Trade Hall and, with the attraction of senior figures Winston Churchill, Leopold Amery, Sir Henry Page-Croft and Lord Hailsham as speakers, it was packed to capacity. Lloyd made a hard-hitting speech condemning the government's reforms which would, he said, result in the handing over of hundreds of millions of Indian people to the 'tender mercies of the Brahmin oligarchy, of Bombay monopolists, of Ahmedabad mill-owners, of usurers more exacting than Shylock, and priests more zealous than Torquemada'.

Lucy had returned to London but early in July 1933 she embarked on the *Liberty* once more. She had hired a new captain, Lionel Dawson, who had recently retired from the Royal Navy. He was probably imagining that his new job would be easy but he had not reckoned on Lucy. She ordered him to bring the *Liberty* into the port of London and anchor the vessel near Tower Pier. When Lucy arrived, Dawson's first impression of his new boss was of a 'strangely impressive but somewhat pathetic little figure'. As she came aboard Lucy waved to some nearby Tower of London Beefeaters, telling Dawson that they had probably heard of her arrival and hence dressed in their best uniforms. However, it was at this point that Dawson fell from grace. The cause of his downfall was Lucy's big untidy leather handbag. As she stepped off the gangway she thrust the bag at Dawson, but when he ordered a cabin-boy to carry it to Lucy's cabin she glared at him and snatched the bag back. There was a short, sharp scene in which Lucy told Dawson to carry the bag himself while he tried to impress upon her that naval officers were not porters. Dawson had failed to realise that to be entrusted with Lucy's handbag was a great privilege and very few beyond Miss Ritchie, Foster the chauffeur, Lord Horder and the captain of the *Liberty* were accorded that honour. But Dawson had sealed his fate and for the next six months Lucy would make his life a misery.

Later, Dawson would publish an account of his time on the yacht under the heading 'Hard to Please. Captain's Difficult Task.' He relates that from the port of London the *Liberty* proceeded down the Thames under sail, he being irritated that Lucy would not tell him their destination until the yacht had steam up. They went first to North Foreland off the coast of Kent but at the end of July a gale forced them into Harwich. Finding the area quiet and pleasant, Lucy would stay at anchor in the River Stour for two months. Dawson, meanwhile, found life on board most irregular. He was expected to be not only captain but also 'steward, butler, sick-nurse, housemaid, bell-boy, and, on lighter occasions, of acting Laurel to her Hardy'. He was frustrated that there was no proper system for obtaining supplies and he had great difficulty in obtaining money from Lucy to buy food for the crew. He resorted to sending a wireless operator ashore to go round nearby farms to buy potatoes and milk. Meanwhile, Dawson found that Lucy did not trust her employees and would spy on them – he probably meant himself.

Lucy had soon tired of Guy Pollock as editor of the *Saturday Review* and wanted Wentworth Day to take over. She invited him to the River Stour and they discussed a new cover for the journal. Roping in the *Liberty*'s carpenter, Lucy called for large sheets of paper and pots of paint to be brought to her stateroom, where she set about creating an eye-catching design in red, white and blue paint from the yacht's stock of paint pots. Lucy depicted the Union Jack 'triumphant' over the red flag of communism: 'And make that Red Flag droop more,' she snapped at the carpenter. 'It's got to feel sorry for itself!' Satisfied at last, she sent the carpenter to London to deliver her work to the printer. Her scheme had to be followed to the last detail, but when the colours from the *Liberty*'s paint pots were difficult to match in ink it was only the first of the myriad of practical difficulties that the printers would face in the coming years. As Wentworth Day wrote, Lucy would transform the *Saturday Review* into a 'flamboyant, hard-hitting, hoydendish termagant' that 'bristled with hard home-truths'. In other words, it became an extension of Lucy's personality.

On one visit to the River Stour that summer, Lucy handed Wentworth Day an envelope with the instruction to take it to her sister in London, and warned him to look after it because it was valuable. Wentworth Day stuffed the envelope into his inner breast pocket and secured it with a safety-pin. As he left in the *Liberty*'s launch a crew member asked him, 'Do you know what you've got in that envelope, sir?' Wentworth Day then learned that he was carrying Lucy's famous black pearls, which were not insured. Back in the River Stour, Lucy was kept awake one night by curlews and suddenly gave Captain Dawson orders to depart. The yacht arrived at Sandgate in the first week of September, anchoring for several days before continuing westwards towards Dorset. All the way, Dawson reported, Lucy 'knew everything – how to steer, how to navigate, how to scrub the decks, how to cook. She told us all our jobs.' Exasperated, he would leave the *Liberty* at the end of the cruise in January 1934.

It was in 1933 that Lucy first became interested in fascism. She, like many others on the British right at that time, had become concerned that capitalism had failed to provide a fair society. Lucy, Allen wrote, disliked democracy, as did many others who had 'risen from the people', and doubted that democratic systems were capable of dealing with the world's problems. For these reasons she was attracted to the idea of leadership by a strong elite, as long as it did not interfere with her own freedoms. She admired the Italian dictator Benito Mussolini, and later Adolf Hitler in Germany, for their achievements in building up their countries and also for their promise to provide a bulwark against Soviet Russia. Lucy delighted in the story of Mussolini having dosed political opponents with castor oil which, among other properties, acted as a laxative. She wrote to the Italian leader: 'You are a wonderful man and have done wonders for Italy. I only wish we had someone to give our Socialists a dose of castor oil as you have dosed your Socialists in Italy.' Mussolini's son-in-law replied politely and Lucy, impressed by this courtesy, named her little Belgian Griffon dog 'Benito'. She also wrote to the *Morning Post* in March 1933 praising Mussolini as a 'strong man who has wisdom and understanding. Bravo, Mussolini! Let us all raise our right hands in Fascist salute to you.'

More ambivalent was Lucy's attitude to Oswald Mosley, Britain's most prominent fascist. Styling himself upon Mussolini, Mosley had launched the British Union of Fascists (BUF) in 1932 in imitation of Italy's National Fascist Party. Mosley visited Mussolini several times and was impressed by his blunt, straight-talking ways and method of rule. While the British had long suffered from 'statesmanship in skirts', Mosley wrote in the *Daily Mail*, it could be said of Mussolini that 'here at least is a man'. At a BUF rally in Manchester in 1933 posters advertised that Mosley would speak 'The Truth at Last', and 2,000 people gathered to hear him declare that 'England is not finished. England is not dead. Send to all the world a message – England lives and marches on.'[44] Mosley's fighting talk attracted many members to the BUF and Lucy too was impressed, for he said what she herself wanted to say.

Lucy's interest in Mosley became known, and in the summer of 1933 a story went round that prompted the well-known cartoonist David Low to produce a cartoon with the title 'Sensational Rumour in Political Journalism'. Published in the *Evening Standard* in September, it showed Mosley at his desk, one arm raised in a fascist salute to pictures of Mussolini and Hitler on the wall, while on other side of the desk sat Lucy, clad as a plump Britannia. In one corner of the cartoon Low depicted himself being asked by another man, 'Is there any truth in this rumour that Lady Houston is going to finance a new paper for Oswald Mosley?' to which he replied, 'Don't know. But it's the solemn duty of all cartoonists to see that there is truth in it as soon as possible.' Although Lucy issued an immediate denial, saying that she was a patriot, not a fascist, there was probably some foundation to the rumour. Stories were going round that Lucy and Mosley, either individually or together, were seeking to buy an island on which to run a radio station. Indeed, Lucy gave Wentworth Day the task of island hunting and he investigated the possibilities of Lundy, 12 miles off the coast of Devon. However, he wrote, Lucy's interest ended abruptly when the Privy Council warned the owner not to sell to her. When questioned by the press, Lucy replied, 'Lady Houston is not buying Lundy Island. England, the island of the blest, is the island she loves.' Lucy then explored the possibility of the *Liberty* becoming a floating radio station, but that idea also came to nothing.

While Oswald Mosley intended to become Britain's Mussolini, Lucy was trying to mould Lord Lloyd into that role, and indeed in 1933 his influence rose to the extent that he and Churchill were together regarded as the unofficial leaders of the Conservative Party's right wing, known at the time as 'Die-Hards'. The two were much in demand, giving hard-hitting and well-received speeches mainly concerned with India and the weakness of Britain's national and imperial defences. Lloyd wrote to Lucy in June that his aim was not so much to attack the government (except on the questions of India and defence) as to try to counteract efforts being made by the government's left wing to gain control of, and then silence, the right. To this end he intended to activate the 'young men of the party and in the country'.[45] But, unlike Churchill, Lloyd lacked the common touch and, one newspaper reported, was still only a 'prancing proconsul' in the popular mind. However, Lloyd seemed to have warmed to the idea of becoming Prime Minister, and he and Lucy worked on a scheme that was intended either to make him leader of the Conservative Party or alternatively of a new party that he intended to form.

In October Lucy wrote to Lloyd from the *Liberty* in characteristically scattershot style. 'Dear Lord Lloyd, Your letter has been opened! I suggest you get some grey sealing wax. I always use it,' she began by way of a greeting. Then she instructed Lloyd to provide her with a programme of his policy and how he proposed to bring it about. Anticipating that he would require office accommodation, Lucy suggested that ground floor rooms might be available in the Belgravia Hotel, which she part owned, or alternatively there was space spare in the *Saturday Review* premises. She was having 'bother' with the *Saturday Review*, she complained, but when it was settled it could become Lloyd's own newspaper and feature a piece from him each week.[46] But this letter agitated Lloyd and put him in a dilemma, for while he wanted Lucy's financial support he could not tolerate being ordered about. He sat down and wrote the first draft of a reply. While, he said, he would keep her fully informed, he needed freedom of action without having to submit all details to her. If she would give him a free hand he would have 'no scruples' about accepting her help, but if she would not then he would rather 'scrape along' on his own. However, Lloyd thought better of sending this and wrote a more conciliatory version omitting the appeal that Lucy leave him alone. But he did indicate that he was not prepared to give Lucy carte blanche, telling her that his campaign planning was well advanced and that he had already found office accommodation in Westminster. He requested that Lucy forward him the promised £5,000 so that he could pay the lease and begin work.[47]

Lucy perhaps detected signs of disaffection, for when she replied to Lloyd's letter the following day she addressed him as 'My dear George'. She was forwarding the £5,000, she said, and asked him to make a 'fighting speech' in the House of Lords in which he would tell the members that they were 'far too beastly polite. Peril – is at our door & yet they make tepid speeches deploring in polite language the danger without even accounting the true culprits Ramsey & Baldwin.' These two, she said, were handing the British Empire to Russia. 'Please dear,' Lucy urged, 'use most unparliamentary language & I am sure you will get many wobblers & harden those already with you.'[48]

But meanwhile Lloyd had spoken to Wentworth Day, asking him whether Lucy was offended by his desire to do things in his own way. When Wentworth Day reported the conversation to Lucy she wrote again to Lloyd, telling him what Wentworth Lucy had said. 'My dear!' Lucy exclaimed to Lloyd, 'I feel rather small.'[49] It was a feeling that she perhaps did not experience very often. Lloyd was embarrassed by Wentworth Day's indiscretion and on 15 October penned an awkward letter to Lucy: 'I don't know a bit what Day was talking about and it only shows how careful one should be never to talk at all to people one does not know well.' All that he had told Wentworth Day, he said, was the outline of his scheme, and that Lucy was assisting him. He had only mentioned that he was 'rather anxious lest you should be disappointed with my way of doing it – that so far as I can remember was what I said to him'. Moving swiftly on, Lloyd gave an update on his progress, for he was busy collecting the support of a 'few real stalwarts' with whom he planned to begin his campaign.[50] But although Lucy would later send Lloyd a further donation of £5,000, the problem of her desire for control would not go away.

Lord Lloyd's star continued to rise and in November 1933 there were reports that he was about to form a new political party that would resuscitate Conservatism. The *Bystander* stated that Lloyd was emerging as a challenger for the Tory leadership: 'He is collecting the young men while he consults with the old.' Lloyd was indeed planning to launch himself, his platform being a dinner held in his honour at the Savoy Hotel in London on 21 November. As it was hosted by the *English Review*, a failing right-wing magazine, Lucy's money probably funded the event. Prior to the dinner the *Daily Herald* reported that there was about to be a 'Diehard Bid for Power', and Lloyd would come out into the open and make a 'bold bid' for the leadership of those Conservatives who were sick of current regime. His programme was 'undiluted Toryism' that opposed the League of Nations and the National Government coalition, and supported rearmament.

The great day came and more than 300 guests – all male and many of them young Conservative MPs – assembled at the Savoy Hotel where, a newspaper reported, the atmosphere 'buzzed with plots to mend or end the National Government'. Lloyd's great keynote speech, entitled 'The Present Crisis in National Affairs', was intended, it was reported, to convert younger Conservatives to his views. Lloyd's moment of glory had come, the eyes of the nation were upon him, and he had a free hand to set out his ideas and agenda. However, Lloyd flopped. He killed his speech from the start by announcing that he would not tell jokes but go into matters in some detail. This, it was reported, caused his audience to 'sit back in something like surprised dismay', which suggests that Lloyd was regarded as a boring speaker. He began by denying current rumours that he intended to form a new party or a new wing of the Conservative Party; he had no such intention. It was not 'new bottles' that were needed but 'stronger wine' in the existing ones. The problem, he said, was not political parties but political principles, and there was frustration and impatience with the complacency of the current political leaders.

After discussing the inadequacy of Britain's defences, matters of British autonomy and his disapproval of the League of Nations, Lloyd revealed his great agenda, which was a new national policy for the revival of British agriculture and industry. He had prepared many facts and figures about pigs, poultry, dairy produce, mutton, market gardening, transport, mines and factories, and said that under his scheme a million jobs could be created. But it did not go down well and the *Birmingham Daily Gazette* headline, 'Lord Lloyd Fails. No Enthusiasm Aroused for His Policy' was typical of much of the press coverage. The newspaper reported that Lloyd's much-heralded bid to lead a Conservative crusade 'failed entirely. If it were intended to rouse enthusiasm for a new drive in nationalism, it missed its mark.' Lloyd's attack on the government's agricultural policy had created resentment and his idea that England could be self-sufficient for much of its food supplies within a few years had been 'openly ridiculed'. The *Yorkshire Post* made a more personal attack. Lloyd, it reported, lacked wit, while his voice was 'not the most persuasive, and such natural vigour as it possesses was strained in his effort to cope with an excess of material'. Lloyd's speech had been long-winded and boring, and his bid for power had apparently failed at its outset. After this, his relationship with Lucy cooled.

Lucy had her own problems with the *Saturday Review*. With such a proprietor it was bound to get into trouble sooner or later, and the first occasion came in November 1933. On 11 November the journal published an article written by Lucy entitled 'The Day of Remembrance. Lest We Forget!' In it Lucy expressed regret that no lessons had been learned from the First World War when soldiers had been sent to their deaths untrained and ill-equipped. Indeed, since then Britain had been 'forced into disarmament' while public money had been squandered on peace conferences. During the war Ramsay MacDonald had urged munition workers to strike and, she asked, could any reader who still mourned the loss of a loved one be sure that their life had not been 'sacrificed through the TREACHERY OF THIS TRAITOR!!' Lucy followed this up with a telegram to MacDonald which read, 'When are you going to sue me for libel? I am waiting. Hurry up.' There was no reply; MacDonald perhaps knew that if he sued Lucy the material that she had collected on his 'anti-British' activities would be publicised and cause him political damage.

However, when the Remembrance Day issue appeared the Federation of London Wholesale Newsagents refused to handle it unless two paragraphs of Lucy's article were cut out. She agreed to this and a second issue was produced, but she found a use for the existing copies. She sent Wentworth Day into central London in search of unemployed men, and in particular those who had served in the First World War, to hire as street sellers. Equipping the men with copies of the banned edition and placards emblazoned with the words 'The *Saturday Review* – Banned for Telling the Truth', Wentworth Day sent them out to sell the journal on the streets. The venture was a great success, he remembered, and 50,000 copies were sold. Only the printers, fearing a libel action against them, were unhappy. The next issue of the *Saturday Review,* published on 18 November, declared that Lucy was unafraid: 'The trouble is that Lady Houston *will* speak the Truth – and all the King's horses and all the King's men cannot muzzle her.' She did not fear legal consequences, the journal reported, and England should be grateful that there was at least one person who came out in favour of the 'old principles of Conservatism' and 'true British Imperialism'. Indeed, the *Saturday Review* regarded the ban as a 'piece of luck' for it had been an excellent advertisement and everyone wanted to read the offending article. At about this time that the *Saturday Review* changed its tagline to 'The only paper that dares tell you all the truth.'

Lucy was delighted with a cartoon published in the *Sheffield Independent* that showed Ramsay MacDonald and Herbert Samuel, then leader of the Liberal Party, boxing. Climbing into the ring was a rotund figure wearing boxing gloves and a vest bearing the name 'Lucy'. The words 'You men are no good. Let me get at him!' were issuing from her mouth. The cartoon's caption was, 'Battling Ramsay (to latest opponent): For heaven's sake keep the fight going, Herbert. Look what's come now!' Lucy ordered 200 copies of the newspaper and bought the original cartoon, which she hung over her bed at Byron Cottage as her proudest possession.

But another item in the 18 November issue of the *Saturday Review* caused a diplomatic incident. After his appointment as German chancellor in January that year Adolf Hitler had begun a programme of rearmament, and in Britain some began to feel that Hitler's Nazis were not so very different from the Germans of the First World War. Wentworth Day had obtained a report, written for a Nazi newspaper, of interviews given by Dr Joseph Goebbels, Reich Minister of Public Enlightenment and Propaganda, and Hitler's right-hand man. The report stated that the basis of German foreign policy would be to make alliances in order to provide land for the expansion of the German race. This, the article explained, was 'necessary' for Germany's existence, and those who opposed the policy were Germany's enemies. The 'revision' of the peace treaties made after the First World War, Goebbels said, was top of the German political agenda and the primary aim was to revise the Eastern frontier. The Nazi plan, Goebbels stated, was to march into the Danzig Corridor and take over Poland, and 'after that the rest will be purely a matter of power'. The article, Wentworth Day wrote, was a 'bombshell', for just at that time the Nazi Foreign Office was assuring Europe that Hitler had no designs on the Danzig Corridor and only friendly feelings towards Poland. Wentworth Day was in no doubt of the authenticity of the report, and the paper proof that he had obtained had been corrected and signed by Goebbels himself. Goebbels's statements were as good as a declaration of war, Wentworth Day wrote, and a few years later Germany would carry out the plan as stated.

The Goebbels article was a great scoop for the *Saturday Review* and Wentworth Day printed it under the title 'The Nazis' Next Step'. When Goebbels got to hear of it he sent a telegram stating that the *Saturday Review* had been the victim of a 'malicious forgery'. He declared that he had 'written no such paper either for you or any other publication ... I expect in fairness that you will immediately stop the issue in question or, if too late for that, you will make known my disavowal.' Wentworth Day held firm. He could only assume, he suggested in the *Saturday Review*, that in the interval since Goebbels had given the interview Hitler's policy had changed. 'We can only feel,' he wrote, 'that Dr Goebbels, like many another statesman, has found cause to regret the hastily-uttered words of unguarded truth.' Wentworth Day invited Goebbels to follow up with another article but received no reply, and in Berlin on the following Monday newspapers attacked the *Saturday Review* for its impudence, lies and violation of journalistic traditions.

There were further repercussions. A Polish embassy official arrived at the *Saturday Review* offices to collect a pile of copies that filled the back seat of the embassy car. The German government instructed Prince von Bismarck, its London ambassador, to call at the Foreign Office and emphasise the negative effect that the article would have on international relations. After this

Wentworth Day was also called in to the Foreign Office, where he explained that he had no doubt as to the authenticity of the article. He thought that on the whole he had handled the matter rather well – until he saw Lucy. She demanded: 'What is all this about?' and Wentworth Day explained that they had a first-class story which had exposed Germany's plans and 'knocked Goebbels silly'. To this Lucy replied, crushingly, 'If anyone is going to knock Goebbels silly I am quite capable of doing it myself!'

In early December 1933, from on board the *Liberty* at Sandbanks, Lucy sent a telegram to Ramsay MacDonald and copied it to the press. Renewing her offer of £200,000 for defence, she now made it specifically for the defence of London which, she said, remained the only European capital unprotected against invasion by air. Prominent political and military figures were voicing their indignation: 'Will the Government still dare to refuse this offer?' Lucy asked. Being again met by silence from the government, twelve days later she penned a 'Manifesto to the Citizens of London', asking 'Which is Most Important, the Safety of London or the Imaginary Dignity of the Prime Minister?' She urged Londoners to pressure the government to accept the money as a Christmas gift to the country. However, she would receive no final response from the government for months.

Denied the opportunity of contributing to air defence, by the end of December 1933 Lucy was backing another aviation project. A highly ambitious scheme was being developed for a non-stop flight around the circumference of the globe on its longitudinal axis, with refuelling taking place in the air. The all-British project was in its early stages but it was hoped that the attempt would take place in the spring of 1934. If successful, the *Sunday Dispatch* reported, it would 'reduce to puny proportions every other event in man's history in the air'. Money, it seemed, was no object, but while efforts were being made to keep secret the identity of the financial backer Lucy was named, and it was planned that the project would be called the 'Houston Round-the-World Flight'. But the problems involved were too formidable and after these initial reports the project disappeared without trace. Not until 1949 would the first non-stop flight around the world be made, by the United States Air Force.

THE BLUDGEON, NOT THE RAPIER

G iven that they shared a stubborn and pugnacious nature it was inevitable that friction should arise between Lucy and Wentworth Day, and by the spring of 1934 her editor had fallen from Lucy's favour. Lucy thought Wentworth Day a 'flibbertigibbett', while he was tired of being on permanent call; whenever Lucy had a bright idea in the early hours of the morning she would call him on the telephone, becoming very annoyed if she failed to reach him. Warner Allen, meanwhile, was still working on the *Saturday Review.* Then in his mid-50s, Allen was well travelled, well connected and an authority on French wines. Although he regretted the vulgar, extravagant and eccentric turn that the *Saturday Review* had taken, he was happy enough in his job and agreed broadly with Lucy's political views. Having gathered from colleagues that Lucy was 'formidable', 'eccentric', 'unreasonable' and 'aggravating', Allen had hitherto avoided her. But when Lucy began to telephone him with her troubles over Wentworth Day he realised that she wanted him to be her next editor. He was alarmed, for he feared that were he to agree he might be held responsible for any libellous statements that she made.

An invitation to visit Lucy on the *Liberty* came in the spring of 1934 and Allen travelled down to Sandbanks in a state of apprehension. He had not met Lucy before and when he entered her stateroom he was awed by her appearance, which included turban and curl. But Lucy wooed Allen, entertaining him to an excellent lunch and serving him vintage champagne – Mumm

Cordon Rouge 1911 – the last bottle left from the days of Robert Houston. After lunch the matter of the editorship was discussed and Allen was relieved to find that Lucy wanted that job for herself, while she intended him to be her 'Managing Director'. In practice, it would become clear that Allen would be allowed neither to manage nor direct, for those were not functions that Lucy delegated to others. In accepting the job, Allen was projected into a close association with Lucy and became involved in many of her activities.

Despite being aged 77 when she took on the editorship Lucy inflicted upon herself a punishing lifestyle, often going without rest and food as she strove to make each issue exactly as she wanted. She drove others as she drove herself, demanding obedience from her staff. Allen, by his own admission, found Lucy a 'terror to work for, often a domineering tyrant, deaf to reason and common sense'. She was capricious and extremely impatient, and did everything at top speed. She never forgot an order she had given and everything had to be carried out to the letter. It was futile to tell Lucy that something was 'impossible' for, as with Houston, it was a word she did not recognise. She always thought that she knew best, and had to have the last word. Like Wentworth Day before him, Allen suffered by being always on call and he too found Lucy's early morning telephone calls the worst trial. Even when Lucy was on the *Liberty* there was no escape, for when the yacht was lying in harbour it was part of Allen's duties to arrange for a telephone cable to be run out to it.

Another source of suffering for Allen was Lucy's love of fresh air. When he went to Byron Cottage to receive instructions in person, even on a cold day, Lucy would often take him out in Houston's big, old-fashioned, open-topped Rolls-Royce, instructing her chauffeur to drive half a mile to a cart track on the edge of Hampstead Heath in order to escape the 'madding crowd'. There they would sit for most of the morning while Lucy issued instructions, but, while she was dressed warmly for the excursion, Allen was often not so well prepared. However, he dared not shiver or blow his nose or else Lucy would scoff at his male delicacy and declare that she had nothing under her fur coat but a nightdress and dressing gown. But if Allen's job was sometimes irksome there were financial compensations. One day Lucy told him that she intended to double his salary: 'You never expected that, did you?' she asked. Childlike in her delight at her own generosity, she drummed her hands on the bedclothes and asked repeatedly, 'Aren't you surprised?' Allen's very real surprise and delight was the 'essence' of Lucy's pleasure, he wrote. Nevertheless, it took him weeks to persuade her to contact her bank and put the change into effect.

Lucy was not well qualified to be a newspaper proprietor or editor. Poorly educated, she had set herself up against those who had had the best education that money could buy, although her high opinion of herself and her own abilities prevented her from understanding the extent of her disadvantage. Dorothy Crisp, a right-wing activist who knew Lucy in the 1930s, wrote that she was 'very far from a fool', but had 'no intellect as the university don understands intellect'. In its place she had 'that kind of peasant shrewdness that puts its finger right on the spot without being able to advance reasons or to argue academically about the proposition'. As her mind had never been disciplined she jumped to conclusions, relying on emotion and intuition rather than reasoning. And now in old age she lacked concentration and was led by whatever whim or feeling came into her head.

When her health allowed, Lucy determined the contents of the *Saturday Review*, read every word that was to be printed, and had the final say on all matters related to production and publication. The journal's content was eclectic, for in addition to opinion articles, true to its name it included reviews of books, films, plays and broadcasting. There were also columns on finance, horse racing and motoring, a round-up of imperial matters and material reprinted from papers such as the *Daily Express* and *Daily Mail*. Lucy had a tendency to accept unsuitable articles and also to reprint her own material across issues, for she believed in rubbing things in. Letters of adulation of Lucy were a major feature of the correspondence columns, and the edition of 10 February 1934, for example, contained three. One began, 'I must write and tell you how much I admire your outspoken criticisms in the *Saturday Review*. It is a pity more newspapers do not speak the truth!' A second urged: 'Madam, Go on, you are doing a power of good,' for few people had as much 'pluck' in attacking 'humbug' as Lucy did. A third advised, 'Take heart, take strength, and take courage!' There were few advertisements and over time, as the *Saturday Review*'s notoriety grew, the larger advertisers dropped out. Eventually the American *Time* magazine, which had a way of putting its finger on things, would report that the journal had 'little advertising except a two-page "Register" of gloomy provincial hotels'. But Lucy did not need advertising revenue.

Lucy spent hours poring over the journal's design and layout, going through many iterations until she was satisfied. She had, Allen wrote cuttingly, an 'indomitable faculty for taking pains, which she had no doubt exercised when she was creating her own dresses'. Lucy 'underlined, rewrote, crossed out, asked for advice, ignored it, told you to mind your own business'. She had 'not been a spoiled beauty for nothing', Allen commented. The cover was always a major concern and wore Lucy's nerves to a frazzle every week. She treated it as a piece of embroidery and spent much time positioning photographs and strips of proofs to the background with pins. It was vitally important to her that the Union Jack, perhaps, or the Prince of Wales's head be positioned exactly as she wished. Text – perhaps Lucy's doggerel or a political parody of a nursery rhyme or comic song – had to be inserted into the design. Sometimes Lucy and Allen would drive to the printers' premises in St Andrew's Street and sit outside in the street in the Rolls-Royce to work on the cover. Unperturbed by the curiosity of passers-by, Lucy cut out photographs with a pair of scissors and laid them out carefully while the master printer attended to her wants. The finished design was sent into the building with the pins in place.

Lucy was proud of her writing ability and Wentworth Day thought that had she not been a millionairess, and had she been able to 'discipline her English', she might have made a 'first-class' journalist. But Lucy could not discipline her English and her style was painful to professional journalists. Her articles, dictated at top speed, contained dashes in the place of full stops, semi-colons and commas, and for emphasis she inserted capitals, italics, bold text, red text, underlining and a variety of fonts at will. Once when Wentworth Day tried to persuade her to change her style Lucy rebuked him: 'Be damned to you and your literary ideas! I'm writing this, not you. That's the way Lady Houston writes and because it's Lady Houston people read it.' She had learned her journalism from Mr Blumenfeld, she said, and he had given her two rules for writing: 'Be Simple' and 'Be Distinctive'. Lucy said she never used long words because she couldn't spell them, and her red type and dashes were definitely distinctive.

Wentworth Day nevertheless admired Lucy for going 'straight to the point as she saw it. She spoke her mind on what she believed to be true.' She regarded it as weakness to praise an opponent or concede that they might have points in their favour but, although she spared nobody, she had no use for people who were frightened to stand up to her. She was a product of her upbringing and, as Allen wrote, her character had been formed in an age when plain speaking was unchecked by refinement or libel laws. As Lucy adhered to those standards in her writing and her political life she was 'coarse, extravagant and contemptuous of the finer feelings – the bludgeon, not the rapier'. In her writing, too, she used plain language, and indeed her best prose was lively, direct and hard-hitting, containing memorable and quotable text. Even Allen admitted that her patriotic fanaticism gave her 'broken and often ungrammatical utterances a suggestion of inspired extravagance'. While she was often laughed at, her public persona, with all its brashness and comedy, gave her wide appeal. For all the paper's obvious faults there were many who agreed with her political views and her articles were probably the main attraction for some *Saturday Review* readers. It became, Wentworth Day said, the 'smart thing' to have the journal in a 'Mayfair flat, a ducal mansion or a stockbroker's house'. And equally it was found in the 'solid households of the suburbs and the cottages of working people'. Nearly eighty years on, it is difficult to judge the accuracy of this profile of the readership.

Press day was an ordeal for Lucy, who invariably upset the arrangements. Her Rolls-Royce or Buick flew between Byron Cottage, the editorial offices in York Buildings and the printers' premises at all hours. As the deadline approached she would continue to work frenetically on the contents and design, and ring the printers at the last moment with alterations which prevented the newspaper from being 'put to bed' until late at night. She seemed neither to know nor care about the problems her brainwaves created; her will was paramount and mechanical concerns and the time factor, which dominated ordinary newspaper offices, had to stand aside. And yet Allen was surprised at how much could be achieved when expense was not a consideration. Predictably, the printers loved her for the overtime money they earned and their enthusiasm was heightened by Lucy's habit of backing her own horses and distributing her betting wins among her employees. They also bet loyally on her horses but often lost money. On one occasion much was expected of Silver Belle, but afterwards Lucy wrote in the *Saturday Review*, probably as an apology to the printers who had backed the horse, 'Silver Belle disappointed us again at Goodwood – if she does not do better next time I shall seriously consider renaming her – Silver-Plated Belle.'

Lucy was concerned less with sales figures than with distribution figures, for she wanted her message to reach as many people as possible. Accounts of the *Saturday Review*'s circulation varied: Dorothy Crisp wrote that it reached a respectable 20,000 copies per week, while Wentworth Day put the figure at more than 60,000. However, Lucy's extravagance on production, advertising and distribution meant that it would be calculated that in 1936 the journal was actually costing Lucy £60,000 a year, or about £1,150 per issue. If Allen tried to warn her about the cost of her latest brainwave she would not listen, but nevertheless grumble when the printer's bill arrived. Allen expressed his horror at Lucy's excessive spending to her solicitor, who only replied, 'Why shouldn't she spend a few thousands on the *Saturday Review*? She can well afford it and it amuses her.'

As editor Lucy needed to be present in London, and when she returned from Sandbanks in the spring of 1934 she would not use the *Liberty* again until the following year. Byron Cottage became Lucy's fortress, both the launchpad of her attacks and a place of refuge. As she grew ever more outspoken, her notoriety increased and she became an object of intense curiosity. Although many people sought Lucy out she saw nobody whom she did not wish to see; however, in addition to Wentworth Day and Warner Allen, the *Saturday Review* brought Lucy into contact with the writers Dorothy Crisp, Comyns Beaumont, Collin Brooks and Meriel Buchanan. As all had the privilege of visiting Byron Cottage and later wrote of Lucy's life there, her last few years are recorded in some detail.

Dorothy Crisp thought the Hampstead house a 'modest residence' for a millionairess and that, with the exclusion of the *Liberty*, Lucy's lifestyle was more like that of someone with an income of only £2,000 or £3,000 per year. But after twenty-five years the house had become a museum of Lucy's past and she was happy there with her memories. She kept up the grounds with their beautiful old trees and gardens full of the flowers that she so loved. Until the early 1930s Lucy occupied the ground-floor rooms, lunching in the dining room or the front hall, but over time she withdrew upstairs to her bedroom. Then Byron Cottage became a testimony to her priorities. She neglected it and the disused ground floor rooms, although kept clean and dusted, grew shabby and descended into a state of disrepair. A close inspection of the china cabinet revealed that broken and cracked items had been pushed to the back of the shelves, no doubt by a careless maid. Such was Lucy's character that, as with her yacht captains and chefs, she could not keep her staff. For example, Beaumont recounted how he had once found Lucy a new private secretary, but soon the girl came to tell him that she had resigned. Lucy, she reported, was always awake by four in the morning and would demand that her secretary accompany her on walks on Hampstead

Heath. The paths were dark and deserted, and even when the night was bitterly cold Lucy would tell the unfortunate girl, 'You don't want to put on stockings. I don't.'

Lucy was particularly hard on her kitchen staff. Good food had always been important to her, and her pride in her cooking abilities came second only to her pride in her political acumen and patriotism. Lucy had a great knowledge of food but her tastes were simple. She liked 'old English' food such as lamb chops, jugged hare, grilled salmon, roast pheasant, turtle soup, lobster and oysters. Broad beans, asparagus and globe artichokes were her favourite vegetables. She began the day with bacon and eggs, and a typical lunch might be steak-and-kidney pudding followed by pineapple and an orange, with a bottle of Guinness to wash it down. For tea she might have Gentleman's Relish sandwiches. Everything had to be exactly to Lucy's liking; her kitchen staff were given precise instructions. Once she employed a top chef but, disliking the porridge he made, she sent Miss Ritchie to the kitchen to make it instead. When the humiliated chef came to ask what her ladyship would like for lunch, Lucy told him that Old Charlie, the *Liberty*'s cook, could cook better than he could. It was not surprising that there was a high staff turnover in the Byron Cottage kitchen. But as the *Saturday Review* increasingly monopolised Lucy's thoughts, her interest in domestic matters declined and 'char-women' became her stand-by. While they were usually to be found scrubbing floors, one day Lucy told Allen that she was 'living entirely on raw eggs, as they are the only dish my "chars" know how to cook'. Few rich women can have lived more uncomfortably.

If other staff fled, two stayed on out of genuine affection for Lucy. Miss Ritchie and Foster the chauffeur had been her longest-standing employees. They had much to bear, however. Miss Ritchie was expected to give Lucy care and attention around the clock, being required to sleep either in Lucy's bedroom or the room next to it. Night after night Lucy would wake her at two or three in the morning and force her to listen to her reminiscences or plans for saving England. From time to time Miss Ritchie found this way of life so onerous that she resigned, only to return later. Foster stayed the course but confided the trials of his job to Wentworth Day. When out in the Buick, he said, Lucy would tap the glass window behind him and say, 'Faster, faster, Foster! We're not driving in a pony and trap!' On one occasion they had been in the Rolls-Royce going at 80mph on the Southampton Road when a small car passed them. Lucy, who did not like to be beaten, said, 'Look at that little car that's just passed us. Pass it! Pass it! Call yourself a chauffeur? Get a move on! Crawling along like this. I'm not going to my funeral yet.'

As time passed Lucy became increasingly confined to her bedroom, which her friend Collin Brooks described as her 'perpetual sick-room'. She had never been physically robust and her medical conditions were chronic but ill-defined; over the years she had suffered from influenza, jaundice, eye problems, vertigo, 'nervous prostration', a weak heart, insomnia and low blood pressure. As age weakened Lucy further, her mind increasingly took over from her body as the sphere of activity and she adopted a lifestyle of invalidism. It afforded certain advantages. She could see and be seen only as much as she wished, and nobody could expect anything of her. It enabled her to exert influence on others, and Allen confirmed that Lucy had 'no scruple to play ill-health as one of her trump cards'. When she told him how hard she fought against illness, how bravely she struggled against depression, and how despite it all she desired to fight for England to the end even he, who did not wholly like her, found it impossible not to feel 'affectionate pity'.

Visitors to Byron Cottage stayed downstairs until they received the summons to ascend to Lucy's room, and on the way up they might have to step round char-women and their buckets. The first impression of the bedroom was pleasant or unpleasant according to the weather. The windows were kept wide open all the year round and in spring the song of blackbirds floated in from the garden while in winter cold winds swept across Lucy's bed. There were occasions when Wentworth Day saw the carpet billowing in the wind and snow on the floor. In the bedroom, as downstairs, the colour scheme of red, white and blue was much in evidence. Copies of the *Saturday Review*, with its patriotic cover, were scattered about, and the room was always full of red, white and blue flowers. In the midst of this was Lucy, a small and round person, either lying in bed or on an adjacent low divan. Beside the bed was a large silver-framed photograph of Houston with his black-dyed beard.

The visitor would have to beware the electric flexes that were coiled about the bed. Some were for standard lamps but others were attached to two or three bell-pushes with which Lucy could summon a servant, secretary or chauffeur, although with her high staff turnover there might be nobody to respond. A great deal of Lucy's activity was conducted by telephone and one flex belonged to a portable telephone. There was only one in the house that could be plugged into points in various rooms, but if a call came for Lucy when the machine was not in her bedroom there was commotion and a long delay. The bedroom was Lucy's office, and her bed served not only as a place to sleep but also as writing desk, easy chair, proprietorial and editorial desk, and all the desks of those newspaper staff in whose roles she involved herself. From the bed Lucy ran the *Saturday Review* and her political campaigns, gave orders, carried out and gave interviews and managed her financial affairs. From here she wrote or dictated letters, telegrams, leaflets and articles, wrote cheques and dispensed charity money. When she needed information she called an expert. She knew them all, Wentworth Day wrote, from 'Cabinet Ministers and financiers to admirals, generals, slum parsons and champions of dumb animals'. Thus Lucy became in her later years a voice from behind the bedroom door.

There were many who made the pilgrimage to Byron Cottage. Politicians came, for in 1934 she told Dorothy Crisp, 'I have had them all up here, Cabinet Ministers and everybody.' She also received her friends, including the Ranee of Pudukota, Lady Cynthia Colville, and the Duchess of Hamilton. Brinckman visited on occasion and also, before the breakdown of their relationship, the Duchess of Atholl, with whom Lucy shared an interest in political and social issues. Here too came the Prince of Wales and Winston Churchill. Lucy invariably met visitors wearing one of her signature turbans of pink, red, white or blue silk, perhaps shot with gold and decorated with an aigrette or a diamond or emerald brooch. From beneath the turban there always peeped a blond curl, artfully arranged. It was, wrote Allen, 'always just where it should be or very nearly so', and from time to time Lucy would inspect it by means of a big silver hand mirror which always lay within reach. Pouting in the mirror, she would push the curl delicately with her finger. Often a fur coat or sable cloak worth thousands of pounds was slung casually around her shoulders or thrown across the pillows behind her head. However, her clothes varied according to her assessment of the visitor. Lucy made an effort for those whom she wished to impress. On one visit, Wentworth Day found her wearing a red turban pinned with a large emerald, and when he commented that he liked the turban Lucy replied complacently, 'So did King George of Greece, when he came to tea the other day.' Upon that occasion, she said, she had been wearing a white dress with a red, white and blue scarf and a white turban. 'How elegant you are,' the King had said. At other times her knees were covered by a Union

Jack bedspread; modelling herself on Queen Victoria, she sat straight-backed against a high pile of while pillows edged with delicate broderie anglaise.

Lucy was little concerned about her appearance when meeting lesser beings. Crisp, for example, was amused to be received by Lucy in bed clad in a 'green-wool sports suit' of jacket and skirt. On Wentworth Day's visits she might be surrounded by buckets and soap suds as the chars carried out their work, and wearing a cotton nightdress – she had two of each in red and white, yellow and white, and blue-check – and wrapped in a large towel. Sometimes she had on a pink silk nightdress beneath a red flannel dressing gown. And yet despite such mundane garb, Wentworth Day mused, she had boxes of the world's most superb silks stored away. Out of the house, too, Lucy could show a strange lack of self-consciousness. She had told the press in 1928 that she put on an old coat to walk on Hampstead Heath, but Wentworth Day described how one day in the 1930s when they were going out for a drive Lucy appeared in a 'heavy, rough, blue tweed overcoat with a Persian lamb collar' and a pair of men's woollen long johns peeping coquettishly from beneath her skirt. When Lucy saw him looking she said stoutly, 'Warm – that's why I wear 'em!'

Youth and beauty had meant so much to Lucy that as she aged she mourned her lost looks. Yet, Crisp thought, although she was 'decidedly plump' and her hair a wig, still her appearance was not absurd, and she possessed the 'most exquisite pink and white skin' that Crisp had ever seen. Lucy had her own beauty regimes. In her later years her morning routine was to wash her face in warm milk and then, while her dog Benito lapped it up, she dusted her face with Brown and Polson's cornflour. She applied it thickly and brushed it off, leaving only the smallest amount: 'There is no poisonous muck in that,' she said. 'I know what I'm putting on my face – something pure, good and fit to eat. That's why I never get spots.' Lucy did not use cosmetics and disliked seeing fully made-up young women. Allen wrote how sometimes she would take a damp bath sponge and scrub it mercilessly round the face of the young visitor, saying, 'You have got a nice natural complexion, my dear: that is the advantage of being English; and you had better make the most of it.'

Lucy loved jewellery but was careless about even the most expensive items. Once day when she was out with Comyns Beaumont in the Buick he eyed her great handbag curiously and she asked him to guess what was inside. When Beaumont could not, Lucy said, 'Jewels, stupid, I never let them out of my sight. There are heaps of thieves lurking about the heath and jewel thieves are cunning rascals.' When he asked why her servants could not look after them, she retorted, 'I would never entrust my jewels to the servants. Only a fool would!' At other times she kept them in a large safe in her dressing room, but once when she was away her chauffeur called Allen to Byron Cottage in a panic, as the safe had been found open. When Allen arrived he discovered that it contained 'rubbish', including 'false hair, false teeth and imitation pearls'. However, there was also a very valuable gold toilet set and some unset precious stones. Allen rang Lucy's secretary and was given a list of the fabulous pieces that should have been in the safe, but there was no correlation between the list and the contents. He was then instructed to contact Scotland Yard immediately. But Scotland Yard were not alarmed for they were used to rich old ladies losing their jewellery and indeed, the detective sent to Byron Cottage speedily ascertained that some time previously Lucy had sent several large cases of jewellery to the bank for safe-keeping.

A complex person with enormous zest for life, Lucy was a woman of extremes and contradictions, with glaring faults and virtues. She was essentially an honest woman who lied about her past. She was a simple woman who was shrewd, a kind woman who was merciless to enemies, and an invalid who presented an indomitable front. She knew that those who were out of sympathy with her views often thought her mentally unhinged, and she once told Beaumont, 'Lots of people think that I am as mad as a March hare. I know these things.' Yet Lucy was not wholly unaffected by public opinion; Crisp thought that much of her flamboyance was a retort to what people thought of her.

Despite being rude, arrogant and dogmatic, Lucy was also deeply religious, taking her Bible readings seriously, listening to radio broadcasts of church services and ending her day with a recitation of the Lord's Prayer. Despite her enormous self-confidence Lucy was capable of humility, and from time to time her religious conscience prompted her to repentance. For example, she and Allen once compiled a list of her benefactions and published it in the *Saturday Review*. Later, Allen asked whether Lucy wished to reprint it but upon going to Byron Cottage he found her with an open Bible. She had been reading, she told him, the story of the 'widow's mite' and the saying that it is 'easier for a camel to go through the eye of a needle than for a rich man to enter the kingdom of God'. Lucy's conscience had been struck and she was in a state of great penitence, regretting her pride in boasting of her generosity. 'My dear,' she said to Allen, 'I am thoroughly ashamed of myself. I ought never to have done it. That list must never appear again.'

Those who knew Lucy and liked her found her sensible, shrewd, sincere and humorous. Large minded and unaffected, she never pretended to be a saint; she would forgive others much, and in particular young people, for she had not forgotten her own youth. One sin that she despised was hypocrisy; she set sycophant traps for the unwary. One day Allen was a target. Arriving at Byron Cottage, he found Lucy wearing a brooch set with a large green stone in the collar of her dressing gown. 'What do you think of my new emerald?' she asked. Allen knew that Lucy possessed fabulously valuable emeralds but was suspicious of this brooch. 'I suppose it is very fine and valuable, but …' he replied cautiously. Lucy was delighted. 'You do not think much of it,' she exclaimed, 'and you are right. You are a better judge of jewellery than I gave you credit for.' She had taken in a lot of people with the brooch, she said, and was wearing it specifically to show them what fools they were. Because she wore it they thought it must be a genuine emerald, but it was obviously only a piece of glass; Allen had passed the test.

Lucy had used many personae over the years and, with much of the actress in her still, she presented versions of herself based on her perception of the person or occasion. She could appear demure and shy, or brazen and coarse-mouthed. To some people she was charming, friendly and informal, while to others she was stiff and formal. Conversation with Lucy was never dull but her visitors had to stay on the alert. Meriel Buchanan, for example, found that Lucy never allowed her to 'equivocate, or quibble or waver', but demanded the same 'forthright honesty, the same undeviating courage with which she herself faced life'. At the smallest indication of weakness Lucy would 'flash out one of her quick, characteristic rebukes' and then give a 'sudden human, brilliant' smile that illuminated her whole face; the attack was forgotten. Buchanan felt the power of Lucy's 'amazing, vivid, virile' personality and her 'shrewd, brilliant eyes', which read her thoughts and probed her weaknesses to the depths.

When Lucy wanted people to do things she would go to great lengths to get her own way. She was particularly adept at bending men to her will, Allen wrote, for 'what she did not know of the male sex was not worth knowing'. Even he, who had a great deal to put up with from Lucy, was influenced by the 'mysterious charm' that had 'fascinated so many lovers'. That charm, he thought, together with a 'capacity for the unexpected', served to command his interest and reconcile him to Lucy's tantrums. Indeed there were many, Wentworth Day wrote, who enjoyed being commanded by her; he too had been 'under the spell'.

Lucy enjoyed the concept of female ruthlessness without reason or mercy, and still relished her ability to control and manipulate men. The last line of a verse by her old friend Rudyard Kipling was always on her lips:

> When the Himalayan peasant meets the He-bear in his stride,
> He shouts to scare the monster who will sometimes stand aside.
> But the She-bear thus accosted turns to rend him tooth and nail,
> For the female of the species is more deadly than the male.

When uttering the line, Allen said, she would 'smack her lips over it with malicious relish', in particular if she was planning an outrageous attack against a hated politician.

Early in 1934 Lucy had backed Dorothy Crisp's scheme for a high-profile meeting that would attack the National Government. Crisp organised the speakers but Lucy was displeased that she had not included Lord Lloyd: 'Ask him now,' she ordered. Crisp's real reason for omitting Lloyd was that he was too controversial, and in any case had 'well passed the hey-day of his appeal'. However, knowing that it was pointless to tell Lucy this, Crisp fell back on a 'very minor though strictly true objection'. She had not asked him, she replied, because he wanted 'such a lot of fuss making of him'. What happened next, Crisp wrote, was 'amazing'. Up to this point Lucy had maintained the usual stiff demeanour that she used with Crisp, but suddenly she dropped the mask. Her face 'lit with glee, her toes curled beneath the bed-clothes and she positively hugged herself as she said: "Of course he wants a fuss making of him. All men want a fuss making of them. I'll show you how to make a fuss of them."' This, Crisp reported, was 'not in the least grotesque', and indeed despite Lucy's advanced age had seemed the 'most natural thing in the world'. Crisp was stunned by Lucy's 'sheer vitality and certainty of overwhelming attraction'. But when Crisp kept her face a polite blank, Lucy quickly returned to her former manner. Afterwards Crisp, knowing nothing of Lucy's past, remarked to a friend that Lucy was the 'sort of person who in France would undoubtedly have become the King's mistress and run both his majesty and the country, to their infinite good'. It was only later, after Lucy's death, that she learned how 'good a shot' she had made.

RULE BRITANNIA AND
DAMN THE DETAILS

I n the year that had passed since the historic overflights of Mount Everest public interest in the expedition had remained high and those involved had been much in demand to give talks and lectures and to write books and articles. In 1934 Colonel Etherton made a European speaking tour and when in Rome was granted a private audience with Pope Pius XI. The pope gave Etherton a special blessing, extending it to the other members of the expedition and in particular to Lady Houston, who had made it possible. Lucy was greatly pleased and the cover of the next issue of the *Saturday Review* bore the headline 'The Pope Blesses Lady Houston', while inside there was a picture of the pope with his hand raised in benediction. An editorial note stated that, coming from a man 'so fully deserving of the title of His Holiness', a blessing was a blessing indeed. However, the note stated, while the pope had blessed Lady Houston for her patriotism she was still waiting to hear from the Archbishop of Canterbury. This was a dig at the archbishop, Cosmo Gordon Lang, whom Lucy liked little and respected less.

Meanwhile, the Gaumont studios had been working to produce a film about the Houston-Everest Expedition, to be titled *Wings Over Everest*. Lucy was to be featured in an introductory sequence which showed her meeting with Clydesdale at Kinrara, and a crew filmed the outside of the house while the inside scene was filmed at Byron Cottage. But after Lucy's scene was completed pressure had been exerted on the Gaumont studio to omit her. When Lucy heard of this she sent for Allen in a 'rage'. Having been sidelined by Lord Astor at the Everest luncheon, she told him, she was now being excised from the film because Gaumont was trying to keep her role from the public. Lucy often complained that there was a conspiracy to deny her credit for her good works, and Allen thought that there was indeed some truth in this although he also knew that she was partly to blame. Lucy dispatched Allen to the Gaumont studios with instructions to declare that she would take the company to court unless the introduction was reinstated: 'My dear,' she said, 'you must make them realise I'm a very dangerous enemy.' But it took Allen several visits before Gaumont assured him that it had all been an unfortunate mistake and that the missing footage would be restored.

At last the film, forty minutes long, was ready and Lucy was invited to a special showing at the studios. That morning she was in a bad temper and all the way there she urged Foster to break speed limits and ignore traffic signals and one-way streets. Upon arrival she was met by Allen and he, Lucy and Miss Ritchie were ushered into a small cinema. Lucy was irritated by a delay in starting the film and she took a dislike to the film's director. At last the film began, but after only a couple of minutes Lucy stood up and declared, 'This is disgraceful. I shall not have it. You shall hear from my solicitors.' Later it was reported that she was displeased because some captions that criticised the new Indian constitution had been left out. Lucy stomped back to her car where a crowd of bystanders, hoping to see a famous film star, was waiting nearby. Lucy blasted the director with the full force of her disapproval while the crowd, not knowing what she was talking about, cheered her on. But driving home she was suddenly in a sunny mood and delighted with her attack on the director: 'The crowd was with me. Did you see how they cheered me? The people are always on my side. I am one of them myself,' she said.

There was probably no alteration made to *Wings Over Everest* before its private premiere on 1 June 1934 at the Curzon Cinema. Lucy attended and was very pleased with the film, which opened with her image and the caption, 'Lady Houston, DBE whose generosity made this great adventure possible.' In the scene depicting her meeting with Clydesdale she is sitting bolt upright in bed backed by a pile of pillows, with a posy pot of flowers on a small table beside her. Turban and kiss curl are in place, and Lucy has two strings of large white pearls around her neck and a fox stole across her shoulders. Clydesdale, wearing not his kilt but a business suit, is seated in a nearby armchair. In the scene he outlined his Everest scheme and the subsequent dialogue between them went thus:

Lucy (demurely): What you tell me thrills me through and through, but I'm not going to help you commit suicide.

Clydesdale: Oh, there's very little chance of that, Lady Houston. We've worked it all out most thoroughly.

Lucy (dubiously): But isn't it most *terribly* dangerous?

Clydesdale (with a glimmer of a smile): No more than walking across Hampstead Heath on a foggy night. But seriously, of course it's the highest mountain in the world. It's true there must be some risk, but isn't it a risk well worthwhile?

Lucy: Of course, it requires a lot of careful consideration. It's an *immense* adventure. That's what appeals to *me*. (Pause, then pushes chin forward and says impulsively): I agree. I'll help you.

It was Lucy's first and last speaking role on film.

A luncheon was to be held to mark the film's release and John Buchan had written to invite Lucy. Her reply, he wrote later, was 'distinctly unusual', for she said that she rarely went to such functions and was not certain that she would attend but in case she did, two seats of honour should be kept for herself and Lord Horder. The luncheon began and Buchan occupied the chair with the Duchess of Hamilton on his left and the two empty chairs on his right. It was not until the coffee stage that Lucy and Horder arrived. Buchan had not met Lucy before and to his surprise he found her a 'timid, gentle little lady bearing no relation to the popular conception of her'. When proposing Lucy's health Buchan told the audience that he had 'prepared a welcome to the modern Boadicea, only to find that here was someone straight from the pages of the Brontes'. But Buchan was not taking Lucy's acting ability into account.

Lucy gave a speech which Buchan found modest, simple and very well-delivered, and it was reproduced in the *Saturday Review*. There, continuing in her guise of timidity, Lucy added, 'Oh! how frightened I was when I made my Maiden Speech at the Luncheon.' But she raised the question of honours, suggesting that awards should be made to the leaders of the Houston-Mount Everest Expedition although, she added, patriotism, honesty and courage were not qualities that appealed to the 'mis-leaders' in the government. Lucy's transparent subtext was the award of an honour to herself and the following month she made a cheeky suggestion in the *Saturday Review*:

The deaths of the Dukes of Wellington and Marlborough have created an unexpected problem for filling the two vacancies that have arisen in the Order of the Garter – As one would be no use to me – I modestly suggest that I be given them both!

This, Allen commented, she wrote in 'that spirit of naughtiness which makes a child stick out its tongue at those who regard themselves as its elders and betters'.

By early 1934 Oswald Mosley's BUF had nearly 40,000 members across Britain. Mosley's most influential supporter was Lord Rothermere, who used his newspapers to publicise the fascist cause in articles entitled 'Hurrah for the Blackshirts' (*Daily Mail*, January 1934) and 'Give the Blackshirts a Helping Hand' (*Daily Mirror*, January 1934). Rothermere praised Mosley's doctrine and leadership ability, dismissing rumours that he would adopt dictatorial methods that opposed Jews, trade unions and Freemasons. The BUF was thoroughly British, Rothermere declared, and respected the traditional political principle of tolerance. Mosley was finding favour, and businessmen and senior figures in government had also joined the BUF. In 1933 and early 1934 the *Saturday Review* promoted the fascist leader by publishing articles written by and in favour of him. For example, on 10 February 1934, Mosley's article 'Our Policy – Britain First!' was accompanied by a full-page portrait with the caption 'Sir Oswald Mosley. The English Fascist Leader who is daily gathering more and more disciples.' However, at this time Lucy was still wary of Hitler, writing to the *Morning Post* on 20 April that he had made a mistake in his persecution of Jews and also in his attempt to 'defy' the Roman Catholic pope. A magazine entitled *The Fascist: The Organ of Racial Fascism*, published by the anti-Jewish Imperial Fascist League, picked up on Lucy's letter, declaring itself amused that a woman who would have remained in obscurity if 'someone had not made money for her to spend' should advise Hitler on how to run Germany.

The *Evening Standard* cartoonist David Low again drew attention to Lucy's association with Mosley by presenting her as his supporter. Although Low interpreted Lucy as a rich, fat, fur-coated fascist, she was flattered by the attention. Buying Low's originals, she reproduced them in the *Saturday Review*, which reported on the 'good humoured guerrilla warfare' between Lucy and Low. Lucy became one of Low's stock figures and in return, he wrote in his autobiography, she assaulted him with '"poems" of calypso quality written in mauve ink' and boxes of cigars. When Low first featured Lucy he had not yet invented his best-known character, 'Colonel Blimp', an elderly, pompous, obese and ultra-nationalistic figure who sported a walrus moustache. Low intended Blimp to be a 'comic figure typifying stupidity' and Lucy, he wrote, had been the colonel's 'premature female counterpart'.

In July 1934 Mosley received a great blow when Rothermere suddenly withdrew his support. Mosley wrote in his autobiography that Rothermere had explained frankly to him that companies under 'Jewish influence' had threatened to stop placing advertisements with his newspapers because of Mosley's anti-Jewish stance.[51] Rothermere's withdrawal put Lucy in a difficult situation. With whom should she side? If she were to side with Mosley and public opinion continued to go against him, her own newspaper might lose readers. After two weeks of indecision Lucy came off the fence. In an article entitled 'Lord Rothermere is Right', she stated that while she did not oppose Mosley's ideology, she objected to him embracing foreign influences. Mosley was far from being a Mussolini and was doing his cause harm by attempting to imitate the Italian leader. English people, wrote Lucy, shied at the word dictator, and for Oswald Mosley to pose as one was a 'mistake'.

Lucy's doctors having recommended rest and change of air, she departed for Scotland in June and placed an advertisement in the *Scotsman*: 'Maid (useful) wanted; accustomed to wait on invalid and sleep in lady's room; no nurse attendant or trained nurse need apply; good long character from similar post indispensable; middle-aged, quick, and attentive; wages £100.' However, Lucy was not such an invalid that she could not entertain a rowdy house party at Kinrara, or indeed launch a new campaign. The British herring industry was in difficulties that summer because for political reasons fish could no longer be exported to Russia and Germany. When at the end of June Sir Murdoch Wood, MP for Banffshire, made an unsuccessful appeal in the House of Commons for financial assistance for Scottish herring curers, Lucy sent him a telegram expressing her sympathy and suggesting that the industry could be boosted if the personnel of the army, navy and air force were supplied with fresh herrings once a week.

Lucy's interest in Scottish herrings prompted the *Aberdeen Press and Journal* to contact her at Kinrara. She told the newspaper that it was a 'scandal and a crime' that 'delicious' herrings, which she preferred to salmon, should be dumped back into the sea or used as manure due to lack of demand. People thought that because the humble herring was cheap it was not good but they were entirely mistaken, and if the price was much higher more people would buy them. She suggested the formation of a patriotic Herring League, with members promising to eat the fish once a week to help the industry. It was, she said, the duty of MPs to take the matter seriously and insist upon action. Although Lucy insisted that 'something should and must be done', little happened. The outcome of Lucy's campaign was unclear but Allen reported that some top restaurants put the fish on their menus. In July the cartoonist Low included her in his roll of honour of 'Britain's Year of Champions'. Lucy, wearing a sash bearing the words 'Miss England', was given the title of 'Special Champ' while a little dog, presumably Benito, was shown peeping from behind her pneumatic form.

Although at Kinrara Lucy was 500 miles from Allen, he was not allowed to relax; she kept in close touch by telegram and the telephone that she had now had installed. That summer of 1934 he had the irritating task of dealing with Lucy's food supply. Everything was sent by rail from the Army and Navy Stores in London, although Allen never could understand why she did not buy her provisions in nearby Inverness. One July day he received a telegram informing him that Lucy, her guests and the whole household were on the verge of starvation. The food parcels had been delayed in transit because the weather was unusually hot, and by the time they reached Kinrara the contents had gone bad. Allen was required to supervise the shipments personally, which involved going to the railway station each time a consignment was to be dispatched, and tipping the guard heavily to take care of it. The parcels had to change trains twice, and Allen had to send the station masters telegrams, warning them to attend to the matter personally. For some time all went smoothly, until a telegram arrived complaining that a leg of mutton had arrived two days late and full of maggots, and the fruit was squashed. Allen's heart sank, but fortunately the weather cooled and the situation eased. Lucy left Kinrara in August, and would never return.

Lucy's racing stable had not been doing well and, doubtless thinking back to the days when Gretton's Sterling and Isonomy had won race after race, she pondered the faults of the modern horse in the *Saturday Review*. The famous horses of the past, she wrote, had usually kept their form but now so many 'high-bred' young thoroughbreds started their racing career by running brilliantly only to quickly fade into 'also rans'. Wondering whether this was the fault of modern methods of training, Lucy moved her own horses from Newmarket to Mablethorpe in Lincolnshire where they were under the care of a new trainer, Jim Russell, who used a system based on the beach environment. Wanting to see her horses in training, towards the end of September, Lucy leased Burwell Hall, a large Georgian house situated on the edge of the Lincolnshire Wolds within easy reach of Mablethorpe. Although the house had fine rococo plasterwork ceilings it was isolated, damp and inconvenient, and Allen found it more difficult to supply food there than to Kinrara. Nevertheless, Lucy loved to see her horses gallop and roll on a long stretch of sandy beach: she believed that sea water and the iodine it contained would benefit them, and in particular their legs and feet.

If the *Evening Standard* found its way to the wilds of the Lincolnshire Wolds, Lucy would have been cheered by a Low cartoon published in October with the caption, 'Judging by the recent Tory conference we may soon be looking for a new Tory leader. The following probable starters have arrived.' Lucy was shown as number three among the 'starters', behind Winston Churchill as one and Lord Beaverbrook as two. She stood, chin out and with her signature Britannia shield at her side, declaring her policy: 'Rule Britannia and Damn the Details.'[52] Low had intended this to show that Lucy had no policy, and was frustrated when she delightedly adopted it as a slogan for the *Saturday Review*.

That winter, back at Byron Cottage, Lucy introduced a new feature into the *Saturday Review*. She was afraid of only one thing – the common cold – and devised her own cure by putting together every remedy that had ever been prescribed for her. The result, Allen thought, was a 'monstrous compendium of elixirs' that was far worse than any cold, but over the next two years 'Lady Houston's Cold Cure' would be reprinted ad nauseam in the *Saturday Review*. There were many stages to the cure, which included sniffing and gargling with Listerine or salt and hot water, taking tablespoons of castor oil, and swallowing Vaseline to stop a cough. Probably remembering the final illness of her brother Tom, Lucy wrote that 'a cold is the forerunner of pneumonia, and bronchitis, and very often ends in death'. A cold, she recommended, should never be neglected: 'You should immediately take every means to fight it tooth and nail.' Many readers wrote letters of praise for the cold cure to the *Saturday Review*; however, as Allen himself wondered if any had been 'written in the office', perhaps not all were genuine.

Lucy's visitors had to be careful not to display any signs of a cold. Once, when Beaumont had a coughing fit, Lucy scolded, 'I refuse to admit anyone to my bedroom with a cold. You are spreading millions of bacilli!' When a few minutes later he coughed again Lucy rang for her maid who fetched a tablespoon and a large pot of yellow Vaseline. Lucy loaded the spoon with Vaseline and held it out to Beaumont: 'Swallow it quickly!' she ordered. Beaumont protested and said that if he did so he would vomit, but Lucy only replied, 'there are three windows and you may have your pick of them if you are sick. Come, swallow it! All you men are cowards in these matters!' Lucy watched with interest and amusement as Beaumont gulped back the Vaseline, but it did stop him coughing.

But 'Old Britannia', as Wentworth Day described Lucy, was tiring. At the end of 1934 she was in a gloomy mood about the state of England and at Christmas sent Edward, Prince of Wales, the gift of a book, *First Over Everest: The Houston-Mount Everest Expedition 1933,* written by members of the expedition. Signing herself 'Lucy Houston', she inscribed the volume:

> Our Prince of Wales
> Whatever ails
> Through storms and gales
> Loves us with a love that <u>never fails!</u>

She marked the passing of the year with a despondent rhyme in the *Saturday Review*:

> O, thirty four, in thy small space,
> What dire events have taken place,
> Of our privileges thou has reft us,
> Only disaster has thou left us.

Lucy saw no more pleasing prospect for 1935. The year, she wrote in the *Saturday Review*, was starting with a 'thick pea-soup fog clouding our mental vision', but if people could see through it they would be staggered by the horrors that appeared. The cover of the New Year issue featured the Union Jack flying proudly while beside it a ragged red flag drooped sadly. Which flag was Britain under, the text enquired? Was it the flag of England's forefathers from the days when 'Britannia Ruled the Waves', or the 'Red Flag of Socialists, Communists, and Bolsheviks' – three terms which had but one meaning: 'Disintegration and Slavery for all Britons.'

Lucy was now a household name. *Saturday Review* readers described her as the 'gloriously fearless Lady Houston' and the 'Joan of Arc of our times', but elsewhere her reputation was not as good. For example, in January the Tunbridge Wells Junior Imperial League staged a mock trial of a libel action brought against Lucy by Ramsay MacDonald, with local people taking the parts. 'Witnesses' were called, with actors representing Lady Astor, Stanley Baldwin, Colonel Blimp, Billie Houston (one of the Houston Sisters comedy duo), Ishbel MacDonald and Oswald Mosley. At the conclusion the verdict was given in favour of MacDonald, who was awarded damages. Then a few weeks later a London newspaper invited readers to contribute two lists, the first the names of six people who interested them and the second the names of six who bored them. The writer George Bernard Shaw came in well out in front as the top bore, followed by the pilot Amy Johnson, Mosley, MacDonald, Greta Garbo, Hitler and many lesser bores. The top polling 'interesting' person was the politician Lloyd George, closely followed by Winston Churchill, Lord Beaverbrook and Gracie Fields. Although Lucy was ranked lower down the 'interesting' list she was sufficiently well known to make the listings.

German rearmament was now well advanced and this, together with the relatively backward state of Britain's military defences, was a hot topics early in the year. In some quarters in Britain there was deep mistrust of the intentions of Hitler and the Nazi regime, and Lucy watched the unfolding situation in Germany closely. She revealed her unease in January with a poem entitled 'The Goose Step'. Among her verses were the following:

The only altar that Nazis
Worship at is Mars's
Or that Scandinavian wallah
Who lived in Valhalla

As for Christianity
They regard it as sheer inanity
And pastors who venture to mention
It incur domiciliary detention

As for that chap who burbles
On the wireless – Dr Goebbels,

The gist of most of his sallies is
'Deutschland uber Alles.'

Hourly the German labours
To live at peace with his neighbours,
And the greater his will to peace is,
The more his army increases.

At this time the dangers inherent in Germany's desire for dominance were apparent to Lucy, but by the time another year had passed she, in line with many others on the British right, would be swept along in a wave of enthusiasm for Hitler and his achievements.

Lord Rothermere envied Germany's military advance and wanted Britain to emulate its progress in aviation. In particular he wanted a British version of the German Air League, which promoted aviation among the people and had 5 million members. Rothermere proposed the creation of a British National League of Airmen, the major function of which would be to warn the country about the dangers of being unprepared for aerial warfare. On the morning of 21 January 1935 Rothermere asked Collin Brooks, a versatile and hard-working 41-year-old *Sunday Dispatch* journalist, for his help. As Brooks recorded in his diary, Rothermere instructed him 'half-jocularly' to 'go and get £10,000 from Lucy Houston' to fund the League of Airmen. Brooks was to tell Lucy that if she donated the money she could be named as founder and her patriotic efforts would receive coverage in Rothermere's newspapers. Such was Lucy's reputation that Rothermere made 'bawdy jokes' about Brooks's 'virtue not being safe with Lady Houston'. Then began a 'farcical day' for Brooks, but it would mark the start of a close friendship between him and Lucy.

Brooks, well connected in the newspaper world, firstly contacted Allen, who told him that Lucy was 'ill, bad tempered, and would see nobody'. When Brooks insisted, Allen said that he would try to fix up an appointment, and they arranged to meet at their club at noon. But that morning when Brooks saw Rothermere again his boss's mind was still running on the bawdy theme: 'Honeymoon successful?' he asked. When Brooks explained that he had not yet seen Lucy, Rothermere cut in: 'Listen, Brooks, when you go out to Hampstead to see your girlfriend call in at a good chemist and buy the necessary medicaments – charge 'em to the office.'

Escaping from Lord Rothermere and his laboured dirty jokes, Brooks met Allen and learned that he had an appointment with Lucy at five o'clock; Allen warned him that she was 'very difficult' to deal with. When Brooks told Rothermere of his date with Lucy he was advised to 'take a good meal of stout and oysters'. Brooks took a taxi to Byron Cottage where, he wrote in his diary, 'you ring an old bell at its gates and a maid comes cautiously down the patch and shoots back two bolts. You are shown into a pleasant old English hall with a wood fire burning and crackling.' Brooks petted Benito while he waited and at length a maid showed him upstairs. Lucy was lying on the low divan wearing her red dressing gown and a red turban, with a red, white and blue scarf around her neck. Her 'puffy old face and her peepy little eyes were like a caricature of her features', Brooks wrote. This, then, he mused later, was the 'famous millionaire harlot' who as a child had run the streets as a gamin and at the age of 16 'married from a chorus'. She had had three 'official' husbands, the last being Robert Houston, who had made his fortune from 'coffin ships', or ships that transported migrants in dangerously overcrowded conditions. Such was the account of Lucy and her late husband then current in society.

Remembering Allen's advice on how to treat Lucy, Brooks greeted her by being 'greasily diplomatic', stooping over her hand and touching it with his lips. There then followed a long conversation during which Lucy denounced Ramsay MacDonald as a traitor under Soviet control, and Brooks concluded that she was a 'good sort – but mad'. When at last Brooks steered the conversation round to the League of Airmen, Lucy seized upon the idea of lending the Kinrara estate for aviation training, although the hilly, wooded landscape made it unsuitable. Lucy 'babbled' on but eventually, pleased with the idea of being named the founder, and attracted by the idea of gaining a voice in the Rothermere press, she agreed in principle to donate £10,000. However, within a few days Lucy discovered that Rothermere would not allow her to attack MacDonald in his newspapers and withdrew her offer. She met Brooks again and complained that Rothermere had deceived her; although Brooks tried to placate her, as he noted in his diary, she was right. As they parted Brooks was amused when Lucy advised him to treat Rothermere 'with sugar', saying, 'be diplomatic, my dear, I know that kind of man'. When Brooks replied, 'I'll do my best, but I'm not Lady Houston,' she 'beamed with pleasure'. Brooks wrote in his diary: 'What a mountebank they make of me!!' But the situation had reached an impasse, and although later that day Brooks spent hours on the telephone to Lucy, she would not give the £10,000.

Within a few weeks, however, Lucy had invited Collin Brooks to join the eclectic group of regular contributors who by now formed the backbone of the *Saturday Review*. With such an owner, the journal naturally attracted those with extreme views, but as she paid her writers well – Brooks alone received £1,200 a year – others with less extreme views were prepared to write as Lucy wished for the sake of selling their work. Several, perhaps not wishing their association with the controversial newspaper to be known, used pseudonyms. Brooks, for example, wrote as 'Historicus', and Comyns Beaumont as 'Kim'. Lucy wrote not only under her own name but also as 'Truthsayer'. Although the majority of *Saturday Review* writers were men, there were two women – Meriel Buchanan and Dorothy Crisp – among the regulars. However, as Lucy mistrusted her youth, Crisp decided to adopt a subterfuge and submit her articles under the name of a friend, Colonel Sir Thomas Polson, an Anglo-Irish septuagenarian and former MP for Dover.

Meriel Buchanan wrote under her own name, and from April 1935 became the second most frequent female contributor after Lucy herself. In Lucy's eyes Buchanan had great credibility for, as the daughter of Sir George Buchanan, the last British ambassador to the Russian imperial court, she had first-hand knowledge of Russia. Buchanan was delighted when Lucy asked her to contribute to the *Saturday Review*, for she admired Lucy's unwavering patriotism and generosity on behalf of England; these enabled Buchanan to tolerate her eccentricities and 'occasional vulgarities'. In her articles Buchanan attacked Bolshevism and supported Mussolini as strongly as even Lucy could have wished in articles such as 'The Russian Menace', 'The Peril of Red Propaganda' and 'England Saved by Mussolini'.

Lucy also indulged her friends by printing their material. Eva Thaddeus was living in Paris from where she wrote Lucy gossipy letters and contributed a regular column, 'Eve in Paris'. An old friend closer to home was Brinckman, and when he visited Byron Cottage he and Lucy reminisced about the old days and mourned over modern politics. Brinckman occasionally submitted a letter for publication but Lucy gave instructions that his contributions should be carefully sub-edited. While she still admired his appearance and style of dressing, she was suspicious, Allen wrote, of his 'intellectual equipment, particularly grammar and spelling', although these were not her own strongest points. Brinckman's letters would have done credit to Colonel Blimp, with one, published in March 1935, beginning:

> I do not know what our daily journals are coming to; yours is the only paper that tells the truth. The others will put in such rotten things as someone seeing a cuckoo very early or a primrose sprouting in December; but anything that contains remarks about our Government or politicians, however cleverly written or truthful, they will not publish, thanks to our so-called statesmen.

In another letter Brinckman criticised the 'deplorable incompetence of the so-called National Government'. At least, he wrote, Germany had a strong leader who had his country's defence at heart, while Britain had 'imbeciles' who had made it the 'contempt of every other country'.

But there was one old friend whom Lucy would not tolerate. When Lucy had first known Violet Hunt she had been a well-known author, but by the 1930s was almost forgotten. She had continued to write, and was working on a biography of nineteenth-century art dealer Charles Augustus Howell, although the book was destined never to be published. The two women had not met for years but several drafts or copies of letters that Hunt wrote to Lucy during the 1930s survive, and reveal the dynamic of their lingering relationship as patron and recipient. Hunt presented herself as ill, self-pitying and financially insecure; living alone, she wrote, gave her much time for 'brooding'. She had sent some reviews to the *Saturday Review* but 'your man didn't like them', she told Lucy. However, she wished Lucy luck with the journal: 'It is spirited – Irish – Are you a bit Irish and do you love a fight? If you don't answer this part sometime I shall think you are angry with me?'

Hunt watched Lucy from afar: 'Anno Domini hasn't touched <u>you</u> much, to judge from the pictures of you in the paper.' And one day she had had tea in the yard of the Bull and Bush inn from where she had looked up the road towards Byron Cottage. She pleaded for an invitation to the 'dear old place', and to see again Lucy's bedroom where Lucy had shown her 'how to use baby powder'. Pathetically, Hunt questioned the way in which Lucy signed her letters as 'L.H.': 'Why are you "Lucy" no more to me, and mine sincerely. It hurts me,'[53] she wailed. But although Lucy had no time for Hunt's unending spinelessness and neediness, she sent her old friend money on a regular basis, albeit with conditions. In one letter Lucy wrote that she had not sent her usual donation because Hunt had ignored a previous stipulation that it was to be spent on a holiday for the sake of her health.[54] When Lucy later relented, Hunt wrote to express her gratitude: 'Your splendid gift came so handy. It was a splendid thing of you to do. And I was afraid from your last letter that you were shocked with me for plaguing you.' She begged Lucy to write her a 'nice' letter and return to being the 'Lucy' that she had been until Hunt was 'naughty' and wouldn't go on the holiday.[55]

In January 1935 Lucy became involved with Randolph Churchill when he decided to run for parliament. At that time the 23-year-old Randolph, employed as a reporter by Rothermere's *Daily Mail*, had been sent to Wavertree in Liverpool to cover a by-election. Only three weeks before polling day Randolph suddenly announced that he intended to enter himself as an independent Conservative candidate. It would become, as the *Liverpool Echo* reported, 'a mad-hatter contest from beginning to end'. Churchill was worried by his son's decision. It was, he wrote to his wife Clementine on 18 January, a 'most rash and unconsidered plunge', for Randolph had no experience of elections and would not take his father's advice. Randolph had not one local constituency supporter and for all his 'personality and political flair' the campaign would be 'amateurish in the last degree'. The Wavertree constituency had traditionally been a safe Conservative seat but Churchill thought it likely that Randolph's intervention would split the Conservative vote and allow the socialist candidate to win.[56] But matters brightened for Randolph when Lord Rothermere gave him support in his newspapers, and his sisters Sarah and Diana arrived in Liverpool to help him.

The idea of Randolph standing for parliament in Liverpool was an irresist-ible combination for Lucy; it brought together Houston's home city and the son of a man she greatly admired. Lucy sent Randolph a cheque for £1,000 to cover his personal campaign expenses with a note that read, 'Here you are my dear Randolph may it bring you luck & to India freedom from that awful blood stained white paper.'[57] Lucy was referring to the White Paper in connection with the India Bill that would be passed later that year. Randolph's campaign would be fought mainly on the issue of India, for Britain's moves towards allowing self-government in India threatened to ruin the cotton industry. 'WAVERTREE stand firm for the Empire. VOTE FOR RANDOLPH CHURCHILL', read the campaign material, and the text was accompanied by a picture of Randolph: young, fresh faced and good looking.[58] Randolph's first speech, given at Wavertree Town Hall on 21 January, was a great success. The venue was packed to capacity and Randolph raised a laugh by describing Lancashire MPs as a 'pretty gormless crowd' who once they got to London were 'dazzled by the big lights' and 'so impressed by meeting a few "nobs"' that they quickly forgot the 'tragic conditions' at home.

Randolph's campaign was further strengthened when the India Defence League threw its considerable weight behind him. Now, Randolph boasted, he would be able to have prominent members of parliament on his political platform, and indeed Lord Wolmer (chairman of the league), Lord Lloyd, the Duchess of Atholl and Sir Henry Page-Croft would all speak for him at Wavertree. Winston Churchill, feeling that he had little choice but to support his son, agreed to give an eve of poll speech. Randolph, Churchill wrote to Clementine, was in the 'seventh heaven'.[59]

The main problem for Randolph's candidature, as the press was quick to point out, was his youth. His backers decided to make a virtue of it, declaring that youth was the new force in politics. Rothermere instructed his journalists to propose that 'servile, wavering old men' were doomed, that youth had genius, and that Randolph possessed the gifts of 'brilliant eloquence, brilliant wit, brilliant courage, brilliant judgment'. Lucy, too, did her bit. On 26 January her article 'Youth at the Helm. What Price Randolph Churchill?' was published in the *Saturday Review*. She greatly admired Randolph, she wrote, for his 'courage and pluck' and willingness to 'fight against all odds for his King and Country'. She accompanied the article with one of her rhymes:

Intelligent Youth
Dealing in TRUTH
Should soon send to glory
The Socialist sham Tory
With his lies tufted and Hoare-y

On 31 January Lucy sent Randolph a telegram that she wanted him to read out on his platform. The supporters of the late Sir Robert Houston, she wrote, should also support Randolph because 'that is what Sir Robert would have done and would have asked them to do if he was now alive'. The telegram also contained a verse that Randolph was perhaps less keen to read out:

When the truth is told to Wavertree
Wavertree will set India free
And Socialist Mac will be up a tree
With all his lies and hypocrisy
Your Indian kinsfolk from over the sea
Are crying to thee
To save them from horrors you cannot see
Gallant Randolph can set them free
For Randolph is brave and Randolph has youth
And is boldly determined to tell the truth
Pitt was premier at twenty three
So why not he?[60]

Puffed up by his own success, Randolph pursued his campaign with energy while his father watched the proceedings anxiously. On 31 January Lord Lloyd arrived at Wavertree and addressed a meeting of nearly 3,000 people. Lloyd's speech seemed reasonable enough but it would effectively end his liaison with Lucy. The following day at Byron Cottage, Wentworth Day and Lucy discussed what Lloyd had said. Wentworth Day argued that Lloyd had taken a temperate line and was sensibly using a 'policy of attrition' to wear down the government's case. But Lucy would have none of it: 'Attrition be damned,' she snapped. 'He shouldn't give the Government any credit whatever, or show them any mercy. He should have blown them sky high.' Lucy then dictated a telegram in which she severely criticised Lloyd's speech. If he believed what he said, she declared, then he was a traitor to his own principles. Wentworth Day, aghast, warned Lucy that if she sent the telegram Lloyd would never forgive her. 'Don't lecture me!' Lucy retorted. 'I shall say what I think. I'm paying for this campaign.' Wentworth Day reminded her that Lloyd had once ruled India and stopped riots in Egypt: 'You can't treat that sort of man like an office-boy.' Undeterred, Lucy sent the telegram.

The following day, 2 February, Lloyd, now back from Liverpool, asked Wentworth Day to call at his house in Portman Square. Wentworth Day found Lloyd angry and upset. He would not put up with such treatment from Lucy, he said, and she had to understand that he would not be dictated to. Although he had spent £8,000 of the £10,000 that she had given him he intended to return the whole sum. Wentworth Day tried to soothe Lloyd, begging him to make allowances for Lucy who was old and thought so highly of him, but Lloyd replied that he had already done so, and this was the end. He handed a cheque for £10,000 to Wentworth Day, who returned to Byron Cottage and threw it down on Lucy's bed. She looked at it and burst into tears: 'Oh! What have I done? What *have* I done?' Wentworth Day replied angrily, 'You've insulted the best man in England. I told you he wouldn't put up with that telegram.' Lucy tore the cheque in half: 'He must keep the money,' she said. As a result of this incident, while Lloyd remained friends with Lucy he would take no more of her money.

When 6 February, polling day, came at Wavertree the worst fears of Winston Churchill came true: Randolph had split the Conservative vote allowing the Labour candidate to win. Randolph came third, with 10,575 votes, but he had done well and the *Scotsman* reported that although he had been helped by the glamour of his name and the influence of his father, the size of his vote was still 'formidable' by any reckoning. Lucy sent Randolph another cheque and a note: 'Here is a little token of admiration for your brilliant & courageous fight <u>for the right</u>.'[61] But once the dust had settled it became apparent that the Wavertree by-election had infuriated Conservatives, damaged the reputation of Winston Churchill and caused a rift between him and Randolph. The seat, stated the *Leeds Mercury*, had been 'thrown away by Churchillian recklessness', and there must be 'no more Wavertrees'.

Randolph, however, had gained a taste for electioneering and was itching for another fight. Another by-election was scheduled to take place at Norwood, a division of Lambeth in London, on 14 March. Norwood was regarded as a safe Conservative constituency and Randolph came to ask Lucy for her support, not for a himself but for a friend, Richard Findlay, whom he would back as an independent Unionist candidate. Winston Churchill did what he could to dissuade Randolph from becoming involved at Norwood but, he wrote to his wife, their son had become 'uncontrollable' and there had been 'sharp words'. Churchill thought it likely that this time neither Rothermere nor the India Defence League would become involved, and reflected gloomily that the best that could be hoped for was that Randolph's campaign would 'come a dreadful flop'.[62]

The Norwood by-election was a lively one. Randolph gave dozens of speeches in support of Findlay, who reciprocated by praising his sponsor Randolph as a 'new force' in politics who might well be the 'salvation' of the Conservative Party. Lucy's role at Wavertree had been low key but now she came out into the open, swamping Norwood with a pamphlet entitled 'Thrown to the Wolves'.

In it she made an all-out attack on the National Government as an 'iniquitous sham' introduced by Ramsay MacDonald in order to destroy Conservatism, helped along by Stanley Baldwin. It was a 'colossal impertinence' for Baldwin to describe himself as the leader of the Conservative Party when he had made Britain's armed forces a laughing stock, while MacDonald was a 'Political Popinjay' who dared not make public speeches even in his own constituency for fear of being howled down. 'Englishmen, Englishmen, have you no shame, no pride, no self-respect?' Lucy cried. With regard to India, Britain had betrayed loyal Indians, for less than half a per cent of the population wanted change even though they had had the 'disadvantage of a Western education, which is utterly unsuited to the Eastern mind'. The government's 'pigheadedness' over India was because politicians had promised the country to Russia in order to keep the Soviets quiet. 'There is something dark and dirty in all this which ought to be unearthed. Who is going to do it? Must it be left to a woman?' she asked. But Lucy was a dubious asset as a by-election ally because she cared little for the rules limiting the amount which a candidate could spend on their campaign. The cost of producing and distributing 'Thrown to the Wolves' must have been considerable and Randolph, fearing that it might be counted in with Findlay's election expenses, made Lucy very angry when he burned much of her literature.

Churchill visited Byron Cottage during the Norwood campaign and, despite Lucy's admiration, did not escape unscathed when she complained to him about Randolph's cavalier treatment of her pamphlets. It was perhaps on this occasion that Lucy told Churchill that he was being too easy on the socialists in parliament and advised him to 'sail in and make mincemeat of them'. When Churchill replied, 'You don't have to live with them every day. I do,' Lucy retorted, 'I never thought you were a coward before.' Churchill was silenced, but was sufficiently broad-shouldered not to bear a grudge. Afterwards Lucy complained to Miss Ritchie, 'I can't get these men to do what I want them to do.' If she was in the House of Commons, she said, she would do and say what she wanted and 'damn the consequences!' When Miss Ritchie replied that MPs had their political reputations to consider Lucy snapped, 'Fiddlesticks! What are their reputations worth compared with the good of the country?' But Churchill's visit had stimulated Lucy and afterwards Allen found her in her 'very best form'.

Without the support of Churchill and the India Defence League at Norwood, Findlay and Randolph were left high and dry, and Lucy wrote to Lord Wolmer to criticise the league for abandoning Randolph. Wolmer replied on 11 March but, irritated by Lucy's confrontation, he was sparing with social niceties. 'I do not think that I merit your criticism,' he began bluntly, 'although I do appreciate the candour with which you write.' He had given his support at Wavertree, he explained, because Randolph had had a chance of winning. But at Norwood Randolph had tried to force Wolmer's hand, introducing an inexperienced candidate and going ahead without consultation. If anyone wanted to criticise Wolmer for not going to Norwood, why didn't they go and speak there themselves, he asked in a dig at Lucy. He ended with a direct attack: 'I wish I could persuade you that we are more likely to influence public opinion by avoiding extravagance in word and action. I refuse to plead guilty to the charge of cowardice because I am not inclined to tilt at windmills!'[63]

Perhaps even Lucy was beginning to understand Wolmer's reservations about Randolph, for he was causing her more trouble. One evening she sent her chauffeur to Norwood with a loudspeaker for the campaign, but he could find nobody to deliver it to: 'The journey was in vain – so <u>tiresome</u>',[64] Lucy wrote to Randolph the following day. But another incident was more serious. Lucy used people such as Dorothy Crisp to spy on those who were spending her money. She took nothing at face value, Crisp wrote, and 'invariably used three or four people as eyes'. Lucy sent Crisp to Norwood to find out what Randolph, Findlay and their friends were up to before she gave any more money. Crisp was a similar age to Randolph's group and so was amused when Lucy urged her to 'be a mother to them!' adding, 'You know, my dear, a woman can make any man do what she wants as long as she lets him think he thought of it all himself!'

After visiting Norwood three times in thirty-six hours, Crisp rang Lucy with her observations. They were negative, for, although she did not record her verdict, she believed – wrongly as it happens – that as a result Randolph received no more money from Lucy. On 7 March Lucy sent Randolph a letter:

> I hear a lot of tiresome gossip going round about Norwood and what several people tell me is that the enemy is circulating a lie that you and Mr Findlay are drinking too much for the constituency to care to vote for you. I tell you this so that you may give them the lie. It is always well to catch a lie and fling it back in the face of the liar.[65]

Lucy was in possession of a letter, written by Dorothy Crisp or another spy, which made an accusation against Randolph, presumably about his drinking. The next day, 8 March, she sent the letter to Churchill with a note: 'I think it is right that you should see it. Can you do anything? It would be disastrous if it becomes an open scandal.'[66] Whatever the accusation, Churchill took it seriously and forwarded the letter to his son, who replied breezily on campaign notepaper. Lucy, he said, had already written to him on the matter and he had told her that it was 'of course the greatest nonsense'. The forwarded letter had been written by a 'foolish young woman who has only been to the constituency about twice and has only seen me once'.[67] Meanwhile, Churchill made his own enquiries and wrote to Lucy that he was satisfied that there was 'no truth whatever in the suggestion'. Lucy need have no further concerns, Churchill assured her. However, like Wolmer, he tried to exert control over Lucy by saying that it would be better that 'with our small forces if in future we tried to act in concert as much as possible'.[68] It was a tactful appeal that suggested his inclusion of Lucy as a political ally while at the same time asking her to consult him before launching into political ventures in the future.

In the event Richard Findlay won only 8.5 per cent of the votes and so lost his deposit. Despite the Norwood fiasco, however, Lucy had not given up on Randolph and afterwards they worked on a plan that Randolph would open the first branch of a new 'Conservative Union' in Wavertree. This, he intended, would eventually become a national organisation which Lucy would fund to run candidates at forthcoming elections. But Churchill saw trouble ahead. Randolph's aim, he wrote to Clementine, was to 'put Socialists in everywhere he can in order to smash up MacDonald and Baldwin', but this would result in 'fury' and cause trouble for Churchill himself.[69] Announcing the venture in the press in mid-March, Randolph said that he had a ten-point plan that would revive the Conservative Party, bring it into closer touch with the working classes, and raise the profile of younger members who were currently 'gagged by the old gang of politicians'. At the end of the month Randolph rashly said that he intended to spend the rest of his 'political life' in Wavertree and, as he was now a ratepayer (Lucy had paid for office accommodation for the Conservative Union), he would seek election to the Liverpool City Council.

While Lucy had been at Burwell Hall in the autumn of 1934 she had received a visitor, Thomas Walker, a suave and well-dressed American.

Having been to Russia several times he had arrived in England that spring claiming to be a journalist and an authority on Russia. He had become acquainted with Lucy's associate the Duchess of Atholl, MP for Kinross and West Perthshire, who strongly opposed the abuses of human rights in the Soviet Union, and when Walker said that he could provide news stories and photographs she provided him with an introduction to Lucy. Lucy, impressed by Walker's credentials, accepted his offer, but the connection would cause her a great deal of trouble.

Sometime early in 1935 Walker visited Byron Cottage bringing three items of intense interest to Lucy – letters purporting to be written to prominent Soviet politicians bearing the signature of 'J. Ramsay MacDonald'. Walker told Lucy that he had just returned from Russia where he had obtained them with great difficulty, and having paid a Russian £300 for each he was keen to sell them on to her. All three appeared to have been written in 1926, the year of the General Strike. The first, dated 11 February, was from MacDonald to Grigori Sokolnikoff, well-known as Soviet ambassador to Britain from 1929 to 1932. Written on MacDonald's private notepaper from his home at Upper Frognal Lodge in London, it was addressed to the headquarters of the All-Russian Co-operative Society (ARCOS) in Moorgate in London, an address that was suspected of being a cover organisation for espionage activities. The letter, dated three months before the 1926 General Strike, read:

> Dear Mr Sokolnikoff.
>   The time does not seem ripe for the movement you suggest. Everything is to be gained by a few months delay. You may count upon me to support you in your noble work.
>   Sincerely,
>   J. Ramsay MacDonald.[70]

This seemed to provide concrete proof that MacDonald had been a key agent in the Soviet instigation of the General Strike.

The second letter, also addressed to Sokolnikoff at the ARCOS offices, was dated a week later and discussed the advance of socialism in Britain and MacDonald's support for it:

> You must recognise that your Russian methods for serfdom and com-munism are not available for use here. Our British workman is more

susceptible to worldly goods and materialist enticements. It is my wish that this country may follow in the same course that you have chosen, but we must have a more intelligent introduction.

The tone suggested that the writer was in a position superior to his addressee, and the comment about British working-class men was unusually deprecating for a Labour leader to make about his rank-and-file members. If genuine and made public, the letter could only discredit MacDonald to his own supporters.

The third letter, dated 5 March 1926, was addressed to Christian Rakovsky, a Soviet diplomatic representative in Britain in the 1920s. Written on House of Commons notepaper, it read:

> Any change which is to readjust the allocation of wealth in Great Britain and which is to establish a system of justice in settling the relation between services and reward must be a sudden and violent change. I hope to see the day, not too far distant, when the King may follow the way of the Czar, but I do not feel too optimistic about the results of the general action planned for May.

In effect, MacDonald was shown to be calling for a British revolution that would overthrow the monarchy and, by implication, lead to the assassination of King George V and his family. In view of the fact that Macdonald was known to be a friend of the King, if the letter were genuine this would be particularly shocking. The letter, as New Scotland Yard's Detective Inspector Smith would write, was 'dynamite'.[71] The Russian letters seemed designed to make Ramsay MacDonald look dangerous to the British right and a traitor to the left. There were also parallels with the so-called 'Zinoviev letter', published in 1924 by the *Daily Mail* four days before the general election. That letter was purported to have been written by Grigory Zinoviev, communist chief in Moscow, to the Communist Party of Great Britain, instructing it to organise subversive activities. The letter had embarrassed Ramsay MacDonald and had helped to bring down his first Labour government.

The provenance of Walker's letters inspired confidence. MacDonald knew Rakovsky well for the two had negotiated agreements at an Anglo–Russian conference in London in April 1924 and, as Sokolnikoff had served as Russian ambassador in London during MacDonald's term of office as Prime

Minister, the two were bound to have met. But the biggest incentive for Lucy to believe that the letters were genuine was that she wanted them to be, for they would provide the evidence against MacDonald that she so desperately desired. It is possible, although unlikely, that Lucy commissioned the letters but if she did, no whisper of it emerged. Whatever the case, she paid Walker for them. About a week later, Lucy showed the letters to the Duchess of Atholl, who recommended that Lucy ask her husband for advice. Lucy then passed the letters to the Duke of Atholl who had them examined by a handwriting expert, who concluded that the signature was a forgery.[72] Early in April the duke sent a note to Scotland Yard requesting that a 'very discreet senior officer' call on him at his house in Elm Park Gardens, for he had 'information about a foreigner concerned in a forgery case against a well-known public man'. An officer duly visited the duke and Scotland Yard then took immediate action by putting out a search for Walker and watching the ports in case he tried to leave the country.[73]

On 12 April Detective Inspector Percy Smith, who specialised in confidence tricksters, was put on the case. In a later account he wrote that he examined the letters, now in the custody of Scotland Yard, and concluded that they contained 'suggestions of treason, revolution and regicide'. At this stage he was unsure as to whether they were genuine, but if they were then Ramsay MacDonald's situation would be serious indeed. But after investigation, although all three pieces of notepaper were found to be genuine, police handwriting experts confirmed that the signature was not. Even so, the quality of the forging was declared to be 'almost perfect … first class'. Smith approached Sokolnikoff and Rakovsky, who denied all knowledge. He then investigated Walker's background and it was established that in America he was known as Robert Green, had committed a variety of crimes including forgery, had served time in the maximum-security facility Sing Sing and, having escaped from prison in Colorado in 1921, was still a wanted man. Walker, Smith concluded, was the 'most amazing confidence man and forger' that he had come across in his twenty years at Scotland Yard.

When Smith tracked Walker down to an 'exclusive private hotel near Knightsbridge' he found the American 'bland, assured, and quite ready to bluff out the authenticity of the letters' but, as his passport was false, Smith arrested him as an 'undesirable alien'. In Walker's hotel room the detective found a curious document: a typed memorandum headed 'Suggested plan of action. To obtain a line on J.R.M. it would be advisable to get in touch with …' There followed a list of names of well-known politicians together with their contact details. It seemed an odd heading for someone to write for their own use; perhaps Lucy had provided it. It was found that Walker had indeed contacted the listed politicians and, Smith wrote, had 'worked conscientiously using his charm and undoubted knowledge of Russia and other parts of the world to impress them'.

When interviewed, Lucy stated that upon first reading the letters she had realised that they were 'most dangerous and defamatory'. She had purchased them, she said, to prevent them from getting into the hands of socialists 'who would use them against the Conservative Party', although the meaning of this is unclear. She added that she had not known what to do with the letters, and twice stated that she had never intended to publish them. This, however, is hard to believe. If the letters became public knowledge, even if they were fake, some people would believe them genuine and great harm would be done to MacDonald. And besides, Lucy told Smith later that publication had been her intention.

MacDonald's solicitors considered what course to follow. On the one hand they wanted the case to be kept quiet, but on the other hand they wanted to take legal action. As Mr Usher, the Prime Minister's political secretary, wrote to MacDonald on 8 April, 'the person who has the best right of action against the man is clearly Lady H. herself, but she for obvious reasons will not prosecute'. By this he meant that if Lucy made a charge of obtaining money by false pretences against Walker it would expose her as falling for a forger's trick. The efforts of MacDonald's solicitors and the British authorities to suppress the existence of the letters demonstrated MacDonald's fear and, as all sides considered what to do, the situation would remain at stalemate for several weeks.

INTRIGUE

Lucy's relationship with Collin Brooks blossomed in that spring of 1935. He wrote later that Lucy liked him for no better reason than that in earlier years he had known Robert Houston in Liverpool, and 'perhaps I amused her'. But Brooks was being too modest, for they had much more in common, holding similar views on current affairs, politics and the world of newspapers. Lucy was also interested in the ideas of the 'English Mistery', a secretive and ritualistic political right-wing guild of which Brooks was a member, which shared some ideas with British fascism and aimed to revive the 'Merrie England' of the Middle Ages. Although Brooks found Lucy eccentric he also thought her 'very sane', with a 'very good mind'. It was a pity, he thought, that she was not 'more readily received and more carefully "tutored" by those who could have made a stateswoman of her'. But, he added, Lucy could not live down her reputation and remained the victim of it.

By April, despite the fact that she was 78, Brooks had fallen under Lucy's spell as a woman. Once when she sent him an autographed photograph of herself and he rang to thank her, they spent forty minutes on the telephone. 'She and I flirt vigorously,' he wrote, 'one forgets the old lady and thinks of the young girl that was once all-conquering.' As she rang off Lucy said, 'You *are* a Dear!' His main memory of Lucy, Brooks wrote years later, was of her voice on the telephone, for they spoke nearly every day and at all hours, and after a sleepless night she would often ring him early in the morning to discuss the news of the day. These, he wrote, were 'not casual or desultory talks' but long conversations of up to an hour. They talked exhaustively, and later renewed their conversation. Lucy always ended her calls with the words, 'May God bless you, my dear,' as if, Brooks wrote, she were a 'Mother Superior dismissing a novice'. The telephone conversations were 'somehow impregnated by a peculiar intimacy' that bound them in a 'queer association of friendship, love, and conspiracy'. Brooks was perhaps the last man whom Lucy loved.

From time to time he visited Byron Cottage, where Lucy loved to serve him with excellent China tea and a special orange cake that she believed was his favourite. He remembered an occasion late one afternoon in Lucy's bed-room when the room was lit only by the flames of the fire. Lucy was tucked up on the divan in her big dressing gown, and the little blond curl protrud-ing from her red turban gave her an 'odd air of coquetry'. As Brooks sat beside her in a big chair with his tea and cake, Lucy explained her religious belief and he found her 'as sincere as a young nun' in her worship of God. One of Brooks's 'best memories' of Lucy was a flashback to her 'harlot' days, which occurred one Saturday morning. Having been promoted to editor of the *Sunday Dispatch*, he was sitting at his desk when Lucy rang to say that she needed to see him urgently. Brooks had no time to go to Hampstead but Lucy said, 'Well, my dear, I'm very sick, but I'll come down to you.' When she arrived in Temple Avenue they sat in the car and talked. Lucy looked 'like some strange idol from a novel by Rider Haggard, wrapped in furs, with her peculiar little headdress'. As they parted he kissed her fingers and Lucy gig-gled and said, 'Do you know, my dear, I've nothing on under this …!' Brooks was alarmed, writing later that 'I didn't know, but having been told, I hurried back to my desk round the corner.'

The silver jubilee of King George V, marking the twenty-fifth anniversary of his accession to the throne, was to be celebrated on 6 May 1935. Postage stamps had been issued and medals struck, and the great day itself was declared a public holiday; parties, fetes, sporting events and pageants were scheduled across the country. As part of its jubilee coverage the *Daily Mirror* asked well-known people the question 'What Will the Next 25 Years Bring to Us?' Lucy was among those whose opinion was solicited, and replied that 'England might easily be swamped and plotted out and become an annexe of Russia, if things continue as they are going on now.' Unsure as to her status in the Russian letters case, Russia was never far from Lucy's mind. Indeed, news of the existence of the letters had leaked out and there had been stories of a 'bombshell' in jubilee week that would smash MacDonald but, although this may have been Lucy's plan, she thought better of carrying it out.

Lucy marked the silver jubilee by taking issue with the strongly social-ist town council of Nelson in Lancashire. When it was reported that the council had declined to arrange jubilee celebrations or provide gifts for children, Lucy declared it 'scandalous'. Why, she asked, should everyone in the town suffer just because of one group? Offering to supply the council with 'medals for traitors', she advised them to 'pack up and go to Russia' where they would be welcomed, and Lucy would pay for single fares for the whole lot. On being informed of Lucy's offer one Nelson Labour Party official joked, 'Are we going by aeroplane or what?' He thought Lucy an interfering busybody: 'If we want to do anything we will do it as we like. We are not going to be told what we have to do by somebody else.' If Lucy came to Nelson, he went on, he would put on his Sunday tie and find her 'four looms and something to do'.

Ironically, however, Lucy's personal celebration of the jubilee would hardly be more enthusiastic than that of the Nelson socialists. She completed the jubilee edition of the *Saturday Review*, for publication on 4 May, before leaving London to spend the summer on the *Liberty*. The issue contained articles on the King as sailor, as sportsman and as emperor, but Lucy seemed more concerned with what she thought were official moves to gag her. The journal's tagline – formerly 'The Only Paper that Dares to Tell You all the Truth' – had been changed to 'The Paper that is not now permitted to Tell You the Truth'. Despite the royal coverage, the focus of the issue was the military weakness of Britain. Lucy's keynote article, given the centre spread and printed in large font, was a passionate appeal for rearmament. She likened the present time, 1935, to the period prior to the First World War when hide-bound, conceited and ignorant politicians had sent 2 million British men to their deaths, unprepared and untrained. The only way to pre-vent another war, she urged, was to be 'PREPARED, DOUBLY, TREBLY PREPARED' militarily, and without this Britain was 'doomed'. With the country in a state of national emergency, Lucy wrote, the jubilee celebrations were just so much 'bread and circuses'.

Unusually, Lucy refused to discuss her summer plans on the *Liberty* with Brooks. He had heard rumours of 'mystery experiments' in which an inven-tor would demonstrate a secret discovery, perhaps a 'death ray', to two retired admirals on board the yacht. But although Lucy would neither confirm nor deny this, Brooks's suspicions were not without foundation. The *Liberty* had gone ahead of Lucy, docking at Swansea on 1 May where, a newspaper reported, the 'greatest secrecy' was maintained over the reason for its visit. In fact, the yacht was collecting inventor Harry Grindell Matthews together with his technician and scientific apparatus. With men and equipment on board the *Liberty* left Swansea to moor at Poole Harbour, where, on 5 May, Lucy joined the yacht.

Lucy had been introduced to Matthews, then in his mid-50s, by Colonel Etherton of the Houston-Everest Expedition. Etherton visited Tor Cloud, Matthews's laboratory high in the hills above Swansea, in the spring of 1935 and produced several articles about the work being carried out there. Governments, Etherton wrote, were keen to learn more of the inventor who was 'revolutionising electrical science and harnessing hidden forces in the air'. He was working on a rocket that could travel at 2 miles per second and might carry man to the moon, and a 'death ray' to kill 'cancer germs'. He was also developing a system of aerial defence for London by which rockets would explode in the air and throw out a network of gossamer-thin steel curtains that would rise to 30,000 feet and bring down enemy aeroplanes.

But it was his maritime project that had brought Matthews to Lucy's attention. She had invited him to Byron Cottage and the two had got on well; Matthews's biographer E.H.G. Barwell wrote that they resembled each other in their outspokenness, their patriotism and their determination. Matthews explained his scheme for an electrical installation capable of detecting submarines 20 miles away that would make Britain impregnable from attack by underwater craft, and it was this system that would be tested on the *Liberty*. The ostensible plan was to cruise across the English Channel and make a covert approach to the French naval base at Cherbourg, where Matthews would test his equipment by secretly picking up the movements of French submarines. Houston, who had so deplored the German submarine attacks during the First World War, would have approved of his yacht being used in this way.

The *Liberty* was due to depart from Poole on its Cherbourg mission on 6 May, silver jubilee day. That morning at 'eight bells', or eight o'clock, the other ships in Poole Harbour hoisted flags to 'dress ship' for the celebration. In a memoir Jim Steele, a former *Liberty* crew member, recalled that Captain Gibb, familiarly known as 'Bully' Gibb, went to Lucy's cabin and asked permission to follow suit, but Lucy ordered him to put to sea immediately. Barwell attributed the yacht's sudden departure to Lucy's fear that the jubilee celebrations might involve fireworks and gun-firing, while she wanted complete quiet. But Wentworth Day later revealed the real reason: Lucy knew that the King disapproved of the behaviour of the Prince of Wales and some of his friends, but in Lucy's eyes the prince could do no wrong.

Once out in the English Channel the *Liberty* steamed slowly westwards until it had passed Land's End, then Lucy gave orders to proceed to Le Havre. En route for the French coast, she called 'all hands on deck', and with the crew assembled outside her door, she ordered them to sing 'God Bless the Prince of Wales', a patriotic song written in 1863 for the marriage of the Prince Edward of her youth. Wentworth Day imagined the scene. Lucy, upright in her chair in her cabin with the doors and windows wide open, and gathered on the deck outside the 'deep-sea sailors, ex-Merchant Navy men, East Anglian herring fishers and spratters and Hampshire yacht hands who had crossed the Atlantic in sail'. Over and over the men repeated the song, the strains ringing out across the English Channel, with the chorus loudest of all:

Among our ancient mountains,
And from our lovely vales,
Oh! let the pray'r re-echo,
God bless the Prince of Wales!

Bottles of best-quality Jamaica rum were ready and each time the men sang the last line Lucy 'spliced the main-brace', or handed out the rum. The singing was kept up until dark and Lucy, perhaps having had her fair share of rum, fell asleep. She had shown a second sign of disapproval against King George V.

The following morning, as the *Liberty* approached Le Havre, Captain Gibb signalled to the shore and a French pilot set out to the yacht in a tugboat. But when Gibb reported to Lucy's cabin she gave new orders. The *Liberty* was to return to England, keeping the ship at sea until the following morning, then enter Poole Harbour and tie up at a buoy near Brownsea Island. When the *Liberty* arrived back at Poole it had traced a large isosceles triangle at sea for no apparent reason. Barwell, mystified, attributed Lucy's decision to leave France to either 'impulse or intuition', but it probably owed more to the fact that she was expecting a visit from Detective Inspector Smith.

At Poole, despite warnings of shallow water from the harbourmaster, Lucy insisted on the yacht being anchored in a certain channel near Brownsea Island. The island was owned by Mrs Bonham Christie, an eccentric animal lover who lived a secluded life and was known locally as the 'Queen of Brownsea'. Mrs Christie, Barwell writes, objected to the close proximity of the *Liberty* to the island's shore and requested that Lucy leave. But meanwhile a swarm of bees had come aboard the *Liberty* from the island and Lucy retorted, 'You take away those damned bees!' The harbourmaster offered the yacht an alternative berth in Shell Bay to the south side of the mouth of Poole Harbour, but there were no submarines to listen to. Matthews was frustrated that he was unable to carry out his experiments but he tried to make the best of it, enjoying the facilities and food on the *Liberty*. Meanwhile, he and his assistant listened on their instruments to the propellers of ships three-quarters of a mile away, and picked up 'leakages' of voices from telephones on land.

Confined to her cabin, Lucy wanted Matthews to entertain her. They shared a sense of the absurd and Lucy was amused by his stories of 'officialdom gone mad', and his account of seals and seagulls being trained to detect submarines. As each day dawned Matthews hoped that Lucy's condition would improve so that they could return to Cherbourg, but nothing happened. Unable to understand Lucy's unwillingness to facilitate his experiments Matthews questioned Lucy, only to be told that when she recovered he could have the yacht to himself to do with as he wished. But Matthews had been aboard the *Liberty* for about three weeks with little result and, with no sign of Lucy's recovery, he packed up his equipment and left the yacht sometime prior to 14 May. Back at Tor Cloud, Matthews was interviewed by a local newspaper about the *Liberty* trip but he only replied, 'With a bit of luck, you will hear something really sensational in a week or two.'

Shortly after the departure of Matthews, on 14 May Detective Inspector Smith arrived. His intention, he wrote later, was to get Lucy's approval to destroy the Russian letters, which were still in the possession of Scotland Yard. He spent three hours with Lucy, and when he told her that the letters were 'obvious forgeries' she only laughed: 'You say they are forgeries, of course,' she declared, 'I am going to publish them.' She cared nothing for the laws of libel or for anything else, she said. However, Smith's account of Lucy's verbal declarations conflicted with the official written statement that she made for him that day, in which she stressed that she had never had any intention of publishing the letters. At the end of the interview Lucy dismissed Smith 'gracefully' and sent him to have tea with Captain Gibb.

While Scotland Yard wanted to destroy the letters, MacDonald's solicitors were keen to obtain them. After Smith's visit the solicitors wrote to Lucy stating that MacDonald had instructed them to request written authority from her that the letters be handed over to them.[74] Lucy was cornered. Whether she had been rattled by Smith's evidence that the letters were forgeries, or whether her legal advisors told her that she had no alternative, she agreed to comply. It must have been galling in the extreme for her to reply to MacDonald's solicitors: 'The letters you refer to are, as you say, obviously forgeries, and were purchased by me in order to prevent any mischief they might have caused.' The solicitors, she wrote, could take this statement as her authority to the police to hand over the letters, but with the condition that they be destroyed. However, this condition caused a problem. When MacDonald received a letter from his solicitors informing him about Lucy's condition he wrote on it, 'Give no promise to destroy.'[75] The solicitors then wrote to the Duke of Atholl. If, they argued, at any time in the future 'some criminally minded or irresponsible person' (Lucy was an obvious suspect) spread rumours about the letters, MacDonald might need to produce them to prove that they were forgeries. If he had agreed to their destruction then that could lead to 'sinister deductions'. It seemed that MacDonald also feared that Lucy might publish copies of the letters once the originals had been destroyed, and there would then be no proof that they had been fakes.

When Lucy continued to insist that the letters be destroyed, Atholl suggested to MacDonald's solicitors that they obtain a certificate from a handwriting expert to the effect that the letters were forgeries, and Lucy would countersign it. She would also promise that she had no intention of using or misusing the letters, provided that the solicitors stated that they had no intention of 'attacking her in any way' in the future. Atholl reiterated that Lucy had never intended to publish the letters, while to drop a 'bombshell' in jubilee week would have been 'quite the last thing' that she would have wished to do. Her loyalty to His Majesty and the Crown was 'proverbial', Atholl said.[76] This sounded reasonable but in reality Lucy would probably have enjoyed publishing evidence of MacDonald's regicidal ambitions during the King's jubilee celebrations. But, with the fate of the letters unresolved, matters were again at a stalemate. Meanwhile, Thomas Walker had been sentenced to six weeks' imprisonment with hard labour for the passport offence, and after serving it was put on a liner for New York, where the police were waiting for him.

After the interview with Smith, Lucy stayed on in Shell Bay where, in the coming days, there were various things to occupy her mind. One was the death of T.E. Lawrence in a motorcycle accident on 19 May. Lord Sempill visited several times, landing his plane on the beach below Studland. But as Lucy sat aboard the *Liberty* trying to come to terms with her humiliating climb-down over the Russian letters, she would have been soothed by the knowledge that, even had she published them, the effect would have been less damaging to MacDonald than in the past. MacDonald's health was in decline and by May it was known that he would soon be replaced as Prime Minister by Stanley Baldwin. In anticipation, on 23 May Lucy wrote to Churchill, 'Now is the cycological [*sic*] moment <u>for you</u>!' – for she wanted Churchill to insist upon the government being called 'Conservative' rather than 'National'. Commenting on the government's new moves towards increased defence spending she told Churchill that, having discovered what he had been telling them for years, politicians were 'actually patting themselves on the back for it'. Characteristically, she added an item of local news: 'It is blowing a gale here and the weather is pretty dirty outside, hardly yachting weather.'[77] Churchill replied a couple of days later. There was little point, he said, in insisting upon the next government being labelled 'Conservative' because most MPs believed that they would be better off under the title of 'National'. However, he was 'so pleased to have played a useful part' in warning of the growth of the German air force, although he regretted that his advice had not been taken in time.[78]

The Russian letters affair dogged Lucy into early June. Although it is not clear whether it was ever sent, at one point MacDonald's solicitors drafted a letter to the Duke of Atholl that suggested that if Lucy would not hand over the letters unconditionally, they would deal with the matter 'in a way which might be unpleasant for Lady Houston'. This appeared to be a threat that MacDonald would take proceedings against Lucy, which would reveal that she had engaged in 'trafficking with a purveyor of forged documents'.[79] Eventually, however, MacDonald's solicitors, wary of taking on Lucy in the courts, entered into an agreement with her by which neither side would use the letters, or knowledge of them, against the other.[80] Lucy would keep her word. The period of MacDonald's settlement with Lucy coincided with the announcement, made on 7 June, that he was stepping down as Prime Minister. Perhaps Lucy consoled herself with the thought that he had resigned out of fear of her. While MacDonald stayed on as leader of the

Labour Party, Baldwin became Prime Minister. In Lucy's view Baldwin was not much better than MacDonald but, despite her best efforts to oust him, his premiership would continue until May 1937 and outlive her.

On 23 June 1935, the forty-first birthday of the Prince of Wales, Lucy made a great display by ordering the *Liberty* to be 'dressed overall' with flags from end to end, thereby rubbing in her refusal to do the same for the King's jubilee. But another jubilee event, the Naval Review, was to take place at Spithead on 16 July. The King arrived at Spithead on the royal yacht *Victoria and Albert*, while members of the cabinet joined the Admiralty sloop *Enchantress*. The military ships of the home and Mediterranean fleets were represented, and 1,000 civilian craft were present. On the Cowes side of the Solent moorings had been allotted to private yachts – but the *Liberty*'s mooring was empty. While rockets fired, flags fluttered, twenty-one guns roared in royal salute and the Fleet Air Arm made a flyover, Lucy remained in Shell Bay, making her third strike against the King that season.

On the day of the Naval Review a by-election was held in Robert Houston's former constituency of West Toxteth. Randolph Churchill had reappeared on the political scene to lend his support to John Cremlyn, the Conservative candidate. Cremlyn was standing against Joseph Gibbins, the Labour candidate who in 1924 had been narrowly defeated by Houston. Randolph's appearance on the scene inflamed the electorate and brought strong opposition to Cremlyn. For example, a van that he used for open-air meetings was attacked by a hostile crowd in the dock area, with poster boards torn from its sides and an attempt made to overturn it. From Shell Bay Lucy telegrammed Randolph's candidate: 'Bravo Cremlyn! You are the man for West Toxteth – a fit and proper successor to my husband, Sir Robert Houston. Good luck and may God be with you. Fight for Conservatism and you will fight for the right.' But it was Gibbins who won the seat with a majority of 5,300 votes. Lucy commented on Labour's win in the *Saturday Review*. Why, she asked, had West Toxteth, so staunch a Conservative constituency in Houston's day, returned a socialist candidate? The answer was simply that Conservative voters saw 'no difference between a Socialist Government and a "National" Government'. It was shortly after the West Toxteth by-election that H.Y. Robinson, an associate of Randolph, went to work for Lucy as her political secretary. Later he would write that 'three weeks were as much as I could stand'. He was aggrieved that no smoking was allowed on board and that, although the yacht had a 'magnificent' gymnasium, he was not allowed to use it. But the final straw came when Lucy ordered him to hire fifty women at £5 a week, dress each one in red, white and blue, and organise them to march around Bournemouth displaying posters which read 'Baldwin is a Liar' and 'Ramsay MacDonald is a Traitor to Great Britain'. Faced with such a responsibility, Robinson packed up and left.

By the end of July, Baldwin, who had been Prime Minister for only a few weeks, was already tired of Lucy and when an opportunity presented itself to contain her his administration took action. In its 27 July issue the *Saturday Review* printed an article with the title, 'Wanted: A *Real* Conservative Leader'. An advertising poster was prepared bearing this title and, as usual, a staff member contacted the bill-posting company to arrange for display. But later the company manager rang back to say that he could not display the posters after all. When pressed, the manager reluctantly admitted that a government representative had informed him that if the company went ahead and displayed the poster 'things would be made very difficult for them *and the Government would not forget*', the *Saturday Review* reported. In practice, Wentworth Day explained, this constituted a threat that companies that continued to handle Lucy's explosive material would lose government contracts for putting up posters for the forthcoming general election. The *Saturday Review* contacted several other bill-posting companies but they too dared not touch Lucy's posters.

Lucy lashed out in an article entitled 'AFRAID!' Baldwin's government, she wrote, was 'afraid of the *Saturday Review* because it TELLS THE TRUTH'. Again inviting the government to prosecute her if she had libelled them, she said that the poster affair had demonstrated that the freedom of the press was a 'myth'. If the government allowed no criticism of itself it was 'NO LONGER A CONSTITUTIONAL GOVERNMENT – BUT AN OLIGARCHY' and the will of the people meant nothing. If the government could not be criticised it was a 'DICTATORSHIP OF THE WORST DESCRIPTION'. Lucy contacted the Duchess of Atholl, who raised the matter in the House of Commons in August, but was told that the allegation that the bill-posting company had been threatened was baseless and hardly needed contradiction in view of its 'fantastic character'.[81] On 3 August Lucy wrote to Brooks that she could not understand the lack of press reporting on the matter and thought that the newspapers 'must all have been got at too'. There was, she reiterated, '<u>no longer</u> a Free Press'.[82]

It was perhaps the sting of the posters episode that caused Lucy to pen a rare reflection on, and justification of, her methods. From Sandbanks on 17 August she wrote to Brooks:

> Many people tell me that I am too crude – too brutal in my attack on the Government and that 'sweet reasoning' might do more but in my experience 'sweet reasoning' never did anything with anybody – much less a hippopotamus hide of Ramsay or a Baldwin – I don't know what you think?[83]

There was, she continued, far too much 'kow-towing to personalities in this Government'. Politicians obviously thought it better, she wrote sarcastically, that the country be undefended than any of them be told that they were 'not as perfect as they imagine themselves'. In Lucy's view this was all wrong. If she attacked a person, she attacked them not as an individual but as a parliamentary representative of the country. It was not right that they should take it personally and get 'huffy'. As individuals MacDonald and Baldwin held no interest for her, and she criticised them only because of their 'Parliamentary attitude towards the country' and because they were not doing their duty. 'I am sure you agree with me in this,' Lucy wrote.

Earlier in the summer Lucy had promised Matthews that he could use the *Liberty* and it seems that he eventually got his chance sometime between late August and mid-October. Lucy had gone to London for a time, having lent the *Liberty*, according to crew member Jim Steele, to 'experimental officers of the Army and Navy'. The yacht collected the officers and large cases of instruments from Swansea and then went to an area 'somewhere between Swansea and Land's End' where the experiments in submarine detection would take place. The officers unpacked the instruments with 'smiles all over their faces', telling the *Liberty*'s crew, 'You men will be proud of serving in this ship at this time, for this is an experiment to surprise the world.' The trials were two days from completion when a wireless message arrived from Lucy ordering the captain to take the yacht to Southampton immediately and discharge the experimental officers there. The captain and officers appealed but Lucy would not be moved. She wanted the *Liberty* at once, she said. The captain had no choice but to obey, but at Southampton he was surprised when a dock official came on board and told him, 'Number 1 dock ready for you, Sir. Lady Houston's orders from London; dry dock.

Scrape and paint below water-line.' After a week in dry dock the *Liberty* was ordered to go on to the eastern shore of Southampton Water and wait for Lucy there, but still she did not arrive and eventually she sent fresh orders to sail round to Poole. For a second time Lucy had scuppered Matthews's submarine experiments. Fortunately for poor Matthews, according to Steele, the Admiralty 'supplied a destroyer to finish the job'.

The BUF had continued to grow until Mosley began to see himself as the country's future Prime Minister and its 'coming dictator'. There was much that appealed to Lucy in Mosley's opposition to socialism and his nationalistic pronouncements, such as 'our first task and duty is to awaken the soul of England again', expressed her deepest yearnings. The government had rejected Lucy's offer of £200,000 for air defence but there was concern that she might give the money to Mosley; Allen had been sounded out by 'certain members of the Cabinet' as to her intentions. The fears of the cabinet members were not without foundation for, as Mosley's prominence increased, his positives began to outweigh his negatives in Lucy's mind. For a while, Wentworth Day wrote, it was 'touch-and-go' whether she would fund Mosley, and by October 1935 she had more or less made up her mind to do so.

Lucy had never met Mosley but sent him an invitation to the *Liberty* at Southampton. Lucy, Mosley wrote in his autobiography, had not the 'slightest idea' what his fascist policies were about but nevertheless their interview went well and they parted on the 'firm understanding' that Lucy would support him financially. Shortly after the Mosley interview in mid-October Lucy left the *Liberty* at Southampton to return to Byron Cottage. As she stepped ashore, did she realise that it was for the last time? After this she became so engrossed in the *Saturday Review* and political matters that she rarely left Byron Cottage.

Lucy was about to send Mosley a cheque for £100,000 when Allen brought to her attention a paragraph in the BUF journal, the *Blackshirt*. It was 'singularly offensive', he recalled, and 'couched in exactly the terms that Lucy would most resent'. It 'sneered at her punctuation, her grammar and her patriotism, at her sense of humour, at her *Saturday Review* and her age – she was old enough to know better', it said. As Allen expected, Lucy was furious, in particular as she had published Mosley's portrait and written nice things about him. However, it was perhaps too great a coincidence that, at the critical moment in which Lucy was about to give a great boost to

British fascism, an incident had occurred to stop her. Lucy wrote angrily to Mosley, accusing him of ingratitude and informing him that she held him personally responsible for the article. Allen for one was happy that the fascists had shot themselves in the foot but it fell to him to take Lucy's letter to Mosley at the BUF headquarters, with instructions to return with an apology. Allen spent half an hour with Mosley, during which time he was struck mainly by the 'extraordinary glassy stare of his dark eyes and his inability to grasp the situation'. Mosley thought he could laugh it off, and said that Lucy ought to be flattered if others used the same plain speech that she used herself. In the end he did write Lucy a letter, but it was more of a lecture than an apology. Lucy was indignant and gave instructions that Mosley and the BUF were not to be mentioned in the *Saturday Review* until further notice. Mosley had lost a fortune and after his abandonment first by Lord Rothermere and now by Lucy he had, as he wrote, had 'more than enough of the whims of the rich'.

The general election was to be held on 14 November 1935, and it may have been at about this time that Lucy tried different tactics with Stanley Baldwin. For weeks on end she sent him letters on lilac notepaper pleading with him to fight socialism and strengthen Britain's defences. For three months the long-suffering Miss Ritchie and Foster the chauffeur had to get up early every morning and drive down to Covent Garden by six o'clock to buy carnations, roses, mimosa and lilies-of-the-valley. Week after week they delivered the flowers to 10 Downing Street, and it was not until she had spent £300 on flowers that Lucy concluded that Baldwin 'wasn't worth a bunch of dandelions'. At one point in all this, Lucy invited Baldwin to tea at Byron Cottage, but his wife came instead. Lucy gave Mrs Baldwin a long lecture on her husband's political failings and after half an hour Mrs Baldwin rose to make her escape. 'I'm sorry you don't approve of Stanley,' she said. 'No, I don't,' Lucy replied. 'He knows it, too!' Miss Ritchie, who showed Mrs Baldwin out, commented to Wentworth Day, 'Poor lady! She looked as though she'd been pulled through a hedge backwards!'

Lucy was planning a general offensive not only against Baldwin but also against Samuel Hoare, Foreign Secretary, and Anthony Eden, Minister without Portfolio for League of Nations Affairs. Eden now replaced MacDonald as the main object of Lucy's vituperation. In his youth he had somewhat resembled Brinckman and now, not yet 40, he was still good looking and known as the 'best-dressed man in the House of Commons'. But looks and elegant tailoring counted for nothing with Lucy if he supported the League of Nations. The League was intended to maintain world peace and prevent war through collective security, disarmament, negotiation and arbitration, but Lucy thought it ineffective, bound up in intrigue, a waste of taxpayers' money, and an excuse to weaken the nation's military defences. In late 1935 Lucy's dislike of the League reached new heights when it condemned Mussolini for invading Abyssinia (today part of the state of Ethiopia). When Baldwin made the League a key election issue, describing it as his 'sheet anchor' and giving his word that there would be no major British rearmament, Lucy furiously dashed off a pamphlet and had 500,000 copies printed. Pleading with Baldwin to turn the country away from socialism and the League of Nations, she wrote: 'Turn over a new leaf, Mr Baldwin, and make the people forget all this Socialistic and League of Nations "Sheet Anchor" nonsense – that has brought us only bitter enmity and will surely bring WAR.'

Lucy believed that the League was controlled by Soviet Russia and in particular by Maxim Litvinoff, Russia's Foreign Minister. When in early November the *Saturday Review* reported on Anthony Eden, Samuel Hoare and Litvinoff attending the League of Nations assembly in Geneva, Lucy condemned Litvinoff as the 'Bolshevik arch intriguer' and a 'wily wire puller' who had Eden as his puppet. The following week, under the heading 'Litvinoff Wants War', Meriel Buchanan described Eden as the 'inseparable companion' of Litvinoff, who had allowed himself to be 'duped and flattered by the serpent tongue', while Hoare was also 'under the spell'. As the British people were being dictated to by Hoare and Eden, Buchanan wrote, in effect they themselves were the 'dupes' of Russia.

Lucy turned her wrath on Eden in October with a pamphlet entitled 'The Serpent in Eden', in which she set him a schoolboy's task of writing out 500 times, 'Fools rush in where wise men dare not tread'. Heaping on further insults, she rolled out another accusation of ungentlemanly behaviour, suggesting that in past times England's gentlemanly statesmen had understood the word 'diplomacy' to mean a 'courteous and supreme politeness'. However, Eden's definition of diplomacy was to bully and threaten, and make 'England' a 'word of contempt among the nations'. Lucy's attacks on Samuel Hoare were less bitter and more calculated to amuse, for she lampooned him by a play on his name with a pamphlet entitled 'Our Champion Hoare'. Lucy made fun of Hoare for being 'FAMOUS for being a beautiful skater – especially when dressed in black silk tights'; Hoare, a keen ice skater, wore jodhpur-type leggings, tight at the knee, when he skated. She also took him to task for his support of the League of Nations. At the Geneva assembly Hoare had said, 'My Country stands by the League,' but Lucy objected because the words suggested that the English nation agreed. Writing as if she, and not Hoare, was the spokeswoman for the country, Lucy stated that 'ENGLAND REPUDIATES THESE WORDS SPOKEN BY SIR SAMUEL HOARE. SHE HAS NO INTENTION OF BEING DICTATED TO BY THE LEAGUE OF NATIONS.'

As if it was not bad enough to be ridiculed as England's 'Champion Hoare', the Foreign Secretary had still more to endure when Lucy devised a further scheme to belittle him. Wentworth Day observed her preparations at Byron Cottage. Probably in reference to the natives of Abyssinia, she had written new words for a popular song of the day and hired a band of four black minstrels to sing them. The men stood on the lawn looking uncomfortable, while through the open windows of the drawing room Lucy conducted with 'tremendous verve' as they sang her lyrics:

> Chelsea voters, mind your eye;
> Take a friend's advice,
> Sir Samuel Hoare has wiped it once,
> Don't let him wipe it twice.
> This sanctions stuff he tries to puff
> Can only lead to gore,
> So if in fight you don't delight,
> Don't vote for Samuel Hoare.

The rehearsals went on for several mornings until Lucy was satisfied, and she then poured each man a tot of rum before sending the men off in a van to Chelsea. There for several days they paraded up and down the street outside Hoare's house singing the song until the police stepped in.

When the day of the general election, 14 November, arrived Lucy made a rare public appearance. Gordon Selfridge was well known for hosting election-night parties at his great department store in Oxford Street. As a keen royalist he had celebrated the jubilee that year by decking out the premises with Empire-themed decorations that included an 80ft statue of Britannia on the roof. Selfridge's parties were famous and Londoners, reported the *Tatler*, regarded them as part and parcel of a general election.

The guest list for this party ran to thousands and featured an eclectic range of people, from politicians such as Lord Beaverbrook and Winston Churchill to film stars such as Douglas Fairbanks Jr and Madeleine Carroll; Lucy was escorted by her old friend Sir Philip Sassoon. The highlight of the party was the announcement of the election results as they came in and, naturally, Conservative gains were wildly applauded. There was jubilation when it was found that the new government would have a majority of 386 Conservative seats, while Labour had only 154. Baldwin continued as Prime Minister but up in Seaham Ramsay MacDonald, who in the previous general election had gained 55 per cent of the poll, now gained only 31 per cent and lost his seat. It was a humiliating defeat for the former Prime Minister.

After the general election, Lucy continued her campaign in support of Mussolini's policy in Abyssinia. When Hoare went to Paris to work with Pierre Laval, the French Prime Minister, on a scheme to end the war between Italy and Abyssinia, Lucy wrongly assumed that Hoare was colluding with the French on sanctions against Italy. Having mocked him with the 'Our Champion Hoare' tag she now sent out sandwichmen with posters that bore the question, 'Why send our Champion Hoare to Paris?' Then, when the 'Hoare–Laval Pact' was drawn up, its terms caused a public outcry and Hoare was roundly condemned. He resigned as Foreign Secretary and was replaced by Anthony Eden. Eden went to accept the seals of office from King George V but, he recorded in his diary, the King told him that he had said to Samuel Hoare 'no more Coals to Newcastle, no more Whores (Hoares) to Paris!' Hoare had not been amused, and this royal jest, despite originating with Lucy, has since been cited as a rare example of George's humour. After his promotion Eden would continue as Lucy's favourite target.

17

PATRIOT NO. 1

As 1936 began the idealised 'England' that Lucy was struggling to sustain was slipping away, for Rudyard Kipling died on 18 January, and King George V two days later. But the accession of the Prince of Wales as King Edward VIII brought Lucy new hope. Edward, the *Saturday Review* commented, came to the throne in a 'troubled hour'. Threats of war endangered the Empire, unsettled the world, and put the fear of strife uppermost in the minds of all. 'Peace!' wrote Meriel Buchanan, 'The world has almost forgotten the meaning of the word. We who knew the security and tranquility of what we now call the "pre-war" days look back on them as belonging to another existence.' Once again the 'Gods of War' were sharpening their swords and the nations mustering their armies. Europe was 'dominated by fear' and a world war seemed 'imminent'.

In times of national danger, an article by Beaumont commented, people looked not to politicians but to the King, and never before had England's monarch needed to command such confidence in his subjects and act as a 'rock' around which they could rally. Edward, continued Beaumont, began his reign knowing his subjects as no other monarch ever had, and they knew, trusted and loved him in return. Edward had all the attributes and virtues of a great King: he was determined, courageous, sincere, modest, kind-hearted, devoted to duty, sympathetic to the 'under-dog,' had a 'horror of shams and snobs' and possessed an 'insatiable thirst for knowledge of everything that would fit him ultimately for the Throne'. Indeed, these were the characteristics that Lucy attributed to herself. Edward was a war hero, sportsman and pilot. He had walked among 'rough men, angry Anarchists and Socialists, out-of-works, and the poorest of the down-and outs', and had always met them 'unaffectedly as man to man'. He had championed the unemployed and learned first hand of the great Empire of which he was now emperor. Nothing, Beaumont concluded, would daunt Edward in doing what he believed to be his duty. Elsewhere, however, there was a lurking fear that Edward might not possess the necessary strength of character for the task that lay ahead.

On 21 January 1936, even as his accession as King Edward VIII was being proclaimed, he broke protocol by watching the event from a window of St James's Palace where he was joined by the twice-married American Wallis Simpson. He later wrote in his autobiography that as the 'polished words of sovereignty and dominion' rang out below they seemed to tell him that his relationship with Wallis had 'suddenly entered a more significant stage'. Indeed, Edward's obsession with Mrs Simpson would end his reign before the year was over. But at this point the abdication was still unthought of and Lucy was full of hope, for she was now a personal friend of England's monarch. She believed that he, her idol, felt as she did about the country and would dedicate himself to promoting the good of all that she held dear.

Meanwhile, Lucy had two more by-elections to fight. Both Ramsay MacDonald and his son Malcolm had lost their seats in the general election and, although Baldwin had allowed Malcolm to stay on in the cabinet as Secretary of State for the Colonies, father and son badly needed seats in order to save face. In January 1936 each stood in a Scottish by-election, Ramsay MacDonald for the 'Combined Scottish Universities' constituency and Malcolm for Ross and Cromarty. Malcolm got off to a bad start, for Baldwin's pressure on the constituency to adopt him as a Conservative candidate backfired when irritated local Conservatives chose Randolph Churchill instead; Malcolm was forced to campaign as a National Labour candidate. Lucy accused Baldwin of wanting to 'foist' the MacDonalds upon Scotland and the only thing that anyone knew about Malcolm, she wrote, was that he was a 'chip off the old block'.

Early in January 1936 Lucy called Wentworth Day to Byron Cottage and instructed him to do what he could to oppose the MacDonalds in their by-election campaigns. He began with the Scottish Universities contest, for which the election would take place at the end of January. The constituents were members of the universities of Glasgow, Aberdeen, Edinburgh and St Andrews and so there could be no public meetings, but Wentworth Day displayed Lucy's posters and sent a pamphlet, 'What the Late Prime Minister Has Done for England', to every graduate of the universities involved. MacDonald, the pamphlet stated, had enforced disarmament and dragged Britain's armed services 'down, down, down to the depths of despair'. Some staider voters took against Lucy's rhetoric and, the *Northern Whig* reported, after receiving the pamphlet a number who had not previously favoured MacDonald decided to vote for him. However, whether Lucy had helped or hindered MacDonald he would gain 56.5 per cent of the poll and so win the seat.

Wentworth Day concentrated his efforts in Ross and Cromarty, assisting Randolph Churchill against Malcolm MacDonald. At the time he was approached by the constituency Conservative Party, Randolph, meanwhile, had been holidaying in Morocco with his father, Lord Rothermere and Lloyd George. There Winston painted landscapes while Lloyd George worked on his war memoirs and Rothermere urged Randolph to drink less. Rothermere succeeded, temporarily at least, for Randolph would tell a Scottish audience that he was a 'tee-totaller'. Randolph may have been glad when the telegram of invitation from the Ross and Cromarty Conservatives arrived on 7 January and, despite his father's opposition, he left Morocco immediately. Although the polling day was not until 10 February the candidates and their agents arrived during the first half of January, for the constituency was large but sparsely populated and there was much travelling to be done to canvass in remote areas. On 8 January Wentworth Day stepped off the train in Dingwall, the small town on the Cromarty Firth that would be the centre of the campaigning, with a wad of banknotes that Lucy had given him to pay Randolph's expenses. Having told the press at the railway station that Malcolm was a 'political nonentity sheltering behind his father's name', he proceeded down the snow-covered streets to the National Hotel. Randolph arrived in Dingwall two days after Wentworth Day and proceeded to the National Hotel which, by accident or design, was the same hotel at which Malcolm MacDonald and his entourage were staying. This press reported that Randolph had hired the hotel's spacious lounge as his campaign base, leaving Malcolm to make do with the smaller private sitting room next door.

On 12 January Lucy telephoned Dingwall with the message that she would support Randolph 'tooth and nail'. Then the following day Lucy sent Randolph another telegram: 'It seems to me that this is a vital crowning point in your career. You must win and I will do all I can to help you.'[84] The election raised great interest in Dingwall for the town did not see many celebrities, and Randolph and Malcolm were both the sons of famous men. But it was the presence of the junior Churchill, with his brash personality, that made a carnival atmosphere. His speeches drew large crowds and his campaign was marked by many boisterous attacks on the MacDonalds. However, he did not adapt well to the rural Scottish environment. For example, he weakened his credibility by not knowing his heifers from his steers, and scandalised churchgoers by holding a fifteen-minute argument with a retired senior official of the Church of Scotland. In the heated dispute it was reported that Randolph shouted angrily, 'I am not going to be hectored, bullied or brow-beaten by any gentleman, however pompous and offensive.'

One evening the people of Dingwall came out in force to hear Randolph speak, and hundreds had to be turned away from the town hall. It was, the *Scotsman* reported, 'one of the liveliest political Saturday nights' in the town's history. At the meeting Randolph was attacked about the distribution of Lucy's leaflets, which featured anti-MacDonald material. When it was alleged that the men who distributed them were paid by Randolph's office he sprang to his feet angrily: 'There are evidently some people who are disposed to believe any lie which they think will injure me.' 'Filthy insinuations' were being made, Randolph said. The uproar continued until two distributors stepped on to the platform and denied that Randolph had paid them, but the truth was that the money had originated with Lucy.

Election day, 10 February, arrived and the count revealed that Malcolm MacDonald had won easily with nearly 9,000 votes – almost 50 per cent of the poll – and was thus able to keep his cabinet seat. The Labour candidate came second and Randolph a poor third, polling only 2,400 votes. The *Dundee Courier* made a triumphant swipe, reporting that Randolph's 'entire stock-in-trade as a candidate was made up of a limitless capacity for impudence, which was put unstintedly on tap'. His methods had 'amused the voters in a period of blizzard and snow-blocked roads', but they had regarded it as nothing more than entertainment.

Once again Randolph's political campaign had come to nothing but, unabashed by his defeat, he wrote to Lucy in March to ask for more money; he was £300 short in his Ross and Cromarty expenses. Lucy paid up but after this gave Randolph no more support. It was perhaps for this reason that in March 1936 he received a court summons to appear in Liverpool: the man who had once boasted that he was a Liverpool ratepayer had accrued rate arrears amounting to £20 12s 1d for his Conservative Union office premises. In court the magistrate asked the clerk, 'Was this the young man who came to Liverpool in a hurry and dashed in to tell people how to run the city?' When the clerk replied that it was, the magistrate commented: 'A nice example he is showing.'

During the by-election, Litvinoff, Russia's Foreign Minister, had attended the funeral of King George V and subsequently held meetings with cabinet members; Lucy's indignation knew no bounds. This, she reminded her readers on 8 February, was the man who had given the 'casting vote' for the killings of the Tsar of Russia, the cousin of the King of England. Buchanan suggested that at his meetings with cabinet members Litvinoff had 'easily duped' Baldwin and Eden, and a 'secret pact' had been made. It was the intention of Baldwin and Eden, she wrote, to 'subjugate and degrade England in bonds of an intolerable and shameful alliance with Russia!' Eden, doubtless exasperated by these accusations which came on top of the offence of Lucy's 'Serpent in Eden' pamphlet, now revealed in public the depths of his contempt for her. During a debate in the House of Commons on 26 February he was asked about the kidnap and selling into slavery of a British subject in Abyssinia. Eden knew nothing of the matter but the questioner persisted: 'Is the right hon. Gentleman aware that this allegation was made recently by Lady Houston in the *Saturday Review*?' To this Eden responded with the four words that he would regret to his dying day: 'Who is Lady Houston?' There was laughter in the House, and as Eden sat down he must have felt satisfied with his withering put-down. But he had not studied his enemy sufficiently and, having played into Lucy's hands, he would now have to pay the price.

The next issue of the *Saturday Review* contained fresh insults against Eden, with Buchanan writing that during his visit to Moscow the previous spring, Soviet ministers had realised that the 'fashionable young man' with 'feminine looks' would be a useful tool. Therefore with 'cunning flattery and ambiguous promises they beguiled his stupidly conceited mind and deluded him, throwing dust in his eyes, entangling him hopelessly in their net of lies'. But Lucy was planning a greater revenge for Eden's insulting question. One morning she rang Collin Brooks at six o'clock to ask whether, in his opinion, it would be libellous to call anybody a 'nancy'? Brooks exclaimed, 'Libellous?

It would be criminal libel, I imagine.' Lucy, pleased to have caught him out, laughed her 'low chuckling laugh' and replied, 'My dear, you're quite wrong. I've taken three counsels' opinions. They are based on the big whatsitsname dictionary which defines it as "effeminate".' Brooks thought that in using the word 'nancy' Lucy was playing not only on Eden's reputation for snappy dressing but also a commonly held view of his status as the 'political pet' of MacDonald and Baldwin.

When the leaflet and associated posters appeared, Londoners, although used to Lucy's material, were nevertheless taken aback to see placards bearing the words, 'This Nancified Nonentity, Anthony Eden'. In her pamphlet, entitled 'Who is Mr Anthony Eden?', Lucy set out Eden's personal 'law' in the style of the edict of an ancient potentate:

I AM ANTHONY EDEN – MY WORD IS LAW AND I ORDER ALL BRITONS TO FOLLOW THE EDEN LAW, WHICH IS TO FIGHT ONLY FOR THE LEAGUE OF NATIONS. THIS DOCTRINE MAY BE DESCRIBED AS EVIL – UNNATURAL – UNPATRIOTIC AND AGAINST EVERY LAW OF GOD AND OF MAN – BUT WHAT DO I CARE? – IT IS THE LAW OF ANTHONY EDEN.

Lucy piled on more insults: Eden was a 'sinister self-worshipping simpleton' and the 'Prince of Ineffectuals'. He was unfitted for his position, she wrote, and now, while imagining himself a saviour and redeemer, he succeeded only in 'braying like an ass'. It would take Eden a long time to live down Lucy's epithet of Nancified Nonentity, Wentworth Day wrote, and never again did he question her identity.

By 1936, with the growing stature and confidence of Nazi Germany, enthusiasm was growing for Adolf Hitler in Britain. In February Germany had hosted the fourth Winter Olympic Games in Bavaria and the event, although marred by the presence of Nazi troops equipped with bayoneted rifles, was a great propaganda coup. Lucy, and many others in Britain, began to warm to Hitler. For example in February, Lucy wrote that the German leader 'with all his faults – is a Patriot – he works for Germany – While England's so-called statesmen ALONE IN ALL THE WORLD SCORN THE NEEDS OF THEIR OWN COUNTRY AND WORK FOR THE LEAGUE OF NATIONS'. When on 7 March German troops marched into the Rhineland, despite the move being in violation of the Treaty of

Versailles, there was significant approval in England where many regarded Hitler as a man of action and a patriot. Speaking in the occupied territory on 12 March, Hitler said that no people desired peace more than the German people, and Germany had one wish only – to be left alone to live and work in peace and quiet. For anyone nervous about Hitler's intentions these were surely comforting words, even if they did not seem to accord with other signals coming out of Germany. While it was not immediately apparent, the Rhineland coup would remilitarise areas along the River Rhine and begin to shift the balance of power in Europe towards Germany.

Lucy was one of those dazzled by Hitler's aura of a strong man dedicated to building up his country and destroying Bolshevik Russia. However, her approval should be seen within the context of the period. Although in the light of subsequent events, they may later have chosen not to recall doing so, many British people took a positive view of the German dictator because of their frustration with what they saw as the stagnancy and even decline of British life. Britain's leaders seemed unable to deal with the country's problems, while in Germany dictatorship had enabled Hitler to rejuvenate the economy and bring pride and a sense of purpose to the country. Germany's new military might had lifted it out of national humiliation to become a great power. It seemed, therefore, that dictatorship might be the way to go.

The *Saturday Review* began to print material favourable to the Nazi regime, with Meriel Buchanan contributing a major article, entitled 'Hitler – the Man of Destiny', for the 14 March issue. While in his own country Hitler had once been laughed at as an 'over-rated and bombastic boaster', Buchanan wrote, he now stood out as a 'lode star, a burning flame above the turmoil and chaotic darkness' of the day. He was the man who, having made Germany dominant in Europe, held the 'destinies of the Great Powers in his hands!' Without Hitler's armies, Stalin's Red Army would be sweeping across central Europe and England would be facing ruin. It was useless, insisted Buchanan, for the British to delude themselves and continue to trust in Britain's supposed superiority; they should recognise that it was the German Führer who had the power to 'dictate peace or war to the world'. Whether people loved or hated Hitler they should acknowledge that in him lay the 'only hope of world security and peace'.

There was light relief for Lucy when in April a new comedy review, *Spread It Abroad*, opened at the Saville Theatre, featuring an affectionate take-off by the actress Ivy St Helier. Miss St Helier wore a pseudo-military uniform with a model aeroplane attached to one shoulder and a model warship to the other, like epaulettes. She held a copy of the *Saturday Review*, and her act included a song with the verse:

> Little Lucy Houston helps her country all she can –
> Singing 'Rule Britannia' in her bath.
> Red and white and blue die-hardy annuals you'll find
> All along her garden path.
> Patriotic dresses, she possesses quite a stack!
> Blows her nose upon a Union Jack!
> Just give her half a chance and she'll show Stanley Baldwin how –
> She's Empire boost'n Houst'n now!'

St Helier's act could not have worked unless the audience had a reasonable knowledge of Lucy, and it demonstrated that Lucy's patriotism, newspaper, garden, politics, desire for rearmament, obsession for red, white and blue, and dislike of Baldwin, were all well known. The *Illustrated Sporting and Dramatic News* reported that 'Lady Houston pays the price (of fame) in this burlesque of Britain's Public Patriot No. 1'. Lucy paid the price again later that month because of the cartoonist Low. With fears of poison gas in the event of an air attack, plans had been made for the issue of gas masks in Britain. Low showed a large figure struggling with a too-small mask, with the caption, 'Gas Item: It seems that gas-masks are to be issued in sizes, so people must be sure to get suitably roomy ones. We don't want Lucy Houston wearing a size 6 in a size 7 mood.'

In May Lucy made a rare public outing when she took a box for the Variety Artists' Ladies' Guild and Orphanage annual evening concert held at the Phoenix Theatre. The singer and comedienne Gracie Fields, guild president and Lucy's Hampstead neighbour, was the star turn. This may have been Lucy's last public engagement.

18

HITLERESS

In 1934 Lucy had opposed the concept of dictatorship, but two years later that was forgotten. When in May 1936 Mussolini's forces captured Addis Ababa and the Italian leader announced that 'Abyssinia is Italian', Lucy had sent an effusive telegram:

TEN THOUSAND TIMES BRAVO BRAVISSIMO: Oh! Splendid man!! I rejoice to know that Your Excellency has triumphed over your enemies in Abyssinia and your enemies in England. All your English FRIENDS congratulate you on your great victory. Long live Italy!

It was perhaps at about this time that Lucy also sent Hitler a telegram:

I want to tell you that you are a wonderful man. You have done wonders for Germany, but the great thing for you to do now is to join hands with Britain and go for Russia. Note well what I have said. Great Britain and Germany together could crush Russia. Russia is the enemy of God and civilisation.

Possibly feeling that he did not need Lucy's unsolicited advice, Hitler sent no reply.

With the examples of Hitler and Mussolini before her, Lucy was frustrated at the comparative weakness of British politicians. She had tried to promote Lord Lloyd and Randolph Churchill but they had not been up to the job, while Winston Churchill was too much his own man to be her puppet.

And besides, even if one of them had become Prime Minister he could easily be voted out. In her frustration at the limitations of the democratic system Lucy saw a solution: England should have its own dictator. It should be a man who was powerful, patriotic and who could not be deposed. There was only one candidate who fitted Lucy's criteria – the King. And so it was that in May 1936 the *Saturday Review* began a campaign calling for Edward VIII to become the dictator of England.

The *Saturday Review* proposed that Edward should follow the pattern set by Hitler and work miracles for England as the Führer had for Germany. This theme was introduced on 2 May with two forthright articles, 'England wants a Dictator' by Comyns Beaumont, writing as Kim, and 'England's Sore Need – A Benevolent Dictator' by Collin Brooks, writing as Historicus. Kim explained the advantages of dictatorship and the freedom of action that it allowed. In contrast to Hitler and Mussolini, he wrote, Baldwin was an insignificant 'Lilliputian', but with permanency of tenure the German and Italian leaders could 'defy the proletariat vote' and rule for the benefit of their countries. 'WHAT WE WANT ABOVE ALL THINGS IN THIS COUNTRY IS AN ENGLISH DICTATOR WHO WILL AIM TO PLACE BRITAIN AT THE HEAD OF THE NATIONS IN WARFARE AND COMMERCE', Kim argued. An English dictator would throw off the chains of the League of Nations and 'rule with an iron fist' to lead England to greatness. It was 'cheap claptrap' to suggest that England would not tolerate a dictator, Kim added, for 'of course she would if that dictator were a great and determined ruler'. Brooks compared the prestige of Germany and Italy to the 'universal distrust and execration' into which 'Baldwin the Blunderer, MacDonald of Moscow, and Pretty Polly Eden' had dragged England. There was only one man who could fit the bill of 'Benevolent Dictator' – the King.

There were already fears at high levels within the British establishment that Edward's enthusiasm for right-wing politics and notoriously weak head would make him a liability in British foreign policy, and in particular in relation to fascism in Europe. Already he was being watched by the intelligence services and his telephone conversations monitored. And now Lucy was urging him to cast off the shackles of tradition and custom, overthrow the country's elected government and take power into his own hands. If he followed her line and bypassed the parliamentary system he would become an autocrat with absolute power and no accountability to voters; Lucy was assuring him that Britons would back him if he did so.

In June a new note of desperation entered the *Saturday Review*. Buchanan wrote that the 'secret power' behind Bolshevism, by which she meant communist Jews, had openly stated that war must erupt in Europe before harvest-time in Germany, i.e. before October. None of the European powers wanted war, Buchanan believed, and therefore the aggression was coming from Russia. Fearing that war was imminent Lucy published an extraordinary apocalyptic call to action, her 'HUMBLE PETITION TO HIS MAJESTY THE KING FROM HIS LOYAL AND DEVOTED SUBJECTS WHO HONOUR HIM AS THEIR ONLY LEADER'. Lucy addressed Edward directly: 'YOUR MAJESTY, YOU ARE A GREAT AND MIGHTY MONARCH. BUT, YOU ARE **MUCH MORE** THAN THAT. A DEARLY-LOVED KING WHO REIGNS BY LOVE IN THE HEARTS OF HIS PEOPLE.' She believed that she expressed the thoughts of millions who looked to him to deliver them from this 'TERRIBLE TIME OF STRESS'. Earlier that year the *Saturday Review* had named Adolf Hitler as 'Man of Destiny' but now Lucy applied the term to Edward: 'WE WANT TO HAIL YOU AS OUR MAN OF DESTINY, WHO WILL FREE US FROM OUR PERPLEXITY – TO REINSTATE US – AND HEAL OUR WOUNDED PRIDE WHICH HAS FALLEN SO LOW.' His enemies, politicians who were 'FALSE AND TREACHEROUS AS HELL', were working to destroy him and the British people by imposing war on an unarmed nation, she wrote. Then, in bold capital letters, came the core of Lucy's plea:

WISE MEN DO NOT DESPISE THE COUNSEL OF A WOMAN; HEAR ME THEN, OH! MY KING, FOR I LOVE YOU AND EVERY WORD I WRITE IS THE INSPIRED TRUTH; THAT IS WHY THEY FEAR ME.

Edward's throne and perhaps even his life were in jeopardy, she warned: 'Remember Russia.' She urged the King to use his 'whip hand' and royal prerogative to rid himself of bad political advisors. Her desire, of course, was to fill their place.

What did Edward himself think of Lucy's desperate call to arms? If he had not approved of the extreme line that the *Saturday Review* took, a word from him would have ensured that Lucy toned it down. But the continuance of Lucy's campaign suggested that either Edward did not care about his reputation and image, or that he was not wholly opposed to the idea of himself as dictator. Edward had been King for only about five months at this point and Lucy may have been wondering at his lack of action, but such was her love that she could attach no blame to him – the fault must lie elsewhere. Certainly behind the scenes, as Edward wrote in his autobiography, in his attempts to act independently he found that he was 'tampering with tradition' for he, more than most people, was a 'prisoner of the past'. Constrained by convention and duty, Edward was reduced to occasionally 'tilting at the creaking windmills of custom'. Less inclined than his royal predecessors to respect his officials, he clashed with those who surrounded and advised him. For this reason he was probably not unhappy that the *Saturday Review* referred to his elected ministers in such negative terms. However, in large part Edward's frustration was owed to the fact that his royal duties kept him apart from Mrs Simpson.

While Edward fretted, the *Saturday Review* warned him of external dangers to his throne. In July Buchanan contributed an article entitled 'Reds Threaten Our King'. Since the murder of the Russian tsar, she wrote, many European monarchies had fallen until only Edward and Leopold, sovereigns of Britain and Belgium, remained. These men were the main enemies of the 'forces of darkness'. A communist, Buchanan reported, had recently stated that, 'We are the supreme masters of Peace and War ... So far we have succeeded in overthrowing most of the thrones of Europe; the rest will follow in the near future.' And now Russia was carrying out 'underground activities' in Britain and elsewhere to 'liquidate' all of Europe's royalty.[85] Lucy tried frantically to galvanise Edward. In early August, Kim wrote in the *Saturday Review* that as parliament became increasingly discredited, the King's 'personal ascendancy' became more pronounced. And Edward, 'discreet but determined', was coming to be seen by ordinary Britons as a bulwark against the 'feeble ineffectiveness' of political parties. But these, of course, were only Lucy's wishes presented as fact. Government ministers, Kim pointed out, were only the 'servants' of the King; Queen Victoria and Edward VII had often acted independently of them. But the fact that Edward might choose to go against the advice of ministers was 'repugnant' to Baldwin.

Meanwhile, with the opening of the 1936 Summer Olympic Games in Berlin on 1 August, Germany launched a great national charm offensive, and in its issue that day the *Saturday Review* praised Hitler's Olympic effort as a 'Heaven-sent opportunity' for the Third Reich to 'impress the world'.

The world's press attended and the *Saturday Review* printed an admiring article about the Berlin Olympic Village, entitled 'Olympic Wonderland' and probably written by Meriel Buchanan. The Germans, the *Saturday Review* reported, had paid great attention to detail, putting much work into 'artistic schemes of furnishing, colouring and decoration' for the buildings, while an official had slept in the village for several nights to test the comfort of the competitors' beds. Each house had its own wine cellar and, although the best of German cuisine was on offer, teams were also allowed to bring their own cooks. Outside the village, special squads had eliminated mosquitoes from the surrounding countryside. One of the Olympic competitors was reported to have said, 'You've got to pinch yourself to find out if it's real.'

At the same time Germany was reported to be a clean, modern country with new buildings everywhere. Whether in the offices of government ministers, in hotels or little country beer gardens, on public transport, in country roads or town streets, there were only 'happy faces' to be seen. Far from being 'brow-beaten, cowed and dragooned by hectoring, overbearing masters', as in Russia, ordinary Germans were united in a spirit of friendship and comradeship, and free from fear. The mention of Hitler's name aroused a 'fervour of adoration', and one old peasant woman, tears running down her cheeks, had said, 'He is a man sent from God to deliver Germany. Where would we be now if he had not come forward to save us?' When the achievements of Nazi Germany were shown to the world, approval of Hitler and his regime was raised in Britain, and in particular among those on the political right.

If Hitler's Germany seemed a heaven on earth, back in Hampstead Lucy yearned for King Edward to step forward and similarly transform England. August had brought the end of his required period of mourning for his father and now he would have more freedom. But, while Lucy was fighting on his behalf, the King himself was counting the days until his forthcoming holiday. It would allow him to escape from the stifling court and the pressure of royal duties and, crucially, to spend an extended period with Wallis Simpson. When Edward boarded the great luxury yacht *Nahlin* that he had chartered for a month's cruise in the Adriatic Sea, his friends on board included Lord and Lady Louis Mountbatten, Lady Cunard, Lady Diana Cooper and her husband Duff Cooper, but the British press did not report that Mrs Simpson was also one of the party.

That summer Lucy's admiration of Nazi Germany and loathing of Bolshevik Russia brought her into conflict with an old friend. Up until now

Lucy and the Duchess of Atholl had been on the same side and in complete agreement over the threat presented by the totalitarian regime in Soviet Russia. But in July their views diverged. While they still agreed on the nature of Bolshevism, the duchess expanded her concern to cover Nazism. In her more sophisticated analysis she identified Hitler's regime as totalitarian and concluded that it was Germany, and not Russia, that presented the greater threat to world peace. In doing so she incurred Lucy's wrath, and a rift developed between the two women.

The duchess disliked Lucy's approval of Hitler and calls for the King to become England's dictator, and the two became embroiled in a public battle of words via the pages of the *Morning Post*, the *Daily Telegraph* and the *Saturday Review*. The debate began when the duchess wrote to the *Morning Post* taking issue with comments made by Lord Queensborough. In her letter she set out Hitler's policies as stated in the unexpurgated version of his book, *Mein Kampf*. The German leader intended, she said, to win the friendship of Britain and Italy before destroying France and subsequently expanding Germany into Russia, and it was therefore only prudent to bear this in mind when considering any peace offer made by him. Hitler, she continued, might also be tempted to invade Czechoslovakia and from there take over Romanian oil fields, the Black Sea and the Mediterranean before turning back in 'overwhelming force' against the Western powers. She called for European nations to unite to present a common front against any aggression that might come from Germany.

Lucy was not having this. The duchess, she wrote to the *Morning Post*, had quoted Hitler but not Stalin, and Bolshevist leaders had for years openly declared it their aim to destroy Britain's power. While it was true that England, unable to defend itself, could easily be wiped out from the air by either Russia or Germany, would the duchess rather be under the heel of Hitler or Stalin? This question forced the duchess out into the open. She could not recall, she replied, that Stalin had made a declaration of aggression which equated with those made by Hitler in *Mein Kampf*. And while she was undecided which 'dictatorial heel' she preferred to be under, as the Nazi heel was closer and 'likely to be of the highest possible type of workmanship', it seemed the one more likely to stamp, and stamp heavily.

Lucy wrote again to the *Morning Post* pointing out Russia's anti-Christian stance. If the Russian people were allowed to speak out, she said, they would say that they loathed Bolshevism. Had the duchess forgotten these things, and did she not realise the 'curse' that Bolshevism brought to civilisation? Five days later, in a further letter, Lucy asked, 'Can anyone deny this fact? – that when the whole German nation cry "Heil Hitler," it is because they adore him as their deliverer from the horrors of Bolshevism.' Russia was more to be feared for Bolshevists had repeatedly declared that their primary aim was to destroy the British Empire: 'I am not one of those who fear Germany, for I believe Hitler wishes to be good friends with England, and I fail to see why his offer of friendship is not gratefully accepted.'

The debate continued. On 22 August the duchess replied gracefully that she had not forgotten the terrible religious persecution in Russia and was most grateful to Lucy for publicising it. But she asked Lucy to 'keep both eyes open – the right one as well as the left', and remember that there were German pastors as well as Russian priests in concentration camps. Germany, she added, had no more freedom of speech than Russia, and she questioned whether the whole German nation adored Hitler. At some point in the row Lucy produced a pamphlet featuring what Allen described as a 'most unflattering portrait' of the duchess together with a 'highly flattering' one of herself, but when he suggested that this was taking an unfair advantage Lucy only giggled.

In the following weeks letters published in the *Saturday Review* also sniped at the duchess. One was entitled 'A Busy Little Body', while another expressed the view that she was 'cleverly trying to fool the British public' about Germany. In another letter her outlook was criticised as being that of a 'provincial schoolmistress', and it was also suggested that she should concentrate on combatting Bolshevism rather than 'bothering about the spread of decent, patriotic movements in other countries'. Lucy, on the other hand, was complimented: Britain did not need a Hitler for it already had a 'Hitleress named Lady Houston'. The duchess had embraced evidence and shifted her position, only to be put down, patronised and ridiculed as a small-minded meddler. The episode sadly highlighted Lucy's shortcomings as a politician and a person. For the sake of her own fixed ideas she was prepared to humiliate and sacrifice an old friend. The only certainties were the old certainties, and to change one's mind was to demonstrate weakness.

After the Summer Olympics Germany staged the Nuremberg Rally, the annual gathering of the Nazi Party, from 9 to 14 September. With Germany buoyed by its sense of national honour and pride, the 1936 rally was particularly impressive. Lucy sent Meriel Buchanan as her representative but in an account written twenty years later, seemingly eager to exonerate herself of approval of the Nazi regime, Buchanan wrote that she had not enjoyed the week at Nuremberg. Even so, she had to admit that the parades and assemblies, put on by Goebbels in a huge stadium to great dramatic effect, were 'magnificent', and calculated to impress foreign visitors. She particularly remembered a great night-time assembly when, as Hitler entered, the stadium was suddenly lit by the 'blue beams of hundreds of searchlights springing up in an arch'. On the final day she was among those invited to a formal reception at which she met the Nazi leaders; when Buchanan shook hands with Hitler she asked him a question that had been put by Lucy but which, unfortunately, she did not record. With hindsight, she remembered that when she looked into Hitler's 'strange mad eyes, lit up by a fanatical glare as he barked out an answer', she felt a 'cold shudder'.

However, at the time Buchanan did not reveal any misgivings; in the next issue of the *Saturday Review* she praised Germany as a 'reborn' country that had 'learnt how to laugh again!' It was free of the fear that consumed Russia, the 'agony' of war-torn Spain, the hatred and unrest of France and the lethargy that gripped England. With the vision of the massed thousands at Nuremberg fresh in her mind Buchanan wrote that German youth had risen triumphant so that now, 'strong and stalwart, virile and sunburnt, young Germany stands in serried ranks, armed and ready to fight for ideals and preserve the new born strength of the Fatherland'. England, she wrote, should cast off the chains that bound it to the 'forces of darkness' and unite with Germany to fight the common enemy, Russia.

That autumn Lucy became involved in two maritime projects. Since the spring the country had been captivated by the romance and mystery of a long-running news story about the *Girl Pat*, a Grimsby trawler that while apparently on a routine fishing trip had taken off to wander the world. The voyage of the *Girl Pat* began on 1 April and, as *The Times* would later report, it never quite seemed to shake off the 'associations connected with that date'. On board were the skipper, 35-year-old George 'Dod' Orsborne, his younger brother Jimmie, and a mate, deckhand and cook. The extraordinary news coverage of the trawler's travels mixed true reports, false reports, speculation, misinformation and probably also disinformation; the truth was that Dod Orsborne, as he later explained in his book *Master of the Girl Pat*, was involved with British naval intelligence. However, there was never a whisper of this in the press at the time.

Orsborne's handler had sent him on a fact-finding mission in the run-up to the Spanish Civil War. The right-wing Nationalist General Franco was attempting to overthrow the left-leaning Spanish Republican government, and it would be Franco's failed efforts to launch a coup that would precipitate the war in July 1936. The plan was for Orsborne to head for Gibraltar, get to know Spaniards there, and pose as a sea captain willing to ship goods from the Continent to Franco's forces in Morocco. While doing so he was to keep his ears open for information that might be of interest to naval intelligence. Orsborne had collected the *Girl Pat* at Grimsby. The boat had been specially designed by naval camouflage experts so that its appearance could be changed as required; with two masts and a dummy smoke funnel that could be raised or lowered, the vessel could appear either as a sailing boat or an engine-powered craft.

Problems had arisen at Casablanca, where Orsborne learned that his misdeeds on a previous mission had caught up with him. Wanted by the Italian, Spanish and French authorities, he abandoned the Gibraltar mission and the *Girl Pat* went on the run. By mid-May the trawler had been reported to the Admiralty as a fugitive, and as such could be arrested by any British warship or merchantman. At Dakar in French West Africa the French authorities learned of Orsborne's identity and removed the ship's compass and charts to prevent it from leaving the harbour. Searching the pockets of an old jacket, however, Orsborne found a cheap school atlas that had the maps marked with meridians. Using this, Orsborne sailed the *Girl Pat* across the Atlantic Ocean. Eventually the trawler was apprehended and taken to Georgetown in Guyana, South America, from where the crew were sent back to England.

What was Lucy's involvement in the *Girl Pat* affair? In October 1936, while still in dock in Georgetown Harbour, the *Girl Pat* had been sold and, although her role was never made public in Britain, the *Montreal Gazette* and other foreign newspapers reported that the purchaser had been Lady Houston. She paid £3,500 and provided an additional £500 to cover the costs of bringing the trawler back to England, where she intended to donate the craft to the crew. The *Girl Pat* remained at Georgetown for several weeks, where presumably the special fittings were removed. Advertisements were placed for volunteers to bring her back to England and, it was reported, Lucy chose a new crew and officers from among 500 applicants. The Orsborne brothers were tried at the Old Bailey, found guilty of stealing the *Girl Pat*, and sentenced to twelve and six months imprisonment; their naval intelligence connection was not revealed. The British government was certainly sensitive about the episode; in 1938 some of the official records of the case would be sealed for a longer period than normal. One of the files, entitled 'EXTRADITION: George Black Orsborne and James Black Orsborne: extradited from British Guiana for theft of fishing trawler *Girl Pat*', was closed for 100 years, not to be opened to the public until 2038.[86]

Also that autumn Lord Baden-Powell, founder of the Boy Scouts Association, wrote to ask whether Lucy would provide money for the rescue of the *Discovery*, which had been donated to the Scouts. The ship had been the one in which Captain Robert Falcon Scott had explored the Antarctic in 1901–04, but she had fallen into disuse and there was talk of her being broken up. However, the Scout Association hoped to save the *Discovery* not only as a memorial to Britain's polar explorers but also a headquarters and training facility for Sea Scouts. Lucy agreed to give £30,000, making a stipulation that her gift must not be revealed until after her death. The mystery benefactor was subsequently known as 'Mr A'.

For months the American press had been hinting at a romance between Edward and Mrs Simpson, but the story had been suppressed in Britain until the King's *Nahlin* cruise. In mid-September the *Saturday Review* celebrated Edward's return from his holiday with the headline, 'Gentlemen, Fill your Glasses and Drink to – the King!' but behind the scenes the seriousness of the affair was becoming more widely appreciated. When in mid-October it was reported that Mrs Simpson was divorcing her husband, it was understood that this would open the way for the King to marry her. Once Lucy heard the rumours she sprang to Edward's defence. In the *Saturday Review*'s 24 October issue she attempted to counteract the image of the King as a selfish pleasure-seeker. The cover featured a large picture of Edward, sturdy and healthy, wearing shorts and a pullover and carrying a squash racquet. The headline was 'A PATTERN FOR HIS PEOPLE TO COPY', and an article promoted the King as a disciplined and serious-minded ruler, almost an ascetic, who sacrificed himself for the good of his country and Empire: 'How many men are there in the King's Realm today – with so frugal, so strenuous, a daily programme as the daily programme followed by his Majesty?' it asked. Edward's regime was described. He awoke at six o'clock and (like Lucy) took deep breaths in front of an open window. He then worked up a sweat by running around the gardens of Buckingham Palace in a heavy pullover. He weighed himself every day and, if the reading was more than 10st 7lb, ran for longer. A cold bath was followed by a breakfast of fresh fruit and weak tea or coffee. As for other meals, 'plain simple food eaten slowly' formed his main diet, and only by his 'RIGID SELF-DENIAL AND SELF-SACRIFICE' could the King keep himself 'FIT AND ABLE TO DISCHARGE THE MULTITUDINOUS DUTIES OF HIS GREAT POSITION'.

Gardening, it was stated, was one of the King's hobbies and he did not disdain digging the soil and rolling and mowing the lawn himself. Bizarrely, the article reported that garden hints 'culled from his Majesty's personal experience' were to be circulated to youth organisations. Lucy's attempt to turn the youth of Britain into gardeners was perhaps an attempt to mimic the work of Germany's Hitler Youth movement. But the Hitler Youth engaged in military-type activities to prepare young men to fight as soldiers, and the call for teenagers to dig the garden was not quite in the same league. 'Cut off this cover and hang it on your walls,' Lucy ordered, for it would remind readers to follow their King's example and make themselves 'STRONG AND WELL' so that England would no longer be 'UNDER THE REPROACH OF BEING A C.3 NATION'.

In November Lucy wrote to Winston Churchill privately to criticise his attitude toward the League of Nations. The League, she wrote, was as 'dead as a doornail and everyone knows it', and by trying to 'resuscitate' it he was doing himself great harm. She added a postscript: 'Please realise that these words are friendly and remember that everything I have foreseen for the last 5 years & more has happened alas!'[87] Three days later Churchill replied. While he did not agree with Lucy's assessment of Hitler's intentions, he said he had considered the course that he was taking with regard to the Nazi 'menace' very carefully, and he invited Lucy to read a recent speech in which he had set out his arguments. However, he shared Lucy's regrets for the 'misguided policy' of the 'MacDonald–Baldwin regime' in defence and foreign affairs.[88]

It was a measure of Churchill's patience with Lucy that he replied at all, for at that time he was preparing for a crucial speech to be delivered in a debate on defence in the House of Commons on 12 November. It would be, the Scotsman would report afterwards, one of the 'most important and remarkable' to have taken place in the House for many years, owing not only to the gravity of the subject matter but also to the 'unusual candour and dramatic revelation' of the speeches. The main feature was Churchill's long and incisive attack upon the government's tardiness over rearmament. He reminded the House that two years previously when he had warned of the dangers of German rearmament he had been censured as 'alarmist' by Conservative newspapers. But since then Germany had spent £800 million per year upon 'warlike preparations', broken treaty agreements, created a 'gigantic' army and air force, introduced military service, occupied the Rhineland and now it was building a large submarine fleet. The German army and air force would soon be stronger than those of Britain and France put together and the Western democracies needed to combine their strength on the basis of the Covenant of the League of Nations. Only when a position of superior force had been achieved should Germany be invited to open a new door to peace and disarmament.

Churchill attacked the government for its irresponsible slowness in accepting the unwelcome fact of German rearmament and clinging to a policy of unilateral disarmament. This, he said, had proved to be 'wrong, utterly foolish, and never to be tried again'. The government, Churchill said, had gone on in a 'strange paradox, decided only to be undecided, resolved to be irresolute, adamant for drift, solid for fluidity, all powerful to be impotent'. Reviewing the deficiencies in the British army and air force, he said that if Britain went on in this way there would come a 'very terrible reckoning'. The time of 'procrastination, of half measures, of soothing and baffling expedients, of delays' was ending and a period of 'consequences' was beginning. Churchill had been 'staggered' by the speed with which the dangers had arisen and by the failure of the House of Commons to react appropriately; unless the House took action it would have committed an 'act of abdication of duty without parallel in its long history'.[89]

Churchill's hard-hitting words would reinstate him as a leading politician – and impress Lucy. A few days later she wrote what would be her last letter to him, saying that if he kept up the attack he could 'demolish' Baldwin in a few weeks and replace him as a 'true' Conservative leader. She had always wanted Churchill, she said, to rise to the heights that he had in his speech and would gladly have funded him to 'turn out' Baldwin. However, she questioned his value as leader if he was tied to the League of Nations: 'Why – when you can be so great – so devastating do you demean yourself by truckling to that unreal thing the League of Nations & that awful little ass Mr Eden? – who isn't fit to black your shoes!' she asked. She believed that Churchill had the support to become Prime Minister, and she had been 'dead right for 5 years & more you cannot bring one word I have written that has not been too frightfully true – & Robert said I was uncannily right over politics'.[90] On 18 November

Churchill replied, somewhat wearily: 'We are agreed on so many things and have so many powerful antagonists, that we ought to be tolerant with one another about differences.' He explained that it was now proposed that the League of Nations should become an 'association of strong and well-armed States to resist an aggressor'. Under this new scenario, he said, Britain would quickly become strong again and he was 'most anxious to marshal all worthy forces behind this process of rearmament'. Churchill appealed to Lucy to support his efforts in the push for rearmament but, knowing her too well, he ended his letter by stating that he did not expect her to agree with him.[91]

On 16 November, the day after Churchill's speech, the King informed Stanley Baldwin that he intended to marry Wallis Simpson and Baldwin replied that the American would not be acceptable – in particular because the Church of England opposed remarriage after divorce. As head of the Church the King was expected to support its policies but Edward declared that he would rather give up the throne than give up Mrs Simpson. Two days later Edward visited depressed areas of South Wales and at Blaenavon in Gwent said that his ministers were giving 'serious consideration' to the introduction of new industries in mining areas. Later he remarked to some miners that 'Something must be done for you.' The King's words made a big impact but Baldwin and others in government took them as a criticism of their economic policy. Edward may indeed have intended to shame his ministers into action, but he had not improved his popularity in government circles.

Lucy believed that Edward should be allowed to marry Mrs Simpson; apart from being a divorcee herself, her support was intensified by the fact that the King's main opponent was the hated Stanley Baldwin. Lucy refused to acknowledge the problems that the Prime Minister faced or accept the general feeling that Edward should put country and duty before personal feelings. The situation churned in Lucy's disturbed mind until it produced a nightmare, which she recounted in the *Saturday Review*. On the night of 27 November, she wrote, she had had a dream that was like a vision. A voice seemed to say, 'England is in great danger and the King must be warned at once. There is a plot to get rid of him by Russia, helped by *The Times*.' The basis of this was that Edward regarded Geoffrey Dawson, editor of *The Times* and supporter of Baldwin, as a great enemy. The King, Lucy said, had to go because of his 'loving, keen, sympathetic, understanding' of the misery in distressed mining areas, and because he had said 'Something must be done.' His popularity and strength of purpose angered the 'POWERS OF "RED

HATE"', which had mustered spiritual evil and given the order that Edward 'MUST BE GOT RID OF.' Lucy had awoken from the dream at two in the morning 'horror-stricken, and trembling'. She had waited impatiently until quarter past six, when she rang for the housemaid who came to light the fire. 'Ellen,' she said, 'I have had a terrifying dream about the King – bring me paper and pen and tell the chauffeur to bring round the car.' Lucy's letter, in which she implored Edward to beware, was delivered to Fort Belvedere, the King's home in Windsor Great Park, by eight o'clock. Still agitated, Lucy then made a flurry of phone calls to tell her dream to Allen, her sister Florence and Collin Brooks. But, she wrote later, her letter did not have the desired effect for the King was 'DECEIVED AND MISINFORMED BY THOSE WHO SHOULD HAVE HELPED HIM'.

When it became apparent that Edward intended to abdicate, Lucy's 'whole being flashed with passionate anger', Allen wrote, and she 'raged as some Greek fury would have raged'. The intensity of her 'daemonic energy' was frightening and she dictated letters, telegrams and articles with fierce energy. Her outbursts, Wentworth Day wrote, came from the 'tired and tortured mind of a very old and gallant lady, who put England and her King first and feared that both were in dire danger'. One letter that Lucy wrote was to Edward's mother, Queen Mary, who was much against her son's abdication. In it Lucy suggested that the Queen go to Cannes at Lucy's expense and bring Mrs Simpson back to stay with her at Marlborough House. In the midst of this, on 30 November, the Crystal Palace, where more than fifty years previously Lucy had appeared on stage as Melissa Smayle, was destroyed by fire. This event could only have added to her sense of apocalypse.

Because of voluntary press censorship, the British public had until now known little or nothing of the unfolding crisis, and when it was made public on 3 December the nation was stunned. Other news stories, Collin Brooks wrote in his diary, were swamped by the royal drama, but of all the people he encountered only Lucy and the Marquess of Donegall, a journalist, were 'thoroughly pro-King'. From what Brooks had heard Edward was so mentally unstable that he might 'do anything', even to the point of replacing Baldwin with Oswald Mosley and thus attempting a 'fascist *coup d'etat*'. Perhaps Lucy had been pushing the King to do this very thing. Brooks ruled nothing out, and in preparing his newspaper for the weekend, he wrote, he had 'even had to allow for a Royal suicide, for the King is obviously out of the realm of rationality and in the realm of nerve storms'.

Edward's 'nerve storms' were in part due to the fact that Mrs Simpson had departed for Cannes to escape the furore, leaving him bereft and miserable at Fort Belvedere.

One afternoon at about this time the King made a secret visit to Byron Cottage. He stayed for an hour; what was said did not emerge but afterwards Lucy made a dramatic move. Later her chauffeur Foster would tell Wentworth Day that Lucy had given him a brown paper parcel addressed to King Edward VIII. Lucy had obviously made a private arrangement with Edward for, following her instructions, Foster had taken it to Fort Belvedere and at the gates given a certain signal on the car horn. The guards let him through and he delivered the parcel at the Fort and waited for an answer from the King. A short time later the King emerged with a letter, written in his own hand and addressed to Lady Houston. The chauffeur took it, saluted, and drove away. But what had been in the parcel, Wentworth Day asked Foster. 'It felt like bank notes,' the chauffeur replied. 'I could certainly feel something under the paper. You and I have handled some big packets of notes for her Ladyship on different jobs.' In Wentworth Day's view the package most likely contained £250,000, for Lucy had frequently told him of her intention to give or leave that sum to Edward. If Lucy had sent the King money she may have intended him to use it to arrange a *coup d'etat* to overthrow the government, as Brooks had suggested was a possibility. Indeed, many Conservative MPs saw the abdication crisis as an opportunity to get rid of Baldwin, although it was thought likely that the King would favour Winston Churchill above Mosley as Prime Minister. But Edward did no such thing; abdication was the quickest means by which he could be reunited with Mrs Simpson.

That weekend many took to the streets of central London, forming crowds outside Buckingham Palace, Marlborough House and the Prime Minister's residence at 10 Downing Street. The atmosphere was tense. It was as if, reported *The Times*, 'awareness that a major event in our history was being enacted had made the people restless'. In Downing Street the waiting press and public were rewarded by the sight of the comings and goings of Baldwin, cabinet ministers, and Archbishop of Canterbury Cosmo Gordon Lang in his clerical garb. Lang, aged over 70, had been a close associate of George V and in the hierarchy of precedence in English society he was above the Prime Minister. Lucy understood that Lang had refused to perform the coronation ceremony unless the King abandoned Mrs Simpson. It would be a 'hollow mockery', Lang had said. Edward disliked Lang, whom, he wrote in his autobiography, he found to too 'worldly' and 'more interested in the pursuit of prestige and power than the abstractions of the human soul'. Fearing the archbishop because of the subtlety of his mind, Edward felt his influence as a 'shadowy, hovering presence' behind Baldwin. Edward's suspicions were correct, for Lang and Baldwin had been holding secret discussions for weeks and the archbishop, intellectually superior to Baldwin, had guided the Prime Minister as they worked together to ensure that Edward stepped down.

People had gathered in central London to make protests. A car circled the statue of Queen Victoria in front of Buckingham Palace displaying a sign 'We Want our King', while a man walked through the crowds with a placard which read, 'For King and the People: No Treason'. In Whitehall, Oswald Mosley's Blackshirts marched up and down displaying a portrait of the King and chanting:

> One, two, three, four, five,
> We want Baldwin dead or alive.

Meanwhile, Lucy did what she could to keep Edward on the throne. She composed a pamphlet, 'The King's Happiness Comes First', which was handed out in the West End, and wrote Edward a personal letter:

> Be of good cheer, Sir – the Country are *with You* … Sir, I am sure you are conquering. I have outside my windows a flying banner – 'The King's happiness comes first,' and last night a lot of young people stood and cheered it and sang 'For He's a Jolly Good Fellow!' They *love* you, my King. Do not desert them.

But all was in vain, for on 10 December, after a reign of 327 days, Edward signed the instrument of abdication at Fort Belvedere to become the Duke of Windsor. The following day he made a radio broadcast from Windsor Castle in which he explained that he felt unable to serve as King without the support of 'the woman I love'. He then left the country for Austria and his younger brother became King George VI. It had all happened so quickly that the next issue of the *Saturday Review*, published on 12 December, had not kept pace. It featured a picture of Wallis Simpson captioned 'The Queen of His HEART', and an article written by Lucy entitled 'Love Conquers

All'. Reviewing the events of the last few days, she wrote that she had hardly eaten or slept for her heart had been full of 'loving sympathy and indignation' for the King in his 'cruel, heart-breaking trial'. Again she blamed the Prime Minister:

> Primed with instructions from Russia – to get rid of the King – Mr Baldwin has had a busy week – backwards and forwards – backwards and forwards – several times a day to hold a pistol to the head of the King, crying, 'Do my will – or – abdicate.' **BUT LOVE IS GREATER THAN HATE**. *And a woman's love has saved the situation.*

But which woman was it whose love had 'saved the situation'? Was it Mrs Simpson, or Lucy and her £250,000? The conspiracy to remove the King, Lucy continued, had failed, 'as it was bound to do', and now the King reigned 'GREATER AND MORE FIRMLY THAN EVER IN THE HEARTS OF HIS PEOPLE'. She focused on the human aspects: 'WHAT A ROMANCE!' No other love story could approach this 'true tale of true love. PROVING – NOT ONLY – WHAT A GREAT MAN THE KING IS – AS KING – BUT WHAT A GREAT AND SPLENDID TRUE LOVER. READY TO ABDICATE HIS THRONE FOR THE WOMAN HE LOVES.' In later years women would weep when they read the love story of Edward and Mrs Simpson, 'FOR ALL THE WORLD LOVES A LOVER'.

It was not until the following issue, published on 19 December, that the *Saturday Review* caught up. With colour banished, the cover bore a full-length portrait of the former King in military uniform and the text, 'What Lady Houston thinks: **Are We Downhearted? YES**'. Then followed Lucy's last poem:

> Goodbye – Goodbye
> We cry with a sigh
> Driven away
> By the law that's a lie
> **Great King and True Lover**
> For you we would die.
> Will you never return, Sir,
> To gladden our eye?

In ten short days, Lucy wrote, the abdication had been rushed through as though Edward were a criminal, and now she mourned him 'FOR HE WAS A GREAT KING AND HE DEALT WELL AND LOVINGLY WITH HIS PEOPLE'. Baldwin was responsible for the King's departure, she wrote, and he should from the first have explained the situation frankly to the people so that they could understand what was happening and 'weighed the pros and cons of what it meant to the Nation'. More than she mourned for the King, however, Lucy mourned for England: 'I FEAR FOR OUR DEAR COUNTRY. This is said with no want of respect to King George VI and Queen Elizabeth – as they both will understand, I know.'

In a scathing article in the same issue, Comyns Beaumont declared that Edward had been got rid of because of demands that he should 'lead his people against the increasing despotism of a dishonest junta of politicians'. However, as Lucy had been a key voice in demanding this, by implication she had been partly to blame for the King's departure. Parliament, Beaumont continued, wanted a King who was a figurehead only, parading with the trappings of royalty and serving as a 'sedative' to the people. Politicians did not want a King who probed too deeply and exposed their 'neglect' as Edward had in South Wales: 'Good God! Such a man is a menace to the well-being of the nation. He is becoming too popular!' Politicians had hated Edward because he saw through their shams and hypocrisies, and so parliament had 'bumped him off in a manner which the most experienced Chicago gangster might envy', and not one MP had queried the constitutional grounds for doing so.

Predictably, Meriel Buchanan implied that the abdication had been part of a plot by 'dark, furtive and secret … forces of international finance' that had been intended to weaken Britain. She, like Lucy, discerned an occult element. Perhaps never before in the history of the world, she wrote, had the 'affairs of nations been so fatally controlled or mis-controlled by Satanic influences; never before has evil flourished with such bare-faced impunity'. The British masses, Buchanan continued, might smile when hidden powers were mentioned but Buchanan knew of 'reliable evidence' that the mystic Rasputin had been financed and used by Russian bankers who, 'no doubt acting under the order of international financiers', had worked to bring down the Russian imperial family so as to prepare Russia for revolution.[92]

Bolshevism, international financiers and Stanley Baldwin – all had been blamed by the *Saturday Review*, but it reserved its most damning attack for the Archbishop of Canterbury. Once Edward had left the country, Lang made a radio broadcast. When coming to the throne, he said, Edward had received from God a 'high and sacred trust', but when the King had surrendered this trust and abdicated he had explained to the people that his reason, in Lang's term, was a 'craving for private happiness'. It was sad and strange, the archbishop continued, that the King should have sought happiness in a manner that was 'inconsistent with the Christian principles of marriage, and within a social circle whose standards and ways of life are alien to all the best instincts and traditions of his people'. Those who belonged to that circle, Lang continued, should know that they stood 'rebuked by the judgement of the nation'. While, Lang said, he had hitherto held back from making these comments, he now felt compelled to do so for the sake of 'sincerity and truth'. Lang's speech did not go down well; many felt that it was tantamount to hitting a man when he was down.

Lucy included herself among those Lang condemned as having low moral standards, and she poured out her scorn in the 19 December edition. Jesus Christ, she wrote, had tried to help women who were 'sinners' (which in context meant prostitutes). Did the archbishop place Mrs Simpson in this category, Lucy asked? If so, he should 'refresh his mind by reading Christ's loving, tender and merciful words: SHE LOVED MUCH'. The archbishop, Lucy continued, 'might perhaps have hesitated to broadcast his harsh judgement on King Edward had he remembered that a greater than he said: "Judge not that yet be not judged"'. These words of Jesus Christ, quoted by Lucy, formed, Wentworth Day wrote, a 'magnificent rebuke; I wonder if the Archbishop was capable of blushing?' This probably reflected rumours about Lang's private life.

The *Saturday Review* of 26 December 1936 would be the last issue that Lucy edited. It had reverted to its red, white and blue cover but the attack on the archbishop was kept up. Lang, Brooks stated, was 'devoid of Christianity' and had been 'unforgiving, unkind and wantonly hurtful', demonstrating the 'vindictive waspishness of a snubbed old man'. On the letters page, Lang was described as 'A Malevolent Prelate' who made 'mealy mouth utterances and malevolent posturings'. He presided over the 'cant and humbug' of Church of England ministers; he was unjust, intolerant, arrogant and a 'repulsive reptile'. David Low, too, took aim at the archbishop in a cartoon captioned 'Col. Blimp's Christmas Circus', published on 19 December. Lang was depicted cavorting on a bowl of ice with the caption, 'Cosmo

Cantuar – Thin ice skating thrill'. Amid various other public people of the day Lucy also appeared, wearing a tutu and feathered aigrette, and balancing delicately on the back of a bear. Her caption was 'Engagement!!!! Extraordinary La Houston – Graceful equestrienne on the Russian Bear (By kind permission of Stalin)'. Above her swung 'Tony Eden – Dashing Young Man on Flying Trapeze'.

In the *Saturday Review* of 26 December Lucy published an open letter to King George. The archbishop's attack on his brother must have hurt him deeply, she said, and Lang and Baldwin would forever be held responsible for the 'DASTARDLY MANNER' in which they drove Edward out of the country. Lucy assured the new King and Queen that she was 'most sincerely and truly' their friend, and she knew that they would not think less of her for her letter. Then, predictably, she gave some advice. Those who had got rid of Edward, she told the King, were deceiving themselves with the 'FOOLISH IDEA' that George would 'ACCEPT THEIR ADVICE UNQUESTIONINGLY AS BEING THE RIGHT AND PROPER PEOPLE TO DICTATE TO YOU THE POLICY YOU MUST FOLLOW'. While these people hoped that he would not 'probe into things' as Edward had done, Lucy anticipated that he would '**astonish and disappoint them**'. Lucy had already begun a campaign to influence the new King.

It was ironic that Lucy's last issue featured her cold cure, for by the time it was published she had caught a cold that would prove fatal. The abdication crisis had taken a great toll on her both mentally and physically and, as Wentworth Day put it, the 'last spurt of demoniac anger signed her death-warrant'. Lucy, who could not stand to be thwarted, felt that she had been defeated by the very forces that she had warned against for so long. Crisp spoke to Lucy after the abdication and found that she had 'lost all interest in life'. Her last words to Crisp were, 'Well, you can go on, my dear, and I'll help you, but it's no good now – it's all finished.' Lucy had had such great faith in Edward as the saviour of country and Empire that with him gone she had lost hope.

On Sunday, 27 December, Lucy rang Collin Brooks at about four o'clock in the afternoon. They had a long talk in which Lucy told him that she was very tired, but she was often tired and Brooks did not think her illness out of the ordinary. However, as it had with Tom Radmall and Lord Byron, her cold tightened its grip. The following day Allen rang Brooks and told him that

Lucy was now 'really ill' with pleurisy and bronchitis; Allen also consulted Brooks, whom Lucy trusted implicitly, about the cover of the forthcoming issue of the *Saturday Review*.

Wentworth Day describes the last few hours of Lucy's life on 29 December. Lord Horder went to Byron Cottage, where he found her in bed with all the windows open, and wind and rain driving through the room. Horder told Lucy that the windows must be shut: 'You've a bad cold already and you've pretty well starved yourself to death.' Lucy snapped, 'I won't have them shut,' to which Horder replied, 'Very well, then, I won't attend you.' Lucy hit back, 'Oh! All right, you can have them shut. Afraid of a little bit of fresh air, are you?' Horder left, probably smarting at the ridiculous jibe, but after he left Lucy ordered the windows to be opened again. Later, she lay in bed quietly singing her favourite hymn to herself until her attendant said, 'It's time for you to go to sleep.' 'Yes, my dear,' Lucy replied. 'It's time for me to sleep – and a damned long sleep it's going to be.' Prophetic words, but perhaps Horder had given her a strong sedative. Lucy died late that evening, 'very peacefully' while unconscious, according to Arthur Wrey. He and Florence had been at her side. There was general agreement that the strain of the abdication had fatally weakened Lucy and Horder was reported to have said, 'My patient went on hunger strike,' and that but for the abdication she would have lived for another ten years. But would Lucy's own verdict have been that she had 'died most mysteriously', the victim of a plot with its origins in Moscow? She left this life exhausted, thwarted and fatally 'downhearted'; England and the Empire would have to carry on without her as best they could.

19

LEGACY

ucy's death, Comyns Beaumont wrote, came as a 'severe shock' to all who knew her. The next day Collin Brooks had lunch with Warner Allen, who told him that her relatives were already arriving at Byron Cottage like 'hungry wolves'. How much, Brooks confided wistfully to his diary, he would 'miss those long telephone talks', and later he wrote that he could have 'better spared a better woman'. But Brooks's mind, in common with many another, quickly turned to Lucy's money. Brooks would lose an 'easy £1,200 a year' and Crisp was also dismayed, for Lucy had left cheques made out but unsigned, one being for a large sum that Lucy had promised Crisp. Another cheque may have been made out to Oswald Mosley, for there was speculation that Lucy had been planning to contribute a considerable sum to help him run 400 parliamentary candidates at the next general election. When questioned the BUF stated that Lucy's death would not affect its plans for candidates, but this did not amount to a denial that it had been expecting a donation. Another question was Lucy's age. Arthur Wrey was no help to the press when in answer to questions he replied gallantly, 'She had no age – no woman has,' but most newspapers speculated that she had been about 65. The matter was settled when a reporter found her birth certificate showing that she had died at the age of 79. Her 'biggest secret', said the press, had been revealed.

The search for Lucy's will occupied many column inches. Wentworth Day, Warner Allen, Collin Brooks, Comyns Beaumont and Lord Sempill were all convinced that Lucy had made a will. Brooks and Allen knew that she had devised a scheme to dedicate her money to the creation of an Empire Trust, and indeed she had got as far as making a pencil draft. Byron Cottage was ransacked, the *Liberty* searched, and even the gardener at Beaufield asked whether there were any hiding places in the garden. There was a brief ripple of excitement a few days after Lucy's death when it was reported that a will had been found, but it was only the one in which she had left everything to Juliana Hoare, and it was invalid because Miss Hoare had died in March 1936. No valid will was ever found. Lucy could perhaps have destroyed it after the abdication having already given money to the former King, or alternatively it may have been removed by person or persons unknown.

Despite the fact that for months Lucy had scarcely been mentioned in the mainstream press she was now featured everywhere. The obituaries were a mixed bag. While some gave a plain account of her life, others were more forthright. *Time* magazine described Lucy as a 'plump, imperious person, voluble to an epic degree'. The *Birmingham Daily Gazette* reported that, with her 'acute sense of the theatre', Lucy had seen in everything an opportunity for a 'vehement personal intrusion'. The *New Statesman* regretted Lucy's passing, for she had rivalled the cartoonist Low in her power of 'making detestable opinions appear ridiculous, and was herself an incarnate argument against the inheritance of wealth'. Elsewhere she was described as a female Colonel Blimp, known by her 'few intimates as a queer, obstinate old woman', who despite her age had dressed like a 'matron of 35'. Lucy was dubbed as 'aggressive' and a 'nuisance'. Her character was described as 'impulsive, wayward, intractable', and 'marked by intense likes and dislikes'. She had had 'half-baked views', made 'comic propaganda', and 'followed her intuitive and untutored impulses wherever they led her wealthy fancy'. She had 'all the right impulses backed by the wrong views'. The *Sphere* concluded that Lucy was let down by her weaknesses, for she 'vainly over-rated her power, her abilities, and her importance. If her heart was big, her mind was sometimes very small.' However, it was also the *Sphere*'s obituarist who gave Lucy perhaps the kindest tribute:

Lady Houston did much good publicly and a great number of private acts of kindness, from a generous and patriotic heart, and I hope the earth will lie lightly on her, and her troubled, unbalanced, courageous spirit have rest.

The funeral, on 4 January 1937, was a low-key affair. The day was cold and wet. Although four policemen were posted on duty outside Byron Cottage, only a few people gathered to watch the funeral cortege depart.

Lucy's body was encased in an ornately carved coffin upon which was a simple brass plate with the inscription, 'Fanny Lucy Houston. At Rest. December 29, 1936.' Placed on the coffin in the hearse was a wreath of yellow chrysanthemums and orchids from Florence, Lucy's only remaining sibling, with a card which read 'To My Beloved Sister'. Another wreath, from Lord Sempill, bore the inscription:

> With love, and in memory of a great friend, who never spared herself, but thought unceasingly of others, and acted courageously in their interests. Her foresightedness and generosity greatly benefited the vital cause of aeronautics.

The cortege proceeded to St Marylebone Cemetery in Finchley where the funeral service was held in the chapel. The plain building held only 200 people but no more than that number turned out and Meriel Buchanan, who was among them, thought it 'pitiful that there were so few to remember her generosity or to pay tribute'. Florence Wrey was too ill to attend but her husband Arthur was there, and he and Lucy's nephew Tom Radmall were the principal mourners. Lord Sempill attended, and Wentworth Day represented Lord Lloyd, who was too ill to attend. Roderick Brinckman represented his father, who was in hospital after an operation, and would himself die later that year.

In the chapel Lucy's coffin was placed upon a catafalque before the simple oak altar upon which two candles flickered. The service lasted for only fifteen minutes; no hymns were sung but there were prayers, a lesson and the reading of Psalm 23, 'The Lord is my Shepherd'. It was drizzling when the funeral party emerged and walked up the slope to the cemetery's Remembrance Avenue where, near the soldiers' plot, Lucy was to be buried. After the coffin had been lowered into the ground, an elderly woman stepped forward and dropped a bunch of violets into the open grave. Violet Hunt had remained faithful to the last. Later Florence and Arthur Wrey would commission a gravestone with the inscription:

> In Very Loving Memory of Dame Fanny Lucy Houston, D.B.E. who passed to her rest on December 29th, 1936. Widow of the late Robert Patterson [sic] Houston, Bart. She was one of England's Patriots and her generosity was unbounded.

303

The Wreys had misspelt Houston's name, but left space for their own inscriptions to be added when the time came.

Such had been the hiatus that the *Saturday Review* of 2 January 1937, the first after Lucy's death, made no mention of her beyond a full-page photograph on the cover; the 9 January issue, with a new-style white cover, contained tributes from the journal's staff and contributors. Meriel Buchanan equated the loss of Lucy with that of King Edward VIII as one of the 'two great tragedies' of the closing days of 1936. Beaumont recounted his first impressions of Lucy on the *Liberty* at Rouen six years previously and paid tribute to her patriotism and her 'robust common sense'. He ended by stating that although Lucy's mind had in many ways been like that of a man, she had also possessed the 'feminine gift of jumping to conclusions rapidly, wittily, and sometimes wrongly. But mainly she was right.'

Without a will, Lucy's solicitors set to work to divide her estate between her relatives. They were in two groups, those in England and those in Australia. There was speculation in the press as to the value of the estate, and £7 million was mentioned. But Lucy's spectacular giving had reduced the value of her English estate to £1,528,083, before death duties. It was also revealed that Lucy had also held estate in Jersey to the value of at least £2 million, although there was no confirmation in the British press of the form that the Jersey estate took. Taking into account the £1.5 million that Lucy had paid on Houston's estate in 1927, she had got through about £2 million since his death.

Lucy's horses were sold and some of her jewellery was put up for auction at Christie's in May 1937. Although only four pieces were presented they were, *The Times* reported, 'of a quality rare even in Christie's rooms'. At some point Lucy had signed over ownership of the *Saturday Review* to Warner Allen, Comyns Beaumont and Collin Brooks, and they hoped to make a go of it as an independent right-wing journal. A notice appeared in the 16 January edition: 'To-day the *Saturday Review* resumes its old position as the leading Conservative weekly. The dictatorship under which its circulation exceeded that of any previous period in its long history is over, and we return to constitutional government.' But the journal would not succeed, and it was generally agreed that Lucy had given it the kiss of death. The *Yorkshire Post* reported that she had 'transformed it into something cheap and strange' and, unable to find a purchaser, the *Saturday Review* closed in 1938.

Byron Cottage was eventually sold in the spring of 1938, while Beaufield continued in the possession of Lucy's nephew Tom Radmall until his death in 1948. More painful was the disposal of the *Liberty*. Since it had last been in commission in October 1935 the yacht had been moored at Cowes, manned by Captain Gibb and a skeleton crew. When she was put up for sale in the summer of 1937 reporters took the opportunity to look round. The *Liberty*, one wrote, was 'spick and span, ready for sea at a few hours' notice; her twin-screw engines clean and shining, and her 270ft of promenade deck spotless'. The handful of crew still aboard were hoping that the yacht would find a new owner: 'She is too grand a ship to die,' one said. But the weeks passed and no buyer came forward. The truth was that the *Liberty* was a glamorous but expensive leftover from another age, and also had the disadvantage of using coal in the days of oil-burning motors. The great yacht was eventually sold for scrap and broken up.

Lucy's legacy is not easy to quantify; the *Oxford Dictionary of National Biography* (2004) assesses her as an 'adventuress'. In her political life there is no hard evidence that she changed public opinion with her street campaigns, posters, leaflets, articles or the *Saturday Review*, although she did provide a focus for those who agreed with her. The results of her support of the Suffragist cause and her work in the First World War are impossible to quantify, as are the value of her gifts, large and small, public and anonymous, to individuals, groups and institutions. But while the outcomes can never be known, the impact on the lives of ordinary people may have been significant. Who can tell the effects down through time, for example, of a life saved by an operation in a hospital wing sponsored by Lucy, or of a family avoiding eviction because her cheque paid the rent? Of Lucy's other donations, her purchase of Ronald Ross's malaria archives for the British Museum ensured their preservation for the nation and, if it is true to say that without Lucy's money the *Discovery* would have been broken up before the Second World War, the ship's survival is owed to her. But by 1953 Lucy's donation had run out and the Boy Scouts could no longer maintain the ship. The *Discovery* was taken over by the Admiralty and used as a training ship but by 1979 was again in danger of being scrapped. Opened to the public as a museum, in 1985 she was handed over to the Heritage Trust in Dundee to become a visitor attraction in the city in which she had been built.

Probably the main legacy of Lucy's life has come to be regarded as her contribution to the development of the Spitfire through her funding of the

Schneider Trophy competition. Allen believed that if Lucy could have arisen from the grave and been told that it was largely owing to her that the Battle of Britain in the Second World War had been won she would have been gratified but not surprised. However, one dissenting voice has been that of Gordon Mitchell, the son of R.J. Mitchell. While it has been suggested, he wrote in his biography of his father, that Lucy's support of the Schneider Trophy competition was instrumental in the production of the Spitfire, the S.6B was:

> essentially only a modified version of the S.6, the major part of the vital experience R.J. [Mitchell] gained from the Schneider Races, later to be of such value in designing the Spitfire, was in fact obtained in 1927 and 1929 with the S.5 and S.6.

But in 1953 an article in the *New York Herald Tribune* stated that the 'whole free world' owed Lucy a considerable debt: 'So who seems loony now, crazy Lady Houston, or the respectable Baldwins, Chamberlains and Simons, whose balanced budgets evoked such universal contemporary admiration.'

Lucy's contribution to the Spitfire's development was certainly promoted by the British film *First of the Few*, a biography of R.J. Mitchell, released in 1942. The representation of Lucy comes in a scene set at a party in 1931 to which she comes ashore from the *Liberty*. In the scene Lucy has a conversation with Mitchell, which later prompts her funding of the Schneider competition. The *Liberty* can be seen offshore, its lights flashing the messages 'Down with the Government' and 'Wake up England' alternately, rather than Lucy's actual original 'To Hell with Ramsay MacDonald'.

Lucy died while the enthusiasm of some in Britain for Nazi Germany was still at its height, and she has gone down in history as an unrepentant fascist and supporter of Hitler. Had she lived, she might have cheered when Germany marched into Czechoslovakia and then Poland in September 1939, still believing Hitler to be the main bulwark against communism. When German bombs fell upon her beloved London she might well have blamed Baldwin and Eden who, controlled by Moscow, had goaded Hitler beyond his endurance. Others who had once enthused about the Nazi regime were later able to change their views or cover their tracks, but death deprived Lucy of that advantage. In his biography, Warner Allen commented that, for all her faults, she did at least see that England was in danger and it was to her 'undying credit' that she did what she could to save the country. Her prophecies of war and ruin were scorned or ignored, but, Allen wrote, if Lucy was wrong in points of detail, she was 'not so wrong as those who scoffed at her'. Lucy, Allen concluded, was 'essentially a character, such as the world no longer moulds, providing a welcome break in the monotony of mass-produced humanity'.

NOTES

Chapter 3
1   Divorce Amendment Bill [H.L.] HL Deb, 28 May 1895, vol. 34 cc431–48.

Chapter 4
2   The house was taken by Lady Susan St Helier, a well-known society hostess and great-aunt of Clementine Hozier, the future wife of Winston Churchill. It would be at a dinner at the house in 1908 that the couple would meet for the first time.

Chapter 6
3   Violet Hunt Papers. 4607 b7 f47. Letter from Lucy to Violet Hunt, undated, about 1926.

Chapter 7
4   Lady Byron, D.B.E. (1920). 'Woman and the Problems of the Future'. In *British Dominions Year Book 1920*. Eagle, Star and British Dominions Insurance Company Limited.

Chapter 8
5   MS-BALDWIN-00159-000-00211-2. Lady Byron to Stanley Baldwin, 16 October 1924.
6   MS-BALDWIN-00159-000-00213. Note, possibly Geoffrey Fry.
7   MS-BALDWIN-00159-000-00214. Unsigned letter, possibly Geoffrey Fry to Miss Lucy Byron, Trianon Palace Hotel, 18 October 1924.
8   MS-BALDWIN-00159-000-00215. Lady Byron, Trianon Palace Hotel, to Stanley Baldwin, November 1924.
9   MS-BALDWIN-00159-000-00216-9. Lord Birkenhead to Sir Robert Houston, 31 October 1924.
10 MS-BALDWIN-00159-000-00228-236. Colonel J.F.C. Carter, Special Branch, to Geoffrey Fry, 14 November 1924.
11 Violet Hunt Papers. 4607 b7 f47f. LH, *Liberty*, St Maxime, to Violet Hunt, 8 Radnor Cliff, Sandgate, New Year 1925.
12 MS-BALDWIN-00159-000-00228-233. Joan Smith to Sir Robert Houston, 1 November 1931.

13 MS-BALDWIN-00159-000-00220-6. Poppy Houston to Stanley Baldwin, January 1925.

14 MS-BALDWIN-00159-000-00220-6. Poppy Houston to Stanley Baldwin, January 1925.

15 MS-BALDWIN-00159-000-00228-234. Geoffrey Fry to LH, 15 January 1925.

16 Violet Hunt Papers. 4607 b7 f47. Poppy Houston, *Liberty*, St Maxime, to Violet Hunt, 8 Radnor Cliff, Sandgate, 12 February 1925.

17 Violet Hunt Papers. 4607 b7 f47-b. LH to Violet Hunt at 8 Radnor Cliff. Undated.

18 Violet Hunt Papers. 4607 b7 f47. Poppy Houston, *Liberty*, St Maxime, to Violet Hunt (undated).

19 Violet Hunt Papers. 4607 b7 f47f. Poppy Houston, Benalder Lodge, to Violet Hunt, 23 October 1925.

20 Violet Hunt Papers. 4607 b6 f13. Gedge, Fiske, and Gedge, Hastings House, Norfolk Street, London, to Violet Hueffer, 8 Radnor Cliff, Sandgate, 8 April 1926.

Chapter 9

21 Violet Hunt Papers. 4607 b6 f13. Gedge, Fiske, and Gedge to Violet Hunt, South Lodge, 80 Campden Hill Road, London, 27 April 1926.

22 Violet Hunt Papers. 4607 b7 f47-a. LH to Violet Hunt at 8 Radnor Cliff. Undated.

23 CHAR 2 164, Winston Churchill to Sir Frederick Ponsonby, Buckingham Palace Privy Purse Office, 5 July 1929.

Chapter 10

24 CHAR 18 72. LH, *Liberty*, St Maxime, Var, France, to Winston Churchill, 4 March 1928.

25 CHAR 18 72. Winston Churchill to LH, 8 March 1928.

26 CHAR 2 164. Sir Frederick Ponsonby to Winston Churchill, 4 July 1929.

27 CHAR 2 164. Winston Churchill to Sir Frederick Ponsonby, 4 July 1929.

Chapter 11

28 GLLD 19/2. LH, Byron Cottage, to Lord Lloyd, 11 November (probably 1930).

29 LH, Beaufield, to Oscar Pulvermacher, 27 November 1930. Quoted in Wentworth Day, p. 91.

30 LH to Oscar Pulvermacher, 3 December 1930. Quoted in Wentworth Day, p. 93.

31 LH to Oscar Pulvermacher, 12 January 1931. Quoted in Wentworth Day, p. 93.

32 LH to Oscar Pulvermacher, June 1931. Quoted in Wentworth Day, p. 97.

33 LH to Oscar Pulvermacher, 29 June 1931. Quoted in Wentworth Day, p. 96.

34 T.E. Lawrence Papers, Bodleian. MS. Eng. d. 3341, fols 922–26. LH, Beaufield, to T.E. Lawrence. 1 March 1932.

Chapter 12

35 Ways and Means. HC Deb, 19 October 1932, vol. 269 cc175–264.

36 GLLD 19/2. LH, Kinrara, to Lord Lloyd, 30 Portman Square, London W, 21 October 1932.

37 GLLD 19/2. Lady Houston, Kinrara, Aviemore, to Lord Lloyd. Undated but probably late October 1932.
38 GLLD 19/2. LH, Kinrara, to Lord Lloyd, 30 Portman Square, London W, 20 November 1932.
39 GLLD 19/2. LH, Kinrara, to Lord Lloyd, 21 November 1932.
40 T.E. Lawrence Papers, Bodleian. MS. Eng. d. 3341, fols 922–26. LH, Byron Cottage, to T. E. Lawrence, 9 January 1933.
41 RDCH 5 11. LH, Byron Cottage, to Randolph Churchill, 1 February 1933.
42 RSCH 5 11. Randolph Churchill to LH, 3 February 1933.
43 Joseph and Stewart Alsop, 'Matter of Fact', *Oxnard Press Courier*, 4 May 1953. Reprinted from *New York Herald Tribune*.

Chapter 13
44 Oswald Mosley, Blackshirt rally, Bellevue, Manchester, 1 October 1933.
45 GLLD 19/2. Lord Lloyd, 4 Queen Anne Street, W.1., to LH, Byron Cottage, 25 June 1934.
46 GLLD 19/2. Lord Lloyd, 4 Queen Anne Street, W.1., to LH, Byron Cottage, 25 June 1934.
47 GLLD 19/2. Lord Lloyd to LH, *Liberty*, Sandbanks, 10 October 1933.
48 GLLD 19/2. LH, *Liberty*, to Lord Lloyd, October 1933.
49 GLLD 19/2. LH, *Liberty*, to Lord Lloyd, October 1933.
50 GLLD 19/3. Lord Lloyd to LH, Sunday 15 October 1933.

Chapter 15
51 Mosley, p. 286.
52 *Evening Standard*, 17 October 1934.
53 4605 b69 f12-17 Ford Maddox Ford Collection. Violet Hunt to Lucy (undated, 1930s).
54 4605 b69 f12-17 Ford Maddox Ford Collection. Lucy to Violet Hunt, 12 November 1934.
55 4605 b69 f12-17 Ford Maddox Ford Collection. Violet Hunt to Lucy (undated, 1930s).
56 CHAR 1 273. Winston Churchill to Clementine Churchill, 18 January 1935.
57 RDCH 5 11. LH to Randolph Churchill, 1935.
58 CHAR 2 246. Wavertree by-election campaign leaflet, 1935.
59 CHAR 1 273. Winston Churchill to Clementine Churchill, 23 January 1935.
60 RSCH 5 11. Telegram LH to Randolph Churchill, 31 January 1935.
61 RDCH 5 11, LH to Randolph Churchill, 1935.
62 CHAR 1 273. Winston Churchill to Clementine Churchill, 23 February 1935.
63 MS.Eng.hist.c.1013. Bodleian, Lord Wolmer to LH, Byron Cottage, 11 March 1935.
64 RDCH 5 11. LH to Randolph Churchill, February/March 1935.
65 RDCH 5 11. LH to Randolph Churchill, 7 March 1935.
66 CHAR 2 246. LH to Winston Churchill, 8 March 1935.
67 CHAR 2 246. Randolph Churchill to Winston Churchill, March 1935.
68 CHAR 2 246. Winston Churchill to LH, March 1935.

69 Winston Churchill to Clementine Churchill, 2 March 1935. Quoted in Soames, p. 388.
70 Texts of the three letters are produced from: Ex-Chief Inspector Percy J. Smith, 'Smith of the Yard, the Coolest Forger Tried to Ruin Prime Minister. Scotland Yard Man Exposes Clever Crooks', *Truth* (Sydney, NSW) 28 September 1952.
71 Ex-Chief Inspector Percy J. Smith, 'Smith of the Yard, the Coolest Forger Tried to Ruin Prime Minister. Scotland Yard Man Exposes Clever Crooks', *Truth* (Sydney, NSW) 28 September 1952.
72 PRO 30/69/1558. Statement by Lucy Houston, *Liberty*, Sandbanks, to New Scotland Yard, 14 May 1935.
73 PRO 30/69/1558. H.B. Usher, Political Secretary to Ramsay MacDonald, to Ramsay MacDonald, 8 April 1935.

Chapter 16
74 GB 133 RMD/1/14/151. Kenneth Brown, Baker & Baker, Solicitors, to LH, *Liberty*, Dorset, 17 May 1935.
75 PRO 30/69/1558. Alfred Baker, Solicitor, to Mr H.B. Usher, Political Secretary to Ramsay MacDonald, 22 May 1935.
76 PRO 30/69/1558. Duke of Atholl to Kenneth Brown, Solicitor, 24 May 1935.
77 CHAR 2 235. LH, *Liberty*, Sandbanks, to Winston Churchill, 23 May 1935.
78 CHAR 2 235, Winston Churchill to LH, 25 May 1935.
79 PRO 30/69/1558. Solicitors to Duke of Atholl (undated, perhaps unsent, on or after 29 May 1935).
80 PRO 30/69/1558. From Duke of Atholl (undated).
81 api.parliament.uk/historic-hansard/commons/1935/aug/02/posters. HC Deb 2 August 1935 vol. 304 cc2984–85.
82 LH, *Liberty*, Sandbanks, to Collin Brooks, 3 August 1935, in author's possession.
83 LH, *Liberty*, Sandbanks, to Collin Brooks, 17 August 1935, in author's possession.

Chapter 17
84 RDCH 5 11. LH to Randolph Churchill, 13 January 1936.

Chapter 18
85 Buchanan, Meriel, 'Reds Threaten Our King', *Saturday Review*, 25 July 1936.
86 HO 144/20690, National Archives. 'Extradition: George Black Orsborne and James Black Orsborne: extradited from British Guiana for theft of fishing trawler *Girl Pat*'. Kew, record opening date: 1 January 2038.
87 CHAR 2/260/113-114; CHAR 2/260/10. LH, Byron Cottage, to Winston Churchill, 6 November 1936.
88 CHAR 2/260/65. Winston Churchill to LH, 9 November 1936.
89 Debate on the Address. HC Deb, 12 November 1936, vol. 317 cc1081–155.
90 CHAR 2/260. LH to Winston Churchill, 15 November 1936.
91 CHAR 2 260. Winston Churchill to LH, 18 November 1936.
92 Buchanan, Meriel, 'Secret Forces Aim to Destroy British Empire', *Saturday Review*, 19 December 1936.

BIBLIOGRAPHY

Allen, Warner (1947). *Lucy Houston, D.B.E.* London: Constable.

Astley, Sir John (1895). *Fifty Years of my Life in the World of Sport at Home and Abroad.* London: Hurst and Blackett.

Barwell, E.H.G. (1943). *The Death Ray Man: The Biography of Grindell Matthews, Inventor and Pioneer.* London: Hutchinson & Co.

Beaumont, Comyns (1944). *A Rebel in Fleet Street.* London: Hutchinson & Co.

Birkenhead, Second Earl of (1960). *F.E.: F.E. Smith the First Earl of Birkenhead, by his Son, Second Earl of Birkenhead.* London: Eyre and Spottiswood.

Brooks, Collin (1950). *Tavern Talk.* London: James Barrie.

Buchanan, Meriel (1958). *Ambassador's Daughter.* London: Cassell & Co.

Campbell, John (1983). *F.E. Smith: First Earl of Birkenhead.* London: Jonathan Cape.

Crisp, Dorothy (1946). *A Life for England.* London: Dorothy Crisp and Co. Ltd.

Crowson, N.J. (ed.) (1998). *Fleet Street, Press Barons, and Politics: The Journals of Collin Brooks, 1932–1940.* London: Royal Historical Society.

Davenport-Hines, Richard (2004). 'Houston, Dame Fanny Lucy (1857–1936).' In *Oxford Dictionary of National Biography.* Oxford: Oxford University Press.

Dickens, Charles (Jr) (1897). *Dickens's Dictionary of London.* London: Charles Dickens.

Douglas and Clydesdale, Squadron Leader the Marquess of, and McIntyre, Flight Lieutenant D.F. (1936). *The Pilots' Book of Everest.* London: William Hodge.

Fellowes, P.F.M., Stewart Blacker, L.V., and Etherton, P.T. (1933). *First Over Everest: The Houston-Mount Everest Expedition 1933.* London: Bodley Head.

Gilbart-Smith, J.W., writing as Denham, Sir James (1922). *Memoirs of the Memorable.* York: George H. Doran.

Hoare, Sir Samuel, Viscount Templewood (1957). *Empire of the Air.* London: Collins.

Lipton, Thomas (1932). *Lipton's Autobiography.* New York: Duffield and Green.

Low, David (1957). *Low's Autobiography.* New York: Simon and Schuster.

Minney, R.J. (1967). *The Two Pillars of Charing Cross.* London: Cassell & Co.

Mitchell, Gordon (2006). *R.J. Mitchell, Schooldays to Spitfire.* Stroud: The History Press.

Mosley, Sir Oswald (2006). *My Life.* London: Friends of Oswald Mosley. http://www.oswaldmosley.com/downloads/My Life.pdf

Nash, Eveleigh (1941). *I Liked the Life I Lived.* London: John Murray.

Orbsorne, Dod (2011). *Master of the Girl Pat.* Charleston: Nabu Press.

Porter, John, and Moorhouse, Edward (1919). *John Porter of Kingsclere: An Autobiography.* London: Grant Richards.

Riddell, G.A. (1933). *Lord Riddell's Intimate Diary of the Peace Conference and After, 1918–1923.* London: Victor Gollancz Ltd.

Soames, Mary (2001). *Winston and Clementine: The Personal Letters of the Churchills.* New York: Mariner Books.

Tennant, Ernest W.D. (1957). *True Account.* London: Max Parrish.

Thaddeus, H. Jones (1912). *Recollections of a Court Painter.* London: John Lane.

Wentworth Day, James (1958). *Lady Houston, the Richest Woman in England.* London: Allan Wingate.

Windsor, Duke of (1953). *A King's Story: The Memoirs of HRH the Duke of Windsor.* London: Reprint Society.

INDEX

The History Press
The destination for history
www.thehistorypress.co.uk